Urban Plants

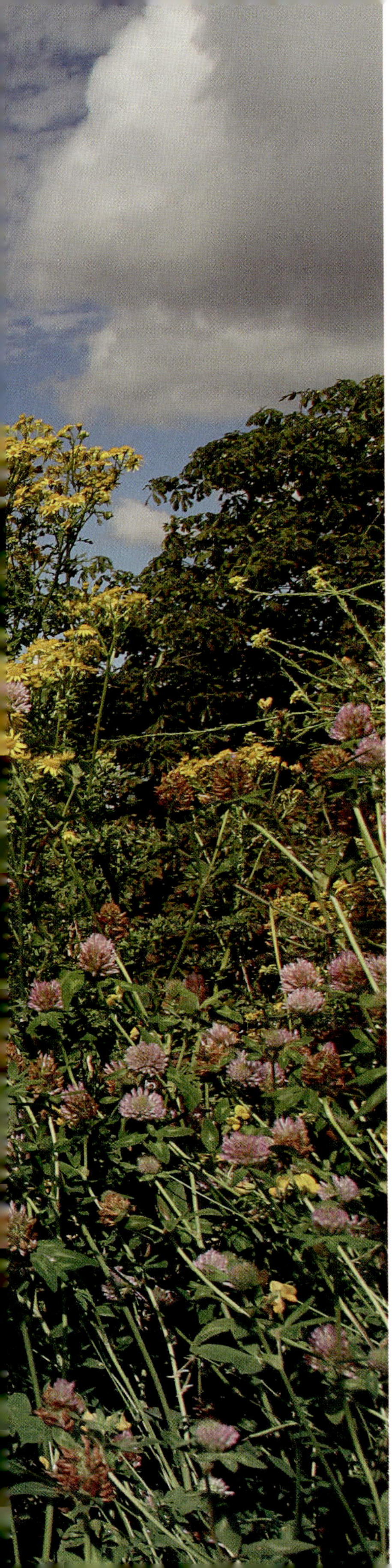

BRITISH WILDLIFE COLLECTION 15

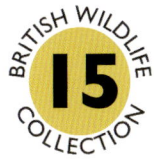

Urban Plants

Trevor Dines

BLOOMSBURY WILDLIFE
LONDON • OXFORD • NEW YORK • NEW DELHI • SYDNEY

To Nev, for his constant support, and Madog, for constantly reminding me to 'be more spaniel'. Diolch o galon.

BLOOMSBURY WILDLIFE
Bloomsbury Publishing Plc
50 Bedford Square, London, WC1B 3DP, UK
Bloomsbury Publishing Ireland Limited,
29 Earlsfort Terrace, Dublin 2, D02 AY28, Ireland

BLOOMSBURY, BLOOMSBURY WILDLIFE and the Diana logo are trademarks of
Bloomsbury Publishing Plc

First published in the United Kingdom 2025

Copyright © Trevor Dines, 2025

Trevor Dines has asserted his right under the Copyright, Designs and Patents Act, 1988,
to be identified as Author of this work

For legal purposes the illustration credits on pages 373–374 constitute an extension of this copyright page

All rights reserved. No part of this publication may be: i) reproduced or transmitted in any form, electronic or mechanical, including photocopying, recording or by means of any information storage or retrieval system without prior permission in writing from the publishers; or ii) used or reproduced in any way for the training, development or operation of artificial intelligence (AI) technologies, including generative AI technologies. The rights holders expressly reserve this publication from the text and data mining exception as per Article 4(3) of the Digital Single Market Directive (EU) 2019/790

Bloomsbury Publishing Plc does not have any control over, or responsibility for, any third-party websites referred to in this book. All internet addresses given in this book were correct at the time of going to press. The author and publisher regret any inconvenience caused if addresses have changed or sites have ceased to exist, but can accept no responsibility for any such changes.

A catalogue record for this book is available from the British Library
Library of Congress Cataloguing-in-Publication data has been applied for

ISBN: HB: 978-1-3994-0749-6; ePDF: 978-1-3994-0747-2; ePub: 978-1-3994-0748-9

2 4 6 8 10 9 7 5 3 1

Design by Susan McIntyre
Jacket artwork by Carry Akroyd

Printed and bound in Dubai by Oriental Press

To find out more about our authors and books visit www.bloomsbury.com and sign up for our newsletters
For product safety related questions contact productsafety@bloomsbury.com

HALF TITLE: Polypody *Polypodium vulgare* perched on a drainpipe in Caernarfon.
FRONTISPIECE: The skyline of Sheffield city centre from South Street greenspace.

Contents

Preface	6
Part One: Setting the urban scene	12
1 Introduction	14
2 A brief history of our urban plants	30
3 Urban botany today	40
Part Two: The roots of urban botany	48
4 Origin of urban plants	50
5 The physical urban environment	70
6 Creation of the urban flora	102
Part Three: A walk through the streets	120
7 Pavements	122
8 Walls	170
9 Urban fallow: waste ground and derelict land	224
10 The grassy bits	270
11 Street trees	298
Part Four: Final thoughts	334
12 The future of urban plants	336
Further study	350
Glossary	352
References	356
Illustration credits	373
Acknowledgements	375
Index	376

Preface

I was lucky enough to have a rather idyllic rural childhood, growing up on farms surrounded by the chalk downs of Wiltshire and Hampshire. My agricultural playground of fields, hedgerows, woods and rivers sparked an early interest in wild plants. Long before my teenage years, I'd become an avid hunter, identifier and recorder of plants, obsessed with everything I could find – from orchids to grasses and from ferns to fumitories. Apart from a few years in Bangor, Gwynedd, while studying for my PhD in botany at university, I've always led a deeply rural life.

Despite this rustic background, or perhaps because of it, I've always found cities to be utterly thrilling and exciting places that ignite within me a deep curiosity. Give me a pavement and I'll gladly scour the cracks for unusual garden escapes. Give me a wall and I'm even happier, scanning the masonry for tiny ferns and other urban cliff-dwellers. Maybe it's the lure of the new and a fascination for the exotic. Maybe it's an admiration for the sheer determination of life to survive in the most extreme and challenging of environments. Or maybe it's the relentless dynamism and flux, the constant coming and going of species that keeps you permanently alert. I relish that sense of anticipation and the thrill of the unknown.

Most of all, cities present me with a landscape full of questions. Why is this plant growing here? Where did it come from and how did it arrive? Will it thrive and spread, or struggle and decline? How can it cope with the extraordinary stresses of city life?

Given that we've always lived alongside plants, it's strange that it's taken us so long to become interested in urban ecology. During the eighteenth and nineteenth centuries, ecology focused on pretty much everything except urban habitats. Indeed, the prevailing view was that 'real ecologists study wild and natural places' (Gaston 2010).

OPPOSITE PAGE:
Urban plants can survive in the most extraordinary spots. Growing high on an apparently impenetrable wall, this Adria Bellflower *Campanula portenschlagiana* forms a tight mound of flowers every spring.

Even today, most people imagine ecologists pulling on waterproofs and walking boots before striking out for the hills, not donning T-shirt and sandals and heading to a city-centre pavement.

Across Europe, the aftermath of the Second World War stimulated an interest in the ecology of bomb sites as plants colonised newly opened urban spaces (Schmidt 2014). But in Britain and Ireland, it wasn't until the 1980s and 1990s that urban ecology really began to take off as a discipline in its own right. As well as a flurry in the publication of city Floras, including those for London (Burton 1983), Dublin (Jackson & Skeffington 1984) and Nottingham (Shepherd 1998), the period saw the production of several landmark textbooks, namely Oliver Gilbert's *The Ecology of Urban Habitats* (1989) and Arnold Darlington's *Ecology of Walls* (1981). These helped put urban ecology in the spotlight at last, and a steady stream of research since then has turned into a flood; globally, the number of urban biodiversity studies more-or-less doubled in the five years from 2012 to 2017 (Rega-Brodsky *et al.* 2022).

Many factors have fuelled this renewed interest. Today, 4.4 billion people (56% of the world's population) are urban, so the ecology of towns and cities is relevant to more of us than ever before (Satterthwaite 2020). We now also appreciate that all the world's ecosystems are

BELOW: Mature trees, including birch *Betula* sp. and False-acacia *Robinia pseudoacacia*, soften the brutalist architecture of the Barbican Centre in London.

influenced by human activity to some extent – no matter how remote they appear to be – and that urban environments represent the extreme end of this continuum of modification. Their study helps us grasp the depth and breadth of human impacts across all habitats. We're also beginning to understand the enormous demands that densely populated human settlements place on rural surroundings in terms of resources, waste processing and sources of pollution. Moreover, we now appreciate the significant benefits that contact with nature has on our health and wellbeing, especially for those living in urbanised landscapes where such contact can be limited. And we shouldn't forget that urban ecology is also just plain fascinating. The unique structure and function of anthropogenic habitats leads to the creation of novel communities, ecological processes and species interactions, all of which require new and often interdisciplinary approaches to their study (Gaston 2010).

Today, urban ecology is flourishing, and the flora of cities is attracting particular attention. Since 1990, more than a third (38%) of all urban biodiversity studies have focused on plants, compared to 19% on birds, 7% on butterflies, 7% on bees and 5% on bats (Rega-Brodsky *et al.* 2022). Whilst botanists might cheer this welcome attention, we must remember that more studies on other taxonomic groups are needed if we're to get a fully holistic view of urban ecology. Plants might be the foundation of all habitats, but they don't grow in isolation.

Scope of this book

With the huge diversity of plants and habitats found in urban areas, it would be impossible to do them all justice here; it would be a little like writing a single book on the botany of 'the countryside'. Although semi-natural habitats such as woodlands, grasslands, rivers, ponds and lakes are extremely valuable and important components of the urban landscape, their botany and ecology are similar to those in rural settings and can be dealt with elsewhere. Instead, this book takes a deep-dive into the other end of the spectrum, focusing on the most anthropogenic habitat of all: the urban built environment.

In what follows, **Part 1 sets the scene**, looking at the history of urban plants and the state of urban botany today. **Part 2 considers the ecology of urban landscapes**, examining the origins of the plants, the unique physical ecology of the built environment, and how these two come together to form the urban flora. **Part 3 then takes inspiration from an imagined walk around the streets** of a typical urban area, exploring five different key habitats and features: pavements, walls, urban fallow (waste ground and abandoned derelict spaces), urban grasslands (lawns, parks, playing fields and verges) and street trees. By studying these in detail, I hope that we might see them with fresh eyes and begin to appreciate how complex and fascinating urban botany can be. Finally, in **Part 4, the future of urban botany is explored**, asking how the flora might evolve, how we should conserve it, and how our relationship with it might change.

The geographic scope of the book is Britain and Ireland but, since urban ecology has been studied in cities across Europe and around the world, we'll draw on this research where it helps us understand ecological processes and plant behaviour back at home.

Botanically, the focus is primarily on vascular plants: the flowers, grasses, ferns, trees and conifers we encounter in urban areas. Some bryophytes (mosses and liverworts) are also mentioned, especially the more abundant urban species. Throughout the book, the focus is on the spontaneous vegetation that has arisen by itself without the help of human hand. As you'll see, I've carefully avoided the word 'wild' because it's so difficult to define, especially in urban contexts. Instead, 'spontaneous' covers most of the plants we'll encounter, and rules out any cultivated and ornamental plants that have been deliberately sown or planted in our gardens and parks or on verges and most green roofs.

This, then, is the story of our urban flora and our relationship with it, the plants you're likely to encounter, and some of the surprises you might want to keep an eye out for. Above all else, I hope it encourages you to look at the botanical neighbours on your streets in a new light and inspires you to get out and explore your own urban patch. After all, you never know what you might find next – as we'll see in the following anecdote that encapsulates many facets of urban botany.

Preface

ABOVE: Grey-cushioned Grimmia *Grimmia pulvinata* is one of the most common urban bryophytes on walls, where its neat tufts have earned it the alternative name Hedgehog Moss.

Part One
Setting the urban scene

Introduction | chapter one

It all started with a mundane trip to the barbers. As usual, I park down near the bike shop in Llandudno Junction so I can enjoy the walk through the streets to check up on what's growing. There's that big, bright clump of Narrow-leaved Ragwort *Senecio inaequidens*, a recent arrival from South Africa, covered in small yellow flowers. There's good old Snapdragon *Antirrhinum majus*, an intense blaze of pink on the corner of the road. And here's my favourite tuft of Wall-rue *Asplenium ruta-muraria* on a garden wall, its neat little fronds poking out from between the bricks. I continue on my way, clocking each old friend and revelling in the spread of new arrivals. Native species jostle for space with plants from all around the world, unlikely pavement partners forming a cosmopolitan mix as diverse as the human communities they live alongside.

I'm a bit early for my short-back-and-sides, so for once I carry on past the barber shop and scout out the car park beyond. Suddenly, nestled at the base of a wall beside a discarded fizzy drink can, a large yellow daisy catches my eye. I'm pretty familiar with all the plants around here, but I've not seen this one before. Now, yellow daisies like this are notoriously difficult to identify – there are so many of them and they all look so similar. My brain struggles to give this one a name, so I greet the plant with a simple 'Oh hello! Who are you then?' It's certainly a garden escape. As an avid gardener from the age of five (sunflowers and broad beans were the first miracles of nature I remember growing), I can put a name to most common garden plants, but not this one. So, I turn instead to a miracle of modern technology and, drawing my mobile phone from my pocket, resort to a bit of artificial intelligence.

My plant identification app asks me to take a photo of the mystery plant. The image is then compared to many thousands of images of plants online (or, according to the app, it is analysed using 'a

PREVIOUS PAGES:
Ivy-leaved Toadflax *Cymbalaria muralis* scrambling over an old brick wall in Ironbridge, Shropshire.

OPPOSITE:
Oxford Ragwort *Senecio squalidus*, a plant that can trace its origins to the volcanic slopes of Mt Etna in Sicily, here growing on a graffiti-covered wall in Bristol.

Urban Plants

ABOVE: Willow-leaved Yellow-oxeye growing at the base of a car-park wall in Llandudno Junction, Conwy.

cascade of deep neural networks on the app's computer cluster', whatever that might mean). A few seconds later a result appears on my screen, and it looks a perfect match.

My mystery plant is Willow-leaved Yellow-oxeye *Buphthalmum salicifolium*, a plant normally found in open woodland and rocky mountain slopes across Central Europe and the Alps through to the Balkan peninsula. There's a picture of it in its native habitat, and I'm immediately transported to a stunning alpine hillside full of wildflowers, a very far cry from a litter-strewn pavement in Llandudno Junction. It's not a common garden plant in the British Isles but is increasingly popular as a good resource for pollinators. Taking a flower back home, I confirm its identity using more traditional morphological means (my key says the 'receptacular scales should be folded around the achenes', which they are). I also learn that, somewhat randomly, potted plants of Willow-leaved Yellow-oxeye were given to each medal winner at the 2022 European Athletics Championships in Munich, so they could 'immortalise themselves in the Munich 2022 Champions Garden'. I bet it looks lovely, a sea of large yellow daisies.

Moments of discovery like this provide the ultimate thrill of urban botany: you never quite know what you're going to find. Whether it's a common wildflower or something entirely new, the lure of the unknown is a powerful force, pulling us from the comfort of our sofas to get outside and see what's there. In the countryside you can be fairly sure what you'll come across, Bluebell *Hyacinthoides non-scripta* and Wood Anemone *Anemone nemorosa* in an oakwood, for example, or Heather *Calluna vulgaris* and Tormentil *Potentilla erecta* on a mountainside. But in our towns and cities the stakes are a little higher. A handful of species – the urban specialists – are very frequent and common in such settings and you'll find them on nearly every street, but by far the majority of urban plants are rather infrequent, making fleeting cameo appearances in the constantly changing urban landscape. And this means there's always the chance of a new discovery.

I checked my new plant with the database of sightings maintained by the Botanical Society of Britain and Ireland (BSBI). Willow-leaved Yellow-oxeye was first recorded as an escape here in 1985,

ABOVE: Willow-leaved Yellow-oxeye in the wild on a mountainside in the Berchtesgaden Alps, Germany.

when Alan Leslie came across it growing on Wandsworth Common, London. It wasn't recorded again until 2007, when it was found at Mile End Ecological Park, London. Then there's a record from Holmes Chapel, Cheshire, in 2009 and another not far from Oliver Cromwell's house in Ely, Cambridgeshire, in 2010. And that's it – just four sites, all in England. I'd found an exceptionally rare urban plant, and a first for Wales too! That's a nice little feather in the cap, thank you very much, and all because I was early for a haircut.

Discoveries of rare alien escapes in towns and cities aren't uncommon, because most botanists still tend to shun urban landscapes, leaving rich pickings for those who take an interest. Many of us prefer to explore more rural settings, often homing in on high-quality habitats and the lure of rare native plants. And perhaps many feel more comfortable with fewer people around watching what they're doing. After all, staring intently at a wall or pavement for even just a few minutes invariably attracts attention from passers-by, and sometimes awkward questions too. Ironically, these are often along the lines of 'are you from the council and can you get them to clear away these dreadful weeds from the street?'

In our comparatively unbotanised urban landscapes, therefore, many unexpected plants can be found in unexpected places. A spectacular example is the appearance of Lesser Tongue-orchid *Serapias parviflora* high on the green roof of an investment bank in central London in 2021. Known from France and one long-gone population at Rame Head, Cornwall, seeds of this Mediterranean orchid could have blown in from continental Europe. Alternatively,

LEFT: In 2021, Lesser Tongue-orchid was one of 165 species found on the 12-year-old green roof of Nomura Bank in central London. The roof is also home to one of only three colonies of Green-winged Orchid *Anacamptis morio* in the English capital.

RIGHT: With hot and dry conditions and infertile soil, the green roof mimics Mediterranean conditions, perfect for Lesser Tongue-orchid.

they might have been transported in soil with mats of sedum planted on the roof (although that's unlikely as the mats originally came from the Netherlands, where the species doesn't occur). Either way, it's thriving in its new home, with 396 plants counted in 2024 (Sean Cole pers. comm.). Research is under way to establish the origin of Lesser Tongue-orchid in this unlikely spot, but at the moment it's a mystery, and that's part of the magic.

A week after I found Willow-leaved Yellow-oxeye, I returned excitedly to see if there were more plants around the town. As I stepped out of the car, my heart began to sink. All along the pavement, the plants had a tell-tale look – a sickly, slightly off-colour appearance as growth stops and tissues begin to break down. The touch of glyphosate herbicide is unmistakable, and my plants hadn't escaped the deadly spray. Flowers and shoots were drooping and leaves were already turning brown. Just a few days after their discovery they'd been killed, and I'm absolutely gutted.

This is one of several signatures of urban botany: transience. Plants that are here today can be gone tomorrow, either damaged accidentally, sprayed with herbicide or intentionally removed by people cleaning up walls and pavements around their properties. Patches of waste ground rich with flowers can disappear overnight as the developers move in. The result is an extraordinarily high turnover of species over time as plants come and go. Urban botanists soon learn not to hang around if they want to photograph or identify a particular plant, as it's likely to be gone in the blink of an eye. Only very rarely do plants persist in the same spot for many decades or centuries, usually on ancient castle walls and abbey ruins, as long as they escape the cleaning, repairing and repointing of the masonry.

Urban areas are meeting places for plants from all over the world. We grow more than 400,000 different species, varieties and hybrids in our gardens (Royal Horticultural Society pers. comm.), and many of these occasionally jump the garden wall and appear on our streets. Others hitch-hike through shipping, rail and road networks, global travellers in our global village. Indeed, just over half our flora (51%) is now made up of alien species (Walker *et al.* 2023). Stand on a city-centre pavement and you can likely find plants from China, Canada, Japan, the Alps, the Mediterranean, Argentina, Mexico, the Caucasus Mountains, South Africa, Australia, North America and New Zealand. Some of these have become true urban specialists, closely associated with us and our built environment. Perhaps the quintessential conqueror of concrete and masonry is Buddleja *Buddleja davidii* (also known as Butterfly-bush, see pages 250–251), and a map of this species clearly shows the positions of our major towns, cities and conurbations.

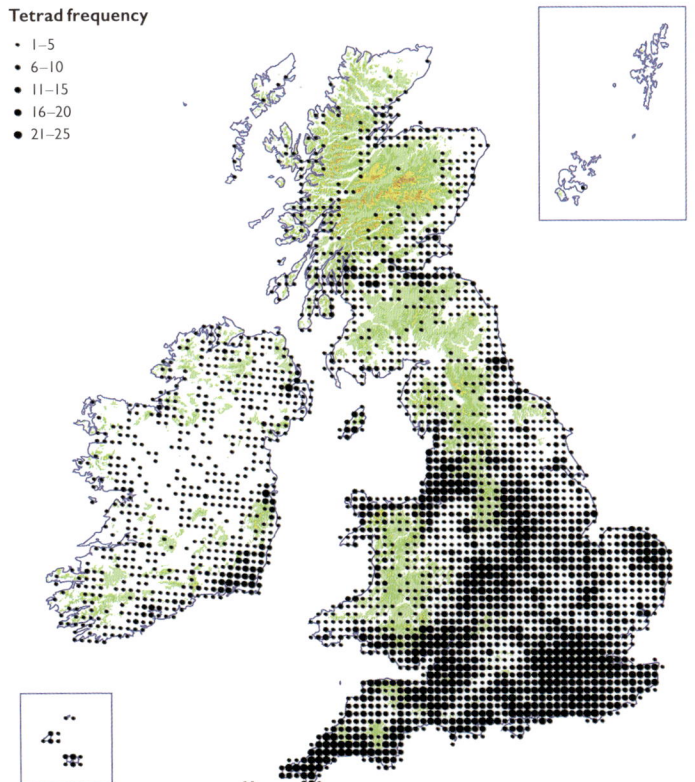

BELOW LEFT: The 2-km square tetrad frequency map of Buddleja from *Plant Atlas 2020*. As well as Greater London, you can make out Cardiff, Swansea, Birmingham, Manchester, Liverpool, Nottingham, Sheffield and Leeds as well as Newcastle upon Tyne, Edinburgh, Glasgow, Dublin and Belfast.

Growing alongside these alien species is a vast array of natives. These aren't just the ruderal 'weedy' elements of our flora, but plants from a wide range of semi-natural habitats including woodlands, hedgerows, rocky cliffs, meadows and pastures, coasts and riversides, ponds and marshes. Each species has its own adaptations and characteristics that allow it to survive, and sometimes thrive, in urban environments. Although alien plants often grab our attention and steal the headlines, native species predominate and make up, on average, 61% of urban floras in Britain and Ireland.

Another hallmark of urban botany is the presence of unique communities of plants, comprising familiar and unfamiliar species from near and far. Ruderal, pioneer communities are particularly common, with plants making the most of opportunities to colonise bare, open spaces. Abandoned urban land is often awash with Oxford Ragwort *Senecio squalidus*, Canadian Fleabane *Erigeron canadensis* and Rosebay Willowherb *Chamaenerion angustifolium*, along with Buddleja, Mugwort *Artemisia vulgaris*, Creeping Thistle *Cirsium arvense*, Ribbed Melilot *Melilotus officinalis* and even pioneer trees like Ash *Fraxinus excelsior* and Sycamore *Acer pseudoplatanus*. Classifying these unique associations, which haven't been comprehensively studied across Britain and Ireland, is a major challenge.

The close juxtaposition of very different habitats is another characteristic of urban environments. Within a few metres you can have a tightly mown lawn, a cultivated flowerbed, a sun-drenched wall, a cracked pavement, an open basement and a blocked road drain. All these habitats provide very different opportunities for different plants to find a home and is one reason why urban environments can have a higher diversity of species than the surrounding countryside (see Chapter 6). This diversity isn't spread evenly across a city, but varies according to historical, geographical, cultural and even socio-economic factors.

So, urban botany is dynamic, exciting and unpredictable. Much of this is driven by the fact that the urban environment is extraordinarily challenging for plants. Soils are usually thin, dry, repeatedly disturbed and often include waste building materials. Or they might be sealed below an impervious surface of concrete paving slabs or tarmac. Summer temperatures can soar, exacerbated by the urban heat island effect, where heat is absorbed by solid surfaces and re-radiated later in the day (see Chapter 5). Water is often scarce and summer droughts can be extreme, while our increasingly stormy climate is leading to wetter winters with more flooding, a situation exacerbated by hard urban infrastructure. Air pollution can reach dangerously high levels, with atmospheric nitrogen dioxide, ozone, volatile organic compounds, sulphur dioxide and particulate matter all having an impact on plants. Add to this liberal doses of herbicide and you can see why it's such a tough life in the city. I often think that most urban plants are as just as stressed as the people they live alongside, and only those species equipped to deal with the extreme conditions can survive.

We humans are, of course, an integral part of the mix. By far the majority of us are urbanites, with some 56.5 million people or 84% of the UK population living in towns and cities (World Bank 2022). Urban settings are therefore where most people come into regular contact with plants and, ironically, where our relationships with them are perhaps most polarised. Plants on pavements, streets and walls are utterly ignored or treated with distain by some people, but loved, cherished and fought-for by others. The urban environment is the most highly anthropogenic of all habitats, entirely created by us, and it evolves with us as society changes over time. It is subject to our whims and our fashions, our wars and our disasters, our policies and our planning rules. Even very subtle changes in our behaviour, such as the parking of e-scooters and e-bikes, can impact plants.

This narrative of constant urban change can be seen everywhere. A few months after my Willow-leaved Yellow-oxeye plants were herbicided into oblivion, I returned to the fateful spot. There, between the pavement and base of the wall, a few small plants were beginning to emerge. Hopefully, they'll survive and flower again next year. Above all else, our urban flora is tough and resilient and, if we give it half a chance, will often return.

BELOW: The corner of this street in Cambridge was once a grass sward, but has been worn away now it's used as a parking place for the city's newly introduced rental e-scooters.

What is urban?

This is one of the questions I get asked most often, but which is very difficult to answer. Each of us probably has a good idea of what 'urban' means, but we probably don't all have quite the same idea. It's one of those slightly intangible concepts that is difficult to pin down. Indeed, there's no agreed global definition of urban (Schmidt 2014).

Dictionary definitions are varied, but they tend to run along the lines of:

Urban – of or in, or belonging to, or connected with, or characteristic of, a city or a town.

So, urban is framed around cities and towns. But what are they? Again, dictionary definitions vary, but in general…

Town – a densely populated, built-up area, where people live and work, containing many shops and places of entertainment, that is larger than a village but usually smaller than a city.

City – any large town, or (in the UK) a large town that has received the title of city from the Crown.

Urban, then, seems to be a built-up, densely populated place where people live and work, and is larger than a village. And a village is…

Village – a group of houses and other buildings that is smaller than a town, usually in the countryside.

So, size is important, but the distinction between 'urban' and 'rural' is a bit more complicated than that as our houses aren't spread evenly over the surface of the land but densely packed into some areas and scattered more sparingly across others. In the UK, areas are described as rural if they fall outside settlements with more than 10,000 residents (Defra 2016). Detailed classifications have been developed to describe patterns of settlement. Defra's Rural Urban

RIGHT: With a population of only about 450 people, the tiny Hampshire village of Wherwell is most definitely rural.

Introduction

Classification of settlements based on population size

Category	Number of settlements	Population size	Examples
Core cities	12	Major population and economic centres	London, Edinburgh, Belfast, Manchester, Leeds, Nottingham, Cardiff
Other cities	24	175,000 or more	Leicester, Swansea, Aberdeen
Large towns	119	60,000 to 174,999	Chester, Great Yarmouth, Dundee
Medium towns	270	25,000 to 59,999	Salisbury, Kendal, Newry, Ayr
Small towns	674	7,500 to 24,999	Falmouth, Oban, Whitby, Llandudno
Villages and small communities	6116	Less than 7,500	Wherwell, Litchborough, Taynuilt, Menai Bridge

Adapted from Baker (2018).

Classification, for example, has ten different categories, including 'Urban Major Conurbation', 'Urban City and Town', 'Rural Town and Fringe', 'Rural Village', and 'Rural Town and Fringe in a Sparse Setting' (Defra 2016). A slightly simpler classification with six categories based purely on population size has been developed by the House of Commons Library (Baker 2018). Using this definition (see table above), any settlement above a population size of 7,500 (i.e. not a village) is classed as urban.

Ecologically, the term 'urban' is perhaps even harder to grasp. Indeed, there is no internationally agreed definition of urban habitat (McIntyre 2000, OECD 2022). In a global review of urban ecology, Rega-Brodsky *et al.* (2022) note that the United Nations' 1955 view

BELOW: Kendal in Cumbria, with a population of around 29,000, is classed as a 'medium town' and is therefore urban.

ABOVE: One of 12 core cities, the largest classification of urban settlement in the UK, Edinburgh has a population of about 530,000.

that 'there is no point in the continuum from large agglomerations to small clusters of scattered dwellings where urbanity disappears and rurality begins; the division between urban and rural populations is necessarily arbitrary' is as true today as it was 70 years ago. Since the 1990s, urban ecological researchers have defined their area of study in a variety of ways, mostly using municipal boundaries (41%), land use (35%) or land cover (25%), while only a few (13%) used population density (Rega-Brodsky 2022).

Part of the problem is that no single community of plants allows us to define urban habitat. For natural and semi-natural habitats like woodlands, heathlands and grasslands, familiar plants come together to form well-defined associations of species that help us recognise them; the National Vegetation Classification (NVC), for example, identifies 12 major types of vegetation, further divided into 286 communities and 578 subcommunities (Rodwell 2006). However, not one of these is uniquely urban, and it's difficult to fit many of them into highly urban built environments. This is largely because the urban landscape is a mosaic of all sorts of different habitats. As well as pavements, walls and waste ground, there can be areas of woodland, scrub, grasslands and meadows, rivers, marshland, ponds and canals. Fragments of these habitats form glorious patchworks, highly jumbled mixtures that bring all sorts of plants together to form a diversity of different communities.

Inside the urban boundary, though, quite large tracts of semi-natural habitats can be found. These areas are vitally important for both urban biodiversity and people, and can be of such good quality they're designated as Sites of Special Scientific Interest (SSSI) and Local or National Nature Reserves (LNRs and NNRs). For instance, in 2022 the Flashes of Wigan and Leigh, a 738ha (1,824 acre) area of former industrial wasteland, became the largest urban National Nature Reserve in the UK, and is on the doorstep of 2.8 million local people. It includes a mosaic of shallow open water, swamp, reedbed, tall-herb fen, wet marshy grassland and wet woodland. To all intents and purposes, this is open countryside, but it's also classed as urban.

So, where do we draw the urban boundary ecologically? One solution is to look at land use. Unlike semi-natural habitats, most of which can quite readily transform into one another over time, urbanisation is very much a one-way street. Once an area has been built upon, the change is almost impossible to reverse. The lifespan of most building materials, such as concrete, bricks, stone, steel, plastics and glass, is so long that it's extraordinarily difficult to completely un-build the built environment. Even in post-industrial sites, urban decay is usually gradual and echoes of urban activity persist for generations.

Taking this land-use approach, the Centre for Ecology and Hydrology (CEH) and Office for National Statistics (ONS) define their Built-up Areas land cover class as any area 'irreversibly urban in character' (ONS 2023, Marston *et al.* 2022a, b). Crucially, this puts population size to one side, so it includes any settlement that's a village, town or city. This definition moves us towards something more ecologically coherent: urban is the built environment and the habitats it contains, regardless of population size. To botanists, this makes more sense; after all, a wall in a village is the same as a wall in a city, and Wall-rue will grow happily on either. Using this definition, the total area of urban habitat in the UK is 2.03 million hectares (5.03 million acres), which is about 8% of the whole UK land area (ONS 2023, Marston *et al.* 2022a, b).

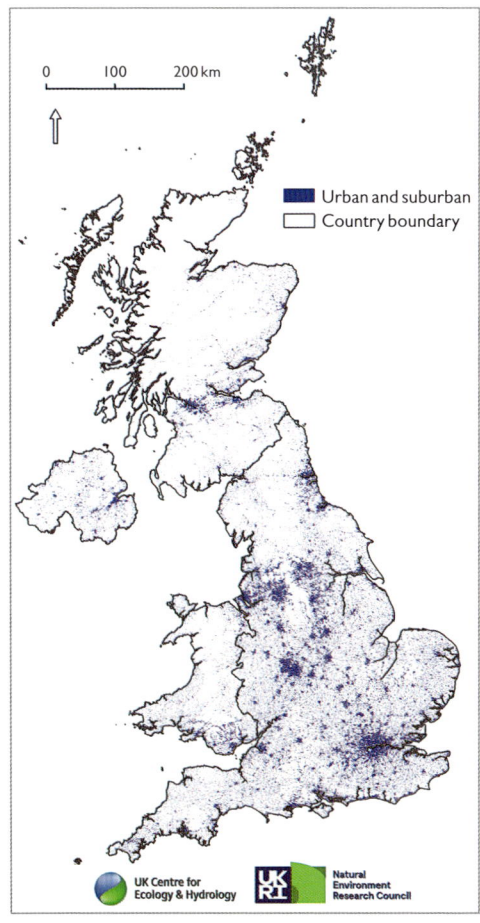

BELOW: The distribution of 'Built-up Area land use' from the Centre for Ecology and Hydrology (CEH) Land Cover Map 2021. Note how closely urban areas match the distribution of Buddleja (see map on page 19).

The remarkable mosaic of urban habitats

Whenever we take a walk around an urban area, we're likely to come across a huge variety of habitats. Some of these are **semi-natural habitats**, such as grasslands, heath, scrub, woodland and marshes. **Urban green spaces** tend to be more highly managed, including gardens and allotments, parks, playing fields, sports pitches and golf courses, churchyards and cemeteries. Aquatic habitats within urban areas, such as rivers, canals, ponds and lakes, are known as **blue space**. The most modified urban habitats are termed the **built environment**, and include walls, roofs, buildings and pavements, car parks, and road and railway infrastructure, as well as derelict, vacant and abandoned urban land. It's a long list.

While three-quarters of the urban area in the UK is made up of urban habitats (the built environment along with urban green space), the extent of semi-natural habitats within the urban boundary often comes as a surprise (ONS 2023). The largest contribution (17.2% of the urban area) is from farmland (351,034ha or 778,466 acres), followed by woodland covering 4.6% (94,385ha or 233,230 acres) and then semi-natural grasslands at 1.2% (23,865ha or 58,972 acres). Freshwater, wetlands and floodplain habitats make up 0.9% (17,837ha or 44,076 acres). These habitats considerably boost species diversity within the urban boundary. I grew up near Salisbury in Wiltshire

BELOW: Urban road verges can support surprisingly good-quality grassland if they're managed appropriately. Pyramidal Orchid often grows in quantity on chalky lime-rich soils, such as this verge in Reading, Berkshire.

ABOVE: Public parks and gardens are often heavily used green spaces in fine weather. Here, Primrose Hill in London becomes crowded on a warm spring day.

and remember exploring the city's wide range of grasslands, from chalk downland on road cuttings with Wild Thyme *Thymus drucei*, Lady's Bedstraw *Galium verum* and Pyramidal Orchid *Anacamptis pyramidalis*, lowland neutral grasslands featuring Common Spotted-orchid *Dactylorhiza fuchsii*, Oxeye Daisy *Leucanthemum vulgare* and Knapweed *Centaurea nigra*, and tall-herb fen vegetation beside the River Avon with Purple-loosestrife *Lythrum salicaria*, Meadowsweet *Filipendula ulmaria* and Ragged-Robin *Silene flos-cuculi*. A similar diversity of habitats can be seen in almost any urban area.

As well as semi-natural habitats, the extent of urban green space can also be surprising, amounting to 121,566ha (300,396 acres) in Great Britain. The majority of this (38%) is made up of publicly accessible parks and gardens (46,665ha or 115,312 acres). To give an idea of what this means on the ground: the average urban person will live 881 metres away from their nearest park or public garden as the crow flies. In comparison, the nearest playing field will be 751 metres away and the nearest bowling green 1,493 metres away (ONS 2023).

A journey into town: the rural–urban gradient

Although we try to draw a line around what is rural and what is urban, in truth there is no such boundary. Instead, there's a continuous gradient between the two, a gradual increase in urbanity (or a decrease in rurality, depending on which way you're heading). In order to appreciate this, we only have to imagine taking a journey from the countryside into a city centre. This route, or at least part of

ABOVE: View of Leeds showing rural–urban gradient from open countryside in the far distance, through the suburbs and city fringes and finally the tall, crowded buildings of the city centre.

it, is something many of us experience regularly as we commute to work or travel into town by road or rail.

For our imaginary journey, let's start at a tiny rural train station. During our trip, we're following a gradient which sees population density (and the infrastructure needed to support it) gradually increase. Individual houses and wide-open fields give way bit by bit to clusters of houses and villages. Roads and road junctions slowly become more frequent, as do railway lines and stations. Towns become larger and closer together, and we begin to pass out-of-town shopping centres and industrial units, and factories start to appear. As population density rises, taller buildings begin to cluster together and residential tower blocks become apparent. As we approach the city centre, shiny high-rise offices and more ostentatious towers crowd the skyline, and there's a tangle of roads, junctions and railways. Suddenly, as our view is completely obscured by buildings and our train passes under bridges and through tunnels, we arrive at our city-centre station.

So, where did urban begin and the countryside end? It's difficult to say. We haven't passed a boundary but have followed a gradient of increasing population and anthropogenic impact. As a result, many environmental conditions have also changed. For example, air and

Introduction

LEFT: This map of open green spaces and private gardens in London shows a gradient of increasing urbanisation (white areas) towards the city centre, but also the sheer extent of green spaces through most of the city. Map from Greenspace Information for Greater London CIC.

soil pollution have increased, nitrogen deposition has increased, soils have become more compacted and sealed below impervious surfaces, and soil moisture has decreased. The atmosphere has also changed, becoming more heated and turbulent (Schmidt 2014).

The rural–urban gradient can be seen readily in visualisations of green space across London. Greenspace Information for Greater London (GIGL) has mapped all green space and habitats in the city, and the most depleted areas do indeed lie towards the centre. However, the map is surprising in just how much green space there is. Remarkably, around 47% of Greater London can be regarded as 'green'; 33% is classed as natural and semi-natural habitat and 14% is vegetated gardens (GIGL 2022, Smith *et al.* 2011). Urban areas are certainly not entirely concrete jungles.

A brief history of our urban plants

chapter two

We have always lived alongside plants, a cohabitation stretching back hundreds of thousands of years. Originally, it was a more intimate relationship, born of our dependency on the living things that sustained us. As humans began to come together and form the earliest Palaeolithic, Mesolithic and Neolithic settlements, plants would have been growing all around us and, quite literally, under our feet. Initially, these would have been **native** species (plants that arrived here at the end of the last glaciation without human help), familiar colonisers of disturbed ground such as Common Chickweed *Stellaria media* and Groundsel *Senecio vulgaris* along with all manner of foraged wild foods like Crab Apple *Malus sylvestris*, Hazel *Corylus avellana* and Hawthorn *Crataegus monogyna* that gained a foothold from discarded fruit.

With the arrival of the first agricultural practices from Europe in the Neolithic (4000–2200 BC) and more settled patterns of living, the range of plants increased. Alongside newly domesticated crops such as Emmer Wheat *Triticum dicoccum* and Celtic Bean, a variety of Broad Bean *Vicia faba*, the first non-native **archaeophytes** appeared. These are plants introduced by humans before AD 1500 (as opposed to **neophytes** that have been introduced since AD 1500). These first arrivals included species such as Shepherd's Purse *Capsella bursa-pastoris* and Black-bindweed *Fallopia convolvulus*. Remains of Hazel are particularly frequent in Neolithic settlements, along with Raspberry *Rubus idaeus*, Blackberry *R. fruticosus* and Crab Apple (Treasure *et al.* 2019). Many more new species arrived through the Bronze Age and the Iron Age up to AD 43, when the

OPPOSITE:
Noble Street Garden, London, where 1940s Blitz damage exposed remains of a Roman fort built around AD 120. Now surrounded by modern office blocks, the site has been planted with wildflowers.

Roman invasion of Britain commenced. Along with food crops such as Spelt Wheat *Triticum spelta* and Garden Pea *Lathyrus oleraceus* were other archaeophytes like Common Poppy *Papaver rhoeas* and Corncockle *Agrostemma githago*, with remains of their seeds often found in domestic midden (rubbish) heaps. Species such as Henbane *Hyoscyamus niger* and Opium Poppy *Papaver somniferum* also appear at this time, suggesting that our relationship with plants included those with medicinal and psychoactive properties.

The Iron Age marks an important turning point in the story, with the emergence of the first proto-urban settlements. During the period 750 BC to AD 43, more than two thousand fortified hillforts, such as Danebury Hill in Hampshire and Tre'r Ceiri in Gwynedd, became established. Towards the end of the period, as Roman influence began to be felt in Great Britain, other fortified settlements known as 'oppida' (from the Latin *oppidum*, a town) were established. Around 24 oppida have been identified, mainly in southern England (e.g. Winchester and Colchester) but also the Midlands (e.g. Leicester) and reaching north to Stanwick in North Yorkshire (Historic England 2018). Although fairly diverse in nature, these settlements all shared certain characteristics. They were centres for local and long-distance trade, for the storage of goods, for the production of crafts and for ritual activities. They had an imported material culture (e.g. pottery and jewellery) and they had separate residences for the ruling elite (Lodwick 2017). Less tied to agricultural activities within the settlement boundary, they are considered by archaeologists to be the first steps towards urbanisation in Great Britain. Indeed, quite a number acted as nuclei for the foundation of Roman towns, some of which survive today. A spectacular example is Calleva, now known as Silchester, in Hampshire (see box on pages 34–35).

During the period of Roman occupation (AD 43–410), towns continued to grow and flourish, despite almost continual warfare with numerous native British tribes. Many towns were established, sometimes near forts to support garrisons of legionaries or on the sites of Celtic settlements. Many modern urban centres, such as Chester, Gloucester and Lincoln, can trace their roots back to Roman origins, and by the end of the period in the fourth century the urban population in Great Britain was about 240,000 people (Acock 2011). In Londinium (London) alone, the population is estimated to have been around 30,000–35,000. With the influx of people from all over the Roman Empire, new species of plants continued to arrive with them, including familiar urban species such as Wormwood *Artemisia absinthium*, Wall Barley *Hordeum murinum* and Red Dead-nettle *Lamium purpureum*. It's also worth mentioning the extraordinary archaeological evidence from Roman and Viking York, where more than 40 different food species alone have been recovered, including cereals, pulses (e.g. Lentil *Vicia lens*), oilseeds (e.g. Opium Poppy), flavourings (e.g. Bog-myrtle *Myrica gale*) and vegetables (e.g. Leek *Allium porrum*). For an entertaining review of these finds, see Hall (2000).

With the fall of the Roman Empire, many towns and cities fell into a period of decline and urban life in Britain doesn't really re-emerge until the seventh century (Palliser 2000). During the Dark Ages and Middle Ages (AD 410–1500), trade routes with Europe strengthened and the dominance of London, York and Edinburgh increased, while Southampton was founded at the end of the seventh century and Hereford in the eighth century (Lambert 2021). New species continued to arrive, such as Horse-radish *Armoracia rusticana*, Prickly Lettuce *Lactuca serriola* and Annual Mercury *Mercurialis annua*, all of which remain common today on disturbed urban land.

During the twelfth and thirteenth centuries, most towns grew much larger; London's population, for instance, swelled from around 18,000 at the time of the Domesday Book (1086) to 45,000 by the end of this period. Many new towns were established as trade and commerce increased. Some of these grew out of existing villages but others were entirely new, simply created by tradesfolk coming together to start a market. From 1348 to 1349, the British Isles were devastated by the first wave of Black Death, and outbreaks continued until around 1665. Despite the dreadful toll, towns and cities actually continued to expand and prosper, often bolstered with an influx of people from the countryside (Lambert 2021).

During the sixteenth and seventeenth centuries, as scholars increasingly turned their attention to the natural world, the first formal observations of urban plants in Great Britain were made. The earliest seem to be in Turner's *The names of herbs* (1548), where he notes that Hound's-tongue *Cynoglossum officinale* 'groweth in sandy groundes and aboute cities & townes' and White Horehound *Marrubium vulgare* 'groweth aboute townes and villages'. Both of these wonderful plants would have been grown by herbalists for their medicinal properties. Today, they're rather unusual and declining species, neither of which are at all common in urban settings.

Urban Plants

Calleva: the first urban flora

The extraordinary preservation of plant material at the bottom of wells in Calleva (Silchester) allows us to peer back in time and reconstruct perhaps the earliest British urban flora. The plant remains have been excavated by a team at Reading University led by Lisa Lodwick (2017).

In the late Iron Age (20 to 10 BC), the settlement was probably established by people from the Atrebates tribe from north-west Gaul in modern France. A major trading centre dealing in goods such as metals, foodstuffs, horses, chariot gear and slaves, it consisted of an inner earthwork enclosing an area of 32ha (79 acres), much of which was occupied with roundhouses and metalled streets, palisaded enclosures and rubbish pits. As many as 161 different plant species have been identified from six different well deposits, two dating from late Iron Age (20/10 BC to AD 55) and four from the late Iron Age/Roman period (AD 43 to 70/80) when the site had developed into a large town with a grid of streets, public baths, a forum basilica and an amphitheatre. Some of these plants would have been growing within the settlement, while others would have been brought in as food or fodder from the surrounding land. They formed distinct groups of species, characteristic of different land uses.

Cultivated plants and crops As well as cereals, Flax *Linum usitatissimum* was the most common crop, along with Celery *Apium graveolens*. Herbs include Dill *Anethum graveolens*, Fennel *Foeniculum vulgare* and Coriander *Coriandrum sativum*. Remains of Olive *Olea europaea* and Sweet Cherry *Prunus avium* were also found.

One of the first steps towards urbanisation in Great Britain, the Iron Age town of Calleva (Silchester) was a well-developed social, economic and political hub, with three distinct areas separated by wide streets. One of these contained the great hall, a unique timber building nearly 50m long.

Disturbed, arable land These formed the largest group of plants (47 species), with Knotgrass *Polygonum aviculare*, Fat Hen *Chenopodium album*, Common Chickweed and Small Nettle *Urtica urens* being most frequent. Other notable species include Corncockle, Venus's-looking-glass *Legousia hybrida* and Opium Poppy. There was also a remarkably high frequency of Deadly Nightshade *Atropa belladonna* and Black Horehound *Ballota nigra*.

Grasslands The second-largest group of plants (36 species), with Creeping Buttercup *Ranunculus repens* and Yellow-rattle *Rhinanthus minor* being particularly abundant, along with Oxeye Daisy *Leucanthemum vulgare*, Common Knapweed *Centaurea nigra* and Tormentil *Potentilla erecta*, and unusual meadow plants like Corky-fruited Water-dropwort *Oenanthe pimpinelloides*. These were most likely components of hay meadows and grazed grasslands.

Wet ground A group of 19 species dominated by Meadowsweet *Filipendula ulmaria*, Common Spike-rush *Eleocharis palustris*, Soft-rush *Juncus effusus* and Lesser Spearwort *Ranunculus flammula*, as well as Common Meadow-rue *Thalictrum flavum*, Ragged-Robin *Silene flos-cuculi* and Water Mint *Mentha aquatica*. These probably grew on floodplain hay meadows, wet grazing pastures or in ditches.

Heathland A small group dominated by Heath-grass *Danthonia decumbens*, Bracken *Pteridium aquilinum* and Gorse *Ulex europaeus*. Fragments of *Sphagnum* mosses were also frequent along with Heather *Calluna vulgaris*. These plants perhaps provide the earliest known evidence for stable-flooring material,

supporting other evidence that suggests oppida were important for managing horses.

These botanical remains paint a picture of Cavella as a bustling trade settlement with a focus on horses for which hay and bedding are required. These were harvested from carefully managed meadows and heathlands in the surrounding landscape and regularly brought into the settlement. It's very likely seed escaped from the hay and gained a foothold in the streets and beside the buildings; we can imagine more robust meadow plants like grasses, Oxeye Daisy, Knapweed and Yarrow *Achillea millefolium* growing around the town. The horses' bedding, rich in dung, would have been piled up in midden heaps and become covered in nitrogen-loving plants, not just native Common Chickweed and Fat Hen, but also new arrivals from mainland Europe like Fig-leaved Goosefoot *Chenopodium ficifolium* and Many-seeded Goosefoot *Lipandra polysperma*. Other new arrivals included herbs and foodplants such as Celery and Coriander, which would likely have been grown inside the settlement walls. Outside, cultivated fields of Flax, Spelt Wheat and Barley supported an increasingly rich and colourful arable flora, and again it's likely that some of these – Common Poppy, Corncockle and Pale Persicaria *Persicaria lapathifolia* – found their way inside the settlement walls.

Rather wonderfully, 43 of the species recorded from the Iron Age and Roman wells are still present in the area, including Black Horehound, Common Poppy, Black-bindweed and Greater Celandine *Chelidonium majus*, which still grows beside the Roman walls where it was probably flowering more than 1,900 years ago.

Urban Plants

ABOVE: The medicinal herbs Hound's-tongue (left) and White Horehound (right) are among the first urban plants recorded in Britain, noted to be growing in towns and villages nearly 500 years ago.

Perhaps slightly more evocative is an observation by Gerard (1597), who noted Navelwort *Umbilicus rupestris* growing on Westminster Abbey, 'over the doore that leadeth from Chaucer his tombe to the olde palace'. Sadly, this plant had gone by 1633. Another famous early record was of London Rocket *Sisymbrium irio*, a native of Western Europe and the Mediterranean. This species was first observed in 1666 when Christopher Merrett described it as growing 'almost everywhere in the Suburbs of London on walls & beside ditches' (Merrett 1666). Then, early in the morning of 2nd September 1666, a fire broke out in Thomas Farriner's bakery on Pudding Lane. Five days later, the Great Fire had destroyed a third of London and 100,000 people had been made homeless. Fires were common in towns and cities at the time and it's a galling irony that such urban disasters provided wonderful opportunities for the spread of ruderal plants through the creation of large areas of bare, open ground for colonisation; in 1667 and 1668 London Rocket appeared in huge quantities, especially around the rubble of St Paul's Cathedral (Ray 1670). It is still to be found on the streets of London, an iconic plant of the city that retains deep cultural links with the capital's history.

From the late eighteenth century and through the nineteenth century, towns and cities underwent monumental transformations as the Industrial Revolution wrought its many changes. Populations swelled as people moved in from the countryside, and building density increased considerably with new housing, factories, municipal buildings and establishments for entertainment, like taverns, music halls and theatres. As the urban population increased, the condition

A brief history of our urban plants

of streets deteriorated and groups of men called Paving Commissioners were given powers to pave, clean and light the streets with oil lamps (Lambert 2021).

It's difficult for us to appreciate the true character of streets in Victorian Britain. As well as throngs of people, most transport was by horse with their accompanying carts and carriages, and livestock was still brought into towns and cities for market. In 1846, for example, 310,000 cattle and 1,600,000 sheep were driven through the streets of London into Smithfield Market alone (Hansard 1849), and by the 1890s around 300,000 horses were on the streets of London. It's estimated that these animals produced something like 1,000 tonnes of dung every day and the streets were soaked with urine. Although young boys were employed to dodge the traffic and scoop up the dung, the problem was never really solved (Jackson 2015). With all these animals came seeds of plants, either attached to their coats or in their feed and dung, and these found a rich substrate in which to grow on the streets.

ABOVE: London Rocket boomed in London following the Great Fire of 1666. It germinates each autumn and winter and is increasing once again in London thanks to our warmer winters.

LEFT: Horse-drawn carriages, trams and carts crowd Threadneedle Street, London, in 1901. Note the hay being carried on the open cart, shedding seed onto the street.

Urban Plants

ABOVE: Sheep and cattle being driven to Smithfield Market over Waterloo Bridge, London, around 1920.

In 1894, the first petrol vehicle was driven on a public road in Great Britain and by 1900 there were around 700–800 cars on the roads. By 1930, this had risen to one million. As horses and livestock disappeared and motorised vehicles came to dominate, our urban roads changed forever. Meanwhile, development of the railway network through the 1800s had led to the construction of 3,926km (2,440 miles) of railway by 1845, carrying 30 million passengers per annum. As well as people, plants also exploited the new road and rail networks to spread far and wide, the most famous example being Oxford Ragwort *Senecio squalidus*, which travelled around Great Britain after reaching Oxford railway station in around 1879 (see pages 256–257).

One of the biggest changes to our urban landscapes came with the Blitz during the Second World War. On 7th September 1940, Germany began 57 consecutive nights of bombing, initially over London but then extending to other major cities. Coventry was among the worst hit, with 503 tonnes of high explosive and 30,000 incendiary bombs dropped on the city. One of the biggest single attacks targeted Bristol on 24th November 1940, when 1,540 tonnes of high explosive and 12,500 incendiary devices fell from the skies (Imperial War Museum 2024). The scale of the destruction is difficult to imagine now. In London alone, more than 70,000 buildings were completely demolished, and another 1.7 million were damaged (Mason 2016). Just one bomb site – Cripplegate in London – was a 39-acre scar through the city, half a mile long by a quarter of a mile wide and left 'with only a few isolated buildings standing' (Jones 1957). Once cleared of the damage, some of these open areas of rubble and earth were sown with seed and planted to create bomb-site city gardens, but most were left alone and allowed to be colonised naturally by pioneer plants (see Chapter 9). With its wind-borne seed, Rosebay Willowherb *Chamaenerion angustifolium* was the most famous of these, turning vast expanses of ruined land a vivid pinkish-purple. Ironically, it was this postwar flowering of such bomb sites across Great Britain and Europe that helped to stimulate an interest in urban botany.

In recent decades, political stability and economic growth have driven urban expansion like never before. This has placed towns and cities in a constant state of flux, a dynamic pattern of growth, innovation, decline, redevelopment and renewal. Some of these changes are small in scale and happen continually; the constant upkeep of urban infrastructure sees pavement surfaces replaced, walls rebuilt and repointed, front gardens converted to car parking, and fragments of abandoned urban land transformed into amenity areas. At the medium scale, individual buildings are often revamped and abandoned plots of land redeveloped, especially given the pressures of the current housing crisis and economic value of vacant plots. Larger-scale changes are less frequent but take place as part of town- and city-centre renewal and grand new infrastructure projects, such as Birmingham's Big City Plan. And, of course, there's the relentless continual expansion of housing, retail and industry on the urban fringe. With all this flux and change, it's little wonder that urban botany can be so thrilling.

ABOVE: Even ten years after the German Air Raids of 1940 and 1941, large areas in many city centres remained undeveloped. Here, the view from Fore Street towards Moorgate in June 1950 shows dense vegetation on the cleared land.

INSET: Rosebay Willowherb became known as Bombweed or Fireweed after its colonisation of urban bomb sites. It remains one of our most common urban plants, an echo of those horrific times.

Urban botany today

chapter three

It could be said that urban botany is undergoing a bit of a renaissance, with a recent surge in popularity. This wasn't always the case. For many years it was generally viewed with distain. Indeed, some considered that it wasn't 'real' botany at all, dealing as it did with what were seen as grim little pavement weeds, many of which were aliens, with little scientific interest or conservation value. Thankfully, attitudes have changed. We are now a thoroughly urban population and many of us are taking more of an interest in the natural environment, especially in light of the heightening biodiversity crisis. We're also realising just how fascinating the urban flora is, with novel species and communities in constant flux, thriving in the most intense of anthropogenic environments. We're appreciating that they can help us understand our impact on all habitats, since none are free from human influence. And we're beginning to treat our alien flora with a little more respect, regarding these species for what they are – simply plants that are on an urban journey with us all.

Today, many individuals and groups of enthusiasts are studying urban floras, either on their own or as part of a natural history society or more informal local flora group. Examples include:

- The London Natural History Society, a large and active group who regularly survey the botany of the English capital (LNHS 2024).
- The Cambridge Natural History Society, who have been intensively surveying the city since 2003 and have recorded around 1,800 species. An account of the botany of the city appears in the recently published *The Nature of Cambridge* (Hill 2023).
- The Urban Flora of Newcastle project, initiated by James Common to record the city flora along with a group of enthusiasts from the Natural History Society of Newcastle (see pages 44–45).

OPPOSITE:
Dandelion *Taraxacum* and Herb-Robert *Geranium robertianum* growing on a derelict urban site in Bristol.

- The Botanical Society of Scotland, who have been recording urban habitats throughout Scotland since 2015. Their checklist, taken from any settlement with a population over 1,000 people, currently runs to 1,150 species. In 2023 they hosted an excellent conference *Urban Floras – a Contribution to Biodiversity* (BSS 2024).

- The Nottinghamshire Wildlife Trust City Local Group, who are celebrating and updating *The Plants of Nottingham* (Shepherd 1998) to see how the flora has changed in the 25 years since its publication (Fry 2023).

- The Hull Natural History Society, who have been recording the wildlife of the city and surrounding areas since 1880. In 2000, Richard Middleton produced *The plants of Hull, a millennium atlas*, which can be found on the society website (Middleton 2000).

- The changing street flora of Cambridge and Aberystwyth, which has been studied in detail over several decades by Chris Preston and Arthur Chater, respectively, most recently in 2023 (Chater *et al.* 2000, Preston & Chater 2024). Chris has also been surveying Cambridge streets each month to investigate the phenology (flowering times) of urban plants (Preston 2020).

Having painted a picture of urban botany being in rather rude health, it's curious that specific Floras have been published for only ten cities in Britain and Ireland: Plymouth, London, Shrewsbury, Derby, Nottingham, Sheffield, Hull, Glasgow, Belfast, Dublin (see Chapter 4 for more details). Seven other county Floras consider their capital city in detail, for example Exeter in *Atlas of the Devon Flora* (Ivimey-Cook 1984) and Leeds in *The West Yorkshire Plant Atlas* (Lavin & Wilmore 1994), while several others consider the broader wildlife of individual cities (such as the wonderful *A Natural History of Aberdeen*, Marren 1982) or of urban areas in their county (such as *Warwickshire's Wildflowers* that covers Coventry, Solihull and much of east Birmingham, Falk 2009). However, that leaves many towns and cities whose urban floras remain largely undocumented.

Even more surprisingly, this volume you're reading now is the first book on British urban botany aimed at bringing this fascinating subject to a wider audience. There are several superb urban ecology books with a strong botanical focus, including Oliver Gilbert's *The Ecology of Urban Habitats* (1989) and Arnold Darlington's *Ecology of Walls* (1981), but these are now more than 35 years old. This book brings the subject up to date, telling the stories of urban plants over what has been an intense period of change. Hopefully, it will also stimulate other people to take a fresh look at urban botany and pay closer attention to the plants on their own streets, pavements and walls.

Urban botany is also thriving on social media, where the hashtag #pavementplants is used to share photos of people's finds, often the most unexpected plants in the most unexpected places. Each one is a wonderful snapshot of our everyday urban plant encounters: 'seen while waiting for the bus', 'caught my eye on my way to work', 'found en route to the corner shop for icy lollies!' and 'spotted as we were leaving the restaurant where we'd been celebrating our eldest son's birthday'. For many people, such encounters are their only daily contact with wild plants, as valuable and rewarding as any wildlife discovery.

Another popular social media hashtag is #morethanweeds, popularised by a project led by Sophie Leguil to change our perception of urban plants growing on walls and pavements. Inspired by the French 2001 initiative *'Sauvages de ma rue'* ('wild plants of my street'), it highlights the role such plants have in our lives with the clarion call that they are indeed more than just weeds. The project aims to spark an interest in urban flora and encourage local authorities to embrace urban biodiversity and manage it in a more sustainable and less damaging way, without the use of chemicals (Leguil 2021).

LEFT: Garden Lobelia *Lobelia erinus* from last year's hanging baskets colonising the pavement in front of Cardiff City Hall, shared by Jude Wood on social media using the hashtag #pavementplants.

A new Flora of Newcastle

Often, it's the passion of a single person that gets a project rolling. James Common has taken up the challenge of recording the urban flora of his hometown, Newcastle upon Tyne. Along with a merry band of helpers from the Natural History Society of Northumbria, he's been surveying all sorts of habitats around the city, including pavements, walls, waste ground, verges and former industrial sites.

Some remarkable and unusual plants have been turning up. Ragweed *Ambrosia artemisiifolia*, from North America, has appeared on the edge of a pond where ducks are fed birdseed. This frost-sensitive species has increased markedly recently as our climate has warmed. Despite being very popular in gardens, Curry-plant *Helichrysum italicum* is a rather uncommon escape but has appeared on a pavement in the city from raised beds along the street. At the other end of the spectrum, Dune Helleborine *Epipactis dunensis* – a very rare native orchid of sand dunes – has appeared under birch *Betula* trees on an old brownfield site. It's a species that's behaving rather oddly in Great Britain, as it's recently begun to appear in all sorts of urban habitats in the north of England and Scotland (see pages 284–285). Another surprise was a remarkable plant of Northern Marsh-orchid *Dactylorhiza purpurella* pushing up between a road gutter and pavement in the city centre, a discovery that James says 'nearly made me drop my bacon roll'.

The project is also revealing some real urban winners, plants on the increase such as Narrow-leaved Ragwort *Senecio inaequidens*, which arrived recently in the city, and Italian Alder *Alnus cordata*, which is continually being planted on streets and amenity areas and seeds abundantly. Another group on the march are the Cotoneasters *Cotoneaster* spp.: James (one of a very small band of self-confessed Cotoneasterphiles) has found 16 different species in the city so far. It's not just aliens on the increase though. Surprisingly, Small Scabious *Scabiosa columbaria*, a limestone grassland specialist, is also popping up in many places as it seems to get sown in wildflower mixes on urban road verges.

Recording the flora of an entire city is a mammoth task. James started surveying in 2022 and by October 2024 had recorded an astonishing 991 species, around 41% of which are neophytes. This is a higher proportion than for other cities (27% on average) and may be a legacy of Newcastle's large Victorian parks which were maintained as naturalistic gardens before being left to run wild, as well as the presence of many bird-sown alien shrubs across the city. James's wonderful blog gives regular updates on progress and his enthusiasm for urban botany really shines through (Common 2022, 2023a, 2023b).

Recording Bee Orchid *Orchis apifera* on the grassy bank of a retail park in Newcastle.

Urban botany today

Curry-plant.

Narrow-leaved Ragwort.

Ragweed.

Northern Marsh-orchid.

Bullate Cotoneaster *Cotoneaster rehderi*.

Taking up the baton to reduce herbicide use on our streets, the Pesticide Action Network has published *Greener Cities: A guide to the plants on our pavements* (PAN 2023), which celebrates pavement plants and gives guidance on how our streets can be managed without pesticides.

A grassroots movement is taking more direct action to raise awareness of pavement plants. The rather wonderfully named #RebelBotanists are taking an unconventional, 'Banksy-esque street art' approach to naming plants found growing on pavements. By chalking the names directly onto pavements and walls, the idea is to spark curiosity in the everyday flowers and highlight the role they play in the urban environment (Rebel Botanists 2024). It's an immensely appealing approach (and let's be honest, who among us isn't a bit of a rebel?) which has attracted a lot of support and attention. Unfortunately, before you reach for your chalk, a note of caution is needed because it's actually illegal to chalk anything on a public pavement, wall, tree or other structure in the UK without prior permission from the local council. This has been granted by a couple of authorities for specific projects, but generally it's not allowed. Whether you embrace the idea or not depends on how much of a #RebelBotanist you are.

RIGHT AND OPPOSITE: The #RebelBotanists movement uses strong images and direct action to raise awareness of pavement plants.

Urban botany today

Part Two

The roots of urban botany

Origin of urban plants | chapter four

Just as cities are melting pots of people from all around the world, so is our urban flora. While the majority of our urban plants are British natives, resident here since the end of the last Ice Age, many others are a reflection today's global village, an eclectic mix of characters that we have drawn together from all corners of the planet. How they come to live alongside us reveals much about our cultural and historical relationships with these species.

As any settlement grows over time, its flora is drawn from three main sources (Williams *et al.* 2009). Firstly, there are native species originally found growing in the area. These can occur in small fragments of semi-natural habitats – woodlands, grasslands and riverbanks, for example – that were once part of the rural landscape but are now surrounded by urban development. These fragments, known as **encapsulated countryside** (Gilbert 1989), are extremely important as they act as pools of urban biodiversity. Sometimes, they can still be home to species typical of ancient woodland and grassland habitats. In Middlesbrough, for instance, populations of Great Burnet *Sanguisorba officinalis*, Pepper-saxifrage *Silaum silaus* and Bloody Crane's-bill *Geranium sanguineum* can still be found in fragments of lime-rich ancient grassland within the city (Allen 2023). Indeed, a satellite photograph of any urban area will show a scattering of small open fields and grasslands, woodlands and rivers entirely surrounded by urban sprawl. This is especially evident on the outskirts, where new industrial estates and out-of-town shopping centres have recently expanded into the rural landscape.

As well as being important in their own right, areas of encapsulated countryside can be a source of species that literally seed themselves

PREVIOUS PAGES:
Hart's-tongue *Asplenium scolopendrium* emerging between the bricks of an old wall in Sheffield city centre.

OPPOSITE:
A pub in Usk, Monmouthshire, prepares for the annual Britain in Bloom competition with tubs and baskets full of plants from all around the world.

Urban Plants

ABOVE: Aerial view of Hemel Hempstead, Hertfordshire, showing 'encapsulated countryside' – remnant fragments of semi-natural grassland and riverbanks that are now surrounded by urban development.

into the surrounding urban landscape. This usually occurs with the more robust components of semi-natural vegetation, the most competitive and adaptable species that can colonise new habitats created by urbanisation. Some of our more resilient woodland flowers, such as Wood Avens *Geum urbanum* and Common Dog-violet *Viola riviniana*, often move out of surviving fragments of old-growth woodland into urban habitats such as pavements, path sides and waste ground.

Secondly, native species that weren't originally found in the area can arrive and spread in novel habitats created by urbanisation. Maidenhair Spleenwort *Asplenium trichomanes* and Wall-rue *Asplenium ruta-muraria* are classic examples, as these ferns of lime-rich rock outcrops would normally be quite rare across large parts of lowland Britain and Ireland. They have, however, found a second home in the lime-rich mortar of masonry walls, readily occupying these entirely artificial rock-faces.

The third source of plants, of course, comes through the arrival, escape and spread of alien species. On average, around 39% of our urban flora is made up of plants we've introduced, a much greater proportion than any semi-natural habitat. Many of these species have a high degree of urbanity, remaining largely restricted to urban habitats and rarely venturing out of the city into rural landscapes. These aliens come together with native species to create entirely new communities of plants, some of which can be considered emblematic of urban habitats; a good example would be pavements that host native Annual Meadow-grass *Poa annua*, Hairy Bittercress *Cardamine hirsuta* and Groundsel *Senecio vulgaris* along with alien Canadian Fleabane *Erigeron candensis*, Oxford Ragwort *Senecio squalidus* and Purple Toadflax *Linaria purpurea*. Such hybrid native–alien communities are uniquely urban and are sometimes described as **recombinant ecosystems**, created by humans deliberately, inadvertently or indirectly and driven by historic cultural factors such as migration, colonisation, trade, globalisation and urban development (Rotherham 2017).

For any alien species to arrive and spread successfully, it has to overcome quite a number of obstacles. There are geographical barriers (the challenge of arriving here in the first place, either intentionally through the horticultural trade, or unintentionally by hitch-hiking on goods or people or livestock), environmental barriers (such as being able to survive in our climate), reproductive barriers (being able to attract pollinators and produce seeds) and dispersal barriers (being able to travel to new places). Sometimes, a species can't overcome all these barriers straight away, but might need to adapt to local conditions or rely on later introductions that include individuals with different genetic characteristics. Only when all these obstacles are surmounted can a species go on to become successfully naturalised, spreading around its newly adopted home. In urban settings, this happens most readily in open, ruderal habitats such as pavements and waste ground, but more vigorous and dominant species can also colonise more closed vegetation like riverbanks and grass verges (Richardson *et al.* 2000).

BELOW: Common Dog-violet is a tolerant and adaptable woodland species that can colonise urban habitats, especially the shaded bases of walls.

Multicultural roots: origins of our alien urban flora

Plants from every continent except Antarctica have found themselves a new home here, largely thanks to our long history of exploration and trade and our legendary obsession with gardening. In a study of alien plants in Europe, Lambdon *et al.* (2008) found that the UK had the second-highest number of alien species, with 1,779 species (a little behind Belgium with 1,969), and the highest number of naturalised neophytes (857 species). Across Europe, they found that most alien species come from Asia (59%), followed by other European countries (53%), Africa (36%), North America (18%), South America (16%) and Australasia (3% – note that these totals exceed 100% because many species come from several different continents). They also calculated that, on average, 6.2 new species arrive in Europe every year.

Pinning down the actual origin of many alien species is not so easy, though, and we shouldn't fall into the trap of assuming that all alien plants are, as Chris Preston puts it, 'somebody else's natives'. Indeed, many aliens don't have 'natural' origins at all, but have been modified by humans long before they arrived on our shores or escaped into the wild. We don't know what proportion of species this applies to, but it's at least 15% of the neophyte flora and maybe as much as 30% or even 50% (Preston 2022).

Many garden plants are highly selected forms of wild species that have been brought into horticulture and selected for their vigour, aesthetic appeal (flower size, shape and colour for example), and ease of cultivation, so much so that they no longer resemble the original wild species. Examples include Dotted Loosestrife *Lysimachia punctata* from Eastern Europe and western Asia, Lilac *Syringa vulgaris* from Southern Europe and Orange Day-lily *Hemerocallis fulva* from China. This form of selection also applies to agricultural crops, such as Lucerne *Medicago sativa* subsp. *sativa*, which was derived from the western Asian subspecies *M. sativa* subsp. *caerulea* (Preston 2022).

Other ornamental garden plants appear to have arisen *de novo* in cultivation, with their exact origins lost in the mists of time. Pot Marigold *Calendula officinalis* is one such species, completely unknown in the wild but probably arising from hybridisation of similar species in the western and central Mediterranean. Another ancient garden plant of unknown origin is Nasturtium *Tropaeolum majus*, widely grown in South America in pre-Columbian times and arriving in Europe as seed from Peru in 1684. Many crops also evolved in a similar way.

Broad Bean *Vicia faba* is entirely unknown as a wild plant, perhaps evolving from a now long-extinct species. Similarly, we know little about the actual origins of Tomato *Solanum lycopersicum* or Quinoa *Chenopodium quinoa*, both from South America. Recent molecular genetic work has thrown up a complete conundrum regarding the origin of Common Millet *Panicum miliaceum*. Grown in China as long ago as the Neolithic around 5000 BC, this important crop species appears to have two ancestors in its genome, one shared with Torpedo Grass *Panicum repens* from Asia and another from Witch-grass *Panicum capillare* from North America. Quite how the genes from a New World species found their way into an Old World crop being developed in ancient China is a complete mystery (Hunt *et al.* 2018, Preston 2022).

ABOVE: Nasturtium appears to have arisen in cultivation in pre-Columbian South America through hybridisation of wild species. The common name comes from the Latin 'naris' (nose) and 'torquere' (to twist), a common effect when the pungent leaves are eaten.

Another group of modified plants includes those that are still evolving on their journey, such as Narrow-leaved Ragwort *Senecio inaequidens* from South Africa. Introduced into Europe multiple times in the nineteenth and early twentieth centuries, this species didn't begin to spread widely until new forms evolved in the city of Verviers, Belgium. Rather than flowering in autumn (as it does in its native range), these forms started flowering in spring, a change that considerably improved seed production and seedling survival. This and other adaptations to our northern climate have allowed it to become one of the fastest-spreading aliens in Europe, but ours is now a very different plant to the original species in South Africa (Lachmuth *et al.* 2010, Preston 2022).

These new perspectives on the origin of alien plants and garden escapes can profoundly alter the way we view them. Rather than regarding them simply as unwelcome foreign invaders, arriving here and taking advantage of the opportunities we've presented them with, the relationship is much deeper and more complex. Many of these species have evolved with us, shaped and forged by our own hands over centuries and millennia, and their lives are intimately intertwined with ours. As Chris Preston eloquently notes, 'for millennia, we've not only been modifying the environment of the planet, but we've been modifying the species too, so we are increasingly living in a world of our own making' (Preston 2020).

From Cwm Idwal to Cwmbran: Welsh Poppy on the move

One of our native wildflowers that I love the most is Welsh Poppy *Papaver cambricum*. On many occasions I've climbed high into the bowl of Cwm Idwal in the mountains of Eryri (Snowdonia) to find it sheltering among huge boulders, cool and damp with its feet in the stream splashing down from the narrow defile of the Devil's Kitchen in the cliffs above. This is a stunning location, a lofty lookout over the lake far below. Welsh Poppy is a scarce plant in such settings, found as a native in only 94 10-km squares in Wales, Ireland and south-west England.

And yet, travel to the heart of many urban areas, from Cwmbran to Cambridge or Carlisle, and you'll find Welsh Poppy growing in the streets. It pops up everywhere, on sunny pavements and dry walls, along verges and on waste ground. In fact, the species has undergone a meteoric rise since the 1900s, a spread that seems to be accelerating (it has increased by 61% since 2000). Across Great Britain, it is now recorded from 1,890 10-km squares, 67% of the total (Stroh *et al.* 2023).

Easy to grow from seed, it's incredibly popular in gardens and this is where the new plants have originated. To understand how such a scarce and delicate native species can spread so vigorously, we need to look at its history and genetics. Although the first cultivated plants, grown in James Sherard's garden at Eltham (Kent) in 1732, were probably of British wild stock, these and other early introductions failed to spread. It wasn't until the twentieth century that the species changed its behaviour.

As well as Britain and Ireland, Welsh Poppy also grows as a native plant in mountainous parts of northern Spain, the Pyrenees and central France. In a study of plants from across its range, Valtueña *et al.* (2011) found that our rapidly spreading garden escapes originally come from the central and eastern Pyrenees. This, it seems, gives them some competitive advantage. Coming from further south in the species' range, maybe they're better able to cope with warmer and drier conditions. Or, like many other garden plants, we might have inadvertently selected more robust forms in cultivation. Alternatively, perhaps we've just introduced them widely to places they just otherwise wouldn't have reached. We don't yet know. What we can say, though, is that Welsh Poppy is another example of the extent to which we've fundamentally modified our flora, turning an uncommon mountain and woodland flower into an urban conqueror.

Native Welsh Poppy growing wild in Cwm Idwal, Eryri (Snowdonia).

Although just 160 microns thick, Welsh Poppy petals are highly pigmented, with special S-shaped cell walls and air cavities that help scatter light and make them appear brighter (van der Kooi & Stavenga 2019).

Escaped Welsh Poppy on a pavement in suburban Sheffield.

Over the garden wall

As might be expected, most of our aliens arrive through horticulture. We are indeed a nation of gardeners; Office for National Statistics' figures show that 83% of households have a garden, the average size of which is 188m^2 (ONS 2020), equivalent to the area of around 16 car-parking spaces. And we fill our gardens with a huge diversity of plants; the Royal Horticultural Society estimates that 400,000 different types of plant (including hybrids and cultivars) are being grown in UK gardens (RHS pers. comm.). It's not surprising that many of these jump over the garden wall, as plants are highly accomplished escape artists. From our hanging baskets and pots spill gaudy annual bedding plants such as Garden Lobelia *Lobelia erinus* (from South Africa), Snapdragon *Antirrhinum majus* (south-western Europe), Petunia *Petunia* × *hybrida* (South America) and Californian Poppy *Eschscholzia californica* (North America). Our rockeries have spawned sprawling perennials like Trailing Bellflower *Campanula poscharskyana* (Adriatic), Yellow Corydalis *Pseudofumaria lutea* (Alps), Mexican Fleabane *Erigeron karvinskianus* (Mexico) and Aubretia *Aubrieta deltoidea* (Sicily, the Balkans and south-western Asia). From our herbaceous beds and borders come numerous hardy perennials such as Green Alkanet *Pentaglottis sempervirens* (south-western Europe), Garden Lady's-mantle *Alchemilla mollis* (south-eastern Europe and south-western Asia), Canadian Goldenrod *Solidago canadensis* (North America) and Atlas Poppy *Papaver atlanticum* (Morocco), as well as bulbs including Montbretia *Crocosmia* × *crocosmiiflora* (a garden hybrid of African parents), Spanish and Hybrid Bluebells *Hyacinthoides hispanica* agg. (Iberian peninsula) and Three-cornered Garlic *Allium triquetrum* (Mediterranean). And finally, our shrubberies have given rise to plants like the ubiquitous Buddleja *Buddleja davidii* (China), Oregon-grape *Mahonia aquifolium* (western North America) and Himalayan Cotoneaster *Cotoneaster simonsii* (Himalaya). All of these are regularly encountered in urban habitats, and new escapes are joining them all the time as horticultural fashions change and our quest for novelty shows no sign of diminishing.

Alongside these ornamental flowers and shrubs, some herbs and vegetables manage to escape, although perhaps considerably fewer than we might imagine given the quantities that we grow in gardens and allotments. The most frequent and familiar is probably Tomato (South and Central America). This is one of the few fruits we eat whole and whose seeds remain viable after they've passed through

ABOVE: Aubretia is one of our most popular rockery plants. The huge (140%) increase in 10-km square records since 1999 reflects both better recording of aliens but also a genuine spread outside gardens.

BELOW: Tomato from tropical South America on a Cambridge street. Plants frequently grow from fruit that's been discarded or dropped.

the human gut. As a result, Tomato plants are particularly common around sewerage works, but also appear regularly in streets from discarded fruits. In Cambridge, it's been noticed that tomatoes often appear alongside pub walls, presumably where the fruit has been regurgitated following a heavy night of drinking; in such spots, they have been referred to as 'vomit flowers' or 'puke plants' (Chris Preston pers. comm.). Occasionally Sweet Pepper *Capsicum annuum* (tropical Americas) and Marrow *Cucurbita pepo* (Central and North America) also arise from discarded fruit, and even Avocado *Persea americana* (Central America) has appeared in a few warm spots in London (see pages 78–79).

Herbs and salad species also appear regularly from seed, especially Borage *Borago officinalis* (Mediterranean) and Garden Rocket *Eruca vesicaria* (Mediterranean region and south-western Asia), while the resurgence in growing herbs and salads has seen an increase in plants like Chinese Mustard *Brassica juncea* (horticultural origin), Root Beet *Beta vulgaris* subsp. *vulgaris* (horticultural origin) and

Origin of urban plants

Coriander *Coriandrum sativum* (northern Africa and western Asia). Another popular Mediterranean fruit has also become a bit of an urban specialist: Fig *Ficus carica* (eastern Mediterranean and south-western Asia) requires mild conditions to thrive and does particularly well in the warm embrace of the urban heat island (see Chapter 5). It's particularly frequent in London, with most records towards the centre of the city. In some northern towns, its establishment is linked to the historical discharge of warm water into rivers and canals, including in Sheffield where the River Don was heated to 20°C thanks to the steel industry, in Leeds where the River Aire was heated by a power station, and along a canal in Liverpool heated by water from the Tate & Lyle sugar refinery (Gilbert 1990).

ABOVE: A large Fig in central London with abundant ripe fruit. Since we lack the wasps that pollinate the fruit, all homegrown figs are sterile. Plants arising spontaneously on pavements come instead from discarded fertile fruits imported from abroad.

From houseplant to city plant

It's easy to imagine garden plants leaping over the fence or wall and becoming established in the streets beyond. But it's much harder to envisage tender houseplants that are cosseted indoors doing the same. This is precisely what has happened, though, with a remarkable range of alien ferns. Since their microscopic spores are easily carried on a breeze through open windows and doors, they just need to find a moist spot and a little extra warmth from the urban heat island

Urban Plants

TOP: Ribbon Fern naturalised in a stairwell at Kew Botanic Gardens.

ABOVE: Tender Brake, which survived on the steps of a basement in Bath for seven years.

to survive. These exotic ferns are usually found in sheltered streets, beneath drainage gratings, on stairwells and in open basements, and are well worth seeking out. Such plants don't always survive for long, however, as they're prone to being cleaned away or succumbing to the occasional harsh winter. If you do find one, take a photograph and get it identified as soon as you can.

The Brake ferns *Pteris* spp. are particularly accomplished escape artists (Crouch 2020, Rumsey & Crouch 2008). The most frequent is Ribbon Fern *Pteris cretica* from tropical and warm-temperate parts of the Old World. A handsome and distinctive species, it's very popular as a houseplant and has become established quite widely in England, especially London. It can't tolerate temperatures below about 2°C, so it prefers warmer urban sites. The closely related Variegated Ribbon-fern *P. parkeri* from Japan, Taiwan and Korea, with a white stripe down the centre of its fronds, is equally popular as a houseplant and has been found in Cambridge, London and Bath. Also in Bath, Jungle Brake *P. umbrosa* from Australia was found in a basement in 2009 and that plant is now over a metre (3ft) across. Spider Brake *P. multifida*, a native of Japan and China, is less common but does occasionally escape (including two extraordinary occurrences down wells inside pubs in Hampshire). Finally, Tender Brake *P. tremula*, from the rainforests of Australia and New Zealand, is a large and spectacular plant but is decidedly frost sensitive, so only grows in the most sheltered locations and rarely persists for long.

Perhaps the most frequent exotic ferns to escape are House Holly-fern *Cyrtomium falcatum* and Fortune's Holly-fern *C. fortunei*. These two are very similar and have been confused in the past, but the majority of plants are probably *C. fortunei* var. *clivicola*. With their long, arching fronds these can form impressive clumps on walls and in basements, but also crop up in woodlands and on coastal rocks.

Another very popular houseplant is Delta Maidenhair *Adiantum raddianum* from tropical America and Africa, a smaller and more delicate form of our native Maidenhair Fern *A. capillus-veneris*. This beautiful fern was first found as an escape by Fred Rumsey when he spotted a large clump growing on a sheltered house wall in Cambridge Street, Pimlico, London in 1997. Unfortunately, and much to Fred's dismay, the house was repointed and repainted within a month of his discovery, leaving no trace of the fern (Rumsey 1998). Today, it's found in a handful of sheltered sites in London, as well as in Bath and Leamington Spa in Warwickshire.

With the booming popularity of ferns as houseplants, more unusual species are escaping. Rasp Fern *Doodia australis*, from Australia and New Zealand, is very striking with its pinkish-red new fronds. A single plant was found by John Edgington on the wall of the Russell Hotel, London, in June 2005, but was lost when the hotel was refurbished after the terrorist bombing a month later (Edgington 2008). More persistent was Sickle Fern *Pellaea falcata*, known for more than ten years on a wall at South Dock in Rotherhithe, London. This small species – along with Button Fern *Pellaea rotundifolia* found on a wall in Mayfair, London – is hugely popular in enclosed glass-bottle gardens or terrariums, an environment that must be even more challenging from which to escape.

TOP: Delta Maidenhair in the basement of Burlington House, London.

CENTRE: Rasp Fern, growing on the wall of the Russell Hotel, London.

BOTTOM: Sickle Fern naturalised on the wall of South Dock in Rotherhithe, London.

The accidental hitchhikers

Horticulture not only brings us alien plants intentionally, but also by accident. Encouraged by our warming climate and the trend for instant 'designer' gardens, there has been an increase in the planting of large, specimen trees and plants imported from the Mediterranean, especially Spain and Italy. These include mature olive trees *Olea europaea* and figs, as well as Chusan Palm *Trachycarpus fortunei*, European Fan Palm *Chamaerops humilis*, Australian Tree-fern *Dicksonia antarctica* and even Sago Palm *Cycas revoluta*. These are invariably imported in large pots, which often come with their own little crop of alien 'weeds' (Hoste & Verloove 2010). A small suite of such warmth-loving hitchhikers – all of which have become more frequent recently in urban areas – are known to have arrived in this way (Leslie 2019, Mark Spencer pers. comm.). They include Mediterranean Nettle *Urtica membranacea* (Mediterranean), Jersey Cudweed *Laphangium luteoalbum* (widespread in the Old World), Spotted Spurge *Euphorbia maculata* (eastern North America), Early Meadow-grass *Poa infirma* (Canary Islands, Western Europe to Mediterranean and China) and Annual Beard-grass *Polypogon monspeliensis* (Macaronesia and Europe to Asia and Africa). Many other less exotic species can easily arrive in pots of soil, including New Zealand Bitter-cress *Cardamine corymbosa* (New Zealand) which is spreading widely through container-grown nursery stock (Stroh *et al.* 2023).

BELOW: Mediterranean Nettle hitching a lift in a pot of European Fan Palm. The plant is already flowering and could easily seed into a garden or street.

Of course, soil rich in seeds can also be moved around when it becomes stuck to the tyres, wheel arches and bodywork of vehicles. This is a very significant, but largely underappreciated, route of introduction. In a study of one of the busiest urban motorways in Berlin (which saw traffic of up to 50,000 vehicles per lane per day), the annual 'seed rain' from vehicles was estimated to be between 635 and 1,579 seeds/m^2/year (von der Lippe & Kowarik 2007). Of the 204 species carried by the vehicles, exactly half were alien, with Bread Wheat *Triticum aestivum* (cultivated origin) and Canadian Fleabane (North America) topping the list, along with familiar invasive species like Buddleja (China), Canadian Goldenrod *Solidago canadensis* (North America) and False-acacia *Robinia pseudoacacia* (eastern North America). Some very unexpected species were also transported this way, including Cape-gooseberry *Physalis peruviana* (South America) and Busy Lizzie *Impatiens walleriana* (Mozambique to Kenya). It's clear that, as we move around, we take all sorts of plants with us.

Feed the birds, tuppence a bag

Another major route of introduction is through seed we put out to feed birds and encourage them into our gardens. Individually, many of us might provide a few bags each year, but collectively huge quantities are involved; the British Trust for Ornithology estimates that around 50 to 60 thousand tonnes of bird food are provided in gardens annually (BTO 2023). That's an awful lot of seed, much of which remains uneaten and falls to the ground.

In a fascinating study to identify the contents of seed mixes, Hanson and Mason (1985) sowed hundreds of samples of birdseed, as well as examining plants growing on the waste tips of a large pet-food distributor in Lincolnshire. They found that 32 species were intentional components, including peanuts, sunflower seeds, wheat, barley and oats and a rich mix of plants like Common Millet *Panicum miliaceum* (Asia), Niger *Guizotia abyssinica* (East Africa), Hemp *Cannabis sativa* (Asia), Aniseed *Pimpinella anisum* (Mediterranean), Canary Grass *Phalaris canariensis* (north-west Africa and Canary Islands) and Buckwheat *Fagopyrum esculentum* (south-western China). However, alongside these were an astonishing number of unintentional hitchhikers that came free with the birdseed. In all, 438 species arrived this way, including exotic imports such as Mexican Poppy *Argemone mexicana* (North and Central America), Bladder Ketmia *Hibiscus trionum* (Europe, Africa and Asia), Caterpillar-plant *Scorpiurus muricatus* (Mediterranean and Asia) and Ivy-leaved Morning-glory *Ipomoea hederacea* (tropical America). Further study

BELOW: Buckwheat might have been cultivated in England as early as Anglo-Saxon times (fifth to the eleventh centuries). As well as appearing in birdseed and grown as a crop, it's also sown for pollinating bees and as a green manure.

Urban Plants

ABOVE: Subtropical Apple-of-Peru is increasing dramatically as a birdseed alien, perhaps because its seeds can survive better in our increasingly mild winters. It's also known as shoo-fly plant as it contains an insecticidal chemical, nicandrenone.

of seed mixes has since brought the total number recorded in the UK to just over 500 species (Hanson 2000). Many of these regularly appear underneath bird feeders, especially the cereal grasses (wheat, barley, oats and millets) along with Niger, Hemp, Buckwheat and Apple-of-Peru *Nicandra physalodes* (Peru). More unusual appearances include Safflower *Carthamus tinctorius* (southern Europe and Asia) and Ragweed *Ambrosia artemisiifolia* (North America).

Amenity planting

As well as plants that unintentionally escape from gardens, vast numbers are planted deliberately in our streets, parks and other non-garden settings. Alongside our familiar and much-loved street trees, the more recent fashion for amenity planting has introduced many other species into the urban landscape. These are the shrubs, grasses and flowers that are often planted in and around retail areas, supermarkets and superstores, industrial estates and office developments, and on roundabouts and in parks. The Horticultural Trades Association (HTA) has produced a list of the top species to plant in such settings, including 50 different types of trees, 100 shrubs and 100 herbaceous perennials (HTA 2010). Alongside the various maples *Acer* spp., alders *Alnus* spp., cherries *Prunus* spp. and rowans *Sorbus* spp., the shrubs include Spotted-laurel *Aucuba japonica* (from East Asia), Thunberg's Barberry *Berberis thunbergii* (Japan), Oregon-grape *Mahonia aquifolium* (western North America), Wilson's Honeysuckle *Lonicera nitida* (China), Mexican Orange *Choisya ternata* (Mexico), Spreading Oleaster *Elaeagnus umbellata* (Himalaya, China and Japan), Escallonia *Escallonia rubra* (Argentina and Chile) and numerous species of Cotoneaster *Cotoneaster* spp. (mainly from China and Himalaya). Evergreen, low-maintenance and often rather dull, these shrubs are usually trimmed into shape with a hedge cutter once a year. Increasingly, some of them are becoming established away from where they've been planted. Oregon-grape, barberries and cotoneasters are particularly prone to this, and the hugely popular Wilson's Honeysuckle is seeding prolifically now that the fertile cultivar 'Fertilis' has replaced the largely infertile 'Ernest Wilson' (Stroh *et al.* 2023).

Several common garden perennials are prominent on the HTA amenity planting list, including various species and varieties of African Lily *Agapanthus*, Elephant-ears *Bergenia*, spurges *Euphorbia*, crane's-bills *Geranium* and sages *Salvia*. Many of these are placed in sunny spots in raised beds, planted borders around seating areas, on roundabouts and in parks, and some readily become naturalised. Mediterranean Spurge *Euphorbia characias*, for example, is a very distinctive plant with spikes of lime-green flowers that appear in winter. It's often planted on roundabouts and around offices and car parks, from where it seeds readily into pavements and waste ground and along the base of walls; since 1999, the number of 10-km square records has increased by more than 570%, with most appearances in south-east England (Stroh *et al.* 2023).

Grasses have become a backbone of low-maintenance horticulture, and the HTA list includes 16 different grasses and sedges for amenity planting. A couple of species, though, raise an eyebrow as they're

ABOVE: Amenity planting beside offices in Bangor, Gwynedd, with a dense mix of Oregon-grape, Thunberg's Barberry, Cotoneaster and Hooker's Hebe.

BELOW: Mediterranean Spurge is popular in amenity planting schemes as it's very drought tolerant and flowers in early spring, as it does in its native Mediterranean range.

Urban Plants

RIGHT: Pampas-grass advancing along the railway line between Llandudno Junction and Conwy, North Wales. It's been known here since 1998 but seems to be spreading more enthusiastically in the last few years.

potentially very invasive. Argentine Needle-grass *Nassella tenuissima*, originally from North America, Mexico, Chile and Argentina, is very popular in gardens for its light, feathery inflorescences, but it's incredibly enthusiastic about seeding into pavements, roadsides, waste ground and other urban habitats. Each plant can produce between 70,000 and 100,000 seeds per year, and the species is regarded as invasive in parts of North America, New Zealand and Australia (Humphries & Florentine 2021). It's spreading rapidly, especially in and around London and westwards towards Reading and Oxford, and 87% of the 370 known records have been made since 2010.

Perhaps even more concerning is the spread of Pampas-grass *Cortaderia selloana*. Infamous as a supposed signal for sexual promiscuity in suburbia, this huge and impressive grass is also popular in amenity plantings. It's native to Argentina, Brazil, Chile and Uruguay but is known to be highly invasive in Australia, New Zealand, South Africa, southern Europe and parts of North

America, including California and Hawaii. Because this plant can get so large (over 3m tall and 1.5m wide), it literally shoulders aside native species in semi-natural habitats and, as well as being nigh-on impossible to remove, well-established clumps are estimated to produce up to one million wind-dispersed seeds annually (Lambrinos 2002). In Britain and Ireland, Pampas-grass has been known from the wild since 1906, but originally the plants didn't produce much seed here. Recently, however, more fertile forms are being grown, and the species is seeding and spreading rapidly in some areas, especially along railways and roads and on waste ground, as well as more natural settings such as dunes and sea cliffs. This spread is probably assisted by climate change, and since 1999 the number of 10-km square records has increased by 240%. As well as all along the south coast of England and Wales, it's now frequent in and around many cities including London, Birmingham, Nottingham, Liverpool and Manchester (Stroh *et al.* 2023). It's even reached the far north coast of mainland Scotland, with a record from a roadside in the village of Dunnet near John o' Groats.

Coming into port

Docks are ideal places for new plants to arrive and escape. Often, seeds come in as contaminants of consignments of grain and other foods, and then germinate if they get spilt as they're unloaded in the port. Now that grain-cleaning technologies have improved and shipping containers are sealed, escapes of such contaminants are much rarer. Giant Ragweed *Ambrosia trifida* from North America and Rough Cocklebur *Xanthium strumarium* from North and South America, for instance, are now extremely rare casuals.

One more recent arrival has been rather more successful. In 1992, Paul Stanley found Bilbao Fleabane *Erigeron floribundus* on a patch of waste ground near Southampton docks, the first record for Britain and Ireland. Originally from Chile, Argentina and Brazil, this rather dull, weedy species certainly doesn't have any horticultural value. Instead, it almost certainly arrived through the docks, with Paul speculating that its lightweight, dandelion-like seed might have hitched a lift from the Continent on a cross-channel ferry, inside an international shipping container, or even on a boat competing in the round-the-world yacht race (Stanley 1996). Curiously, Sylvia Reynolds also discovered it in 1992 near the port of Rosbercon on

ABOVE: As well as their intended cargoes, shipping containers can easily carry plant seeds around the world. This is Southampton Docks, Hampshire, where Bilbao Fleabane from South America first arrived in Britain in 1992.

the River Barrow in County Wexford (Reynolds 1997), while in 2008 the first record for Northern Ireland came from Belfast Ferry Port. Today, this species has moved into all sorts of urban habitats to become one of our fastest-spreading urban plants (see pages 158–159).

Botanic gardens

A final route of introduction is through botanic gardens, those melting pots of global floral diversity. Kew Gardens, for example, boasts a collection of more than 27,000 living plant taxa built on 260 years of global exploration and collection, while the Royal Botanic Garden Edinburgh is home to more than 13,500 living species. These huge collections of new and novel plants are prime sources of escapees. This is because, alongside well-known garden-worthy plants from all around the world, they're home to many other species that are of medicinal, cultural, conservation or taxonomic interest.

To give a brief chronology of those that are known to have escaped from Kew, Garden Arabis *Arabis caucasica* (from southern Europe, North Africa and Asia) was first recorded outside Kew's gates in 1855, followed shortly afterwards by Gallant Soldier *Galinsoga parviflora* (South America) in 1861. A few years later in 1869, Pineappleweed *Matricaria discoidea* (Asia) jumped the walls. Although small and rather inconspicuous, this species then launched one of the most remarkable invasions in British history. Assisted by the

LEFT: After escaping Kew Gardens in 1861, Gallant Soldier became so frequent in the streets and waste places around Richmond it was known as Kew Weed.

spread of its tiny seeds in soil carried on feet and vehicles, it has become one of the most ubiquitous weeds of disturbed soil, paths, gateways and waste ground everywhere. Finally, this species was followed in 1919 by Californian Brome *Ceratochloa carinata* (western North America) which has now spread to cities including London, Oxford and Manchester. In Scotland, the Royal Botanic Garden Edinburgh has spawned fewer escapes, but Spreading Mouse-ear-hawkweed *Pilosella flagellaris* subsp. *flagellaris* (Western Europe) may have originated from here in 1869, finding a home on the banks of a nearby railway, from where it has spread through the central belt of Scotland (Burton 2021).

Into the urban landscape

We are really only just beginning to appreciate the depth and complexity of the relationship between ourselves and urban plants. Everything we do has an impact, and nowhere is this more acute than in the built environment where we live, work and play. Alongside our own native species, we've nurtured and carried with us thousands of alien plants. Together, this broad pool of species has to cope with one of the most extreme environments on Earth. In the next chapter, we'll explore the physical nature of the urban landscape, and how it creates unique challenges that test the mettle of every plant growing in the city.

The physical urban environment

chapter five

Constantly changing and evolving over time, and constructed from a bewildering range of materials, urban habitats are highly complex, with an incredible diversity of places where plants can put down their roots. The juxtaposition of a densely built-up physical environment and its correspondingly dense human population leads to the creation of unique environmental conditions. Let's start with one of the best-known ways that cities modify the physical environment: the urban heat island.

It's hot in the city

In the early 1800s, London was already a vibrant, chaotic city, a kaleidoscope of neighbourhoods in a largely rural landscape (Schwarz 2001). However, it was still tiny, occupying an area of just 30 square km or 11.5 square miles (Greater London today occupies around 1,582 square km or 611 square miles). It was here that Luke Howard, a young pharmacist and budding climatologist, made a series of daily observations from weather stations inside and outside the city from 1806 to 1830. Despite its small size, he noticed that 'we find London always warmer than the country, the average excess of its temperature being 1.579° [deg F]'. This was equivalent to an increase of around 0.9°C, a slight but consistent effect. The increase was evident throughout the year but was most pronounced in winter, from November to March. He also noted that the increase 'belongs, in strictness, to the nights', which averaged about 2°C warmer than the surrounding country (Mills 2008).

This was the first ever measurement of the urban heat island (UHI), a rise in temperature in urban areas compared to the surrounding rural landscape. Howard concluded that 'the temperature of

OPPOSITE:
Sunset over London in January, showing pollution trapped in warm air above the city as a strong winter urban heat island begins to develop.

Urban Plants

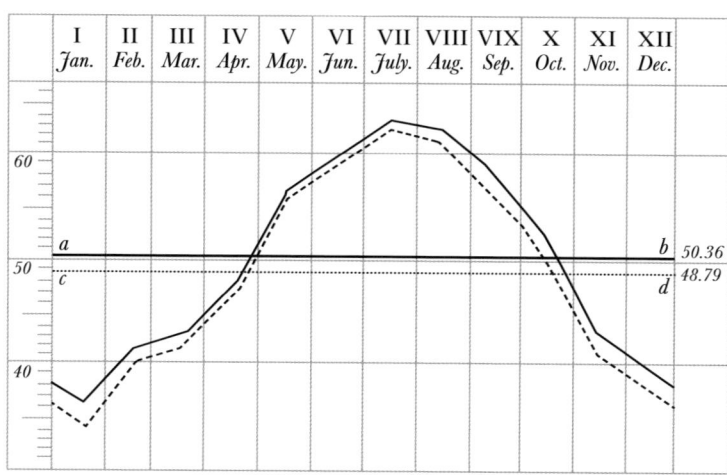

RIGHT: Luke Howard's 1806–1830 measurements of daily temperatures in London (solid line) and surrounding countryside (dashed line) showing the urban heat island for the first time. Graph from Mills (2008).

the city … partakes too much of an artificial warmth, induced by its structure, by a crowded population, and the consumption of great quantities of fuel in fires'. At that time, these sources of heat included innumerable domestic hearths as well as foundries, breweries, mills and even steam engines.

Howard observed that in summer the sun takes over and warms the city air more than the countryside. He identified three causes. Firstly, the vertical surfaces of the city reflect and radiate heat. Secondly, buildings impede light summer winds, trapping warmed air close to the ground. And thirdly, moisture evaporates much more rapidly in urban settings than the countryside, so less is available to cool the air. Howard's accurate understanding of the mechanisms involved, derived from his passion for careful observation, is quite staggering. His observations are entirely supported by modern analysis of the complex fluxes in long- and short-wave radiation from urban surfaces (Kershaw 2017, Mills 2008). The two main causes of UHIs are still regarded as solar radiation absorbed and re-radiated by urban structures, and direct heat generated by anthropogenic factors (Rizwan *et al.* 2007). While steam engines may not contribute as much heat today as they did in the 1830s, we have added a multitude of new heat sources including vehicles, air-conditioning units, industrial processes and all manner of electrical gadgets and devices that require cooling. We've also added considerably more air pollution, which reflects some incoming radiation away but also traps heat under a layer of haze. The height and density of buildings have also increased beyond anything that Howard could have imagined, often forming deep and narrow **urban canyons** that are

The dynamic structure of the UHI

Urban heat islands are frequently described as a dome of warm air that sits above a city. Buffeted by the prevailing wind, they're often lozenge-shaped, with a plume of warm air pushed downwind. They develop best in conditions of light winds and clear skies, particularly at night when heat is lost rapidly from the surrounding countryside but buildings and surfaces continue to radiate heat. UHIs are made up of three main layers (Kershaw 2017):

Urban Surface Layer The ground layer, including the heated surfaces of walls, roads, pavements, roofs and other surfaces which can reach extraordinary temperatures on hot summer days.

Urban Canopy Layer Extending from the ground to the tops of roofs and trees, this is the layer in which we spend our lives. It can include very turbulent air swirling around buildings and mixes surface-layer air with air above the city buildings.

Urban Boundary Layer This is the air above the city buildings and, as it drags over the 'rough' structure of the city below, it also becomes turbulent. It mixes warmed urban air with the surrounding atmosphere, creating the dome of warm air sitting over the city that constitutes the UHI.

Urban areas are constructed from materials with a high thermal mass, meaning they absorb and store a lot of heat. During the day, the sun warms these surfaces and the air, creating thermals that rise up and in turn warm the top of the Urban Boundary Layer. This temperature inversion traps heat, pollution and water vapour down below. During the night, surfaces slowly cool and lose their stored heat into the Urban Boundary Layer. Tall, narrow streets with lots of opposing vertical surfaces, such as densely crowded office blocks and skyscrapers towards the city centre, take the longest to cool down. As the cooling continues, the warmer Boundary Layer above the city descends to just a few hundred metres high. Thermals are still created from the cooling surfaces, but these are now too weak to break up the capping inversion layer. It is the persistence of this capping layer, trapping heat in the city below, that means the UHI is most pronounced at night when the surrounding countryside has cooled much more rapidly (Kershaw 2017).

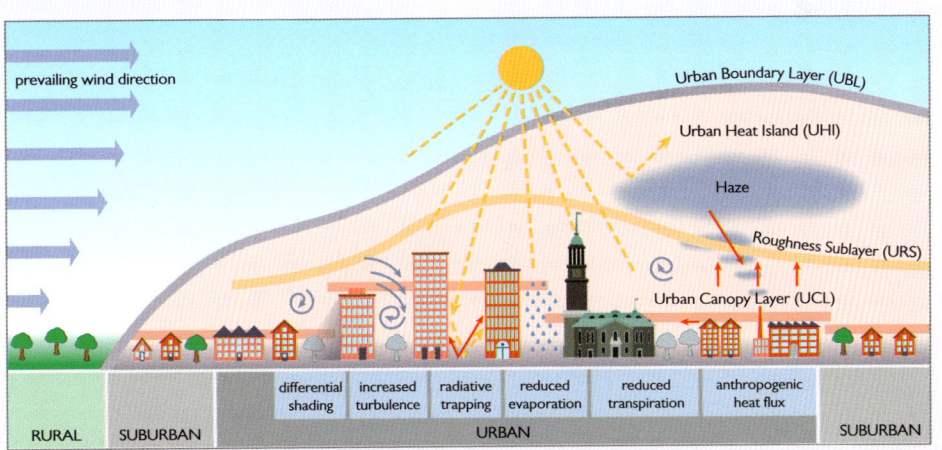

Formation of the urban heat island, showing sources of heat and interactions between the Urban Surface Layer (the ground), the Upper Boundary Layer and the Urban Canopy Layer. Diagram from Betchel & Schmidt (2011).

ABOVE: Urban canyons like this one in London considerably increase the area of heat-absorbing materials and can trap anthropogenic warmth, releasing it slowly well into the night and helping to maintain the urban heat island.

very effective in trapping and storing heat (Oke 1982). Overlying all of these is the impact of climate change, which has the potential to create even higher UHI temperatures (Hulme *et al.* 2002).

The amount that urban temperatures are raised above the surrounding rural landscape (i.e. the intensity of the UHI) can be rather difficult to pin down, as it depends on the time of day, month and year, the prevailing weather conditions and the methods of measurement (Rizwan *et al.* 2007). Despite this, satellite data from around the world have shown that from 2003 to 2020 the median surface temperature of urban areas globally was raised by 2.5°C compared to rural areas. Industrial parts of cities were often seen to be hotspots (quite literally) because excess heat from industry, wide expanses of dark surfaces (such as car parks) and reduced vegetation cover combined to produce strong localised heat islands (Mentaschi *et al.* 2022).

Urban heat islands in British cities

Nearly 200 years since it was first measured, London's UHI has steadily gained in intensity. By the 1960s, it was raising city-centre temperatures by around 5°C, and by the end of the last century it reached about 7°C. As well as urban development, these gains are fuelled by increases in air pollution, population and traffic (Lee 1992). Extreme weather events can push things even further – a summer heatwave in 2003, for example, led to a difference of 9°C (Kershaw 2017). Such heating isn't equally spread across the city, but varies enormously depending on the local fabric of the urban landscape. During the same heatwave, very densely built-up areas reached 6.0–8.7°C above the surrounding countryside, while large parks and green areas were actually cooler, sometimes by as much as -1.5 to 0.5°C (Holderness *et al.* 2013). These phenomena are known as urban cool islands, and usually occur in the morning when surfaces are slow to warm up and cool streets are heavily shaded by surrounding buildings and trees (Yang *et al.* 2016).

During the summers of 2007 and 2008, the intensity of Manchester's UHI was measured at 5°C at night and 3°C during the day, while daytime surface temperatures could be elevated by more than 10°C (Smith *et al.* 2011). Surface heating again matched

The physical urban environment

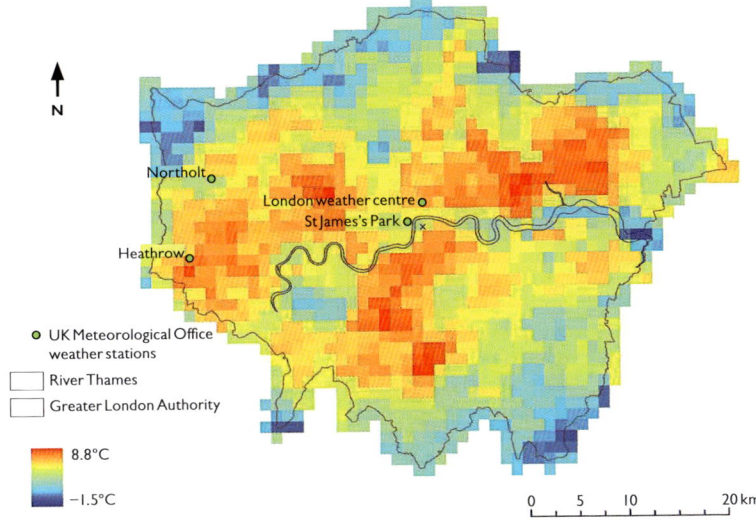

LEFT: Estimated surface temperatures across London on 8th August 2003, showing uneven development of the UHI. Parks and other green areas are considerably cooler than areas dominated by hard surfaces. Map from Holderness et al. (2013).

the fabric of the ground below, with areas of dense buildings and infrastructure being associated with the highest temperatures. As with London, the intensity of Manchester's UHI is increasing (at a rate of 0.21°C per decade), possibly linked to a reduction in the extent of vegetation (Levermore 2018).

Between 2013 and 2014, the highest intensity of the UHI in Birmingham was 8.6°C, comparable with maxima in London and Manchester. The development of the UHI was closely linked to wind speed; under very light winds of 4.8km/h (3mph) the UHI intensity was about 1.5°C, but this came down to 0.4°C when winds increased to 17.7km/h (11mph) (Bassett et al. 2020). Indeed, warm urban air can be pushed downwind to cover surrounding rural areas; in the 2003 heatwave, temperatures downwind of Birmingham were found to be up to 2.5°C warmer than those upwind (Heaviside et al. 2015).

The urban heat island and plants

The reason for all this detail about the UHI is that it has a profound effect on the urban flora. Plants are very sensitive to temperature, with many aspects of growth and development controlled by ambient temperatures and by diurnal temperature ranges from day to night. Budburst, flowering, seed germination and leaf fall are all clear responses to temperature, but others are less obvious. The rate of growth of pollen-tubes in winter-flowering Crocus *Crocus* spp., for instance, is twice as high at 20°C than at 6°C (McKee & Richards

ABOVE: The garden shrub Forsythia was used to demonstrate the impact of the urban heat island in Hamburg in 1955. More recent studies show that urban plants across Europe flower around four days earlier than rural plants.

1998), while the final size of Beech *Fagus sylvatica* leaves is influenced by average May temperatures (Meier & Leuschner 2008).

Changes in the timing of events like flowering or budburst (phenology) caused by the UHI have been observed many times in cities around the world (see Zipper *et al.* 2016 for examples). One of the first was a citizen science experiment in Hamburg (Germany) in 1955, when participants noted earlier flowering of Forsythia *Forsythia × intermedia* shrubs growing in densely built-up areas compared to those on the outskirts of the city (Franzen 1955, as quoted in Schmidt 2014).

Looking at flowering times across ten European cities over a longer period of time, Roetzer *et al.* (2000) found that, on average, Forsythia and Snowdrop *Galanthus nivalis* flowered around four days earlier in urban settings. Two later-flowering species, Wild Cherry *Prunus avium* and Apple *Malus domestica*, flowered 1.8 days and 1.5 days earlier respectively, suggesting that the earlier-flowering species might be more affected by higher UHI temperatures.

In a study of London Plane *Platanus × hispanica* and Dwarf Cherry *Prunus cerasus* in Rennes, France, Mimet *et al.* (2009) showed that flowering time followed the temperature gradient of the UHI, even responding to local reductions in the UHI caused by large urban parks. They also found that urban areas experienced a narrower diurnal day–night temperature range and this affected the timing of budburst across the city, which occurred more unevenly over a longer period of time. By contrast, rural trees were regularly subjected to lower night temperatures, and this appeared to synchronise their budburst. Clearly, there are very complex physiological mechanisms controlling the timing of budburst and flowering, and while the raised temperatures of UHI generally bring these dates forward, they can interfere with other aspects of growth and development.

The overall length of the growing season (i.e. the number of days of active growth in a year) also influences plant growth. Using satellite data and ground sensors in the city of Madison, Wisconsin, Zipper et al. (2016) found that the urban growing season was on average 4.8 days longer than in the countryside, an effect caused by the amount of impervious land cover such as paving, concrete and road surfaces. Large urban green spaces were less affected, with a growing season 2.4 days longer than the countryside. They suggest that this 'cool park' effect might be important in creating refugia for species that are less well adapted to the UHI, or for species that rely on finely tuned phenological processes for their survival.

Perhaps the most impressive impact of the UHI on plants comes from Hamburg, Germany, where Betchel & Schmidt (2011) looked for evidence of a 'floristic heat island'. The distribution of more than 900 native and naturalised alien species from 15 years of recording was correlated with Ellenburg temperature values (Ellenburg et al. 1992). These values indicate the preferred temperature requirements of each species on a scale from 1 (e.g. cold-loving arctic-alpine plants) to 9 (e.g. warmth-loving Mediterranean plants). They found a strong correlation between the strength of the UHI and Ellenburg temperature values, with more warmth-loving (thermophilous) species growing in the centre of the city and cooler-growing species further out. Remarkably, they were even able to construct a map of the intensity of the UHI by mapping average Ellenburg temperature values across the city. This pattern of heat-loving plants was seen in both native and non-native species, so the effect wasn't just caused by alien species from warmer climates growing in the city centre. They also found that the highest average Ellenburg temperature values were in areas lacking vegetation cover (such as industrial areas, the old city centre and areas of dense housing), reinforcing the close link between the nature of the urban fabric, the UHI and the local flora.

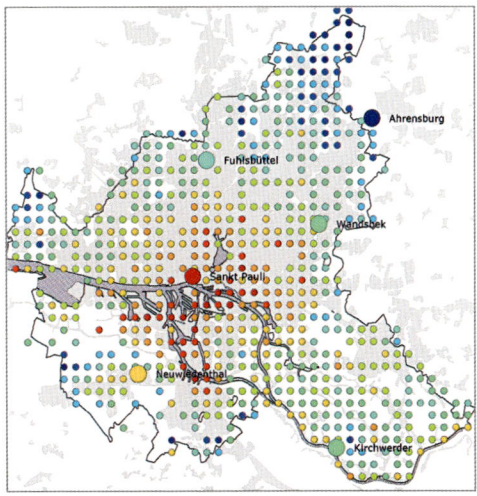

BELOW: The 'floristic heat island' in Hamburg, Germany, revealed by mapping the average preferred growing temperature (Ellenburg temperature value) of 904 native and non-native species. Red dots show the highest temperatures, dark blue the lowest. This closely matches the intensity of the UHI. Map from Betchel & Schmidt (2011).

Jungle London

As we've seen, the UHI has a profound effect on what can grow in urban areas. Indeed, Mark Spencer, BSBI Recorder for Middlesex, now describes London as 'essentially a Mediterranean city'. Even small amounts of warming considerably increase the chances that semi-hardy, Mediterranean or even semi-tropical plants will survive outdoors. Because they're so unlikely and unexpected, finding them provides moments of real excitement for the urban botanist.

As a keen gardener, I know just how thrilling it is to push horticultural boundaries. Many exotic and slightly tender plants have been planted outside by brave gardeners willing to try their luck. Once considered impossible, these days many people routinely grow Japanese Banana *Musa basjoo* and Darjeeling Banana *Musa sikkimensis* outdoors, and large specimens of the former now regularly flower and fruit. Others have tried Bougainvillea *Bougainvillea glabra*, the subtropical climber from South America familiar to anyone who has holidayed in the Mediterranean or tropics, the houseplant China Doll *Radermachera sinica*, a subtropical tree from mountainous regions of southern China and Taiwan, and even Tree Tobacco *Nicotiana glauca*, a warm-temperate shrub from Argentina and Bolivia. All these have survived outside in London gardens long enough to become large specimens, although they haven't yet become established from seed.

However, several exotic fruit trees do grow from discarded or bird-dispersed fruit. If you're a fan of Avocado *Persea americana* mashed on your toast in the morning, you might be thrilled to learn that London is now home to quite a few large specimens. A native of Central America

This Japanese Banana in Beckton, east London, has survived outside for 15 years and fruited at least three times.

An Avocado plant that has appeared spontaneously in Spa Fields Park, Islington, probably from a discarded stone. It's so vigorous it has been pruned back, but is regenerating quickly under the intense gaze of Baloo.

from Mexico to Costa Rica, some of these are more than 10 years old and capable of producing fruit. Although they prefer temperatures of 15–26°C, mature plants of the hardiest cultivars can survive brief lows of -2°C. Plants found on pavements are likely to have arisen from discarded stones.

Another iconic London plant is Loquat *Eriobotrya japonica*, a large evergreen tree or shrub from south-central China cultivated for its fragrant flowers, edible orange fruit and handsome leaves, which are used to make a herbal tea. The fruit and tea are popular with Turkish and Cypriot communities, and most plants in London are found near where they live, such as around Hackney. A subtropical or warm-temperate species, it grows best where winter temperatures don't drop below -1°C.

Several other exotic-looking species fruit regularly in the warmth of the UHI and are becoming established more frequently. One of my favourites is Blue Passionflower *Passiflora caerulea*, a large vine found as a native from Bolivia to Brazil and northern Argentina. Climbing to 20m (65ft) high, it can grow up to 9m (29ft) a year. Although its leaves and stems are often killed by winter frosts, it readily resprouts from the roots, which can survive lows of -10°C. However, its yellow-orange, egg-shaped fruit require warm conditions to form and, as anyone with a Blue Passionflower will know, most are produced after a long, hot summer. In 2013, I had an unforgettable meeting with one of the largest-known specimens in Great Britain, growing on waste ground in Plumstead, south London. Clambering over shrubs to more than five metres (16ft) high, it was covered with flowers and absolutely buzzing with bumblebees and honeybees collecting pollen and nectar. Spontaneous examples of this species are becoming more frequent as our climate warms, not just because it fruits more often but because warmth is required for germination; at 21–26°C seeds will germinate in 1–2 weeks, but take up to 10 weeks at lower temperatures.

One of the fastest-growing plants that almost always looks exotically out of place in the British

Loquat often arises from fallen, discarded or bird-dispersed fruit.

Increasingly encountered in urban settings, Blue Passionflower is said to represent the passion of Christ, with ten petals for the ten apostles present at the crucifixion, three stigmas for the three nails used, five stamens for the five wounds and the ring of filaments for the crown of thorns.

Isles is Tree-of-heaven *Ailanthus altissima*. A subtropical to warm-temperate species originally from China and Taiwan, its leaves can reach nearly one metre long (35in) on a trunk that can grow one to two metres (3.3–6.6ft) per year. Although it prefers temperatures from 7 to 18°C, it can actually survive lows of -35°C and has become so invasive it's sometimes called the Tree-of-hell (see box on pages 318–319).

By creating buildings and surfaces that trap, absorb and then slowly release heat, and by combining this with all the heat we generate through our own activities, it's clear that the UHI has a very profound effect on the climate of urban areas, and in turn on the species and plant communities that can grow there. But that's not the only way that our towns and cities shape the physical environment.

Urban rainfall

As well as temperature, urban areas can modify patterns of rainfall, sometimes in quite dramatic ways. One of the first such observations is in *The Beginning of a Thunderstorm* (Horton 1921), when it's noted that 'some thunderstorms over some cities … originated immediately over the city and did not travel far outside their limits on days when there were no other adjacent thunderstorms' (quoted by Atkinson 1968). This intriguing idea – that cities might be able to spawn their own thunderstorms – was investigated more thoroughly by Atkinson (1968) when he looked at what he called 'thunder rain' over London. We've probably all experienced thunder rain when we've been caught in one of those torrential summer downpours from towering cumulonimbus clouds, formed through convection over hot surfaces. Using data from more than 600 rain gauges across south-east England from

BELOW: Thunder rain falling from a cumulonimbus cloud as a storm approaches Glasgow during the 2023 heatwave.

ABOVE: Although an unwelcome nuisance for pedestrians, water splash from vehicles can benefit some pavement plants that prefer moisture.

1951 to 1960, Atkinson found that London generally received around 80mm (3.2in) of thunder rain a year compared to 60mm (2.3in) outside the urban area. The most intense effect was seen over Covent Garden in central London, which received about 100mm (3.9in) of thunder rain a year. In contrast, some rural areas to the east of the city received only 40mm (1.5in) of thunder rain. Atkinson supposed that three mechanisms might contribute to the generation of urban thunderstorms: the extra warming produced by the UHI, increased air pollution leading to more condensation nuclei, and increased air turbulence due to the structure of buildings.

The modification of rainfall by cities has not been studied as thoroughly as the UHI, mainly because rainfall is so dynamic and depends on a wide range of interrelated factors. However, a review of 85 studies around the world by Liu & Niyogi (2019) has shown that cities can change patterns of rainfall quite significantly. On average, urban rainfall (not just thunderstorms) is 16% higher than in the surrounding countryside. Curiously, though, areas 20–30km (12–18 miles) downwind of the city can receive around 18% more rain, as moderate winds often push cumulus clouds produced over the city into surrounding areas. In high winds, urban buildings can even create a turbulent barrier as storms pass over the city, splitting them in two in a process known as storm bifurcation. As a result, rainfall is reduced over the city but considerably increased downwind as the storm reconverges over flatter, more open ground.

With climate change predicted to bring more storms, increased rainfall and more flooding, urban planners and engineers have obvious challenges managing drainage and run-off. These issues are compounded by the sheer quantity of sealed surfaces in urban areas, and the loss of vegetation caused, for example, by the conversion of front gardens to hard standing for car parking. You might think increased urban rainfall always means wetter soil conditions for plants, but perversely that isn't the case, as we carefully engineer the urban landscape to drain water away as quickly as possible.

In Hamburg, Schmidt (2014) found that while the number and proportion of warmth-loving urban plant species increased with higher annual temperatures, they declined with increasing rainfall, suggesting that thermophilic species tend to favour the warm *and dry* conditions that are typically found in urban habitats. This supports the portrait of the 'perfect urban plant' by Thompson and McCarthy (2008), who showed that successful urban species tend to prefer dry conditions. It's not always that straightforward, though. While Canadian Fleabane *Erigeron canadensis* prefers hotter, drier conditions, these traits might be limiting its spread northwards. On the other hand, Bilbao Fleabane *E. floribundus* appears to relish slightly cooler, wetter conditions, making it more adaptable to the British climate. It certainly seems to be spreading more rapidly in urban habitats and is now overtaking Canadian Fleabane in some areas (Mundell 2000, Stroh *et al.* 2023, Mark Spencer pers. comm.).

Under scenarios of increased rainfall and therefore higher humidity, moisture-loving urban plants like Mind-your-own-business *Soleirolia soleirolii* are likely to increase. This is certainly already happening, as this species is being found more often in damp spots at the base of walls, along shaded pavement and road gutters, and in damp lawns. It's also thriving in the north of its range, with significant increases in cities such as Newcastle upon Tyne (Common 2023b).

Wind turbulence

Walk down any city street during windy weather and you're likely to be buffeted and blown around by turbulent, wind-tunnel-like gusts created by tall, closely spaced buildings. Wind speeds inside these urban canyons can be astonishing, and sudden gusts of 15 metres per second (30mph) or more can blow people off their feet and pose a risk from flying debris (Mittal *et al.* 2018). Some of the highest speeds are created when winds are channelled down narrow streets, when they blow above high buildings and create severe turbulence in the street below, and especially when they're funnelled from large open spaces through narrow gaps between buildings, a phenomenon known as the venturi effect. These latter gusts are usually highly localised; we've probably all experienced that moment when it's practically impossible to walk against the wind in one spot but it's completely calm just a few paces away. Wind speeds in urban areas are governed by highly complex interactions between air flowing above buildings and the morphology of the urban landscape, with the shape, dimension and relative positioning of buildings, roofs, streets, trees, roads, open plazas and parks and other structures all playing a part (Santamouris *et al.* 2008).

The most obvious direct impact of high winds on plants is an increased risk of broken branches. While all trees are susceptible to storm damage, those in urban canyons may be subject to even more intense gusts as wind is funnelled between buildings. In such settings, it is sometimes possible to see evidence of wind pruning, where a tree or shrub is bent away from the prevailing wind through constant damage to upwind twigs and branches. On the other hand, though, street trees are a fundamental solution to reducing wind speeds in urban canyons as they provide a permeable filter that slows air movement. High winds can also increase evapotranspiration (the loss of water from leaves), which can be even more severe when combined with an intense UHI, placing considerable stress on street trees.

Much less apparent, but much more important, is the critical role wind plays in the dispersal and spread of urban plants. Many of the most successful species produce very small, lightweight seeds dispersed by the wind (a process known as **anemochory**); just think of the little parachutes attached to seeds of plants like Oxford Ragwort *Senecio squalidus*, Canadian Fleabane, American Willowherb *Epilobium ciliatum*, Dandelion *Taraxacum* agg. and Red Valerian *Centranthus ruber*. Such seeds can be carried huge distances, especially in turbulent conditions when they may be lifted up into strong airflows above rooftops. In one study of Rosebay Willowherb *Chamaenerion angustifolium*, 20–50% of airborne seeds were observed to be floating more than 100m above ground and were likely to be dispersed over hundreds of kilometres (Solbreck & Andersson 1987). Indeed, turbulent updraughts seem to be especially important for long-distance dispersal; in Dandelion, Tackenburg *et*

RIGHT: Each seed, known as an achene, of Dandelion is adorned with a beak (the umbrella shaft) topped with around 115 radial fibres (the spokes). This gives them extraordinary lift in gusts of wind, essential for long-distance dispersal.

al. (2003) found that convective updraughts were absolutely critical for spreading seeds more than 100m from the parent plant, whereas strong lateral side winds didn't have the same effect. Such side winds were common in flat meadows, while convective updraughts are likely to be more frequent in urban settings where buildings and urban canyons generate turbulence. It seems that strong turbulent gusts are good for spreading dandelions around.

Long streets that funnel winds down their length also provide opportunities for rapid linear spread, a process often assisted by turbulence from passing traffic. In such situations, even heavier seeds, like those of Knotweed *Polygonum aviculare*, may be blown along smooth pavements and roads. The astonishing spread of Danish Scurvygrass *Cochlearia danica* along salted rural and urban roadsides has undoubtedly been assisted though the seed being carried along in the wake of speeding vehicles (Dines *et al.* 2012).

Air pollution

Just as the UHI traps warm air over a city, so it traps gases and particles in the air, reducing the quality of the air we breathe. Air pollution is a major threat to human health, linked to a wide range of illnesses including cancer, asthma and cardiovascular diseases as well as diabetes, dementia and obesity; in the UK, it contributes to about 44,000 deaths a year (Kershaw 2017). Many different chemicals and substances contribute to air pollution, some of which have a major impact on plants, even if their effects aren't always immediately apparent.

Oxides of nitrogen

Oxides of nitrogen (NO_x) come from burning fuel and are mainly emitted by vehicle exhausts, but also from construction equipment, garden machinery, industrial processes and power plants. Much of the NO_x in the air gets deposited, either directly (dry deposition) or through rain (wet deposition). Unlike the benign nitrogen that makes up a large part of the atmosphere, this so-called reactive nitrogen basically behaves like fertiliser for plants, enriching the soil and encouraging growth. For large, robust species such as Stinging Nettle *Urtica dioica*, Creeping Thistle *Cirsium arvense* and Broad-leaved Dock *Rumex obtusifolius*, this 'fertiliser rain' is a boon, giving them a distinct competitive advantage over smaller species, which they dominate and literally push aside. Against this behaviour, more delicate nitrogen-sensitive species such as Harebell *Campanula rotundifolia* and Tormentil *Potentilla erecta* struggle to survive.

Some of the highest rates of NO_x deposition are, of course, along roadsides. Looking at vehicle gas emissions on a range of roads across Scotland, Cape et al. (2004) found that concentrations of ammonia (NH_3) fell by 90% at 10m from the road edge – 15m for nitrogen dioxide (NO_2). Taking into account all the nitrogenous gases produced by exhausts, they calculated that the edge of a busy dual carriageway could receive an extra 8kg of nitrogen per hectare per year, while for a motorway this could rise to 15kg per hectare per year above background levels. For any plant, this is an awful lot of extra fertiliser. It's no surprise, then, that some of the fastest-spreading urban roadside plants, like Cockspur *Echinochloa crus-galli* and Hemlock *Conium maculatum*, have a distinct preference for very nutrient-rich soils. Nitrogen-tolerant bryophytes can also be abundant on street trees next to busy roads, and some are increasing; White-tipped Bristle-moss *Orthotrichum diaphanum* often forms dense swards on tree trunks and can be the dominant bryophyte in such situations, while the much less common Marble Screw-moss *Syntrichia papillosa* appears to be increasing rapidly (Duckett & Pressel 2019) and has become abundant in cities such as Bristol (David Hawkins pers. comm.).

ABOVE: Cockspur, a nitrogen-loving grass native to continental Europe, Asia and North America, has undergone an extraordinary increase since 2000, being recorded from an additional 734 10-km squares in Britain and Ireland.

As well as enrichment, NO_x also makes soils more acidic and can be directly toxic to plants, with high concentrations causing damage to leaf tissues, changes in physiology and reductions in growth (Dise *et al.* 2011). In fact, nitrogen deposition has been a bit of an elephant in the room for decades. The profound changes it has wrought – modifying how some species behave and changing vegetation communities over time – have been largely overlooked (Plantlife 2017). It's had such a major impact that this is now regarded as the third-greatest threat to biodiversity, after habitat loss and climate change (Payne *et al.* 2017).

Vehicle exhausts are of course a complex cocktail of potentially toxic chemicals, including heavy metals and polycyclic hydrocarbons (PAHs), which are deposited on roadsides as particulate matter. It might be significant that a study of 13 common roadside plants, including White Clover *Trifolium repens*, Meadow Buttercup *Ranunculus acris*, Daisy *Bellis perennis*, Dandelion and Wild Parsnip *Pastinaca sativa*, found that most of them were largely tolerant to these pollutants, often through adaptations in leaf structure such as thicker cuticles, longer hairs and fewer stomata (Kováts *et al.* 2021).

Volatile organic compounds

The burning of fossil fuels in vehicles and industry also produces volatile organic compounds (VOCs), chemicals that give the strong smell to petrol and diesel. A huge range of human-made chemicals also contain VOCs, particularly those that are required to evaporate or dry quickly. These include solvent-based paints, glues and sealants, varnishes and polishes, disinfectants, pharmaceuticals and refrigerants, as well as cosmetics and many hobby products. Because of their potential impact on human health, some of these chemicals are now controlled and being replaced with alternatives.

Many living plants also produce VOCs, known as biological VOCs or BVOCs. These include terpenoids, alcohols and carbonyls produced by the leaves of plants to defend against herbivory and to communicate with other plants nearby (think of the strong smell when you tear or crush the leaves of pine trees, tomatoes and cabbages). They're also produced by flowers as scents to attract pollinators and by ripe fruit to attract fructivores for dispersal. Ironically, street trees can be a particular source of BVOCs in urban areas, and often actually contribute to air pollution. Large quantities of isoprene, for example, are produced by Black Poplar *Populus nigra*, Aspen *Populus tremula* and Pedunculate Oak *Quercus robur*, while monoterpenes are produced by Beech *Fagus sylvatica* and most conifers (Fitzky *et al.* 2019). The production of these chemicals is in contrast to the many benefits of street trees (see Chapter 11).

Ozone

The biggest problem with VOCs and BVOCs is that they help produce ozone (O_3). In summer, when high-pressure weather keeps pollutants close to the ground, intense UV radiation from the sun interacts with NO_x and VOCs to produce ozone at ground level. This very dangerous, invisible gas can damage our lungs and airways, but also seriously damages plant tissue.

Ozone enters leaves through stomata and oxidises plant tissues (the same effect as when a cut apple turns brown). As tissues die, leaves become speckled with yellow and brown dots between the veins, weakening the plant, stunting growth and increasing susceptibility to pests and diseases. Eventually, leaves turn yellow and fall early. Particularly ozone-sensitive plants include Harebell, Cowslip *Primula veris* and Cock's-foot *Dactylis glomerata* as well as trees such as beech *Fagus*, birch *Betula* and oak *Quercus* (IPC Vegetation 2017). Ozone damage is often overlooked, as symptoms can be mistaken for disease or drought. In severe cases, though, a damaged plant will appear quite sunburnt, with bronze or brown stippling and shading on the most sun-exposed leaves.

BELOW: This Tulip-tree *Liriodendron tulipifera* leaf has become bronzed following exposure to ozone. Often overlooked, such damage can make leaves look diseased or sunburnt.

Ozone also changes patterns of plant growth. An increase in average ozone concentration from 30ppb (parts per billion) to 70ppb has been shown to bring forward peak flowering time of Common Bird's-foot-trefoil *Lotus corniculatus* by six days, but reduces the number of flowers on Harebell by 40% and on Small Scabious *Scabiosa columbaria* by 20% (Hayes *et al.* 2012). Reduced flowering inevitably leads to reduced seed set and, therefore, a smaller population size. Unfortunately, despite annual fluctuations due to the weather, urban ozone in the UK looks to be steadily on the rise, with the highest ever average level of 66.8μg/m^3 recorded in 2023 (Defra National Statistics 2023a).

Sulphur dioxide

On 5th December 1952, during a period of unusually cold, calm, anticyclonic weather, a combination of smoke from burning coal and fog settled over London. The worst in a long series of such 'pea-soupers', it was said to be impossible to drive or see your hand in front of your face. The smog even seeped indoors, with concerts and films abandoned as visibility decreased. Five days later it cleared, but during the Great Smog and the months that followed, it's now estimated that 12,000 people died from illnesses and respiratory diseases, four times more than thought at the time (Bell *et al.* 2004).

The Met Office calculates that 5,000 tonnes of smoke particles, 10,000 tonnes of CO_2, 700 tonnes of hydrochloric acid and 70 tonnes of fluorine compounds were emitted into the atmosphere during the Great Smog. Most dangerous of all, though, were the 1,850 tonnes of sulphur dioxide (SO_2) that turned into 4,000 tonnes of sulphuric acid (Met Office 2023). This transformation happens quite readily when SO_2 comes into contact with water in the air and, once formed,

RIGHT: Shield Lichen is relatively tolerant of sulphur dioxide but can still find urban areas difficult to colonise because acid rain has acidified the base-rich bark of trees on which it grows.

ABOVE: Ludgate Circus, London, shortly after midday on 6th December 1952. The Great Smog is so thick that the bus emerging from Fleet Street needs headlights and is led down the road by a London Transport inspector (on the left) carrying a fog flare.

the sulphuric acid is breathed into our lungs, or washed out of the atmosphere as acid rain.

The impact of SO_2 and acid rain on plants and lichens is well known. Because they lack a protective cuticle, certain lichens are particularly sensitive and have declined or disappeared entirely from many urban areas over the last 100 years. Even relatively tolerant species, such as Shield Lichen *Parmelia sulcata*, can be impacted – because it lives on trees with lime-rich bark (such as Ash, Field Maple, Apple, poplars and willows) and this substrate can become so acidified that the lichen can't grow (Gilbert 1986).

To some extent, vascular plants are protected from SO_2 by their waxy cuticle, although the gas can enter leaves through stomata. At high concentrations, leaf tissues are rapidly killed, but more often the effect is cumulative from long-term exposure to lower concentrations. This can result in reduced growth, lower crop yields and increased senescence (WHO 2000). In one experiment, plants of Red Clover *Trifolium pratense* were grown at different points along a 38km (24-mile) rural–urban gradient from Ascot to central London. As levels of SO_2 deposition increased along this transect, the dry weight of shoots and roots per plant decreased, as did the number of flowers (Ashmore *et al.* 1988).

Bryophytes as indicators of air pollution

Compared to lichens, bryophytes are rather underappreciated as indicators of air pollution. Although they can be more conspicuous and are slightly easier to identify, four times as many papers were published about the effects of pollution on lichens than on bryophytes in the 1980s (Adams & Preston 1992).

The influence of sulphur dioxide on bryophytes has been known for decades. In the late 1960s, Oliver Gilbert studied the mosses impacted by the dark satanic mills of the lower Tyne Valley, Northumberland. At that time, SO_2 emissions were near their peak thanks to the density of housing in colliery towns and burning pit heaps. He found that bryophyte diversity fell gradually as he approached the centre of Newcastle upon Tyne, an area he described as 'a bryophyte desert' with just a third of the species present in rural areas (Gilbert 1968).

On acidic sandstone walls, some of the first species to disappear on his journey into town were Cylindric Beard-moss *Didymodon insulanus*, Swan's-neck Thyme-moss *Mnium hornum*, Silky Wall Feather-moss *Homalothecium sericeum* and Common Feather-moss *Kindbergia praelonga*, all of which are particularly sensitive to pollution. A mile further in, Cypress-leaved Plait-moss *Hypnum cupressiforme* disappeared. In the suburbs, wall-top bryophytes became very scare, with only Wall Screw-moss *Tortula muralis*, Capillary Thread-moss *Bryum capillare* and Redshank *Ceratodon purpureus* remaining common, although the former two were largely confined to mortar. In contrast, two very tolerant species, Golden Thread-moss *Leptobryum pyriforme* and Bonfire-moss *Funaria hygrometrica*, suddenly appeared and became more frequent as pollution increased.

Swan's-neck Thyme-moss, a species very sensitive to SO_2 pollution.

The physical urban environment

Bonfire Moss is highly tolerant of SO_2 pollution.

After a little experimentation, Gilbert suggested that most bryophytes are unable to exist where average winter SO_2 levels exceed $50\mu g/m^3$.

Today, average SO_2 levels have plummeted to just $16\mu g/m^3$ (Loader et al. 2001) and the urban bryophyte flora is recovering in a spectacular fashion. Surveys of trees in London have shown that 26 out of 30 epiphytic species once regarded as extinct due to SO_2 have now returned, including Smooth Bristle-moss *Lewinskya striata*, Dilated Scalewort *Frullania dilatata* and Frizzled Pincushion *Plenogemma phyllantha* (Duckett & Pressel 2009, 2019; for more on epiphytic mosses, see Chapter 11). On tiled roofs and tarmac, Intermediate Screw-moss *Syntrichia montana* is making a comeback and White-tipped Bristle-moss has appeared on concrete walls all over London, while Sessile Grimmia *Schistidium crassipilum* and Anomalous Bristle-moss *Orthotrichum anomalum* are reappearing on walls and other surfaces made of limestone (Adams & Preston 1992, Duckett & Pressel 2009). These changes in London have been mirrored across the UK, with large recoveries in many sensitive species. Not all bryophytes have benefited, though; Common Pincushion *Dicranoweisia cirrata* is a calcifuge of sandstone walls and acidic bark that was widespread under high SO_2 deposition as substrates became more acidic and competition from other mosses decreased, but the fall in levels appears to have reversed its fortunes.

Common Pincushion is an acid-loving moss now suffering from improved air quality.

The Great Smog of London was a turning point in attitudes towards air pollution, bringing into sharp focus the harmful effects of atmospheric pollution and helping to usher in the Clean Air Acts of 1956 and 1968. Since then, emissions of SO_2 in the UK have seen an extraordinary decline of 98%, down from 6.5 million tonnes in 1970 to just 120,000 tonnes in 2022. This reduction comes mainly from power stations switching from coal to cleaner fuels like gas, stricter controls over sulphur in vehicle fuels, and the general decline in heavy industry (Defra National Statistics 2023b, London Assembly 2022).

In response to this breath of fresh air, some species are making remarkable returns. Indeed, the fall in SO_2 has probably had the single-most profound impact on our urban flora of anything in the last 50 years. By the 1970s and 1980s, leafy lichen species began to reappear in London suburbs and then in 1989 came the astonishing discovery of two very sensitive species, Sea-storm Lichen *Parmotrema perlatum* and Inflated Beard Lichen *Usnea cornuta*, on trees on Hampstead Heath (Adams & Preston 1992). Although the bark chemistry of some older trees may still be too altered to support many lichens, diverse communities of lichens are now being found on younger oak trees whose bark escaped the worst of the SO_2 pollution (Llewellyn *et al.* 2020).

Unlike tree bark, the surfaces of many old walls and pavements constructed of lime-rich concrete, mortar and limestone have now

BELOW: Many urban walls are being recolonised with lime-loving ferns now that SO_2 levels have fallen.

returned to their original pH. People have noticed lime-loving wall ferns, particularly Maidenhair Spleenwort *Asplenium trichomanes*, Hart's-tongue *A. scolopendrium* and Wall-rue *A. ruta-muraria*, appearing in or returning to urban areas where they've not been seen for decades (Edgington 2003). Most spectacular, though, is the explosion in Rue-leaved Saxifrage *Saxifraga tridactylites*. Since 2000, this endearing little calcicole has been popping up more often on walls and pavements in many towns and cities and, with its reddish leaves and sprays of white flowers in early spring, is a very welcome addition to the community of annuals growing on walls and pavements (see box on pages 194–195).

Particulate matter

Particulate matter (PM) comprises a large group of air pollutants that are now recognised as causing significant damage to our health. This is a diverse category of pollution because it comes from so many sources and includes tiny droplets as well as solid particles.

The largest particulates, known as PM10 because they measure 10 microns or more in diameter, include brick and stone dust from building sites, soil and mineral dust that gets kicked up from roads, and particles of vehicle tyres and brake linings. They often contain heavy metals and alkaline elements, as well as fragments of plants and insects, pollen, fungal spores, bacteria and viruses. Smaller PM2.5 particles frequently originate through condensation, coagulation or nucleation of gases and include particles of salt from sulphur and nitrogen oxides. They also include volatilised metals, smoke particles and fumes from vehicle exhausts and power plants (Grantz *et al.* 2003). Being so small, they're able to penetrate deeper into our lungs and potentially cause more damage.

Vegetation can be affected by PM in many ways. Heavy coatings of road, brick and cement dust on leaves can inhibit photosynthesis, damage leaf surfaces, break down waxy cuticles and inhibit transpiration

BELOW: Roadworks and construction sites can be intense sources of particulate matter. As well as large-particle dust from cutting the road surface, this machine's exhaust is emitting fumes rich in small particles.

(Rai 2016). Cement dust can also raise the pH of leaf surfaces to a strongly alkaline 12, enough to destroy waxy cuticles, penetrate tissues and kill the leaf. Long-term deposition of dust on leaves can reduce growth and flower production and cause premature leaf fall (Farmer 1993, Grantz *et al.* 2003). Dust can also block stomata, raising leaf temperatures and impacting photosynthesis and respiration (Farmer 1993, Rai 2016). More dramatically, PM rich in heavy metals such as copper, cadmium and sulphur can cause chlorosis, a yellowing of leaves as chlorophyl and photosynthetic pathways are damaged (Rai 2016). Significant impacts also come from nitrates, sulphates, aluminium and direct toxic effects from acids, alkalis, trace metals and salts (Grantz *et al.* 2003). In addition, mycorrhizal fungi, which are so important to the functioning of plants, seem to be impacted by heavy metals in complicated ways. While cadmium and zinc can reduce mycorrhizal density (Cairney & Meharg 1999), lead was found to reduce some sensitive species of mycorrhizal fungi but increase others (Chappelka *et al.* 1991).

The hard landscape: surface, soils and rock

What lies beneath our feet as we pound the streets is complicated stuff. We can largely ignore it in our everyday lives, but for plants, the nature of this substrate is critical. As well as providing a medium for growth, urban soils supply plant nutrients, absorb, store and release water, and capture and process contaminants such as pesticides, heavy metals and atmospheric nitrogen (Bullock & Gregory 1991). Let's work our way down from the topmost surface, through the soil and down to the bedrock to see how each layer can influence plant growth.

Urban surfaces

The surface of the built environment is possibly one of the toughest places on which to eke out a living. All manner of building materials are used, from concrete to bricks, from paving slabs to polished granite, and from tarmac to steel and glass. Designed to endure, most of them weather and decay slowly, releasing very few minerals and nutrients. However, despite extremes of heat and cold, flooding and drought, it's not impossible for plants to get a foothold. Prime real estate for establishment includes spots where surfaces do eventually weather and crumble (such as mortared joints in walls, old brickwork

The physical urban environment

and areas of thin asphalt) and where detritus can collect (in between paving slabs, on the flat tops of walls and in road drains, for example). Many factors affect this **bioreceptivity** of urban surfaces and control the rate and extent of colonisation by plants, with specialist plant communities adapted to the prevailing conditions eventually becoming established (Lubelli *et al.* 2021).

On the ground, impervious hard surfaces of cement, paving stones and asphalt often completely smother the soil below, creating what are known as **sealed soils** or **sealed surfaces**. Cut off from the elements, these soils suffer from reduced absorption of water and nutrients and impaired exchange of oxygen, carbon dioxide and other elements. On average, just over a quarter of a city's land area (26%) can be covered by impervious surfaces like pavements and buildings (Nowak & Greenfield 2020), while in some city centres this can rise to 80% (Blair & Launer 1997). The proportion of impervious sealed soils has important implications for the management of run-off and flooding; more than 90% of rainwater runs off a typical asphalt pavement, hence the recent interest in developing materials like porous asphalt which allows water into the soil below and reduces run-off by 50% (Hou *et al.* 2020). The extent and distribution of sealed soils obviously has a direct impact on plant populations, as most plants can only grow in patches of open soil.

BELOW: Suburbia can have a high proportion of sealed soils, especially when front gardens are converted to hard standing for parking.

Soils

Urban soils are highly modified by human activity; just think of the mixture of topsoil, subsoil and builders' rubble used to create a suburban road verge, for instance. You'd imagine this degree of human influence would make them easy to define as uniquely urban, but actually most 'natural' soils are modified by us to some extent, especially through agricultural practices like ploughing. Most definitions of urban soils therefore tend to emphasise the role of non-agricultural activities in their formation, such as 'a soil having a non-agricultural, man-made surface layer more than 50cm thick, that has been produced by mixing, filling, or contamination of land surfaces in urban and suburban areas' (Craul 1992, cited in Effland & Pouyat 1997). If you really need to impress your friends down the pub, the formation of urban soils is known as **anthropedogenesis** (literally 'human soil formation').

One important signature of urban soils is that they're extremely heterogeneous in nature and highly diverse (Effland & Pouyat 1997). Within a small urban area you might find: a cultivated, humus-rich loam in a front garden; dry, infertile soil sealed beneath a pavement; silt-rich, wet, fertile soil in a drainage ditch; and a skeletal brick rubble substrate on a patch of waste ground. There might also be more 'natural' soils nearby that are typical of woodlands, grassland or riverbanks. This diversity of soils is a major driver of plant diversity. In a study of 15 urban parks in Belgium, for example, Cornelis & Hermy (2004) found that on average there were nearly 11 different soil types per park, and that plant diversity was directly related to soil diversity.

Another characteristic of urban soils is that they're prone to repeated and significant modification from our activities (Schmidt 2014). Construction of buildings, roads, car parks, pavements, plazas, railways and drains, as well as their regular repair and maintenance, all lead to repeated excavation, mixing, backfilling and infilling that disrupts the processes of soil formation and evolution. Owners of newly built houses often find that their gardens consist of a shallow layer of imported topsoil or turf lying over a jumble of dry builders' rubble. Indeed, urban soils can be made up of **garbic** materials (landfill of mainly household and organic waste), **spoilic** materials (spoil from industrial mining, dredging and road construction) and **urbic** materials (earthy mixtures including building rubble,

The physical urban environment

ABOVE: Building work in Newcastle upon Tyne demonstrates the complexity of urban soils, with a mixture of 'urbic' materials including rubble, concrete, construction waste, metals and plastics, as well as imported topsoil.

construction waste and other artefacts). These long-lasting artefacts, typical of urban soils, include materials created or modified by us such as bricks, broken slabs, concrete, pottery, glass, insulation materials and pieces of metal and plastics (Effland & Pouyat 1997, Lehmann & Stahr 2007).

Despite their high diversity and heterogeneity, urban soils do have some characteristics and properties in common (Lehmann & Stahr 2007). Most urban soils tend to be young, being repeatedly relocated, disturbed and mixed due to multiple episodes of construction. They often have elevated levels of contaminants and can be highly compacted as a result of construction work, the weight of buildings, pavements and walls, and through high vehicle traffic and pedestrian footfall. They also tend to be rather dry, especially when sealed below impervious surfaces. On the more positive side for plant growth, they're generally alkaline (often containing construction residues like concrete), can be high in organic carbon (particularly soils in horticultural settings and when derived from imported topsoil), relatively fertile thanks to the deposition of atmospheric nitrogen and the use of fertilisers in gardens and amenity areas, and tend to be warmer than average because of the UHI. These traits will, of course, exert a strong selection pressure on what can grow, favouring some plant species but hindering others – there's no way that the typical urban soil described above could support Bog Asphodel *Narthecium ossifragum*, for example. In determining the characteristics of 'the perfect urban plant', Thompson and McCarthy (2008) found that the most successful urban species prefer moderately fertile, alkaline and dry soil, rather neatly matching the list of characteristics above (see Chapter 4).

Because topsoil is often imported into, or moved around, the urban landscape, it also plays a critical, but often very underappreciated, role in the dispersal of species. In a study of 15 samples of soil that were being sold, moved and transported around west Cornwall for housing developments and gardens, Robinson *et al.* (2018) estimated that if you were to cover an average-sized garden (190m^2) with imported topsoil, you would typically introduce 2.2 million seeds. Ninety different species were germinated from the samples, and by far the most abundant was Buddleja *Buddleja davidii*, with more than 250 plants germinating from 14% of the samples. Clearly, moving soil around means you're moving species around, and urban soils can have extremely rich soil seed banks. Indeed, seed longevity is one of the key strategies that enables certain species to thrive in the urban landscape.

Urban soils are precious resources and deliver many benefits. They filter and store water, especially if they're rich in organic matter, and can help alleviate flooding. They sequester carbon and atmospheric nitrogen and can trap contamination such as heavy metals and particulate matter. Like many things in the urban environment, urban soils have been somewhat overlooked in the past but are now being taken more seriously.

Geology

Beneath the soil, the underlying geology is the foundation of all our towns and cities. Although often buried out of sight, the nature of these rocks can fundamentally shape the places where we live. They modify both the geography of the land and the evolution of our settlements, determining, for example, where rivers can be crossed, where valuable minerals and coal can be mined, where fishing boats can find a safe harbour and where defensive castles can be built (Margottini & Spizzichino 2014.). The word 'bedrock' implies a hard material, but many areas of eastern and southern England are underlain by various soft clays, such as the Oxford and Kimmeridge clays of the Upper Jurassic. In low-lying and coastal areas, these are often in turn covered by a thick layer of glacial till or boulder clay – a mixture of clay, sand, boulders and rocks deposited by retreating glaciers at the end of the last ice age. In more northern and western areas, the solid bedrock itself lies just under the soil or even comes to the surface.

Sometimes, geological features exert a strong influence on a city's character. One of the best examples is in Edinburgh, where Arthur's Seat and Castle Rock form part of a series of hills made of basalt, dolerite, ash and agglomerate formed by volcanic activity in the Carboniferous period, 342–335 million years ago. The rocky crags dominate the city, with Arthur's Seat forming much of Holyrood Park and Castle Rock providing the imposing location of Edinburgh Castle. Being of such contrasting geology to the rest of the city (which is mainly underlain by sedimentary sandstones), the volcanic rocks are home to very different and special plants including Sticky Catchfly *Silene viscaria*, Maiden Pink *Dianthus deltoides* and Forked Spleenwort *Asplenium septentrionale*.

Geology also dominates the landscape in Bristol, where precipitous cliffs of Carboniferous limestone form the Avon Gorge along the western edge of the city. More than 500 species of plants thrive in the lime-rich soil here, including specialities such as Bristol Whitebeam *Sorbus bristoliensis* at its only known site in the world, and Bristol Rock-cress *Arabis scabra* and Round-headed Leek *Allium sphaerocephalon* at their only native sites in the British Isles. In Plymouth, an outcrop of Devonian limestone forming Plymouth Hoe is home to other unusual lime-loving plants such as Field Eryngo *Eryngium campestre*, Toothed Medick *Medicago polymorpha* and a Mediterranean species of thistle, *Carduus pycnocephalus*, which, having been naturalised here for 155 years, is now affectionately known as Plymouth Thistle. In a similar eponymous vein, John Ray and Francis Willoughby reported that a 'wild white catchfly', discovered in 1669, was so abundant on the Triassic sandstone walls and rocky cliffs of Nottingham Castle that the species became known as Nottingham Catchfly *Silene nutans*.

BELOW: Sticky Catchfly growing on the volcanic basalt crags of Arthur's Seat, Edinburgh. Only 18 populations of this species are known in Great Britain, making this one of the rarest native plants in an urban setting.

Urban Plants

RIGHT: The 'wild white catchfly' growing on the Triassic sandstone walls and cliffs of Nottingham Castle became known as Nottingham Catchfly. Sadly, the plant was last seen on the castle walls in 1926, although attempts are now being made to reintroduce it.

BELOW: Commonly called London Yellow Stock, these traditional bricks made of local brickearth (a type of loess) have a characteristic colour thanks to the addition of chalk, and are often speckled black through the addition of ash and cinders, known as 'spanish'.

Often, the most visible manifestation of the underlying geology comes in the walls of the buildings. The honey-coloured cottages of the Cotswolds, for example, are built from Jurassic oolite, a form of limestone laid down in warm, shallow seas some 175–155 million years ago. In areas of chalk, which is generally much too soft to build with, older buildings may be faced with knapped flint, nodules of very hard silica found embedded in the chalk in the Cretaceous, 145–66 million years ago. In a very broad sweep across Great Britain, buildings in towns and cities including Exeter, Monmouth, Hereford, Chester, Glasgow, Stirling and Perth are constructed from Devonian Old Red Sandstone (419–358 million years old), giving them a beautiful soft, reddish-rose colour. And Aberdeen is known as Granite City from the local stone, an exceptionally hard Ordovician igneous granite (470 million years old) which is so weather resistant that even the oldest buildings still look brand new. Where hard stone isn't available for building, such as the London Basin, bricks are made from the local clay or loess, a mixture of clay and silt that was laid down by wind in the Late Pleistocene 129,000–11,700 years ago.

Usually, the local building stone itself doesn't directly influence the wall flora. On most walls, plants tend to flourish first on the relatively soft, lime-rich mortar

ABOVE: An old wall in Bangor (Gwynedd) constructed from very hard, acidic Ordovician siltstone (478–449 million years old). The thin joints between the stones are filled with lime-rich mortar, allowing dense colonisation by Maidenhair Spleenwort.

used to construct them. On very old walls built of limestone, though, ferns such as Rustyback *Asplenium ceterach* and Maidenhair Spleenwort will eventually grow out on the stone itself, along with bryophytes such as Wall Screw-moss *Tortula muralis* and Silky Wall Feather-moss *Homalothecium sericeum*. In areas where walls are constructed from unrelentingly hard acidic rocks, the flora tends to be forever confined to the mortar between the stones.

Stress in the city

When we marvel at tiny plants like Rue-leaved Saxifrage flowering profusely on a wall or in a pavement crack, we can forget how impossibly stressful and hostile urban environments are for them. The challenges, from high temperatures and drought to pollution and skeletal soils, are numerous and sometimes intense. In addition, urban environments are highly fragmented, dynamic and subject to constant change. On top of all of this, we seem to have a perverse passion for repeatedly poisoning, killing and cutting down plants, a mission that's achieved all too effectively with an arsenal of weapons from mowers to herbicides and strimmers to hot foam guns.

It's a wonder that anything survives. But it does and, remarkably, it often thrives. In the next chapter, we'll take a look at how plants respond to and interact with this abiotic urban environment, creating a flora that's in constant flux as the city evolves and changes.

Creation of the urban flora

chapter six

Walk around any urban area and you'll encounter all manner of plants. The flora of every town or city is shaped by a variety of geographical, cultural, historical, economic and social factors, all of which act to modify the native and alien species that were either already there, or that have since arrived. Under the steady and inexorable growth of the built environment, the original pool of native species is gradually whittled down, leaving only those able to cope with the new conditions. This native flora is augmented by the spread of new arrivals, the alien species we wittingly or unwittingly introduce. Together, all these species face the unique challenge of the abiotic built environment, harsh and unrelenting in character but full of opportunity for those adapted to survive.

Some of the processes that shape the urban flora, like habitat fragmentation, will be familiar to anyone that's worked with the conservation of semi-natural habitats in more rural landscapes. Others, such the planting of expensive and fashionable horticultural plants, are more typically urban phenomena. In this chapter, we'll explore how these fascinating processes work together to shape and create our unique urban flora, and we'll attempt to put some figures on the number of species we might find on our streets.

Shaping the urban flora

As we saw in Chapter 4 (Origin of urban plants), the species that can potentially inhabit any urban area are drawn from a very large pool. In all, 3,445 native and alien plants were mapped in the *Plant Atlas 2020* (Stroh et al. 2023), but over 9,000 taxa are recorded in the BSBI distribution database, including many rare aliens, hybrids and

OPPOSITE:
A rich community of species growing in front of boarded-up houses awaiting redevelopment in Liverpool.

microspecies. Almost any of these could, in theory, grow in our cities. But, of course, many don't. Restricted by all sorts of environmental, historical and cultural factors, the actual number of species in any individual town or city is much smaller. As settlements grow over time, occupying more space and evolving into ever more complex urban landscapes, four separate filters operate to narrow down and shape the species pool. The species that remain are likely to have certain competitive advantages that help them to survive (Williams *et al.* 2008).

The first of these filters is **habitat transformation**, where the original landscape of natural or semi-natural vegetation is irrevocably modified by construction of the built environment. Clearance of woodland, drainage of wetlands and marshes and the 'concreting over' of meadows, pastures and heathland inevitably means that species are lost. In a study of local extinctions in Middlesex and Cambridgeshire, Preston (2000) found that as the countryside was engulfed by the spread of suburban London, most extinctions were of smaller, less competitive species of open habitats and infertile soils. These were plants such as Common Rock-rose *Helianthemum nummularium*, Chaffweed *Lysimachia minima*, Round-leaved Sundew *Drosera rotundifolia* and Pennyroyal *Mentha pulegium*, habitat specialists that just aren't cut out for urban life. As well as these losses, many more native species decline as

RIGHT: Round-leaved Sundew has precise ecological requirements and cannot cope with habitat transformation and fragmentation. In London, it was last seen on Hampstead Heath in 1960.

urbanisation advances, continually thinning out the flora until only the most adaptable species remain. The scale of this loss depends on the original starting point; a settlement developing in an area of species-rich habitats will lose more species than if the area is already degraded by intensive agriculture. In Middlesex – the most heavily urbanised of any county thanks to the relentless expansion of London – 186 native and archaeophyte taxa have become extinct since 1666. That's nearly 12% of London's native and archaeophyte flora, a terrible toll that will only get worse as the effects of habitat loss, climate change, invasive species and pollution bite ever harder (Mark Spencer pers. comm.).

But it's also important to remember there are two sides to habitat transformation. As semi-natural habitats are destroyed, new urban habitats such as walls, pavements, gardens and waste ground are created. These often lie beside each other in very close juxtaposition, a heterogeneity of contrasting urban habitats that allows many different species to become established. In this way, urban areas can potentially have a higher diversity of species than before, although the quality of these habitats tends to be reduced and they're often dominated by ruderal and early-succession communities.

The second filter is **fragmentation**, where areas of species-rich habitat become surrounded by more inhospitable land. Cut off and isolated from their neighbours, fragmentation is dangerous because

LEFT: A plant of shallow water on acidic, infertile peat, Marsh St John's-wort *Hypericum elodes* is the latest casualty of urbanisation in London, lost from its last site in February 2024.

it reduces connections between organisms, breaking ecological processes such as pollination, seed dispersal and gene-flow and making populations more vulnerable to loss and change (see page opposite).

The third filter comes from the unique physical characteristics of the urban environment itself (see Chapter 5). These **anthropogenic modifications** include elevated temperatures from the urban heat island, high levels of atmospheric pollution (such as nitrogen and particulate matter), thin and skeletal soils that are often sealed below hard surfaces, and even altered patterns of wind turbulence that may modify seed dispersal. These modifications tend to increase gradually in intensity as you follow a gradient from rural to urban, reaching a peak in city centres where conditions can be truly inhospitable for plants (Schmidt 2014).

Which species survive best in these urbanised conditions? This is an interesting question because it suggests there might be a suite of characteristics, or traits, that mean some species will perform better in urban habitats than others, the 'perfect urban plants' if you like (as mentioned in Chapter 4). By looking at around 800 species growing at different levels of urbanity, from open countryside to fully urban settings in Sheffield and Birmingham, Thompson and McCarthy (2008) found that successful urban species tend to be tall and robust, prefer lime-rich, calcareous soils that are dry and moderately fertile, and grow in open, sunny habitats. Surprisingly, they discovered that these traits were shared between native and alien species, so this is likely to be a universal portrait of the perfect urban plant.

The final filter, which is rather peculiar to urban habitats, is **human preference**. Urbanisation creates a concentration of new anthropogenic habitats that are highly managed and controlled by us, including garden borders and lawns, allotments, parks, sports fields, planted road verges, amenity plantings and even green roofs. These entirely artificial habitats are dominated by horticultural and amenity plantings, in other words the plants that we prefer to grow. Our voracious appetite for horticultural novelty means there's a steady stream of new alien plants to be found. For the last 48 years, every edition of *BSBI News* has included a section – 'Adventives and Aliens' – dedicated to documenting these new arrivals across Britain and Ireland. Recent editions, for example, include reports of Treasureflower *Gazania rigens* from coastal areas of southern Africa naturalised at a seaside park at Sheringham on the north Norfolk coast (Berry 2022), Purple Mullein *Verbascum phoeniceum* from south-east

Fragmented urban lives

In our daily lives, we can pretty much go wherever we want, using a bus or train, taxi or tram, or even use our own legs to get around by cycling or walking. But for plants it's very different. Their urban landscape is highly fragmented and full of barriers. Intense fragmentation – the separation of places where survival is possible from those where it's not – is a hallmark of urban environments. Hospitable patches of habitat (such as gardens, parks, verges, woodlands, waste ground and pavement cracks) are separated by inhospitable structures like buildings, roads, car parks and wide expanses of concrete, tarmac or paving, with tall buildings also presenting considerable barriers to dispersal (Gorton & Shaw 2022).

Fragmentation plays a critical role in the dispersal of seed, spores and pollen. Plants have evolved all manner of mechanisms to aid dispersal, often taking advantage of vectors including wind, birds and animals, gravity and water. For plants with a limited **dispersal kernel** (pattern of dispersal), staying close to their parents is their survival strategy and fragmentation is not so important. But plants with a wide dispersal kernel need mechanisms to overcome fragmentation, and long-distance dispersal events are essential to circumvent barriers and expand the range of a species (Gillespie *et al.* 2012, Gorton & Shaw 2022).

Fragmentation can cause plants to adapt quickly to the urban environment. For instance, Holy Hawksbeard *Crepis sancta*, a species found across continental Europe and central Asia, produces two types of seed. Some have a dandelion-like pappus for long-distance dispersal on the wind, while others lack the pappus and simply fall to the ground close to the parent plant. In Montpellier, France, Cheptou *et al.* (2008) found that plants in small, isolated populations on pavements tended to produce more wind-dispersed seeds, while those in large, continuous populations on waste ground produced more seeds that fell close to their parents. Remarkably, this shift in dispersal pattern appeared within just a dozen generations, reducing the chances of inbreeding in small, highly fragmented pavement populations.

Fragmentation can also have big impacts on how plants perpetuate themselves. Common Toadflax *Linaria vulgaris*, for example, reproduces sexually by seed and also clonally through vegetative means. Bartlewicz *et al.* (2015) found that smaller, more urban populations in the city of Leuven, Belgium, were genetically less diverse, produced fewer seeds and relied more heavily on vegetative reproduction compared to larger, more rural populations. As a result, urban populations were more likely to be made up of just a few clonal plants, with sexual reproduction becoming less important.

In highly fragmented urban settings, Holy Hawksbeard changes the way its seeds are spread, relying more on wind dispersal to carry it to new sites.

Urban populations of Common Toadflax turn to vegetative reproduction, reducing seed set, genetic diversity and gene-flow.

Europe and south-western Asia naturalised in grass near Wareham Station (Dorset), and Crocus-leaved Romulea *Romulea bulbocodium* from southern Europe and northern Africa planted on a clifftop at Beachlands, Sussex (Berry 2023b).

Our preferences for certain garden plants, shaped by changing horticultural fashions, exert a strong selection pressure on the species that we might come across. In the early 1990s, for instance, a new bedding plant from South Africa known as Bacopa *Chaenostoma cordatum* became the 'next big thing' to grow in pots, hanging baskets and window boxes. It's a colourful trailing plant with small, neat leaves and a continual procession of large blue or white flowers. Every year, millions of plants are grown outside pubs, restaurants and tea rooms, the seeds dropping into the pavements below. Bacopa has quickly become established on our streets; one of the first records was from 'tarmac under window boxes' at Birmingham Children's Hospital in 1997, and it's now been recorded more than 280 times. Nearly 80% of these records have been made since 2010. Who knows what will come next? It's difficult to predict the next horticultural fashion, but it could soon become naturalised on a high street near you.

BELOW: Bacopa became popular as a bedding plant in the early 1990s and is increasingly encountered as a pavement escape. This plant, found in 2023 below a hanging basket in Llanrwst, was the first record for Denbighshire.

The influence of affluence

It might not seem obvious at first glance, but social and economic influences have an impact on urban plant diversity. In Phoenix, Arizona, Hope *et al.* (2003) found that variations in plant diversity were linked to levels of family income and the age of housing. For family income the relationship was very clear: in neighbourhoods where this was above the median for the city ($40,750, or £41,770), plant diversity was twice that of less wealthy areas. However, it was not possible to say whether wealthier residents simply prefer to live in more affluent areas with more plant diversity (more green spaces, trees and amenity plantings), or whether they encourage more diversity through their own horticultural activities (in other words, they can afford larger gardens with more varied planting). Plant diversity was also higher in areas of newer housing, but this appeared to reflect a trend for more drought-tolerant desert-style planting in Arizona, and a move away from water-demanding monocultures of grass lawns and fast-growing trees for shade. Even small income-related actions, such as being able to afford seed mixtures to feed garden birds, can influence the character of the urban flora. Such cultural shifts, though subtle and particular to different historical and geographical situations, are likely to be at work in other cities around the world.

The link between socio-economic factors and urban vegetation becomes stronger over time, as new neighbourhoods tend to be structurally similar at first (land is cleared of vegetation and new housing constructed to standard criteria) but gradually develop their own cultural identity depending on the profile of their residents. In urban areas of south-eastern Australia, Luck *et al.* (2009) found a surprisingly strong link between levels of education and vegetation cover, with percentage cover increasing by about 1% for every additional percent of the population with a university degree. This was found to be more important than household disposable income, although the two are connected. Other studies have shown that while income determines the amount of land in private ownership, education determines how much of the land is actually vegetated (Troy *et al.* 2007). It may be that higher levels of education tend to increase knowledge and awareness of environmental and land management issues, which in turn fosters a desire to act, such as creating a wildlife-friendly garden, a community garden or planting trees. These aspirations are also more likely to be realised because higher levels of education tend to lead to increased wealth (Luck *et al.* 2009). Of course, the flipside of this is also true, leading to some of the most disadvantaged demographic groups living in neighbourhoods with the lowest levels of vegetation cover and species diversity. As is so often the case, levels of education are directly linked to access to nature and to the considerable mental health and wellbeing benefits such contact brings.

If residents' socio-economic status has a direct role in determining urban vegetation cover and species diversity, then working to reduce inequalities can perhaps have knock-on benefits for the environment. Local-government planning plays a critical role in the equation too, of course, and many planning factors, such as the density of housing, the provision of gardens and green spaces, the density of cars and parking, and the management of street trees, can all influence the environmental quality of urban areas (Luck & Smallbone 2010).

National and local planning policies can combine with social and economic factors to create some very unexpected outcomes for plants. An extraordinary example comes from London, where the current housing crisis is leading to the loss of pondweeds *Potamogeton* spp. The demand for affordable housing is far outstripping supply (in 2023 the average house in London was priced at £528,000, GLA 2023), so people are turning to alternative, cheaper options for accommodation. According to the Canal & River Trust, there

BELOW: London's canals are increasingly being used to support cheaper forms of accommodation. More boats means more shade and disturbance, reducing the growth of pondweeds and other aquatic plants.

are now 4,315 boats on London's waterways, an increase of 86% since 2012. With so many vessels on the canals and rivers, they're having to moor end-to-end and side-by-side several boats deep, heavily shading the plants on the substrate below. In addition, boat propellers are churning up the substrate and creating turbidity, clouding the water and further impacting plants. As a result, pondweeds and other water plants are declining on many busy sections of the canal network (Mark Spencer pers. comm.).

Reactions to urbanisation

Different plants respond to urbanisation in different ways. Many species die out rather quickly, others survive and cope for longer, while a few will positively thrive. Species exhibiting similar responses to urban stresses can be grouped as urban 'avoiders', 'adaptors' or 'exploiters' (Elmqvist *et al.* 2008, Geschke *et al.* 2018). As an area begins to be transformed by building and development, some plants are unable to cope with the first inklings of urbanisation and quickly disappear. These **urban avoiders** are mostly native plants like Tormentil *Potentilla erecta* and Sanicle *Sanicula europaea* that are very rarely found in urban settings. They tend to be late-succession habitat specialists that require a very precise set of environmental conditions to survive, conditions that are quickly altered by the imposition of disturbance and urbanisation. **Urban adaptors**, however, are more tolerant of urban conditions and can withstand some habitat modification and disruption. As well as being common in rural areas, they remain frequent even under moderate levels of urbanisation. This group includes many early-succession native and non-native

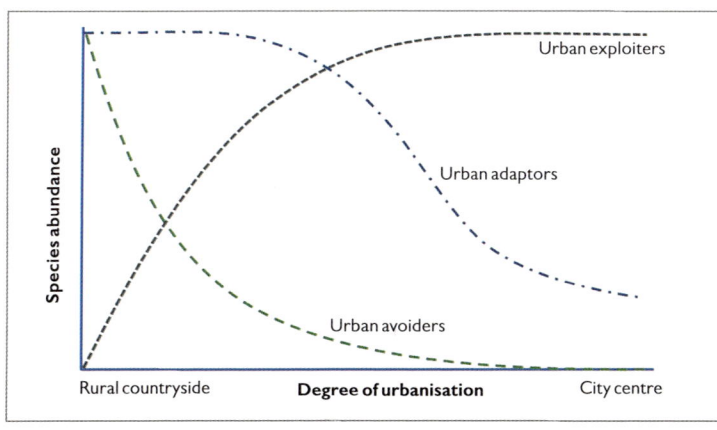

LEFT: As urbanisation increases, urban avoiders cannot cope with the changing conditions and so decline. Urban adaptors cope better with the new conditions but struggle under intense levels of urbanisation. Urban exploiters, though, are highly adapted to urban life and even thrive in the city centre.

And the most urban species is…

Urban plants live in highly unnatural environments. Various attempts have been made to measure this 'unnaturalness', including **hemeroby** (degree of human impact), **urbanity** (tendency to occur in cities or areas of urban land), **ruderality** (ability to survive repeated disturbance) and **stress tolerance** (ability to survive factors restricting growth). These measures help us identify which species are most strongly restricted to urban habitats. After all, many abundant urban plants, like Dandelion *Taraxacum* agg. and Common Nettle *Urtica dioica* are just as common in rural settings. So which species are mostly urban?

Using data collected for 902 species from 2,508 1-km squares across Great Britain, Hill et al. (2002) compared characteristics of species found in rural areas to those in the urban centres of Sheffield and Birmingham. By combining various scales including urbanity, ruderality, stress tolerance, competitive ability and **annuality** (the proportion of annuals), they were able to work out which were the most urban species – the real urban exploiters. The top species, occurring predominantly in 1-km squares with 50% or more urban land cover, were:

- Buddleja *Buddleja davidii*, 75%
- Prickly Lettuce *Lactuca serriola*, 74%
- White Melilot *Melilotus albus*, 64%
- Ribbed Melilot *Melilotus officinalis*, 59%
- Russell Lupin *Lupinus* × *regalis*, 58%
- Canadian Fleabane *Erigeron canadensis*, 58%
- Canadian Goldenrod *Solidago canadensis*, 56%
- Michaelmas-daisies *Symphyotrichum* spp., 56%
- Wormwood *Artemisia absinthium*, 56%
- Large-flowered Evening-primrose *Oenothera glazioviana*, 54%
- Oxford Ragwort *Senecio squalidus*, 50%

It'll be no surprise that Buddleja tops this list, as it's such an inveterate urbanite. Indeed, it's so abundant along railways and pavements, on walls and around waste ground and derelict buildings that it has become an icon of the built environment (see Chapter 7). Found mostly in 1-km squares with at least 75% urban cover, it's only occasionally encountered in rural areas. When you think about it, this is also true of other species on the list; when did you last see Wormwood, Canadian Fleabane and the two melilot species growing in deeply rural settings, for example?

In developing an index to measure the 'unnaturalness' of urban communities, however, Hill et al. (2002) discovered that the proportion of urban land cover (urbanity) alone wasn't very helpful, because so many urban species are also common in rural areas, particularly native species like Creeping Thistle *Cirsium arvense*, Ribwort Plantain *Plantago lanceolata* and Dandelion. Instead, it was found that measures of annuality (the proportion of annuals) and **xenicity** (the proportion of alien neophytes) worked much better, showing that the most highly urbanised of plant communities are dominated by ruderal annuals (particularly arable weeds) and have a high neophyte diversity. When these measures are combined, some of the most characteristic urban plants emerge as Buddleja, Canadian Fleabane, Oxford Ragwort and Wormwood.

Buddleja is common on walls, and one is often left wondering where all the roots are to support such large, leafy stems.

species such as Groundsel *Senecio vulgaris* and Red Valerian *Centranthus ruber* as well as robust mid-succession species such as Meadow Buttercup *Ranunculus acris* and Common Knapweed *Centaurea nigra*. The final group are the **urban exploiters**. These plants are relatively uncommon in rural areas but become increasingly frequent in urban settings. Well adapted to disturbance and urban conditions, this group is dominated by alien, early-succession species such as Canadian Fleabane *Erigeron canadensis*, Wormwood *Artemisia absinthium*, White Melilot *Melilotus albus* and Shaggy-soldier *Galinsoga quadriradiata* (see page opposite).

Biotic homogenisation and random introductions

So, as places become progressively more urbanised, some of the original species die out, others hang on and survive, while a few thrive and spread. The gradual replacement of the original native flora (which tends to be diverse, local and specialised) with fewer but more generalist native species, along with the arrival of a uniform suite of urban alien species, can mean urban floras start to become rather similar, a process known as **biotic homogenisation** (McKinney & Lockwood 1999, Luck & Smallbone 2010). This suggests that urban floras eventually all tend to look the same, but experience tells us this isn't usually the case; I know that the flora of Salisbury in Wiltshire is very different to that of Bangor in North Wales. In reality, while many species are common across urban areas, biotic homogenisation is often counterbalanced by the neophyte flora, which is highly diverse and continually augmented with new – albeit often transient – species (Schmidt 2014).

Indeed, cities are ideal foci for the arrival, movement, escape and spread of aliens; they are centres of trade and traffic including ports, roads and railways, and they have very high densities of domestic gardens, as well as allotments and botanic gardens (Wittig 2004, see Chapter 4). The rather random establishment of particular neophytes from these sources can give different cities their own distinctive character. Canadian Goldenrod, for instance, is especially abundant in and around Birmingham, and Gilbert (1989) suggests this might be due to divisions of the plant being shared around city allotments in the nineteenth century. Similarly, the only real stronghold outside London for Goat's-rue *Galega officinalis* is Sheffield, and this may be a legacy of nurserymen selling cheap plants of this and other vigorous

Urban Plants

ABOVE: The abundance of Canadian Goldenrod around Birmingham may hark back to the nineteenth century when it was shared among allotment owners, whose 'guinea gardens' were rented for one guinea a year.

garden plants door-to-door in the city's poorer suburbs early in the twentieth century. The plant has persisted throughout the city and is now spreading outwards along road verges.

Gradient of diversity

Counterintuitively, urban floras tend to be more diverse than the surrounding rural countryside because small-scale habitat heterogeneity is so high, creating a wide range of anthropogenic and semi-natural habitats. This has been demonstrated by the Urban Flora of Scotland project, coordinated by the Botanical Society of Scotland since 2015. Their results suggest that urban diversity is indeed higher than surrounding rural areas. Although there is much variation between towns, urban 1-km squares are home to a median of 130 species, while nearby rural squares have a median of just 90 species (Grace 2020).

Let's once again take a journey from rural areas into the city centre and see what happens to plant diversity along the route. In the farmed landscape around the edges of town, the flora often tends to be rather depleted because agricultural production is at its most intense. Moving towards the city centre, the suburbs are usually

Creation of the urban flora

home to the highest levels of plant diversity as it's here that the richest mixture of urban and semi-natural habitats is found. With more space for new developments and high levels of redevelopment, suburban areas are also prone to more disturbance, encouraging the growth of a wide range of ruderal species. These relatively affluent areas also have more room for large gardens, allotments, parks and playing fields, all of which boost local plant diversity. Carrying on with our journey, plant diversity begins to drop as housing density increases, habitats become more fragmented and pollution increases. Gardens get smaller and there are fewer other green spaces. When we reach the city centre, diversity drops dramatically. This is because it's been urbanised for the longest period of time, with the highest density of buildings, pavements, roads and sealed soil surfaces as well as the highest levels of pollution. As a result, urban avoiders will have disappeared long ago, urban adaptors will be struggling, and only the toughest of urban specialists will be thriving (McKinney 2008).

A good example of this gradient of diversity comes from Plymouth, where Kent *et al.* (2001) found that the lowest diversity – just 49 species per 1-km square – was in the city centre where older pre-1930s housing was dense, gardens were small, green spaces were infrequent and impervious surface cover was at its highest. By contrast, the suburbs featured newer post-1960 housing with larger gardens planted with lots of non-native species alongside open parks,

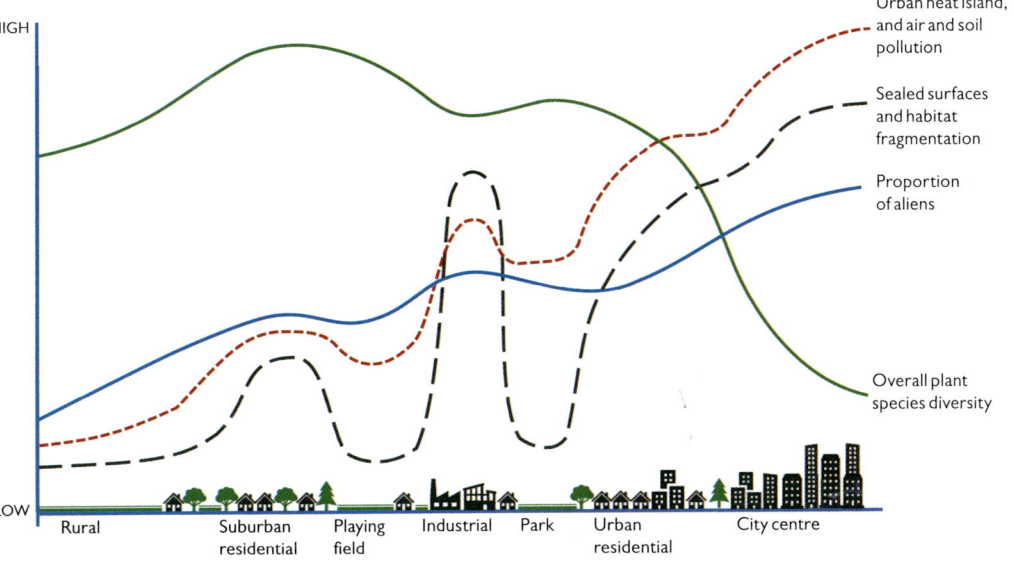

BELOW: Gradient of urbanisation from rural to city centre, showing changes in plant diversity in response to shifts in the physical environment as urbanisation increases. Note local impact of individual features on the ground such as industrial areas and green parks.

many fragments of woodland and scrub, and fragments of arable and semi-improved grassland. As a result, diversity was much higher, with 458 species per monad (1-km square). In contrast, intensively farmed areas on the very edge of the city were less diverse, with 397 species per monad.

Counting all the species

One of the most frequent questions people ask about urban botany is 'How many species grow in our cities?' (Or, perhaps rather more often, 'How many are growing in *my* city?') Unfortunately, this is an almost impossible question to answer, since most urban floras have not been studied in enough detail for us to know; I don't think anyone has counted the number of species found growing in cities like Winchester, Wakefield or Wrexham, for example. Another difficulty is that urban floras are never static, but constantly changing and evolving as new species arrive and spread, while others decline and disappear. This dynamism applies at even the smallest of scales. Walk down any street in any town and you'll be able to find and list a certain number of plants. But you can bet your bottom dollar that if you walk the same street again several weeks later you'll spot a few new species, and probably miss others that were on your original list. Some of this is just human nature (even the best botanists miss things), but much of it is down to the extraordinarily rapid flux in species. Multiply these changes up across all the streets of an entire city and you can begin to see how difficult it is to pin down precise numbers.

Around the world, urban floras are extremely diverse. In the largest global review of 110 cities, Aronson *et al.* (2014) found the number of vascular plants ranged from 269 (Ganyesa, South Africa) to 2,528 species (Philadelphia, USA), with the median coming in at 766 species. In total, 14,240 species were found growing in cities, representing 5% of global plant diversity. This study also identified the world's most cosmopolitan urban plant which, if you've ever wondered what it might be, will probably come as no surprise. Being found in 96% of cities around the world, Annual Meadow-grass *Poa annua* takes the crown. This small ruderal annual is *the* most successful urban plant, growing in a remarkably wide range of habitats including walls, pavement cracks, grassy lawns, verges, flowerbeds, allotments, shady woodland paths, riversides and the margins of ponds. Wherever the ground is cultivated or disturbed,

Creation of the urban flora

LEFT: Annual Meadow-grass is the single-most common urban plant in the world. It arose as a hybrid between Early Meadow-grass *P. infirma* (from Mediterranean areas) and *P. supina* (from the mountains of central and northern Europe) possibly as little as 10,000 years ago as glaciers retreated from southern Europe (Mao & Huff 2012).

you're likely to find it. Not far behind Annual Meadow-grass in the global league of urban plants are Shepherd's-purse *Capsella bursa-pastoris* (95% of cities), Common Chickweed *Stellaria media* (94% of cities) and Ribwort Plantain *Plantago lanceolata* (93% of cities).

In Britain and Ireland, urban floras are similarly diverse. Again, pinning down figures is difficult as numbers constantly change. Floras or checklists have been published for just 17 towns and cities (see table overleaf). This is a tiny proportion (1.3%) of the 1,184 settlements identified as towns and cities (Baker 2018; see Chapter 1). It's important to note that the species totals in these Floras aren't directly comparable with each other; in each study the urban areas have been defined in different ways and they cover very different date ranges. But, despite this, they do give an idea of the diversity of our urban vascular plant flora. They vary from 306 species in Dublin to 3,569 in London, with the average at 910 species. Of these, around 61% are native species and 39% aliens.

The high proportion of natives might come as a surprise as urban floras are often thought to be dominated by our frequently more eye-catching exotic aliens. The two notable exceptions to this are the up-to-date counts for London and Cambridge, which have many more aliens than natives; this may reflect the influx of neophytes in recent decades and the fact that many new alien species tend to appear in southern England first, thanks to the warmer climate and

Total number of species and proportions of natives, aliens, archaeophytes and neophytes in 17 towns and cities in Britain and Ireland

Town or city	Year	Total spp.	Natives no.	Natives %	Aliens no.	Aliens %	Archaeophytes no.	Archaeophytes %	Neophytes no.	Neophytes %	Source
Plymouth	1999	829	561	68	268	32	78	9	190	23	Kent et al. (2001)
Exeter	1984	473	331	70	142	30	66	14	76	16	Ivimey-Cook (1984)
Brighton	1980	529	347	66	182	34	85	16	97	18	Hall (1980)
London	2024	3,569	1,393	39	2,176	61	187	5	1,989	56	Mark Spencer (pers. comm.)
Cambridge	2024	1,491	622	42	869	58	121	8	555	37	Jonathan Shanklin (pers. comm.)
Birmingham	1971	565	400	71	165	29	71	13	94	17	Cadbury et al. (1971)
Shrewsbury	2011	467	303	65	164	35	64	14	100	21	Whild et al. (2011)
Leicester	1988	563	373	66	190	34	74	13	116	21	Primavesi & Evans (1988)
Derby	1989	605	403	67	202	33	68	11	134	22	Futter & Raynes (1989)
Nottingham	1998	784	494	63	290	37	86	11	204	26	Shepherd (1998)
Sheffield	1988	1,418	820	58	598	42	128	9	470	33	Shaw (1988)
Leeds	1994	410	295	72	115	28	46	11	69	17	Lavin & Wilmore (1994)
Hull	1998	696	423	61	273	39	91	13	182	26	Middleton (1998)
Newcastle	2024	991	524	53	467	47	61	6	406	41	James Common (pers. comm.)
Glasgow	2000	1,197	663	55	534	45	90	8	444	37	Dickson et al. (2000)
Dublin	1984	306	198	65	108	35	41	13	67	22	Jackson & Skeffington (1984)
Belfast	1997	582	384	66	198	34	54	9	144	25	Beesley & Wilde (1997)
Averages		910	502	61	408	39	83	11	314	27	

Towns and cities in Great Britain, and those in Ireland, are listed geographically from south to north.

density of the human population. Of the average urban alien flora, the majority are neophytes (79% of all aliens), suggesting that most are horticultural garden escapes, such as Mexican Fleabane *Erigeron karvinskianus* and Spanish and Hybrid Bluebells *Hyacinthoides hispanica* agg. While archaeophytes make up a smaller proportion (21% of all urban aliens), they include some very common plants like Red Deadnettle *Lamium purpureum*, Petty Spurge *Euphorbia peplus*, Common Poppy *Papaver rhoeas* and Greater Celandine *Chelidonium majus* that were introduced with crops or as medicinal plants and which relish the disturbed soils of urban habitats.

Into the streets

Urban ecology has emerged from the shadows to become a thriving area of research. And, as more and more of us live in cities and take an interest in the wildlife around us, we're beginning to study and record our urban flora in much more detail. This is important, because understanding how plants respond to urbanisation illuminates the impact we're having on all habitats, as none are untouched by human hand. It's also exciting, as this is where species are at their most dynamic, with new finds to be made nearly every time we step out onto the streets.

In the next few chapters, we'll take a detailed look at five habitats and features that you're likely to come across when taking a walk around town. Highly urbanised and characteristic of the built environment, we'll see how they're created, what's special about their ecology, which plants they support and the threats they face. So, let's now head into the streets and take a close look at pavements, walls, waste ground, the grassy bits and the street trees.

BELOW: Spanish and Hybrid Bluebells, with their broad leaves and wide bell-shaped, china-blue flowers, frequently escape from gardens and are now the most common bluebells in urban areas. Here, they're becoming naturalised at the base of a wall in Cambridge.

Part Three

A walk through the streets

Pavements | chapter seven

When many of us were children, it's likely we played the game of walking down a pavement and avoiding – at all costs – the cracks between the slabs. Although light-hearted, this distraction has its roots in deeper traditional folklore: narrow gaps, like those found between stones and in tree trunks, were boundaries between the earth and other, much darker, underworlds. The hiding places of malevolent spirits, to touch such gaps was to invite bad luck, illness, fairies or even the devil himself into your life. Best to avoid them altogether, or at least push your little brother or sister onto one instead.

For the urban botanist, however, these gaps are an irresistible source of wonder, constantly attracting our attention and drawing us down to ground level. Who hasn't walked down a street and noticed the plants growing between the cracks in the pavement? Rather than portals into the spiritual underworld, these gaps are openings into the very earth itself, a place to get roots down into the soil below and eke out a living in what is otherwise an incredibly harsh environment. When you're growing on a pavement, these gaps become your only opportunity for life.

Pavements are, of course, our main walking routes and where we most regularly come into contact with urban plants. Because pavements usually run along the front of houses and gardens, or shops, pubs and restaurants with window boxes and hanging baskets, there's plenty of opportunity for escape, with a multitude of alien plants spilling out and seeding themselves. This makes pavements rather thrilling habitats to explore, as you never quite know what you'll encounter in your next few steps. Often, it depends entirely on what the nice people at Number 13 have decided to plant in their hanging baskets this year, maybe Lobelia *Lobelia erinus*, Cape-jewels

PREVIOUS PAGES:
Common Ragwort *Jacobaea vulgaris* and Common Mallow *Malva sylvestris* growing together on waste ground in Brighton, Sussex.

OPPOSITE:
A robust plant of Cat's-ear *Hypochaeris radicata* rooting through a crack in a concrete pavement.

ABOVE: A London street with a rich and attractive pavement flora, including native Herb-Robert *Geranium robertianum* and Annual Meadow-grass *Poa annua*, and aliens including Purple Toadflax *Linaria purpurea* from Italy and Bilbao Fleabane *Erigeron floribundus* from South America.

RIGHT: Every gap in the paving offers an opportunity for plants to become established, such as this Procumbent Yellow-sorrel *Oxalis corniculata* from South-East Asia, growing in the cracks around a manhole cover in Deganwy, North Wales.

Nemesia strumosa or Petunia *Petunia × hybrida*. Pavements are often the first routes of escape from gardens, and many new British and county records for non-native species come from pavements. In a single edition of 'Adventives and Aliens' in *BSBI News*, for example, there is the first record of Atlas Poppy *Papaver atlanticum* for North Devon, the second of Throatwort *Trachelium caeruleum* for Dorset, first of Cape Snapdragon *Nemesia fruticans* for East Norfolk and the first of Malling Toadflax *Chaenorhinum origanifolium* for south-west Yorkshire, all growing on pavements and all seeded from nearby gardens (Berry 2023a).

Pavements epitomise urban habitats. Because we walk them so often and find so many different plants on them, they've become a metaphor for the urban environment itself. On social media, #PavementPlants is the most frequently used hashtag associated with urban botany, with thousands of posts showing the plants people have found growing around their feet. Pavement plants appear to delight and thrill us, a demonstration of the sheer resilience of nature.

Of course, not everyone is a fan of pavement vegetation. Councils are often highly sensitive to criticisms of their pavements being full of 'weeds' and looking unkempt, and there is a widespread and deeply held belief that if such plants are not controlled regularly, maintenance costs will soar and pavements will quickly become overrun and unusable. In order to allay such fears, thousands of pounds are spent by councils on herbicides every year to maintain the neat-and-tidy look. All too frequently, a strip of dead or dying plants can be seen along the foot of walls, pavement edges, fences and railings and around the base of trees and lampposts, the glyphosate ghosts of once-thriving plant communities. This obsession with tidiness is a major driver of urban biodiversity loss, impacting not just the vegetation but also the invertebrates and other wildlife they support.

ABOVE: This plant of Cape-jewels *Nemesia strumosa*, originally from South Africa, probably seeded into the pavement crack from plants grown in the hanging basket in the background the previous year.

What is a pavement?

To a civil engineer, a pavement is *any* surface constructed to take *any* type of traffic, whether that's people, animals or vehicles. This very wide definition includes all manner of surfaces including roads, cycle paths, racecourses, railways, airport runways, town squares and even football fields and golf courses. But to most of us in everyday life, a pavement is something much more specific: it's the flat, impervious and hard-wearing pedestrian surface forming the corridor alongside roads, buildings, private properties and other land.

The width of pavements is probably something few of us have ever considered. In Highways England's wonderfully technical *Design Manual for Roads and Bridges: CD 143 Designing for Walking, Cycling and Horse-riding*, the absolute minimum width is stated as being 2.0 metres, but the 'desirable' width is specified as 2.6 metres, while pavements beside walls and buildings should be 25–50cm wider to improve clearance (Highways England 2021). How this guidance applies in the real world would probably have never been of interest to anyone until, that is, the arrival of Covid-19. Suddenly, the requirement for 2m of social distancing meant that pavement width became an important question. After analysis of many British cities, one study found that 30% of pavements are a surprisingly generous 3m or more in width, 36% are 2–3m wide, and 34% are a slightly uncomfortable 2m wide or less (Bark 2020). This probably rings true on the ground, as we all know places where the pavement seems unnecessarily wide and is a pleasure to walk down, while others feel too narrow and unsafe beside a busy road.

The variation in pavement width often has a historical basis, as streets have evolved to accommodate different forms of transport over the ages. In the seventeenth century, when horses and carts ruled the carriageways, there was often little or no demarcation between the road and pavement. Large numbers of people would have spilled across the carriageway, and, if a pavement was differentiated at all, it was done with a simple line of bollards or kerbstones. It wasn't until the 1760s that pavements as we know them today began to be installed, mainly to separate people from the road to improve safety and cleanliness. Although granite setts (small cut blocks) were the most popular form of paving, wooden blocks were also used as they were quieter under horses' hooves and caused them fewer injuries. In some areas, such as the parish of St George in Marylebone, London, 70% of the streets were paved in wood during the 1890s (Save Bloomsbury 2020). This form of paving didn't last long, though, as the wood soaked up the copious quantities of urine from horses and other livestock, creating a strong stench of ammonia, and harder-wearing surfaces were eventually needed to take vehicle traffic (Jackson 2015).

Pavements are not always narrow, and often widen out into much broader areas. When streets are pedestrianised, tarmac road surfaces are usually replaced with paving slabs, setts, bricks or cobbles to make them more inviting to walk over. Similarly, the wide expanses of open market squares, town squares, plazas or seaside promenades often employ a variety of paving materials and colours arranged in patterns to make them more attractive. Front gardens are also often paved over to provide parking for cars, substantially increasing the area of sealed surfaces in a street.

Anatomy of pavements

Technically, pavements need to provide two things: a very hard-wearing, flat surface so they don't need constant maintenance, and excellent drainage; after all, none of us likes to get our feet wet. Drainage is also important to prolong the life of the pavement, as areas that constantly collect puddles of water are likely to degrade more quickly. Pavements tend to have an impervious, sealed surface, and they are dry. Both of these aspects have a huge bearing on their ecology.

The Highways England *Design Manual* lists 14 different materials of varying suitability for pavements (Highways England 2021). Each surface has different properties that affect the ability of plants to become established, including porosity, the proportion of gaps and surface temperature. The list includes hard-wearing materials such as tarmac, asphalt, flagstones and concrete, but also more porous surfaces such as gravels and aggregates and grass turf reinforced with rubber or plastic grids (note that tarmac is a mixture of aggregate and tar, which is derived from crude oil, while asphalt is a mixture of aggregate and bitumen, a substance created from the distillation of coal or wood).

Tarmac, asphalt and concrete pavements are laid as wet mixtures and – once cured and hardened – produce a virtually impenetrable continuous surface with almost no gaps for plants to get established. However, despite their durability, continual use and wear mean fractures eventually begin to appear in the surface. Concrete is the most hard-wearing and can last 50 to 100 years. Tarmac is much less durable and generally lasts between 12 and 15 years, while asphalt is surprisingly weak and can begin to degrade in as little as 3–5 years, being particularly susceptible to the effects of water, sunlight (which oxidises the binding) and oil and petroleum from vehicles. Degradation is fastest where the asphalt or tarmac is thin, such as at the edges of a pavement, in corners by walls, and around manholes and other obstacles. Here, it often crumbles into a gravel-like state which

BELOW: The thin, degraded edge of this tarmac car park in Dublin is somewhat permeable to the substrate below, allowing a small community of plants to become established, dominated by Pineappleweed *Matricaria discoidea*.

can, in fact, be a very good place for plants to become established. Indeed, although tarmac looks a forbidding habitat, it's an excellent substrate for many bryophytes, and species like Cylindric Beard-moss *Didymodon insulanus*, Silver-moss *Bryum argenteum* and Tufted Feather-moss *Scleropodium cespitans* can flourish on its surface. Perhaps these plants should be known as 'tarmacophytes'?

Across areas of paving, the density of gaps (and therefore plants) depends on the size of the paving materials used. The largest are flagstones, usually cut from natural sandstone or limestone, or made from concrete. Paving blocks, bricks and setts are smaller and typically made from clay or concrete, often coloured with metallic oxides, and come in a huge range of shapes and designs. The grouting used between paving materials also has a strong influence on how hospitable the pavement is to plants. If the grout is soft and porous (sand, for example), plants can become readily established. But hard grouts like specialist jointing compounds and resins will produce an impermeable surface as solid and durable as the paving stones themselves. Often, rather weak mixtures of sand and cement are used which can degrade after a few years and provide an excellent substrate for plants, while small setts are frequently laid down so tightly that no grout is needed, just a brushing of dry sand to fill the gaps.

The substrates underneath pavements, laid to provide a stable surface on which to place the paving material, are generally very free-draining and infertile. Highways England (2021) stipulates that at least a 15cm-deep layer of compacted crushed stone aggregate is employed, sometimes with an extra 5cm of sand, usually laid directly on top of the subsoil. It would therefore be difficult to call what lies beneath the pavement soil, as it tends to lack any biological component and is almost entirely mineral in nature. In time, this substrate can become more humic as small amounts of decaying vegetation and roots work their way down between the gaps, but in general the sealed nature of the paved surface severely hampers the development of anything we'd recognise as soil.

BELOW: Dandelions *Taraxacum* agg. taking advantage of the open sections of a porous pavement, designed to reduce run-off by allowing more rainwater through to the substrate below.

The impermeable nature of most pavements comes at a considerable cost. Around 90% of rainwater quickly runs off the surface and has to be diverted into drains,

ABOVE: A sustainable drainage system in central London, with a strip of open soil between the pavement and road. Alongside the garden plants are a few spontaneous species, including Greek Dock *Rumex cristatus* with its large reddish-brown seedheads.

gutters and culverts. As climate change brings more extreme storms, rainfall and flooding, the focus has now shifted to producing much more porous pavement surfaces. Known as sustainable drainage systems (SuDS), these simple techniques help reduce flooding by letting water pass through the paved surface into the ground. Most of the principles employed echo natural processes, aiming to manage water quantity by allowing it to enter the ground, improve water quality by filtering out pollutants, and provide biodiversity benefits by maintaining the water table and creating opportunities for wildlife. The *SuDS Manual* (Woods Ballard 2015) describes detailed solutions including pervious pavements, large soil-filled tree pits and strips of pavement-edge vegetation that act as filters. These often work hydrologically, but usually have limited value for wildlife as they're filled with all sorts of garden plants primarily designed just for pollinators. In many cases, they're lost opportunities for encouraging the spontaneous and durable urban flora that's much better adapted to urban life.

The reason I've included all this detail about pavement construction is that it really matters for plants. The substrate, the condition of pavement surface, its permeability and the density of gaps all influence the potential for colonisation. The importance of these factors was investigated in a study in the city of Blois (Bonthoux *et al.* 2019). One of the first cities in France to ban the use of herbicides on its streets back in 2012 (a restriction extended to all French towns and cities

ABOVE: Despite the ban on herbicides, pavements in the ancient centre of Blois, France, have low species diversity and vegetation cover because the streets have been urbanised for more than 600 years and now experience high levels of trampling on impervious surfaces.

BELOW: An all too familiar sight: pavements are often, and repeatedly, dug up to access services below, disturbing the substrate.

in 2022), the street flora here is particularly well developed, despite ongoing manual methods of control such as hand-weeding. The research team surveyed nearly 49km (30 miles) of pavement and compared three different types of surface: new pavements with intact asphalt or cement pointing between paving stones, older pavements with cracked asphalt or degraded pointing between stones, and unsurfaced pavements with bare sand. More than 300 species of plants were recorded in total across the city, and pavement type was by far the most important factor in determining species richness. Older, cracked pavements were found to have twice as many species as newer, intact pavements (18 species on average compared to 9). Bare sandy pavements, though, supported the most species (22 on average) thanks to their loose, porous surfaces over the soil below. Species richness was also highest when one side of the pavement bordered a grassy park, verge or garden rather than a wall or road. The study also found that pavement diversity and vegetation cover depended on the type of neighbourhood. The richest, best-developed floras were encountered in areas of large industrial and commercial buildings built in the 1960s, followed by those in areas of low-density nineteenth-century detached housing and areas of detached housing with gardens built in the 1990s. The lowest plant diversity and cover occurred in areas of high-density housing and flats built between 1950 and 2000, and in the ancient city centre, which has been heavily urbanised since the fifteenth century and where pedestrian traffic is highest.

Of course, pavements are rarely composed of one type of surface. Walk down many streets, especially older ones, and you'll notice a mix of materials with sections of paving giving way to asphalt or other surfaces and back again. These differences accumulate over time as repairs and maintenance take place; just think of how many times pavements are torn up and repaired to access water, electricity, gas, sewage and telecommunications services below. Pavements can therefore be surprisingly heterogeneous habitats, and this heterogeneity helps drive plant diversity.

However, the pavement surface itself is only part of the story. Look casually down any street and, at first glance, you'll probably just notice the road, a pavement and the walls of buildings. But peer more closely and you'll see that streets have an intricate anatomy, one that provides a wide range of micro-niches for plants to occupy. Moving from the middle of the road to the buildings, you might come across:

- a gutter along the edge of the road, sometimes constructed of a different material;
- a raised edge of kerbstones, again made of a different material;
- kerbside drainage holes that might be open or blocked with alluvium;
- open areas around the base of trees (so-called 'tree pits');
- manholes, bollards, signposts, wastebins, postboxes, lampposts and all manner of other street furniture;
- vertical edges along the base of walls;
- open edges along fences to gardens or parks;
- downpipes from gutters into drains that might be open or blocked with alluvium;
- steps going up to front doors or down into basements;
- open basements;
- gateways and paths going into gardens;
- forecourts of shops, garages and other establishments;
- and areas of gravel or open soil between pavements and walls.

ABOVE: Where this section of a Dublin pavement has been repaired, soil has been used as infill between the paving stones rather than cement, allowing Annual Meadow-grass, Dandelion and Greater Plantain *Plantago major* to colonise.

All these structures offer different conditions for plants in terms of substrate, availability of moisture, levels of fertility, light, temperature and trampling. A kerbside drain full of alluvium provides a deep, moist, fertile substrate where large plants of Smooth Sow-thistle *Sonchus oleraceus* can grow. Just a few centimetres away beside the base of a wall, the pavement might have a thin layer of dirt that's infertile, sun-baked and intensely droughted, where only tiny winter annuals

Urban Plants

RIGHT: Pavements offer a surprising variety of micro-niches for different plants. Here, the trampled surface on the right with bryophytes and Annual Meadow-grass gives way to a highly vegetated gutter with Toad Rush *Juncus bufonius* and the base of a wall with Ivy-leaved Toadflax *Cymbalaria muralis*.

RIGHT: A remarkable shaded basement beside an Edinburgh street, where the sheltered conditions are home to at least 22 species including Japanese Anemone *Anemone × hybrida*, Mexican Fleabane *Erigeron karvinskianus*, Petty Spurge *Euphorbia peplus*, Welsh Poppy *Papaver cambricum* and Buddleja *Buddleja davidii*.

like Common Whitlowgrass *Erophila verna* can survive. Pavements can support a surprisingly high diversity of plants because of this juxtaposition of micro-niches.

Wherever there's an opening in the pavement surface, or even the slightest accumulation of substrate or detritus, plants will root. This is particularly the case at the base of walls, where the gap between the pavement and the wall readily fills with humus, dirt and general street detritus. It's also where seeds naturally come to rest, and where water running down the wall provides considerably more moisture than the open pavement. Of all the pavement micro-niches, this is the one where most plants are found.

Ecology of pavements

Exposed to very extreme conditions, pavements are one of the most challenging environments in which plants can attempt to get a foothold. Their hard, flat, cracked surfaces are rarely mirrored in natural habitats, except perhaps some outcrops of limestone pavement or coastal rock platforms. But even these are very different, with largely untrodden surfaces and deep fissures that collect soil and provide shelter to plants. When you think about it in these terms, urban pavements are very unusual, with a particular set of ecological characteristics that make them especially difficult for plants.

Heat

Pavement surface temperatures are generally warmer than air temperature, particularly in summer, because solar radiation is absorbed, stored and then re-radiated as heat, contributing to the UHI (see Chapter 5). The amount of heating depends on several factors, but especially sunshine intensity, ambient air temperature, wind speed, the thermal mass of the material (its ability to absorb, store and release heat) and even its colour, as a dark asphalt surface will absorb much more heat than pale concrete (Qin *et al.* 2022).

In summer, pavements can become unbearably hot. During the 2022 summer heatwave in Spain, stone pavement surfaces in Santiago de Compostela reached 55°C, enough to cook any vegetation. However, using a thermal heat-imaging camera, Miguel Serrano from Compostela University found that the plants filling the gaps between the stones were remarkably cooler, at around just 30°C (Cortizo 2022). Some of this 25°C difference was due to evapotranspiration from the leaves; as the water evaporates, it takes

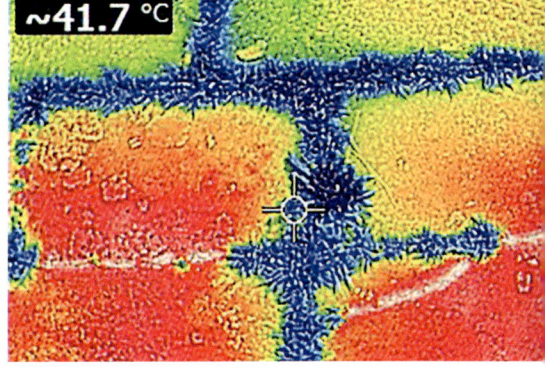

BELOW: Thermal-camera images of a pavement in Santiago de Compostela, Spain, during the summer 2022 heatwave, showing significant cooling from the vegetation. The plants include Procumbent Pearlwort *Sagina procumbens*, Buck's-horn Plantain *Plantago coronopus*, Early Meadow-grass *Poa infirma* and Procumbent Yellow-sorrel *Oxalis corniculata*.

ABOVE: Mediterranean Nettle, a warmth-loving species basking in the radiated heat from the pavement and wall of the Sir Isaac Newton pub on Castle Street in Cambridge.

heat with it, cooling the surface. In addition, the plants don't absorb and store heat in the same way as the surrounding stone or concrete and, even though they're tiny, they still reduce heating by shading the surface below. Even so, this amount of cooling is remarkable and hints at the benefits such urban vegetation can bring.

Since pavements store and radiate so much heat, they're a good place to find warmth-loving (thermophilous) aliens, especially along the base of walls where the warming is at its most intense. A good example is Mediterranean Nettle *Urtica membranacea*, a frost-sensitive species found, not surprisingly, around the Mediterranean. It was first recorded in the British Isles in 2006, when Ann Boucher visited Warwick to celebrate her Golden Wedding anniversary and noticed over a hundred plants growing between a pavement and the base of a wall (Boucher & Partridge 2006). It's now been found at more than 50 sites, from Penzance High Street (Cornwall) to a B&Q car park in Elgin (Moray), and has been known at two sites in Cambridge for at least eight years (Leslie 2019). Some of these plants may have arrived by hitching lifts in large pots of olive trees, palms and other garden plants imported from southern Europe (see Chapter 4).

Moisture

With their high proportion of sealed surfaces, pavements can be extremely dry habitats. The surface is designed to drain very rapidly after rainfall. At least 90% of the rain falling on a standard asphalt pavement runs off, although permeable asphalts can reduce this to 40% (Hou *et al.* 2020). Most of this run-off goes straight into gutters, drains and underground drainage, never reaching the soil. In a study of different pavement surfaces in Delaware, Ohio, Kelley (1999) found that the average soil-moisture content below all the surfaces was just 10–12%, compared to 20–60% for open loam field soils nearby. Perhaps surprisingly, soil moisture remained relatively equal throughout the year, suggesting that soils under pavements can be in a more-or-less permanent state of drought. Only when pavement

LEFT: Common Cornsalad is one of many winter annuals on pavements. A native species, it's often grown as a garden salad known as Lamb's Lettuce.

surfaces began to degrade after several years did significant amounts of water penetrate through to the soil below.

Under drought conditions of hot weather with little rainfall, pavement plants quickly wilt and eventually die, despite the occasional summer downpour. By contrast, more prolonged rainfall during cooler weather from autumn through to spring keeps the uppermost layers of pavement gaps more-or-less continuously damp. This pattern of winter wet and summer drought mirrors coastal sand dune habitats, where winter-wet sandy soils rapidly become droughted in spring and early summer. Dunes are rich in winter annuals, plants that germinate in autumn, grow through the winter and flower in spring, shedding their seed and dying before the heat of summer. It's no surprise that pavements also support communities of winter annuals, especially Thale Cress *Arabidopsis thaliana*, Common Whitlowgrass, Rue-leaved Saxifrage *Saxifraga tridactylites*, Danish Scurvygrass *Cochlearia danica*, Scarlet Pimpernel *Lysimachia arvensis*, Fern-grass *Catapodium rigidum* and Common Cornsalad *Valerianella locusta*. The winter growth of such species is often controlled by their germination requirements; dormant seed is shed in spring, but this dormancy is lost during the summer after which they become capable of germinating, but only at low temperatures (Baskin & Baskin 1970, 1983, Roberts & Lockett 1978). The mass-flowering of these small annuals in early spring can be quite a sight, with pavements bordered with a miniature floral garland for a few weeks before the plants turn to seed and die.

New to the neighbourhood

Several unusual annuals with distinct Mediterranean affinities have recently begun to spread rapidly in urban areas of Britain. Perhaps the most famous is Early Meadow-grass *Poa infirma*, a species once restricted to the warmest parts of the south-west (Cornwall, the Isles of Scilly and the Channel Islands) where it grew in trampled grassland on clifftops, tracksides, picnic sites and dunes. In the 1980s and 1990s, it suddenly set out on a remarkable expansion eastwards and inland, not only colonising similar habitats elsewhere but also moving into towns and cities, particularly London, Cambridge, Colchester, Canterbury and Brighton. In such settings it grows on pavements, trampled grass verges, disturbed ground and at the base of trees and walls. There's little doubt its spread has been assisted by our warming climate and its discovery of the UHI, along with the movement of seed on tyres and footwear, but it may have also been bolstered by new colonisations of the species from Europe.

Early Meadow-grass growing on the cobbled edge of a pavement in Cambridge.

More recently, Four-leaved Allseed *Polycarpon tetraphyllum* has started to follow in the footsteps of Early Meadow-grass. This tiny annual originally grew on south-facing, frost-free, drought-prone banks, shingle and sand at a handful of sites in Jersey, Dorset and south Devon. Since 2000, it also suddenly began appearing on pavements, along the bases of walls and on gravel driveways, especially in London, Cambridge, Aldershot, Herne Bay and other towns in southern England. New sites are appearing every year, and again it seems to be exploiting the UHI, with dispersal assisted by vehicles and feet.

A dense cushion of Four-leaved Allseed in central London.

Another very rare plant with urban intentions is Jersey Cudweed *Laphangium luteoalbum*. First recorded from the Channel Islands in 1689, it was known from just a handful of scattered sites in England until it began to spread in about 2000.

Jersey Cudweed beside the Grand Union Canal where it joins the River Thames in Brentford, London.

It's now recorded from 125 10-km squares, an astonishing 50-fold increase. The majority of these are in London, but it has popped up in places as far and wide as Eastbourne, Northampton, Liverpool, Edinburgh, Belfast, Dublin and Wexford. The discovery of what was once such an extreme rarity in mundane urban settings is undeniably thrilling. As well as receiving a boost from our warmer climate, its seeds may be spreading to new sites in aggregate for hardcore or hitching a ride with potted garden plants.

Compared to these species of predominantly droughted soils, Annual Beard-grass *Polypogon monspeliensis* prefers wetter conditions. This beautiful grass grows in damp, cattle-trodden grazing marshes and the edges of brackish pools and saltmarshes around the coast of southern and eastern England. About as far-removed as you can get from dry, urban pavements, it has nonetheless spread well inland over the last century and is now found in many urban settings, including pavements, the base of walls, waste ground, road verges and railway lines. Its spread may be assisted by vehicles carrying the seed, as well as its inclusion in birdseed mixtures.

Finally, another grass of damp habitats has become one of the fastest spreading of all urban plants. Water Bent *Polypogon viridis*, originally from southern Europe, Asia and northern Africa, was first found in Guernsey in 1860. For decades the Channel Islands remained its stronghold, until it suddenly began appearing in urban settings in south-west England in the 1980s, and Ireland in the 1990s. Since the early 2000s, its 10-km square distribution has increased 15-fold and it's now incredibly common on pavements, the bases of walls, waste ground and along roadsides in towns and cities right across England and Wales. It continues to move north, with many new records from Edinburgh and Glasgow since 2016. This spread has been helped by warmer winters and the movement of seed on vehicles and footwear and in building materials.

What's fascinating about all these species is that few people could have foreseen their rapid and dramatic colonisation of towns and cities. Our flora is unpredictable but also highly opportunistic, allowing even the rarest plants to take advantage of new habitats should the chance arise. It's impossible to say which species might be next to take up life in the city, but all are intriguing additions to our pavement flora.

Annual Beard-grass sprawling across a pavement in Panton Street, Cambridge.

Water Bent growing out from a wall above Regent's Canal in central London.

ABOVE: A large specimen of Opium Poppy growing on Chesterton Lane, Cambridge. Originally introduced during the Roman period, many different-coloured cultivars are popular in gardens.

Many other types of annuals grow on pavements. Unlike winter annuals, they germinate opportunistically at any time from early spring through to late autumn whenever conditions are suitable, although this can make them vulnerable to summer droughts. With thin soils and bare, open areas, pavements are very much pioneer habitats and are dominated by communities of ruderal species. These early-succession pavement pioneers include annuals of disturbed ground such as Groundsel *Senecio vulgaris*, Opium Poppy *Papaver somniferum*, Pineappleweed, Petty Spurge *Euphorbia peplus* and Wavy Bitter-cress *Cardamine flexuosa*, along with familiar arable flowers including Common Poppy *Papaver rhoeas*, Shepherd's-purse *Capsella bursa-pastoris*, Sun Spurge *Euphorbia helioscopia* and Common Fumitory *Fumaria officinalis*, as well as annuals of thin, droughted soil like Squirrel-tail Fescue *Vulpia bromoides* and Slender Sandwort *Arenaria leptoclados*.

Trampling

Pavements are designed for walking, so it's no surprise that one of the main impacts on plants is trampling. In the busiest parts of cities, pavements receive hundreds of thousands of footfalls every day; Westminster, for example, can see traffic of over a million people every day (753,000 workers and 260,000 tourists and visitors, City of Westminster 2017). This is one end of the extreme, of course, and most streets will be very much quieter, but even low levels of pedestrian traffic have an effect on plants. This can be seen clearly on most pavements, where plants tend to be restricted to the edges where we don't walk.

Trampling has several direct and indirect ecological effects. What little substrate there is on a pavement gets kicked around and constantly disturbed, so it tends to be unstable and accumulates in less-trodden areas. It also becomes severely compacted underfoot. While compaction reduces conditions for good root growth, it also limits the activity of nitrifying bacteria, leading to a build-up of organic nitrogen (Lundholm 2011). Walking on plants also damages them directly, crushing leaves and stems and restricting growth. As a result, only those species well adapted to trampling can survive. These tend to be small plants with tough tissues and prostrate growth or leaves in flat rosettes. Some can regrow quickly following damage and they often have multiple growing points (axillary buds) located close to the ground, out of the way of the footfall.

Indeed, pavements tend to be dominated by plants with just a few growth strategies. Most are **hemicryptophytes** (perennial herbs with buds on the soil surface such as Dandelion), **cryptophytes** (perennial herbs with buds located under the soil surface such as Common Horsetail *Equisetum arvense*) and **therophytes** (annuals that perennate as seeds such as Thale Cress). Occasionally, there are also **chamaephytes** (shrubs with buds on perennial shoots close to the soil surface such as some *Cotoneaster* species). These represent different strategies for survival (Raunkiær 1934) and most pavement communities will include a mixture of these life forms.

In a study of 163 pavements from 34 municipalities across Flanders in Belgium, Fagot *et al.* (2011) found that the intensity of trampling had a direct and significant impact on the flora. The pavements were all unsprayed and consisted of small paving stones. In the average 100m square, highly trampled pavements supported 7.7 species, while those of intermediate use had 9.5 species and those with low trampling had 12.3 species. Vegetation cover, however, didn't quite match this pattern, with an unexpectedly high level of coverage on the most intensely used pavements (18.4% cover) compared to intermediate (9.2%) and low use (23.1%) pavements. Although surprising, it seems that cracks in the most heavily trampled pavements are dominated by low-growing mosses and Procumbent Pearlwort, which form almost continual cover of the paving gaps. In contrast, pavements with low trampling were dominated by occasional larger plants like Greater Plantain, Dandelion, Daisy *Bellis perennis*, White Clover *Trifolium repens* and Perennial Ryegrass *Lolium perenne* that didn't form continual cover.

The width of paving gaps also had an influence on species diversity and coverage. Pavements with wide gaps (over 5mm) supported 11.3 species per 100m^2 and had vegetation cover of 15.4%, compared to pavements with narrow gaps (0–2mm) with just 7.1 species per 100m^2 and cover of 6.5%. This underlines the importance of niche availability in determining pavement flora, with a high density of wide gaps leading to more species and greater cover of vegetation (Fagot *et al.* 2011).

The flora of the most heavily used pavements often echoes that of rural gateways heavily trampled by livestock, where only the most trampling-tolerant species can survive. Such plants include Procumbent Pearlwort, Shepherd's-purse, Annual Meadow-grass, Greater Plantain, Knotgrass *Polygonum aviculare*, Scentless Mayweed

ABOVE: Pineappleweed relishes trampled sites – be it pavement or field gateway – and is mainly spread through seed carried around on footwear and tyres.

Tripleurospermum inodorum and Pineappleweed. Two coastal species that are tolerant of heavy trampling – Early Meadow-grass and Buck's-horn Plantain – are also spreading on urban pavements. Many of these species have long-lived seed that can survive for years in the seed bank, appearing whenever the substrate is disturbed.

Pavement refugia

The considerable impact of trampling is best demonstrated by the exuberant growth of plants in any areas where footfall is reduced. These **pavement refugia** are where plants can at last flourish unhindered, with vegetation often reaching its greatest luxuriance. The most frequent such refugium is where the flat pavement meets the base of a vertical wall. We almost never actually set foot on this narrow strip of ground for fear of scraping our shoulders on the wall, so it escapes most of the footfall. Another extremely important pavement refugium is the open soil around the base of street trees. These so-called 'tree pits' often look like minute gardens, and can support many different species, making them critical in supporting populations of pavement plants (see Chapter 11). Another example is where the pavement runs along the edge of the road or cycle lane. Here, the kerbstone and a slight drop in levels means we step out into the road over a narrow gutter. This untrampled gully readily fills with detritus and collects run-off, creating damp and fertile conditions for plants to grow.

ABOVE: A Dublin lamppost and signpost create a small pavement refugium, where Great Willowherb *Epilobium hirsutum*, Common Chickweed *Stellaria media* and False Oat-grass *Arrhenatherum elatius* are sheltered from the footfall.

Other pavement refugia are more subtle. Street furniture such as lampposts, postboxes, signposts, bollards and planting containers can all have a halo of plants growing around them, as we tend to avoid such obstacles while walking. Other areas of pavement can be permanently fenced off with railings, allowing the rapid establishment of shrubs like Buddleja and fast-growing trees such as Sycamore *Acer pseudoplatanus*, Ash *Fraxinus excelsior* and Tree-of-heaven *Ailanthus altissima*. The same is true of temporary scaffolding and areas of building work, which are often fenced off for many more months than originally planned. Even abandoned bicycles chained to a kerbside post or fence can shelter a growth of vegetation beneath them.

All these sites are important as they give plants a vital opportunity to flower, set seed and spread out to the rest of the street. Sometimes, it only needs one or two individuals to do this. A single plant of Spear Thistle *Cirsium vulgare*, for example, can produce around 8,000 seeds and, while the vast majority of these won't germinate or reach flowering size, if only one or two individuals do so then the species has a chance to survive on the street. In this way, pavement refugia can help the long-term survival of a species, regularly re-seeding the surrounding pavements.

These refugia also show what pavements would turn into if we didn't walk on them. The Covid-19 pandemic lockdowns gave us a glimpse of what such a post-apocalyptic world might look like. Many people noticed pavement plants where few had been seen before, as if a great tide of vegetation had been released from the relentless footfall.

Social media was flooded with posts illustrating the greening and flowering of pavements eerily empty of people. This quick response of plants reveals the resilience of our urban flora, persisting for many years as small populations of stunted individuals until opportunities for more exuberant growth come along.

Nitrogen pollution

Lying right beside the carriageway, pavements are subjected to particularly high levels of pollution from vehicle exhausts, especially oxides of nitrogen (NO_x), ammonia (NH_3) and particulate pollution. The edge of one dual carriageway in Perth, Scotland, was shown to be receiving 8kg of nitrogen per hectare per year above background levels (Cape *et al.* 2004, see Chapter 5). That's enough to considerably modify the flora. For this reason, much of our pavement vegetation is rather robust and weedy in character, dominated by nitrogen-demanding plants such as Common Nettle *Urtica dioica*, Cleavers *Galium aparine*, Spear Thistle, Groundsel and Common Chickweed. And it's not just the native species; many aliens that thrive on pavements are also nitrogen loving, including Opium Poppy, Oxford Ragwort and Cockspur *Echinochloa crus-galli*, a robust annual grass from warm-temperate and tropical areas of Europe, Asia and North America which is spreading extraordinarily quickly in urban areas and along motorways and main roads.

RIGHT: Silver-moss is an extraordinarily tolerant bryophyte. As well as pavements and tarmac, it has a marvellous reputation for being the most common moss to colonise vehicles, often growing in the crevices between the windows and bodywork and even on windscreen wipers.

Only a few bryophytes can tolerate the high levels of nitrogen, trampling and intense summer drought of pavements. Perhaps the most common is Silver-moss *Bryum argenteum*, a very beautiful plant that grows in tight mats of slender shoots with white tips, hence the common name. Often seen filling the gaps between paving slabs, it frequently occurs with other small, trampling-tolerant species like Annual Meadow-grass and Procumbent Pearlwort.

Dispersal

Above all, pavements are, of course, places of movement. We can easily carry seeds with us on our footwear and clothing as we walk around town; the turn-ups of trousers are especially efficient at capturing and dispersing seed, as are the muddy soles of our footwear. Animals are also superb vectors of plants, with seeds becoming trapped in the fur and paws of cats, dogs, foxes and other urban mammals. And, as we all know when a bus, lorry or car zooms past at speed, pavements are subjected to considerable levels of turbulence. They therefore act as corridors through which species readily move around the urban environment, and observant botanists can sometimes track the rapid spread of new arrivals along their nearby streets.

Effective dispersal is critical for pavement plants because the habitat is so intensely fragmented, with large areas of impenetrable surface and little open substrate in which to root. Opportunities for getting a foothold can be few and far between, often tens or even hundreds of metres apart, and being able to bridge such gaps effectively gives a species a considerable ecological advantage. Species with heavy seeds that drop close to the parent plant (such as Hedge Woundwort *Stachys sylvatica*) find it difficult to spread quickly, while those that produce large quantities of small, readily dispersed seeds can move around quickly and occupy any available nooks and crannies in the pavement surface. Such species tend to be pioneers and are characteristic of early stages of succession.

The pattern of dispersal around a plant is known as the dispersal kernel (see Chapter 6), and describes the probability of a seed landing at different distances from its parent. Dispersal kernels are fascinating, as the movement of seed often has more than one phase, with different mechanisms coming into play at different times. An excellent example is Procumbent Yellow-sorrel *Oxalis corniculata*, a small but highly invasive species from South-East Asia which

RIGHT: As well as highly effective seed dispersal, the creeping stems of Procumbent Yellow-sorrel also root at the nodes, making it one of the most pernicious garden and pavement weeds.

is increasing rapidly on urban pavements. Originally grown as a rockery plant, its spread in the last few decades appears to have accelerated, with many new occurrences in the English Midlands and northern England, especially from Birmingham to Sheffield (Stroh *et al*. 2023). Much of this success is down to its two-phase method of dispersal. Firstly, seeds are ejected explosively from their capsules; in one greenhouse experiment, individual plants were found to disperse 800 seeds to a distance of five metres (16.5ft) in a 24-hour period (Holt 1987). Secondly, these seeds are also sticky and become readily attached to animals, birds, insects and us. This second phase of long-range dispersal allows the species to move much greater distances.

There are many different forms of seed dispersal. Broadly, they are split into two categories: **autochory**, where seed is dispersed without any external assistance (for example, seed dispersal by means of gravity alone, known as **barochory**) and **allochory**, where an animal vector, the wind or any other form of external help is employed to disperse the seed. Some of our most frequent pavement plants, such as Wood Avens *Geum urbanum*, Cleavers and Wall Barley *Hordeum murinum*, are very effectively dispersed on the coats of animals, a method known as **epizoochory** (literally 'upon an animal' dispersal). Wood Avens and Cleavers (also known as Sticky Willy or Goose-grass) have seeds with hooked spines that help them fix to any passing animal, and we all know how effective that can be. Like several other species of grass, seeds of Wall Barley have rasp-like **awns** on their **spikelets** that work their way into the coats of animals. Dogs can suffer terribly from these seeds becoming embedded in their skin and paws, and dog owners often call on councils to eradicate Wall Barley and other grasses on pavements to alleviate the problem.

We can be extremely effective carriers of seed, and this is known as **anthropochory** (human dispersal). As well as carrying seeds of Cleavers, Wood Avens and Wall Barley on our clothing, we're also good at moving seeds on our footwear. In one study, Wichmann *et al.* (2008) coloured seeds of Wild Cabbage *Brassica oleracea* and Black Mustard *B. nigra* bright pink and measured how far they were carried by the dirty boots of walkers on a rural coastal path in Dorset. Although more than half the seeds fell off within five metres (16.5ft), many were regularly carried a distance of 5km (3 miles) or more. While urban pavements are not usually quite so muddy, seeds will still be carried long distances on our footwear. In addition, it's likely that we bring many seeds back to town when we return from muddy countryside walks, especially if we jump into a car or catch a train or bus to get us home.

Indeed, vehicles have been shown to transport seed over considerable distances, in some cases more than 100km (60 miles). Mud that accumulates under wheel arches, around mudguards and on tyres contains seeds picked up from wherever the vehicle has been. To find out which seeds might be carried this way, Hodkinson & Thompson (1997) collected mud from the wheel arches of 200 cars in University of Sheffield car parks. In all, 37 species germinated from the mud, the most common being Greater Plantain, Annual Meadow-grass, Rough Meadow-grass *Poa trivialis*, Common Nettle and Pineappleweed. All these ruderal species produce small, long-lived seeds and are characteristic of roadsides and pavements.

A slightly more dramatic way of spreading seed around is **ballochory**, or explosive dispersal. As well as Procumbent Yellow-sorrel, several other common pavement species have seedpods that,

ABOVE: A Wood Avens seedhead, showing the hooked spine of each seed that attaches to animal coats (epizoochory) and human clothing (anthropochory).

BELOW: Seeds of Wall Barley stuck in the mesh fabric of a trainer. These can easily be transported many kilometres before falling out.

Urban Plants

LEFT: Seedheads of Cut-leaved Crane's-bill. In the centre, the cup-shaped structures holding the seed have sprung upward (dehisced), flinging the seed away from the plant. Unexploded (undehisced) seedpods can be seen on the left and right.

RIGHT: By uncoiling quickly when wet (in as little as one minute) and coiling up again slowly as they dry, the corkscrew awns of Common Stork's-bill can bury the seed to a depth of one centimetre.

when ripe, explode due to internal pressures that have built up in their tissues. Anyone that's pulled up plants of Hairy Bitter-cress *Cardamine hirsuta* from their garden when the pods are ripe will know how readily they explode on touch, scattering seed up to five metres (16.5ft) away. Herb-Robert and Cut-leaved Crane's-bill *Geranium dissectum* employ a slightly different and very elegant mechanism. The 'stork's-bill' structure that appears after flowering consists of a long beak with five cup-shaped receptacles at the base, each of which holds a single seed. When ripe, a strip of tissue down the side of the beak ruptures and suddenly springs upwards, taking the cup with it. The seed is thrown from the cup, rather like a cricket ball being thrown from a bowler's hand, and the seed can be flung five metres (16.5ft) or more from the plant. Once on the ground, the seeds are often moved again by ants and other invertebrates. In the closely related Common Stork's-bill *Erodium cicutarium*, each seed has a long awn-like structure which coils up in the way of a corkscrew. Once on the soil surface, these uncoil when wet and coil up again as they dry, literally screwing the seed down into the soil ready for germination (Stamp 1984).

Another fascinating and important form of dispersal, known as **myrmecochory**, involves ants. Seeds of myrmecochorous plants have a special structure, a parcel of food known as an **elaiosome**. Rich in fatty lipids, these make the seeds highly attractive to ants, who collect the seeds and carry them back to their colonies where the elaiosome is fed to developing larvae. The intact seed may be discarded underground or near the edge of the nest at the surface. Either way, the plant has been dispersed by a very effective mutualistic relationship with ants. Pavements are often hot, dry and sandy, making them perfect ant habitats, and these insects often nest underneath paving slabs. A surprisingly large number of pavement plants are myrmecochorous, including Creeping Thistle *Cirsium arvense*, Spear Thistle, Greater Celandine *Chelidonium majus*, Petty Spurge, Sun Spurge, Three-cornered Garlic *Allium triquetrum*, Red Dead-nettle *Lamium purpureum*, Common Fumitory, Selfheal *Prunella vulgaris* and Ivy-leaved Speedwell *Veronica hederifolia* (Lengyel *et al.* 2009, Pemberton & Irving 1990). Again, ant-dispersed species sometimes employ two modes of dispersal; the explosive capsules of Common Dog-violet *Viola riviniana*, for example, can disperse seed up to 2.4 metres (8ft), but if Red Ants *Myrmica ruginodis* are present the seed can be carried up to 3.2 metres (10.5ft) from the parent plants (Fokuhl *et al.* 2019). This might help explain why this woodland species is such an unexpectedly successful colonist of pavements.

A key method of dispersal on pavements, especially considering the turbulence created by vehicles passing beside them, is wind. Known as **anemochory**, a variety of adaptations allow seeds to catch the breeze and travel large distances. We're all familiar with the parachute of a Dandelion seed, a structure known as a pappus that has around 100–180 hollow fibres spreading out from a tube attached to the seed. If you've ever tried to tell the time by blowing the seeds from a Dandelion clock, you'll know that a soft breath doesn't work: a good hard puff is needed to get the seeds aloft. There's a firm ecological basis for this. In modelling the dynamics of Dandelion seed in open meadows, Tackenberg *et al.* (2003) found that highly turbulent gusts of wind of around 9–12 km/h (5.6–7.3 mph) were more effective than steady horizontal winds in removing the seed from the capitulum. Once airborne, 95% of the seeds landed within 10 metres (33ft) of the parent plant, but some (0.05%) travelled 100m and a few (0.014%) travelled more than 1km (0.6 miles). Urban settings are highly turbulent, with passing vehicles, irregular building shapes and urban

BELOW: Seeds of Greater Celandine are unusual in having such a large and prominent yellow elaiosome. Ants carry the seeds to their nests to feed these lipid-rich appendages to their larvae, helping to disperse the plant.

canyons, so more dandelion seeds are likely to be carried long distances. Since dandelions produce so much seed, a large proportion will colonise nearby pavement gaps, while smaller numbers caught up in turbulence will allow long-distance dispersal to take place. This may be why members of the daisy (Asteraceae) family, including sow-thistles, thistles, daisies, groundsels, ragworts and fleabanes, are so prevalent on pavements.

A few pavement species exhibit more unusual methods of getting around. One form of wind dispersal involves the whole plant or inflorescence, rather than just the seeds or seedpods, being moved. Similar to the famous tumbleweeds of American prairies, these plants become detached from their roots and roll around in the wind, shedding seeds as they go. Tall Rocket *Sisymbrium altissimum* and False London-rocket *S. loeselii* are known to do this and are sometimes called Tumble Mustard and Small Tumble Mustard respectively. Both these neophytes are generally declining, although for some reason False London-rocket appears to be increasing in Nottingham (where it has been known since 1963) and nearby towns. The inflorescences of Hedge Mustard *S. officinale*, a species almost always associated with human activity, often grow in a ball shape and may also be blown around by the wind. Dispersal by water (**hydrochory**) is also quite common and often occurs as seeds are washed along roadside gutters or splashed around by heavy rain.

Finally, a special form of establishment is exhibited by Shepherd's-purse. The sides of its small, inflated seedpods (the purses) fall

LEFT: Like most plants in the daisy family (Asteraceae), each seed of this Prickly Sow-thistle *Sonchus asper* has a tuft of hairs known as a pappus that catch the wind and help dispersal.

RIGHT: Shepherd's-purse is so-named for its seed capsules, each resembling a purse holding tiny coins. 'Bursa' is Latin for a pouch or purse made of animal hide, while 'pastoris' comes from 'pastor', meaning a shepherd or herdsman.

away when ripe and most seed drops within 50cm of the plant. However, once the seeds get wet, they produce a sticky mucilage and can become attached to the feet of birds and mammals, to be transported much larger distances. Furthermore, this apparently innocuous little species has a rather sinister side. The mucilage, rich in polysaccharides and cellulose, also attracts nematodes in the soil. These are then poisoned, possibly from nematocidal glucosinolates in the mucilage, providing the seeds with additional nutrients in the soil when first germinating. The effect of this so-called protocarnivory appears to be more pronounced on infertile substrates (Roberts et al. 2018), which may well help establishment on very thin, poor pavement soils.

Top 12 pavement plants

Being one of the most interesting, prominent and accessible of all urban habitats, you might imagine that the flora of pavements has been rather intensively studied. After all, what could be more fascinating than observing the comings and goings of plants on the streets where we live? Unfortunately, this isn't the case. Most published city Floras record plants using grids of rather large squares (usually 2-km square tetrads or 1-km square monads) and, while habitat preferences might be mentioned for individual species, few provide any detailed analysis of the vegetation communities that make up specific urban habitats. Thankfully, several excellent studies on the flora of streets have been published and, although they include other street habitats including walls, grassy areas and flowerbeds, these do shed valuable light on the nature of pavement plant communities.

The most comprehensive street studies come from two very different towns. In Cambridge, Chris Preston and (the sadly late) Philip Oswald studied the flora of 16 local streets, totalling about 4km (2.5 miles) in length, in 1998–99 and again in 2023. The number of species increased dramatically between the two surveys, from 235 in 1998–99 to 297 in 2023 (Preston & Chater in prep.). In a different four-year study of flowering times on eight Cambridge streets in 2016–19, Chris Preston recorded 262 species (Preston 2020). Meanwhile, over on the west coast of Wales, Arthur Chater has surveyed 54 streets in the centre of Aberystwyth, totalling 4.2km (2.6 miles), in three periods: 1970–73, 1998–99, and again in 2023. The totals for each period were 108, 121 and 131 taxa respectively, with 192 taxa recorded across all three surveys (Chater *et al.* 2000, Preston & Chater in prep.).

Another detailed, systematic survey of pavement flora was undertaken by Oliver Pescott from 2012 to 2014 (Pescott 2016). Looking at the streets of Sheffield, he recorded 183 species from the pavements within 16 randomly selected Ordnance Survey grid squares of 500m^2. The 862 records collected come from the pavement itself and any plants rooted at the edges of the paved area, including those beside walls, grassy strips, kerbstones and around pavement furniture, giving a snapshot of the flora at that particular time.

These studies give an indication of the richness of our pavement flora. Excluding those that are restricted to walls (see Chapter 8), we can estimate that around 110–250 species grow on the pavements of the average city (although this, of course, is a very small sample from just three cities and is likely to vary enormously between different places). In reality, a vast proportion of the British terrestrial flora could potentially grow on pavements, even if only for short periods. Indeed, our pavement flora is characterised by a small number of species occurring frequently, but a huge number of infrequent species that come and then go. This ever-changing cast of transient species is seen in the most recent Cambridge survey, where 46 (18%) of the 262 taxa recorded were seen only once in four years, and more than half of these were of single plants, including Busy Lizzie *Impatiens walleriana*, Broad Bean *Vicia faba* and Argentine Needle-grass *Nassella tenuissima* (Hill 2022, Preston 2020). Hunting for these rare and elusive 'singletons' has almost become a sport in itself for some urban botanists, who are always chasing the thrill that comes with new discoveries. This pattern of a few very common and frequent species versus many rare fleeting appearances is one we'll note again with other urban habitats (see Chapters 8 and 9).

Looking at the results of the Cambridge, Aberystwyth and Sheffield surveys, a dozen species emerge as our most frequent pavement plants. These top 12 could, perhaps, be regarded as the quintessential pavement flora, the core community of plants that are likely to be found on the vast majority of British pavements. There will, of course, be many regional variations, with some species swapping places in the list and others appearing in some towns and cities, but it's likely this top 12 will almost always be growing on pavements near you. The table opposite lists the species in descending frequency, as averaged from the three surveys.

Top 12 pavement plants

Species		Frequency (%)	Status	Life form
Annual Meadow-grass	*Poa annua*	99	Native	Annual
Dandelion	*Taraxacum* agg.	93	Native	Perennial
Procumbent Pearlwort	*Sagina procumbens*	91	Native	Perennial
Groundsel	*Senecio vulgaris*	89	Native	Annual
Smooth Sow-thistle	*Sonchus oleraceus*	86	Native	Annual
Common Chickweed	*Stellaria media*	81	Native	Annual
Greater Plantain	*Plantago major*	81	Native	Perennial
Petty Spurge	*Euphorbia peplus*	71	Archaeophyte	Annual
American Willowherb	*Epilobium ciliatum*	71	Neophyte	Perennial
Knotgrass	*Polygonum aviculare*	67	Native	Annual
Shepherd's-purse	*Capsella bursa-pastoris*	62	Archaeophyte	Annual
Hairy Bitter-cress	*Cardamine hirsuta*	41	Native	Annual

Frequency is the average percentage occurrence on pavements in surveys of Cambridge, Aberystwyth and Sheffield. Note the high proportion of native annual species.

Highlighting the ephemeral, ruderal nature of pavement plant communities, eight of the dozen on the list are annuals, species that can respond quickly to changing and challenging conditions. They do this by seizing the opportunity to germinate throughout the year and rapidly producing large quantities of seed that can be dispersed widely. It's not surprising that Annual Meadow-grass tops the list, as it has been reported from 96% of 110 cities surveyed around the world (Aronson *et al.* 2014) and is a truly cosmopolitan species (see Chapter 6). It is, perhaps, the perfect pavement plant; a mature specimen can produce 20,000 seeds in as little as six weeks from germination, and plants are highly tolerant of trampling, being able to regrow when repeatedly cut as low as 6.5mm (Grime *et al.* 1992). It has also developed resistance to some herbicides, including paraquat and glyphosate, allowing it to reappear from the seed bank within a few weeks of spraying, although such resistance has not yet been reported from the British Isles. As an aside, the seeds of both Annual Meadow-grass and Early Meadow-grass are an important source of food for urban birds. In summer, you'll often see large flocks of birds like Feral Pigeon *Columba livia* and House Sparrow *Passer domesticus* pecking over the browning ground where carpets of meadow-grasses have gone to seed.

Urban street phenology

Walk down any street, even in the depths of winter, and you'll almost certainly find something in flower. Phenology usually focuses on single events such as the date of first flowering, but following such phenomena as they unfold throughout the seasons reveals much more about the biology and ecology of these plants and their responses to the environment, weather events and climate change.

In a unique study of street phenology, Chris Preston surveyed the flowering of plants in eight streets in Cambridge every month for four years from 2016 to 2019 (Preston 2020). The 4.8km (3-mile) route through mostly residential areas of housing and gardens also included shops, restaurants, churches, offices and parking areas. More than 9,900 records were collected, 43% of which were from pavements, 18% from areas of grass, 13% from flowerbeds, 13% from areas of gravel, 7% from walls and 6% from the soil around the base of trees and under hedges.

Chris recorded 262 species in all. Not surprisingly, Annual Meadow-grass was the most frequent plant in flower, found in 94% of the 384 individual street surveys (i.e. eight streets surveyed in 48 consecutive months), followed closely by Pellitory-of-the-wall *Parietaria judaica* at 92% and Groundsel at 87% of streets surveyed. In contrast to these super-abundant plants in flower, 18% of species occurred just once, mostly as individual plants.

Six species flowered abundantly throughout the year. This street safari 'Big Six' were Annual Meadow-grass, Groundsel, Shepherd's-purse, Petty Spurge, Common Chickweed and Pellitory-of-the wall. Another group of seven year-rounders were interesting for having reduced flowering in summer or autumn, often after they'd succumbed to droughts. Small Nettle *Urtica urens* and Sun Spurge *Euphorbia helioscopia*, for example, flowered less between April and June, while Green Field-speedwell *Veronica agrestis* flowered sparsely between June and August.

Other species flowered over a period of months but peaked at different times. In March and April a small cohort of six species peaked around Easter, including Common Whitlowgrass, Common Field-speedwell *Veronica persica*, Red Dead-nettle and Dandelion. Several others, such as Herb-Robert, came into their own a little later in May,

Sun Spurge can often be found in flower all year round.

Red Dead-nettle flowering in winter with a dusting of frost.

but then a great wave of peak-flowering occurred in June, with 16 species including Daisy, Greater Celandine, Wood Avens, Barren Brome *Anisantha sterilis* and Dove's-foot Crane's-bill *Geranium molle*.

Both Red Valerian *Centranthus ruber* and Wall Barley also started their main flowering in June, followed by another wave of 13 species reaching peak flowering in July. These high-summer species include Ivy-leaved Toadflax, Garden Lobelia, Common Mallow *Malva sylvestris* and Nipplewort *Lapsana communis*. As summer slipped into the school holidays, flowering took a little dip, but Greater Plantain peaked at this time, as did Canadian Fleabane *Erigeron canadensis*.

Late summer saw an upturn in flowering and a final flourish of colour on the streets, with 14 species reaching peak flowering in September. Mexican Fleabane was at its best at this time, along with Purple Toadflax, Great Willowherb *Epilobium hirsutum*, Yellow Corydalis *Pseudofumaria lutea*, Wall Lettuce *Mycelis muralis* and Argentinian Vervain *Verbena bonariensis*, as well as less conspicuous species like Knotgrass and Fat-hen *Chenopodium album* agg. Some of these, such as Wall Lettuce, are 'long-day' species, requiring a particular length of daylight hours to trigger flowering.

Others, for instance Knotgrass, are spring-germinating annuals that only reach flowering size in late summer, while flowering in Fat-hen is stimulated by a reduction in daylight hours.

During Chris's four-year study, extremes of weather exerted a strong influence on flowering. The most prolonged period of winter weather was the infamous 'Beast from the East' in February and March 2018, which reduced flowering to an all-time low and suppressed minimum flowering for a month longer than usual. This was followed by an intense drought and heatwave in summer 2018, with very little rain in June and July. This caused a distinct dip in flowering during August. However, when rain eventually returned in August, plants responded quickly with even more abundant flowering than usual in September.

The annual application of herbicide in April or May also had a significant impact, although some plants, such as Ivy-leaved Toadflax, were able to recover and others, like Hairy Bitter-cress, re-seeded themselves quite quickly. Other influences on flowering came from the frequency of mowing lawns and changes in land-use, such as the closing off of a gravel parking area on Green's Road, allowing many more plants to flower than normal.

Purple Toadflax flowering in late summer.

Common Mallow flowering in Cambridge in 2018 despite severe summer drought.

Urban Plants

ABOVE: Petty Spurge is one of a handful of urban species that can flower all year round. An archaeophyte, the first evidence for its presence here dates to the Iron Age.

ABOVE: Annual Meadow-grass is so common in urban areas we frequently don't notice it. On the most heavily trampled pavements it's often the only species that can grow.

BELOW: Feral Pigeons feeding on a mixture of Annual Meadow-grass, Perennial Rye-grass *Lolium perenne* and Wall Barley in central Dublin.

The year-round blooming of five annuals on our top 12 list helps to explain why they're so successful (see 'Urban street phenology' box on previous pages). These species, namely Annual Meadow-grass, Groundsel, Common Chickweed, Petty Spurge and Shepherd's-purse, produce roughly the same quantity of flower for 12 months of the year (Preston 2020). In addition, Hairy Bittercress also flowers every month, but less abundantly from July to September. These species are predominantly self-pollinating annuals that can flower regardless of daylength. Their seeds can also germinate almost immediately, and the plants can mature and shed their own seed in just one or two months. It's this combination of characters that has helped them become so dominant on urban pavements.

The perennial species on the list are also well adapted to pavement life. Dandelions produce very deep taproots that readily penetrate the substrate below, and regenerate from buds just below soil surface, so they can hunker down in the cracks between paving stones and escape the worst of the trampling. They also produce prodigious quantities of wind-dispersed seed. In contrast, Greater Plantain has shallow, fibrous roots, but the similar mode of growth and very tough, fibrous leaves make the species extremely tolerant of trampling. A robust plant can produce 14,000 seeds within six weeks of germination. Procumbent Pearlwort takes a slightly different approach, keeping very low and tightly adpressed to the ground. It doesn't fare well in dense vegetation, so it exploits the relatively bare and open substrates of pavement gaps, out of the way of trampling. In this manner, it can actually thrive in areas of extremely high footfall where other flowering plants simply can't cope (Fagot *et al.* 2011). Its flowers are also self-pollinated and sometimes don't open fully (a characteristic known as facultative cleistogamy), so seed production isn't dependent on the presence of pollinators, which might find busy pavements an environment too challenging and harsh to visit.

Given the perceived abundance of urban aliens, it might come as a surprise that only three aliens are on the list. Two of these, Petty Spurge and Shepherd's-purse, are archaeophytes, having arrived with farmers as arable crop husbandry spread from continental Europe. Shepherd's-purse first appeared in the Neolithic (4300–2000 BC), while Petty Spurge came much later, in the Iron Age (800 BC–AD 43, Preston *et al.* 2004). It's remarkable to see these two species, so closely associated with ancient farming, now exploiting the toughest of anthropogenic habitats.

The only other alien on the list, American Willowherb *Epilobium ciliatum*, is a neophyte, introduced from North

ABOVE: As well as being tough and fibrous, leaves of Greater Plantain are rich in mucilage that help protect them from trampling.

BELOW: Procumbent Pearlwort is one of the few vascular plants that can colonise extremely trampled pavements, hunkering down in narrow gaps between paving stones alongside bryophytes.

ABOVE: Although they're not the easiest group of plants to identify, American Willowherb is the most common of several species of willowherb that regularly grow on pavements.

America. First recorded in the British Isles in 1891 from the draw-down zone of Cropston Reservoir in Leicestershire, it didn't begin to spread widely until the 1950s but has since become one of our fastest-spreading and most common aliens (Preston 1988). Its flowers are self-pollinated and seeds germinate from spring to autumn. In favourable conditions, plants can reach flowering size in just over a month and are capable of producing thousands of seeds, each furnished with a tuft of hairs to assist long-distance wind dispersal. These are all characters for urban success. Although the plants are perennial, reproduction is mostly by seed and on droughted pavements they usually behave as annuals. This is another species that has developed resistance to herbicides in some countries and this, along with its persistent seed bank, allows it to rebound quickly after spraying.

Quite a few other aliens lie just outside the top 12. These include the fleabanes from North and South America (Canadian Fleabane, Guernsey Fleabane *Erigeron sumatrensis* and Bilbao Fleabane – see pages 158–159), Procumbent Yellow-sorrel from South-East Asia, Barren Brome from southern Europe and Buddleja from China.

The dominant pavement flora in several other European cities is remarkably similar to our own. In a survey of Blois, France, Bonthoux *et al.* (2019) found that Annual Meadow-grass topped the list (out of 307 species), followed by pearlworts, Dandelion, Groundsel, Beaked Hawk's-beard *Crepis vesicaria* and fleabanes. Hairy Bitter-cress and Smooth Sow-thistle are on the top 12 list too but, perhaps because of the open sandy nature of many pavement surfaces in the city, they are joined by Sticky Mouse-ear *Cerastium glomeratum*, Thyme-leaved Sandwort *Arenaria serpyllifolia*, Common Whitlowgrass and Cat's-ear *Hypochaeris radicata*. In a survey of pavements across Flanders, Belgium, Fagot *et al.* (2011) found the top five species to be Annual Meadow-grass (91% of samples), Procumbent Pearlwort (80%), Canadian Fleabane (74%), Dandelion (64%) and Greater Plantain (57%). This suggests that the commonest elements of pavement floras in north-west Europe are fairly uniform, drawn from a rather narrow suite of native species that can cope with pavement conditions, along with a cohort of aliens that have become cosmopolitan pavement colonists.

All change on the streets

The repeated surveys of streets in Cambridge (1998–99 and 2023) and Aberystwyth (1970–73, 1989–99 and 2023) reveal the extraordinary level of change in the street flora over the past few decades (Preston & Chater in prep.). The turnover of species is remarkably high, with 39% of species seen in the three Aberystwyth surveys recorded just once, and 48% of species in the two Cambridge surveys spotted only on one occasion.

In Aberystwyth, some of the plants to increase the most are Cat's-ear, Sticky Mouse-ear, Daisy, Herb-Robert, Keeled-fruited Cornsalad *Valerianella carinata* and Black Nightshade *Solanum nigrum*. Most of the increasing species are native ruderal annuals. In contrast, Broad-leaved Willowherb *Epilobium montanum* and Hoary Willowherb *E. parviflorum* have declined, as has Greater Plantain.

In Cambridge, an intriguing mix of species have increased. These include native Cat's-ear and Sticky Mouse-ear, which also increased in Aberystwyth, but also more aliens that are known to be increasing quickly in south-east England, such as Water Bent, Early Meadow-grass, Guernsey Fleabane (see pages 158–159) and Procumbent Yellow-sorrel. The plants that have declined the most are even more interesting. Once frequent, Oxford Ragwort *Senecio squalidus* has completely disappeared from the streets surveyed, mirroring a national decline that has recently become apparent (see pages 256–257). More inexplicable are the disappearance of Elder *Sambucus nigra* and a sharp decline in Rosebay Willowherb *Chamaenerion angustifolium*. Preston and Chater speculate that these might be affected by a decline in derelict land or a general tidying of streets, and that the reduction in Elder could also be because there are fewer Starlings *Sturnus vulgaris* bringing in berries from the surrounding countryside. A similar decline in Garden Lobelia might be down to changing horticultural fashions; if gardeners, restaurant owners and publicans don't plant *Lobelia* in their hanging baskets each year, they quickly vanish from the streets.

Another trend apparent in both towns is an increase in roadside halophytes, salt-tolerant species that have colonised roads thanks to the spreading of salt in winter. These include plants like Sea Fern-grass *Catapodium marinum*, Lesser Sea-spurrey *Spergularia marina*, Sea Pearlwort *Sagina maritima* and, most famously, Danish Scurvygrass *Cochlearia danica*. This latter species has exploded across Aberystwyth, increasing from four streets in the early 1970s to 51 streets in 2023.

The rise and rise of the pavement fleabanes

Walk down any urban street, especially in England and Wales, and you're likely to find at least one species of fleabane. Regarded by some as rather dull and weedy in character, these aliens have nonetheless launched one of the most spectacular colonisations of the urban environment. Four species from North and South America are commonly found on our streets.

Canadian Fleabane *Erigeron canadensis*
According to one apocryphal story, this species was accidentally introduced into Europe around 1670 in the body of a stuffed bird from North America. As they watched the little seeds float off out of the window, the importer of the specimen could never have foreseen the impact they'd have on European ecology (Wurzell 1994). The species was first reported from London in 1690 and by 1869 was regarded as one of the city's most common weeds (Trimen & Dyer 1869). It began to spread elsewhere and by the 1960s had occupied much of the area from the Wash to the Isle of Wight. Today, it's our most widespread fleabane, found throughout most of lowland England and Wales, with a scattering of records in northern England and Scotland. It now seems to be undergoing a decline, and is rapidly being overtaken by Guernsey Fleabane in London and Bristol (Mark Spencer pers. comm., David Hawkins pers. comm.).

Guernsey Fleabane *E. sumatrensis*
First found naturalised at Chalkwell in south Essex in 1974, this species had reached at least 40 urban sites in London by 1986 (Wurzell 1988). Already well established on pavements, paths, factory forecourts, canal towpaths, roadsides and along the base of walls, the alarm about its potential future spread was raised from yellow to red alert, with a prediction that 'suburban colonization is likely to take place exponentially faster' and posed a threat to the flora of the English home counties (Wurzell 1994). Although still mostly restricted to urban

Canadian Fleabane in Caernarfon, Gwynedd.

habitats, it has spread rapidly around London and the south coast of England and is increasing in the Midlands, with a scattering of records from Wales and Scotland.

Bilbao Fleabane *E. floribundus*
This species was first found in 1994, thoroughly naturalised on waste ground near the docks in Southampton, Hampshire. It's uncertain how it arrived but it is likely to have hitched a ride on a ferry or inside a shipping container, although its finder speculates it could even have come on a boat competing in the round-the-world yacht race (Stanley 1996). For the next few years it popped up around southern Hampshire and London, but then took off, reaching most of southern England, the Midlands and South Wales by 2010. It continues to spread rapidly northwards and westwards and is the commonest species in Ireland.

Argentine Fleabane *E. bonariensis*
For about 150 years this species occurred sporadically as a casual, and it wasn't until 1993 that naturalised plants were found in London. The origins of the early introductions are uncertain, but it's likely that it arrived in bales of wool imported from South America, which was

Bilbao Fleabane growing in central Dublin.

Argentine Fleabane.

then cleaned and the resulting waste (known as shoddy) was spread on fields as a nitrogen-rich mulch (Wurzell 1994). These early introductions failed to persist in our cool, damp fields, but by 1993 some settled in the drier, warmer streets of central London, especially around Euston Station, and found the conditions much more to their liking. Since then, it has spread rather slowly, mainly in London (it still occurs near Euston Station), around Bristol and Newport, and in Birmingham, and is currently much rarer than the other three species.

Subtle differences in the ecology of the four species have influenced their spread. Argentine Fleabane is the most heat-demanding, often seeking out the warmest spots between sun-baked pavements and walls. Guernsey Fleabane and Bilbao Fleabane are also thermophiles, but less so, allowing them to spread further north and west. Canadian Fleabane, the least heat-demanding of them all, copes better with colder and wetter sites and has therefore spread the furthest. All these species appear to have spent a few years 'settling in' after their arrival, with successive generations perhaps becoming more adapted to our climate before taking off.

Herbicide resistance might also have helped their spread. Canadian, Guernsey and Argentine Fleabanes have all developed resistance to glyphosate in Europe (De Prado et al. 1997, Qasem et al. 2023, Sansom et al. 2013). However, the routine application of herbicides on pavements, especially around the base of trees and along the base of walls, is a rather ineffective method of control as plants are invariably missed behind parked cars, lampposts, bicycles and on neighbouring private land. Such plants can each produce around 200,000 seeds, allowing rapid recolonisation of pavements.

We might think that the rise of these pavement aliens is of little consequence. However, Canadian Fleabane growing in European cities has a very significant impact on native flora; at high densities plants can reduce native plant diversity from about ten species per square metre to just four (Shah et al. 2014). This suppressive effect comes from large plants shouldering aside smaller species, but also from allelopathic phenolic compounds. These suppress germination of other species and also reduce the diversity of soil mycorrhizal fungi that help other species to grow (Shah 2010, Shaukat et al. 2014). Since the flora of pavements is already rather depauperate, the impact of the fleabane is amplified.

The overall impression that emerges from these resurveys is of a relatively stable 'core' of street species (including many of the top 12 pavement plants listed above) which may change slowly over time, combined with an astonishing flux of less common species. The majority of these are garden escapes, which by their very nature introduce an inherently random element into the flora. It's worth noting that many of these fail to reach maturity on the streets, or only ever occur as single plants. To paint a picture of such species in Cambridge, examples include seedlings of Passionflower *Passiflora caerulea* from plants trained up walls, Garlic Chives *Allium tuberosum* from a flowerbed, seedlings of Silver Maple *Acer saccharinum* from a tree overhanging the street, Austrian Chamomile *Cota austriaca* from a wildflower seed mix, and one plant of Petunia *Petunia × hybrida* from no apparent source. If these surveys show anything, it's just how eclectic and changeable our pavement flora can be.

Our age-old war with pavement plants

We've always had an uneasy relationship with the plants that grow spontaneously at our feet. In order to control unwanted plants, Greek philosopher Democritus (460–370 BC) suggested the use of lupine-flower soaked with hemlock juice. Others tried salted water and human faeces, or even turned to religious rituals and folk magic (Mesnage *et al.* 2021). Today, the control of pavement 'weeds' has become a highly polarised issue. People seem to either love them, cherishing their tenacity as a symbol of nature's power to 'rewild' the built environment, or they loath them, striving instead for a sterile, 'neat-and-tidy' world in which every pavement plant must be removed.

Throughout most of our urban history, we've relied on intensive weeding by hand and other, mechanical means to remove wild plants from our streets. This painstaking and backbreaking work was often undertaken by the poorest and least appreciated classes of society, with vagrants, the infirm, children and older people shouldering most of the burden. Sometimes the work was turned into a source of income, or at least a scant escape from the poorhouse or starvation. In Victorian London, weeds were collected and sold in bunches to feed pet songbirds such as canaries, goldfinches, linnets, redpolls and greenfinches, pairs of which were often kept in little wire cages by young men as gifts to their betrothed. A remarkably vivid account of this most desperate of lives is given by social diarist Henry Mayhew (*London Labour and the London Poor 1851*, as quoted by Jackson 2012), who tells how the poorest costermongers (sellers of fruit and vegetables from street handcarts) would collect large quantities of chickweed, groundsel and plantain early each morning to sell throughout the day:

> *I cry 'chickweed and grunsell' as I goes along ... I've been at the business about eighteen year. I'm out in usual till about five in the evening. I never stop to eat. I'm walking all the time. I has my breakfast afore I starts, and my tea when I comes home ... We most generally raise a pennyworth, some how, just to boil the kettle with ... I am a walking ten hours every day – wet or dry ... I can't go much above one mile and a half an hour, owing to my right side being paralysed. My leg and foot and all is quite dead. I goes with a stick ... I walk fifteen miles every day of my life, that I do – quite that – excepting Sunday, in course. I generally sell the chickweed and grunsell and turfs, all to the houses, not to the shops.*

ABOVE: The Groundsel Man collecting chickweed and groundsel, by H. G. Hine and E. Whimper, from Henry Mayhew's *London Labour and the London Poor* (1851).

The sheer quantity of plants collected is astonishing. Mayhew estimates that 5.6 million bunches of groundsel and 1.1 million bunches of chickweed and plantain were being sold annually in London in the 1850s. Although these retailed for just a few pennies (a bunch of 60 heads of plantain would make between one and four pence), the combined value of the trade then was around £14,000, equivalent today to more than £1.1 million – an extraordinary amount to raise from handfuls of weeds (Jackson 2012).

In towns and gardens from around Tudor times onwards, weeding was generally a task assigned to women. Although these 'weeding women' were often employed seasonally and usually paid half the rate of their male counterparts, it was one of the few ways that respectable working-class women could earn a wage, especially if they were unmarried or widowed (Parker 2022). Over time, the hand-weeding of paved areas and other open spaces by women became a common sight in towns, as illustrated in George Henry Boughton's 1882 painting *Weeding the Pavement* (pictured overleaf).

As towns and cities expanded through the nineteenth century and the area of paving dramatically increased, it became clear that other methods of control would be needed. French botanist Sophie Leguil has uncovered an 1831 recipe in the *Journal des connaissances usuelles et pratiques* (Journal of usual and practical knowledge) for a 'method

ABOVE: Women shown removing weeds from a paved quayside in the Dutch town of Hoorn in George Henry Boughton's painting, *Weeding the Pavement* (1882).

to kill grass that grows in garden alleys and between cobblestones in courtyards'. The alarming concoction involved boiling 60 litres of water in an iron cauldron with 12 pounds (5.4kg) of lime and two or three pounds (0.9 to 1.3kg) of sulphur. The journal promised that this mixture would, perhaps not surprisingly, 'purge the soil of rebel herbs for several years'. The recipe also made its way across the Channel and is quoted in several English publications for anyone wanting to clear the 'very injurious as well as unsightly' plant growth from between the stones of pavements (Leguil 2020).

Soon, other chemicals were being deployed. One of the first modern chemical herbicides was Bordeaux Mixture, a formulation of 6% copper sulphate used to control Charlock *Sinapis arvensis* and other weeds in crops during the nineteenth century, while the first commercially available herbicide was sodium arsenite, sold as a miracle chemical called Eureka (Leguil 2020, Mesnage *et al.* 2021). Hugely popular for its ability to 'kill the weeds and brighten the gravel', Eureka was so toxic that it wiped out bacteria, insects and most other forms of life it touched. Occasionally, it was used for more nefarious means; when Mabel Greenwood died suddenly in the early hours of a June morning in 1919, her husband tried to blame a gooseberry tart served at supper the evening before, but suspicion eventually fell on him lacing a bottle of port with Eureka taken from the garden shed (Unsolved Murders 2023).

Since then, an arsenal of herbicides has been developed, from infamous early chemicals like DDT and 2,4-D, to modern mixtures of paraquat, atrazine and, especially, glyphosate. Initially intended for agricultural crops, use of most of these chemicals quickly spilled into non-agricultural settings including gardens, road verges, playgrounds, parks, cemeteries, sports fields and pavements. While the use of highly toxic DDT was banned in the UK in 1986, and paraquat in 2007, more than 30 different herbicides and herbicide mixtures are still employed in amenity settings and on roads and railways. A report into their use in the UK amenity sector (local authorities, transport infrastructure and golf courses) by the Food and Environment Research Agency (FERA) found that pure glyphosate was by far the most commonly used herbicide, with councils and their contractors applying at least 110,460kg of the chemical in 2018. Glyphosate mixtures with other herbicides accounted for 93% of all herbicides used (120,556kg). Looking specifically at pavements and other hard surfaces, 11,510kg of herbicides were applied in 2018, of which 98% were either glyphosate or glyphosate mixtures (Garthwaite *et al.* 2020).

ABOVE: An alarmingly jolly advert for Eureka, an arsenic-based weedkiller that exterminated nearly everything it came into contact with. Unfortunately, this occasionally included unwanted family members.

With so much herbicide being splashed about it's not surprising that some species are fighting back and have evolved resistance, especially annuals that produce many generations in quick succession. Glyphosate resistance has been reported for many pavement species in many different countries. Although it's not yet been confirmed whether such variants occur in Great Britain, resistance has been reported in Canadian Fleabane (11 countries), Argentine Fleabane (9 countries), Guernsey Fleabane (4 countries), Perennial Rye-grass (3 countries), Cockspur (2 countries) and Wall Barley (2 countries). Single cases of herbicide resistance have also been reported for Annual Meadow-grass, Ribwort Plantain, Smooth Sow-thistle, Prickly Lettuce *Lactuca serriola* and Compact Brome *Anisantha madritensis*. As can be seen from this list, resistance is particularly common among grasses (Poaceae) and daisies (Asteraceae), plant families that are especially frequent on pavements (Heap & Duke 2018, Torra *et al.* 2022).

Eradicating our endemic ragworts

In 1979, an unusual form of ragwort was spotted in the city of York. Looking like a hybrid between Oxford Ragwort and Groundsel, that's exactly what it turned out to be. The new combination of chromosomes meant it didn't readily back-cross with either parent, and this genetic isolation warranted its elevation to the status of new species. It was named *Senecio eboracensis*, or York Ragwort, after Eboracum, the Roman name for York (Lowe & Abbot 2003, Lowe & Abbot 2004a).

During the 1980s and 1990s, large numbers of this unique, endemic plant were found in the city along the embankments of the River Ouse, around construction sites and car parks, and along street pavements. However, over a period of years urban redevelopment destroyed some sites and the over-zealous application of herbicides gradually eradicated others. In 2000 the last 11 plants were recorded and soon afterwards the plant was formally declared 'extinct in the wild'. York Ragwort has the rather dubious honour of being, as Kevin Walker puts it, 'probably the shortest-lived addition to the British flora', having been exterminated within 21 years of being discovered (Walker 2007).

Thankfully, seeds of the plant had already been taken into storage at Kew's Millennium Seed Bank. After several initial attempts at reintroduction, large numbers of plants were grown by Andy Shaw at the Rare British Plants Nursery in Wales to bulk up seed. Plants have now been reintroduced to several sites in York and this emblematic plant flowered again in its hometown in 2023.

As if the extinction of one unique urban *Senecio* with herbicides wasn't enough, another is heading the same way. Between 1925 and 1955, plants collected from a handful of sites in Denbighshire and Flintshire turned out to be another new species also derived from hybridisation between Oxford Ragwort and Groundsel. Although it had the same parents as York Ragwort, it formed in a different way involving a doubling of its chromosomes (Lowe & Abbot 2004b). Named Welsh Groundsel *Senecio cambrensis*, it was found at around 30 sites in North Wales, such as the village of Mochdre (Denbighshire) and on pavements, wasteland and docks at Leith, Edinburgh.

York Ragwort growing in cultivation prior to reintroduction.

York Ragwort flowering in the city of its origin again in 2023.

Today, only five populations are known to survive, some with just a few plants appearing each year. In Mochdre, regular herbiciding of the pavement edges finally eradicated the plant in 1993, the same year it was also last seen in Edinburgh. It still hangs on in and around the town of Chirk, Denbighshire, growing on pavements, verges and around bus stops. But even here it's losing its battle against glyphosate. Every year, the familiar brown line of dead vegetation appears along the base of walls, pavement edges and beside railings and fences and under hedges, exactly where the plants like to grow. The few that do survive (and it's sometimes just one or two individuals) are usually sheltering behind obstacles such as lampposts and parked vehicles which protect them from the spray. Thankfully, the Species Recovery Trust is now working to prevent this unique species being declared 'extinct in the wild'.

A single plant of Welsh Groundsel sheltering from the herbicide behind a lamppost in Chirk, Denbighshire.

ABOVE: The tell-tale signs of glyphosate use. Note that the highly susceptible Red Valerian *Centranthus ruber* on the left is already dead, while the Pellitory-of-the-wall *Parietaria judaica* on the right is showing a little more resistance and might even pull through.

ABOVE: Glyphosate is often used along pavements and edges, ostensibly to keep them neat and tidy, and safe and accessible. Invariably, the vegetation will return in a few months.

Herbicide resistance has also been reported in Mind-your-own-business *Soleirolia soleirolii* – a small, carpeting plant with tiny leaves on creeping stems. Originally from islands of the western Mediterranean, it prefers warm, damp conditions and is very popular in gardens as it covers bare soil and fills gaps between paving stones. Unfortunately, it can do this a little too enthusiastically and frequently escapes, spreading to pavements, steps, the base of walls, around drains and gutters, and on damp lawns and shaded banks. It has developed remarkable resistance to a very wide range of weed killers. One study tested it against 23 herbicides and found that only two offered total control and four provided partial control; the other 17, including glyphosate, showed little impact (Foo *et al.* 2010). Little wonder it's spreading so quickly as to become one of our more frequent pavement plants.

As well as destroying individual plants, and occasionally entire species, repeated herbicide applications have another important ecological impact on pavement plant communities – they stop succession. As new pavement surfaces weather and become bioreceptive, the first colonising species arrive, filling in the gaps between the stones and making the most of surface cracks. These tend to be small and highly stress-resistant and trampling-tolerant plants, including bryophytes such as Silver-moss, Capillary Thread-moss *Bryum capillare* and Bicoloured Bryum *B. dichotomum*, and the smallest of flowering plants such as Annual Meadow-grass, Procumbent Pearlwort and Thale Cress. As these species become established and contribute to the build-up of organic matter, larger, more competitive species arrive, like the fleabanes, ragworts and sow-thistles, along with vigorous grasses such as Water Bent and Barren Brome.

ABOVE: Mind-your-own-business *Soleirolia soleirolii* is one of the most herbicide-tolerant plants. Sadly, the origin of this species' unorthodox common name has been lost. It's also known as Mother of Thousands, Baby's Tears and Corsican Curse.

Left to their own devices, this process of succession would continue, and pavements would eventually become colonised with large, woody plants. Rapidly growing trees and shrubs such as Sycamore, Ash, Silver Birch *Betula pendula*, Buddleja, Tree-of-heaven and Rusty Willow *Salix cinerea* subsp. *oleifolia* can become established within just a few years. This quick succession can easily be witnessed on any paved areas that have been fenced off for building work for a few years, where a rather wonderful urban scrub can develop.

However, the regular application of herbicides and other street weeding, as well as the continual trampling and occasional intense drought, means that few individual plants will survive on a pavement for more than two or three years. Once plants reach a certain height, people begin to react negatively towards them; overgrown pavements are perceived to be neglected, untidy and sometimes even dangerous (in one case, a Grass Snake *Natrix helvetica* was spotted in long grass beside a pavement, leading to the rather unlikely fear that venomous Adders *Vipera berus* might also lurk in the undergrowth). Such vegetation, it is argued, must be removed, and councils often do so in the light of complaints from residents. This resets the ecological clock, starting the process of succession again. Communities of ruderal annuals and short-lived perennials that do survive are therefore held in a permanent state of suspended succession, unable to develop into more complex mosaics of different vegetation types.

The flipside of herbicide use and weed control is that pavement communities are continually maintained as highly adapted communities of ruderals that would otherwise be lost. Succession is not always a good thing for plant diversity, which can decline as larger, more competitive species become established. On pavements, the use of herbicides doesn't justify the outcome, as wider impacts on other wildlife are enormous, but it's true that some communities of small, ruderal plants would be lost if all methods of weed control came to an end.

Thankfully, though, the regular use of glyphosate on pavements is now being questioned and many local councils are reconsidering their approach. Going completely herbicide free might seem an improbable aim, but we only need to look to our European neighbours to see that it can be done. Both France and Luxembourg have completely banned the use of pesticides in non-agricultural settings, including on pavements and in playgrounds, cemeteries and green spaces. Similarly, Denmark has banned pesticides on paved surfaces, parks and other green areas, while in Belgium the use of glyphosate without a licence has been banned (PAN 2022).

In Great Britain, all public authorities now have a duty to preserve the biodiversity in their jurisdiction, for example through the England Environment Act 2021 and the Nature Conservation (Scotland) Act 2004. Reducing the use of herbicides is an easy step in the right direction, especially when council budgets are tight. According to the Pesticide Action Network, more than 100 UK councils had either banned the use of pesticides, or pledged to reduce their use as of 2024, including East Devon, West Suffolk, Cambridge, Birmingham, Newcastle, Shetland, Derry and several London councils (PAN 2024). Many of these are now exploring other methods of weed control that often involve removing excess plant material and detritus. These include manual hand-weeding or hoeing, mechanical removal with street-brushing machines, the use of mulches, dense plant cover and weed-suppressing membranes to reduce weed growth, and treatments using hot foam (a biodegradable foaming agent heated to more than 70°C), acetic acid (vinegar) and gas flame guns or even electricity (PAN 2021). Such techniques vary in their effectiveness, although hot foam applications can achieve results comparable to those of glyphosate (Antonopoulos *et al.* 2023).

In an excellent little publication on pavement plants, the Pesticide Action Network has highlighted how the London borough of Lambeth has worked with the local community to reduce the use of herbicides (PAN 2023). Once committed to eradicating as many weeds as possible, Lambeth Council originally treated 580km (360 miles) of

Pavements

ABOVE: Clearing pavement weeds in Castle Street, Cambridge, using teams to dislodge plants with spades and hoes, then clearing the material away with brushing machines. It's labour intensive, but better than using herbicides.

pavements with glyphosate annually, along with 80 parks and 100 housing estates. After an approach from Incredible Edible Lambeth (a community food-growing network), the Council committed to ending the use of glyphosate in parks and housing estates in 2019 and phasing out pavement spraying at the end of 2021. However, a scheme was established where residents could opt out of spraying if they removed weeds from their own streets; this proved to be so popular, with 130 streets taking part, that the ban on pavement glyphosate was brought forward to May 2021. Since then, the residents have embraced their greener streets and enjoy living alongside more wildlife. Each year, the streets are given a 'deep clean' with mechanical sweepers to remove excess vegetation and remove detritus.

A ban on the use of herbicides on pavements also came into force in Cambridge in 2023, after a few years of trials to evaluate alternative methods of weed control. Here, street-cleaning teams are now deployed to remove excess growth using a combination of spades and hoes to dislodge plants, followed by brushing machines to pick up the material and clear gutters. This is pretty slow and labour-intensive work and some of the rather grumpy workforce would probably prefer to return to the use of herbicides if they could (Chris Preston pers. comm.). Such methods are effective in removing excess growth but, importantly, leave roots and seedlings untouched, leading to rapid regrowth and recolonisation. Only time will tell what impact these techniques have on the ecology of our pavement flora, or how accepting we are of them.

Walls
chapter eight

We are surrounded by walls. They form our homes, enclose our gardens, mark out our property and shape every single building where we live, work, shop, visit and pass in the street. They keep our possessions safe inside and keep the weather out. They hold back banks of earth and help support structures spanning roads, rivers and railways. Walls can tower more than 100 metres into the sky or raise a single step by just a few centimetres. And yet, despite framing our lives on all sides, these most interesting, diverse and ubiquitous of habitats are perhaps some of those we notice the least. Most people probably never stop to look at a wall.

For those of us that do (and I admit to having a peculiar fascination with them), there's much more to a wall than you might realise. There can be nooks and crannies in the surface, gaps or crumbling mortar between the stones or bricks, and a flatter top with different materials and structures. All these offer opportunities for wildlife. Washed regularly with rainwater, the top of a wall will usually be drier than its base, a gradient of moisture from top to bottom which will suit a range of different species, while a leaking gutter will create its own seepage zone with more opportunities to live. Then there's the direction the wall is facing; the south side hot and baked dry in summer, the north side cool and damp in the gloom of an eternal shade. All these factors mean walls offer a wide range of conditions for plants to grow, and there are an awful lot of walls around when you start noticing them.

The most famous wall in Great Britain, built by Roman Emperor Hadrian more than 1,900 years ago, stretches 117km (73 miles) from Wallsend (Tyne and Wear) to Bowness-on-Solway in Cumbria. Originally, Hadrian's Wall was between four and six metres tall and around three metres wide, with facing stones set in soft mortar and a core of earth, clay and stones. A very substantial fortified structure, it had lookouts, milecastles and garrison forts about

OPPOSITE:
A rosette of Great Mullein *Verbascum thapsus* growing on an old brick wall in Canons Ashby, Northamptonshire.

Urban Plants

ABOVE: Probably the most famous wall in Great Britain, Hadrian's Wall supports a rich flora including Harebell *Campanula rotundifolia*, Wild Thyme *Thymus drucei* and rarer species such as Green Spleenwort *Asplenium viride*.

every 11km (7 miles). Romans are famous for introducing many new crops, foods and medicinal herbs into Great Britain, and there has always been a romantic notion that some of these plants could still be found growing on Hadrian's Wall. At the fort of Carvoran, the early seventeenth-century historian William Camden (as quoted by Witcher 2013) describes how:

> *There continueth a settled perswasion among a great part of the people there about, and the same received by tradition, that the Roman souldiers of the marches did plant heere every where in old time for their use certaine medicinable herbes for to cure wounds.*

Most persistent of these rumours was that Chives *Allium schoenoprasum* had been planted in crevices along the wall. Despite no evidence for this, the story has turned into established fact and is often recounted in visitor leaflets. Other species are implicated too; in Maria Hoyer's *By the Roman Wall* (1908), she recalls a visit to Chester's fort (Cilurnum):

> *Also we looked with longing eyes at the little clusters of* Erinus hispanicum *(or* alpinus*) growing upon the walls, that tiny Spanish plant which has sprung up since the excavations, and which is believed to be a legacy from the Asturian Cohort, the Second Ala of which was long stationed at Cilurnum.*

Since the Asturian Cohort came from an area of northern Spain where Fairy Foxglove *Erinus alpinus* is particularly abundant as a native wild plant, it was assumed that Roman soldiers brought the pretty pink flower with them to Hadrian's Wall (Witcher 2013). Others have meticulously plotted the route the plant might have followed from the high passes of the Pyrenees, with seeds being carried all the way on the boots of the Twentieth Legion. As utterly improbable as these associations might sound, they still capture popular imagination and the plant is still known locally as 'Roman Wall plant' (Mabey 1996). In reality, Fairy Foxglove arrived here on horticultural hands rather than Roman boots. An alpine and subalpine species of mountainous countries including Austria, France, Italy, Morocco and Switzerland, it's a relatively recent arrival, being introduced into British gardens in 1759 and first recorded in the wild in 1862, long after the last Roman legion had departed (Grace 2023, Chris Preston pers. comm.).

ABOVE: Hailing from mountainous areas of Europe and north Africa, Fairy Foxglove has a distinctly northern distribution in Great Britain, being most frequent in northern England and southern and south-western Scotland.

Gardens are actually one of the most important sources of plants growing on walls, largely through our love of alpine and rockery plants. We grow thousands of different species, the vast majority coming from mountainous areas where rocky and cliff habitats predominate. Already adapted to growing on vertical surfaces, these alien plants come well equipped to survive on walls. Only a handful have actually escaped to become widely established on walls, but those that have are real masters of the masonry.

As Oliver Gilbert puts it in *Rooted in Stone* (Gilbert 1992a), the British Isles are home to some of the finest examples of wall vegetation in Europe. This is largely due to our mild, wet, oceanic climate which encourages the growth of sometimes spectacular communities of plants, especially in northern and western Britain. If the ancient walls of castles, abbeys, churches and historic towns in these areas escape repointing, rebuilding and cleaning, they can be clothed in a tapestry of ferns, bryophytes and flowering plants, lending real character and interest to a town or city. By contrast, the drier, warmer, more

Urban Plants

ABOVE: An old wall covered with Red Valerian, Ivy-leaved Toadflax, Ivy *Hedera helix* and Maidenhair Spleenwort *Asplenium trichomanes*. Walls like this considerably enhance the urban environment by providing seasonal displays of colour and resources for invertebrates.

RIGHT: Despite being cultivated here for around 325 years, Trailing Snapdragon has only been recorded at about 100 sites since the year 2000, including the walls of Buckingham Palace in London.

continental climate of southern and eastern areas discourages luxuriant growth, and wall vegetation becomes restricted to more shaded north- and east-facing surfaces.

Walls are unique, cliff-like features forming the vertical fabric of the urban environment. At least 360 vascular plant species, or 10% of our total flora, have been recorded growing on walls in Britain and Ireland (Preston *et al.* 2002). Many of these are infrequent or transient occupants, plants like Trailing Snapdragon *Asarina procumbens*, originally from France and Spain, which is a rare escape from gardens. At the other end of the scale, a small number of species are very common and enthusiastic wall plants, transforming vertical spaces in a most eye-catching way. These hanging gardens play an incredibly important role in urban areas; a wall clothed in Trailing Bellflower *Campanula poscharskyana*, Red Valerian *Centranthus ruber*, Mexican Fleabane *Erigeron karvinskianus* and Ivy-leaved Toadflax *Cymbalaria muralis* not only provides an arresting, flower-filled sight but also helps to soften the harsh surfaces of the built environment.

Incidentally, that name '*muralis*' crops up repeatedly with plants that grow in such locations, as *murus* is Latin for wall. As well as Ivy-leaved Toadflax, there's Wall Whitlowgrass *Drabella muralis*, Annual Wall-rocket *Diplotaxis muralis* and Wall Lettuce *Mycelis muralis*. It's also where the word for a wall painting, or mural, comes from, and I often like to think of our wall flora as a living mural, an ever-changing painting on the vertical surfaces around us.

While we're on the subject of names, all plants growing on rocks are known as **lithophytes**, or 'rock plants'. Those that are actually attached directly to the rock surface, like mosses and lichens, are classed as **epilithic lithophytes** (literally 'upon-the-rock rock-plants'), while those that root into the cracks and crevices of the surface, such as most flowering plants, are **endolithic lithophytes** (literally 'within-the-rock rock-plants'). This latter group are also known as **chasmophytes**, meaning 'plants of chasms or clefts'. Given that we regularly call plants growing upon other plants **epiphytes**, it's rather strange that we don't refer to all these wall plants more regularly as lithophytes. Maybe it's time we showed our living cliffs a little more respect, and give our lithophytes the love they deserve.

BELOW: Founded in 563, the interior of Iona Abbey has a very cool, damp atmosphere. Its walls are home to several large clumps of Sea Spleenwort, protected from the slugs and snails that often plague plants growing outside.

What is a wall?

A wall can be quite easily defined as a continuous vertical structure, often made of brick or stone, that is usually much taller than it is wide, and which encloses or divides something such as property or an area of land. In the context of urban plants, we're almost exclusively dealing with external walls, those surfaces forming the outside of buildings and

ABOVE: Retaining walls, like this one beside the Rochdale Canal, can support lots of vegetation as water and nutrients seep through from the earth behind. Note that the most abundant growth is along small ledges in the stonework where detritus has collected.

the freestanding walls that enclose gardens and other property and are exposed to the elements. But, very occasionally, walls inside buildings can support plants. Few species are able to cope indoors, but some tough ferns with leathery fronds, such as Hart's-tongue *Asplenium scolopendrium* and Black Spleenwort *A. adiantum-nigrum*, can tolerate the low light and heightened humidity of these environments. If you venture to the spectacular Benedictine Abbey on the island of Iona in the Inner Hebrides, for example, several fine clumps of Sea Spleenwort *A. marinum* can be seen adorning the walls. Here, they probably benefit from the rather damp, oceanic climate and the crumbling mortar in the walls of the unheated abbey.

Retaining walls, built to hold back banks of earth, are very different to freestanding walls and the walls of buildings. Because one side sits permanently against a substrate, they tend to be wetter and more nutrient-rich. Often, they're not vertical but lean into the slope, and this dramatically changes their character. Such walls hang on to water, debris and humus much more readily than a vertical wall, allowing them to support more vegetation. This tends to be rather weedy in character, though, with more grasses, shrubs and vigorous nutrient-demanding species. Such walls are often seen supporting old Victorian railway bridges and embankments and can be clothed in dense, fast-growing vegetation that needs to be cleared away frequently.

Anatomy of walls

How walls are built underpins their ecology, and there are three main elements to their construction. If we work from the ground up, first come the **footings**, the foundation on which the wall sits. These are usually made from cement poured into a trench to provide a solid, level surface on which to build the wall. Footings are often two or three times the width of the wall and go down into the ground one third the height of the wall. The nature of these footings can influence what grows at the bottom of a wall – a prime spot for colonisation – and how closely plants can root into the soil beside the wall.

Next, the **vertical wall** itself is built from successive layers of bricks or stone held together with a cement mortar (dry-stone walls are built without mortar, but these are unusual in urban settings where stability is important for safety). There's a huge variety of building styles, techniques and finishes, but all aim to create a wall with vertical sides and more-or-less smooth surfaces. Construction materials may vary within the same wall (brick with flints or brick with stone, for instance) and the ends of walls are sometimes finished with a contrasting material. Over time, repairs to walls using different materials can lead to lots of different surfaces and opportunities for colonisation.

BELOW: This old wall in Caernarfon, Gwynedd, is constructed from various types of brick and local stone and topped with a cement capping. It appears to have been repaired several times over the years.

Finally, the top of a freestanding wall is generally finished with a layer of **coping or a capping**. Architecturally, there is a slight difference between the two. A coping sits on top of a wall and comes over the edge and sometimes slightly down the sides, helping to shed rainwater away from the wall. A capping, however, sits on top of the wall with its edges flush with the width of the wall. Copings are more often used on buildings (rather than freestanding walls) to prevent water ingress and reduce rain running down the surface. Copings and cappings are sometimes made of the same material as the wall, but more often are a different type of stone or brick or are made of concrete. The amount of water running down the wall is critical in terms of their ecology, so cappings and copings play an important role in what grows on walls.

Ecology of walls

The ability of a wall to support vegetation depends on many factors, including construction materials and techniques, exposure to the elements and shading, the slope of the sides (inclination), and the age of the wall and its degradation over time. These all contribute to the **bioreceptivity** of the wall surface – its ability to support plant growth (Lubelli *et al.* 2021). Two of the most important factors affecting bioreceptivity are the presence and movement of moisture within the wall, and the composition of the mortar. Bioreceptivity changes dramatically over time as the wall ages; mortar, in particular, begins to degrade after just a few years and becomes more receptive to plant growth. As with pavements, we're rather obsessed with clearing vegetation from walls. Indeed, an important factor determining plant growth on walls is how accessible they are; if a wall can be reached easily it can be cleaned and repointed regularly. Often, it's the parts of a wall that are out of reach that carry the oldest, most diverse and luxuriant vegetation.

Bricks, stones and mortar

Much of the ecology of a wall depends on the materials of its construction. These often give built environments their distinctive regional look, such as the knapped flint walls of Hampshire and Wiltshire, the honey-coloured ironstones of the Cotswolds or the reddish hue of Old Red Sandstones characteristic of Scottish cities like Stirling and Perth. Many different types of native stone from all around the British Isles, or even abroad, have been brought together as building materials. The much repaired and rebuilt King's Lynn Town Wall, for example, includes cobbles of ancient igneous and metamorphic rock from Sweden and Finland, thought to have arrived as ballast used in medieval shipping (Hoare *et al.* 2002). With their diversity of textures, mineralogy and weathering, walls can provide a diversity of habitats for plants. Some are much better than others in this respect. A precisely engineered face of polished granite will be so hard and unrelenting there will be little foothold for any plants for many decades to come. In contrast, a wall of sandstone blocks pointed with lime-rich mortar will be open and porous, beginning to decay relatively quickly and offering all sorts of nooks and crannies, as well as a welcome dose of lime from the cement, allowing many plants to get established.

ABOVE: As well as looking beautiful and full of character, this wall of Devonian Old Red Sandstone with a thick lime mortar has eroded over time to provide many micro-niches for plants to establish. Note the variety of size of stones used, and the textures of different weathered surfaces.

ABOVE: Walls of notable buildings, such as this one in the grounds of Winchester Cathedral, Hampshire, were often built with a variety of materials carefully arranged to provide pattern and texture. In this case, knapped local flints are interspersed with limestone blocks and layered between local red bricks.

As well as a diversity of native stone, manufactured bricks can be made from dried clay, concrete blocks and breeze blocks from sand and gravel or crushed stone mixed with cement, and cinder blocks from coal ash mixed with cement and aggregate. In a wall, these may be left in their raw, naked state or covered with all manner of renders and stuccos – mixtures of cement, sand and water and other aggregates – used to protect the wall. However, perhaps the most important part of any wall for plants is the mortar used between the joints. Mortar tends to decompose more rapidly than the bricks or stones, so this is where most plants get their first foothold. Walls on very old buildings often support more plants than modern ones because they'd have been built using lime mortar, which degrades much more rapidly than modern mortars like Portland cement (Francis 2011, Gilbert 1992a). Again, many different types of mortar are available using various quantities of cement and sand and, sometimes, lime. Various other compounds may be added to the mortar, including additives and plasticisers that make the mortar more viscose, sticky, flexible or water resistant. Mortar is usually more

ABOVE: Modern city-centre buildings, such as this bank in Edinburgh, are often faced with expensive granite slabs with almost no gaps between them. Highly resistant to weathering, they will remain plant-free for many decades.

porous than the stones or bricks it is bonding together, so it's generally the weakest part of any wall. Because of this it is often replaced or reapplied once it begins to crumble – repairs that are usually disastrous for any plants that have their roots in the masonry.

Wall surfaces

The physical structure of walls provides three main surfaces on which plants can grow. Firstly, the **flat top** of the wall, with or without coping stones or finishes, offers a very different microhabitat to the vertical sides. Rainwater is more likely to collect and remain here for a short while, and a thin layer of decaying humus can quickly accumulate, supplying a foothold for many species. The top of a wall is therefore often the first place that plants become established.

Secondly, the **vertical sides** of the wall obviously provide the largest surfaces on which plants can grow. Their bioreceptivity depends on how the wall is constructed and the materials used. In one novel experiment, Lubelli *et al.* (2021) cemented different types of brick together with different types of mortar impregnated with seeds of Ivy-leaved Toadflax and Yellow Corydalis *Pseudofumaria lutea*. They found that most growth was supported by the most porous brick and mortar combinations. When wetted, the porous bricks absorbed lots of water and acted like a reservoir for the mortar, which gradually drew water out from the bricks by capillary action and retained it long enough for plants to grow. This fascinating insight suggests the movement of water inside a wall is quite dynamic. Rather than imagining them as solid, impervious and dry structures, we should instead think of them as sponges and reservoirs of water, with complex fluxes of moisture within and between the building materials and the external environment. Whenever water is present inside a wall, plants will be able to grow on its surface.

As a rule of thumb, the sides of older walls have a more diverse and abundant flora than new ones. As weathering takes place, the mortar crumbles, the stones or bricks themselves break down and humus accumulates in the nooks and crannies, providing a foothold for plants. An old wall of rough bricks with decaying mortar will have far more places for plants to get established than a newly constructed wall with a face of highly polished granite.

Finally, the **base of the wall**, where it meets the soil or pavement, is one of the favourite spots for urban plants to grow. Although such

ABOVE: This new breeze-block wall might look impossibly hostile, but the flat top is already being colonised by Wall Screw-moss *Tortula muralis*. A line of spore-bearing sporophytes can just be seen along the top.

Walls

LEFT: Ivy is usually rooted in soil at the base of the wall, forming large plants that can spread out over the stonework. This example in Conwy, North Wales, is rooted in a particularly fertile spot inside a damp tunnel.

plants aren't growing on the wall itself, they do benefit from radiated heat as well as an increased supply of water and nutrients washing down the wall surface. The seeds of plants growing on the wall surface often fall here under gravity, producing a line of vegetation that softens the junction between wall and pavement. You'll frequently see Ivy-leaved Toadflax growing in this spot.

Underground, soil or builders' rubble often abuts the concrete foundations. This creates a place for climbing plants to become established, exploiting the deeper more fertile soil lying next to a vertical support. Our two species of Ivy, Common Ivy *Hedera helix* and Atlantic Ivy *H. hibernica*, are the classic plants to make the most of this opportunity, using short, adventitious roots from their vertical stems to climb walls (see box overleaf). In such situations, Ivy often completely clothes the stonework, eliminating all other wall plants but also providing important food and shelter for other wildlife. Its tangled stems are always full of invertebrates, especially snails and woodlice, and offer nesting sites for birds. In autumn, the flowers are a valuable source of pre-hibernation nectar and pollen, particularly for hoverflies, wasps and bees such as Ivy Bee *Colletes hederae*. During winter, the calorie-rich winter berries are beloved by birds including thrushes, Blackbirds *Turdus merula*, Starlings *Sturnus vulgaris* and Blackcaps *Sylvia atricapilla*.

How to climb a wall

Plants employ many different strategies to help them climb, including twining stems (e.g. Honeysuckle *Lonicera periclymenum*), tendrils (e.g. White Bryony *Bryonia dioica*) and curled leaf petioles (e.g. Traveller's Joy *Clematis vitalba*). However, all these rely on other structures, like tree branches, to provide support. Only a few plants attach themselves directly to the flat surface of a wall, and none do it quite so effectively as Ivy. As anyone who has tried to remove Ivy from a wall will know, it can be *incredibly* strongly attached, so much so that pulling at the stems often brings away chunks of brick and render. How it achieves this bond is quite remarkable.

On open ground, Ivy stems are weak and grow flat, spreading far and wide in their search for something to climb. While most plants grow towards the light, Ivy stems in this phase actually grow away from the light (**negative phototropism**), as darkness is more likely to be caused by a trunk or a wall to climb (Wyka 2023). When they've found a vertical structure, they press against it and begin to grow upwards.

These climbing stems then produce clusters of short, brown attachment roots (1–5mm long) that are covered with microscopically small root hairs, about 10 microns in diameter. As the root hairs elongate, their tips become flattened and spoon-shaped, with tiny pimples on their surface containing a special glue. On touching the wall, the 'spoons' push against the surface and spread out, bursting the pimples and excreting the glue. This adhesive is a mixture of nanoparticles made up of at least 19 different sulphur- and nitrogen-rich hydrocarbons that create extremely strong hydrogen bonds with the surface (Zhang *et al.* 2008). Now attached at their tips, the root hairs dry out, twisting and curling up and pulling the main root and stem towards the wall. The short attachment roots also become lignified (woody), increasing their strength, and flatten out, expanding the area of contact with the wall. Although the bonding operates on a microscopic level, the collective strength of thousands of glued root hairs is phenomenal, easily enough to support the weight of the rapidly growing plant (Melzer *et al.* 2010).

Although most Ivy plants are rooted in soil at the base of the wall, smaller individuals can grow in nooks and crevices without reaching the ground, surviving independently on their own network of adventitious roots. When large plants are cut at the base to stop them growing, some small branch fragments can persist for years if they're sufficiently rooted into the wall surface (Darlington 1981).

The small, brown attachment roots of Ivy on a wall in Conwy.

Water supply

The availability of water is perhaps the most important factor in determining what grows on walls. On vertical surfaces, rainwater drains away very quickly and what's left evaporates rapidly, especially on sunny walls in summer. In order to tap into the meagre supplies of moisture, most vascular plants sink their roots deep into any cracks and crevices in the surface to reach the reservoir of water inside the wall.

Wall plants often have other adaptations to store water or cope when it's in short supply. Many are succulent and store water in their thick, fleshy leaves. The stonecrops *Sedum* spp. are superb examples, including the widespread Biting Stonecrop *S. acre* and White Stonecrop *S. album*, as well as English Stonecrop *S. anglicum* and Rock Stonecrop *Petrosedum forsterianum* that are more frequent in western areas. These small, mat-forming plants tend to occur on the tops of walls where conditions are driest. Other succulents are popular garden plants, such as Reflexed Stonecrop *P. rupestre* from southern Europe. This species was being grown here as early as the sixteenth century and commonly escapes onto walls, particularly in England and Wales. Such succulents are becoming more popular in gardens as we experience drier conditions through climate change, and several others like Caucasian Stonecrop *Phedimus spurius* and Thick-leaved Stonecrop *Sedum dasyphyllum* are joining the more familiar species on our walls.

As well as being able to store water, many of these stonecrops change the way they undertake photosynthesis in periods of hot, dry weather.

LEFT: Biting Stonecrop has tiny, succulent leaves, helping it to survive dry conditions on the tops of walls. It can grow from fragments of stem or even individual leaves that fall and root.

LEFT: Reflexed Stonecrop has succulent leaves with a bitter, astringent taste that were once eaten as a salad. Highly tolerant of drought, it's especially popular on green roofs.

RIGHT: As well as its fleshy leaves, Caucasian Stonecrop also has thick, fleshy stems that store water. This plant was photographed in early spring; later in the year the leaves often turn red and it bears bright pink flowers.

Normally, stomata on the leaves open during the day to allow the entry of CO_2 for photosynthesis. In drought conditions, though, this can lead to excessive water loss. They therefore switch to Crassulacean Acid Metabolism (CAM) photosynthesis, whereby the stomata only open at night. During this time, CO_2 is absorbed and stored inside the cells as malic acid, which is converted back to CO_2 during the day when light is available for photosynthesis (Kluge 1977, Starry *et al.* 2014). This switch to CAM photosynthesis has also been detected in the succulent leaves of Navelwort *Umbilicus rupestris* which, although more frequent in the wetter parts of western Britain and Ireland, tends to grow on dry, sun-baked walls (Daniel *et al.* 1985). By keeping their stomata closed at night, these plants significantly reduce water loss, allowing them to grow in much drier conditions.

Other wall plants have different morphological adaptations to help reduce water loss. If you have ever tried to dig one up, you will know that plants of Red Valerian have very long, thick taproots. These can penetrate deep into crevices in the wall, seeking out reservoirs of moisture. At the surface a thick, woody rootstock develops, enabling the plant to store water in periods of drought. Pellitory-of-the-wall *Parietaria judaica* takes a slightly different approach, producing many small leaves (reducing total leaf area) each of which is covered in hairs to trap air and reduce evapotranspiration.

Another way to avoid summer droughts is to grow during the cooler, wetter months, from autumn through to spring. Just as is the case with pavements, winter annuals are especially common on walls (see Chapter 7). Often, small communities of these pioneer plants

LEFT: Being able to switch to Crassulacean Acid Metabolism (CAM) photosynthesis allows Navelwort *Umbilicus rupestris* to thrive in very hot, droughted sites, such as this south-facing wall of dark, heat-absorbing stones.

get a foothold in shallow accumulations of humus and detritus. It's not uncommon to find Rue-leaved Saxifrage *Saxifraga tridactylites* in this position, mimicking how it frequently grows on natural rocky limestone cliffs (see box on pages 194–195). Along with it might be other winter annuals such as Thale Cress *Arabidopsis thaliana*, Fern-grass *Catapodium rigidum* and Common Whitlowgrass *Erophila verna*, and other annuals more typical of open, disturbed ground such as Thyme-leaved Sandwort *Arenaria serpyllifolia*, Annual Meadow-grass *Poa annua*, Sticky Mouse-ear *Cerastium glomeratum*, Shining Crane's-bill *Geranium lucidum* and Wall Speedwell *Veronica arvensis*. Together, these can create colourful communities of plants flowering on walls in early spring.

Since water is such a limiting factor you might imagine that the bottom of the wall, which receives most of the rainwater washing down the surface, would be where most plants grow. Rather unexpectedly, this appears not to be the case. In a survey of 50 walls more than two metres (6.5ft) high in Dundee, Ballinger (2020) found that most species grew higher up. While 31 species were found on the very tops of the walls, 38 were seen one to two metres above ground, but only 22 species were found in the first metre above ground level.

BELOW: Red Valerian has a deep, thick taproot that is able to penetrate crevices in walls, although it can be difficult to imagine where these plants find the room to grow.

Urban Plants

RIGHT: Ripe seeds of winter annuals like this Common Whitlowgrass are shed in late spring. Their dormancy is only broken by summer heat, allowing them to then germinate at low temperatures in autumn and winter.

BELOW: A remarkable seepage zone on a wall in Bangor, Gwynedd. The opening at the top supports a large clump of polypody *Polypodium* sp., with Rue-leaved Saxifrage below. The long green streak of bryophytes includes Creeping Feather-moss, Wall Screw-moss and Lesser Bird's-claw Beard-moss.

The reasons for this aren't entirely clear, but may relate to applications of herbicide, traffic pollution and the use of road salt, rather than the availability of water.

A more regular and constant supply of water on walls comes from leaking gutters and dripping downpipes. It's quite entertaining to hunt these out in most urban settings, as they're revealed by a tell-tale streak of vegetation down the wall. The wetter conditions of these seepage zones encourage growth, especially of moisture-loving liverworts such as Common Liverwort *Marchantia polymorpha* and pleurocarp mosses like Lesser Bird's-claw Beard-moss *Streblotrichum convolutum*, Creeping Feather-moss *Amblystegium serpens* and Common Feather-moss *Kindbergia praelonga* that spread out over the masonry. Seepage zones often have very precise gradients of moisture and, therefore, are home to different plants. The drier outer edges that are only occasionally flooded are frequently colonised by algae, staining the wall black or red. More central areas are colonised by plants that can cope with alternating very wet and dry conditions, and Rue-leaved Saxifrage is often surprisingly common, growing in profusion as if relishing a damp rock-face. In the middle of the seepage zone, some wet-wall communities can be quite luxuriant because, as well as being damp, they receive nutrients from decaying detritus collected on the roof and in gutters. As a result, it's not unusual to find rather large wetland species such as Hemp-agrimony *Eupatorium cannabinum*, Great Willowherb *Epilobium hirsutum* and even Purple-loosestrife *Lythrum salicaria*.

As mentioned earlier, retaining walls tend to receive more water and nutrients than freestanding walls, as well as soil spilling down from embankments above. The result, as Oliver Gilbert puts it, is that 'the typical wall vegetation becomes adulterated by species characteristic of other habitats, often waste places' (Gilbert 1992a). In a survey of walls and buildings in the Isle of Ely, Cambridgeshire, Ron Payne notes that plants such as Hogweed *Heracleum sphondylium*, Lesser Burdock *Arctium minus*, Field Horsetail *Equisetum arvense* and Field Bindweed *Convolvulus arvensis* were found mainly or exclusively on retaining walls (Payne 2005).

Light and aspect

Since most wall plants have their origins in open rocky and cliff-side habitats, they generally require good levels of light to grow; walls heavily shaded by trees, hedges and buildings rarely support a rich flora. However, it's not always as clear-cut as that and there's a close relationship between light, aspect, temperature and moisture. So, south-facing walls tend to be sunny but prone to heat and drought, while north-facing walls are more shaded but cooler and wetter.

How this impacts plant growth depends on where you are. In parts of south-east England with a very dry climate, the severe stress of summer heat and drought restricts plants to spots shaded at midday. This is especially true of ferns. In a survey of walls in Middlesex, for example, Kent (1961) found that 57% of walls with Hart's-tongue faced east, 38% faced north and only one wall (5%) faced south. Maidenhair Fern only grew on north-facing walls, and Polypody *Polypodium vulgare* only on east-facing walls. In western parts of Britain and Ireland, the cloudier and wetter oceanic climate allows plants to become established on both sides of the walls, although those on the south tend to grow smaller and less luxuriantly. In areas lying between these two extremes, many plants will generally avoid the hottest south-facing walls and instead are more likely to appear on walls facing north and east (Gilbert 1992a).

Common wall mosses

Look at any wall and you're likely to find at least a few bryophytes. A small group of mosses adapted to cope with periods of wetting followed by intense drying form a community regularly found on the tops of sunny walls. Generally, they make the most of the mortar, but can colonise bricks and stones as these weather and age. Such mosses are incredibly beautiful plants that deserve a closer look; they're not too difficult to identify and are good to get to know. A few of the more common species are given below; for more tips on identification see Pilkington (2011).

ABOVE: Grey-cushioned Grimmia.

Grey-cushioned Grimmia *Grimmia pulvinata*

One of the commonest wall mosses, this is also one of the most stunning. It forms neat little cushions almost exclusively on the flat tops of walls, inexplicably avoiding the vertical sides (perhaps it prefers to hold on to surface water for a little longer). The grey appearance comes from the long, silvery hairs on the tip of every leaf, giving the moss a distinctive whiskery look. The young spore capsules are also distinctive, curving back on themselves to become partially buried within the leaves. It's moderately tolerant of air pollution so is frequent in urban settings.

Wall Screw-moss *Tortula muralis*

Often growing alongside Grey-cushioned Grimmia, this species can look similar when dry. In this state the leaves twist and curl, their long silvery hairs giving the plants a hoary appearance, but when wet the broad leaves expand and it looks very different. The narrow spore capsules are also very distinctive, being carried on fine, long stems (setae) above the cushions. This is probably the commonest moss on walls, even growing on quite fresh mortar just a few years old. On acidic walls it's pleasingly restricted to bands of mortar.

ABOVE: Wall Screw-moss.
BELOW: Anomalous Bristle-moss.

Anomalous Bristle-moss *Orthotrichum anomalum*

Normally found growing in colonies of very neat little rounded tufts on the tops of walls, this moss is usually a rather dull green and rather unremarkable. But in winter and spring the conspicuous reddish-brown hairy capsules appear, looking like tiny coconuts sitting just above the leaves. Never growing on acidic rocks, this species occurs in urban areas on mortar, concrete and limestone blocks.

Great Hairy Screw-moss and Intermediate Screw-moss *Syntrichia ruralis* subsp. *ruralis* and *S. intermedia*

These two attractive species form loose tufts or cushions that appear more 'leafy' than many other wall mosses, especially when wet. Their broad leaves, each tipped with a prominent hair, give the shoots a star-like appearance. They can be difficult to tell apart unless they're growing together; Great Hairy Screw-moss tends to be larger with bright golden-green, recurved leaves, while Intermediate Screw-moss is smaller and often a duller green with more erect leaves. Both species are calcicoles, growing on mortar and lime-rich rocks.

ABOVE: Great Hairy Screw-moss in centre-left, surrounded by Intermediate Screw-moss.

Thickpoint Grimmia *Schistidium crassipilum*

Growing as a dense low cushion or spreading patch, this is a very common moss of wall tops. It has a slightly spiky appearance, with a short silvery hair on each leaf tip. It's another species that's most conspicuous in winter and spring, when the large reddish capsules appear among the leaves. Once these open they're even more striking, with a vivid red mouth and fringe of peristome teeth.

ABOVE: Thickpoint Grimmia.

Wall Thread-moss *Bryum radiculosum*

One of the few *Bryum* species that grows on hard surfaces. This common species produces compact mats or cushions of tight-packed stems, with thickly matted root-like rhizoids at the base of the plant bearing tiny tubers. The small, dark green, shiny leaves don't twist or curl when dry. In early summer the sporophytes are particularly distinctive, wine-red in colour and looking like unevenly inflated balloons. It's a very strict calcicole, only ever growing on mortar, limestone and other hard base-rich substrates.

Silky Wall Feather-moss *Homalothecium sericeum*

This species is quite unlike the others because it's a pleurocarp, forming wide, spreading mats rather than the neat little cushions of acrocarp mosses. It has a distinctive golden-green colour when dry, turning more apple-green when wet. The long, creeping stems often spill down the sides of the wall, attaching themselves to the stones and brickwork with small, root-like rhizoids. When wet, the branches and leaves spread out, giving the plant a beautiful feathery appearance. It looks very different when dry, as the leaves and branches curl up and twist.

ABOVE: Wall Thread-moss.
BELOW: Silky Wall Feather-moss.

It's worth noting that after rainfall, walls under tree canopies often remain wetter for longer. This means they can support more shade-tolerant bryophytes; Woodell & Rossiter (1959), for instance, noted that in Durham, Creeping Feather-moss *Amblystegium serpens* only occurred on a few damp and deeply shaded walls.

Dispersal

Walls present an interesting challenge for plants when it comes to dispersal, as the vertiginous nature of the habitat means gravity is the predominant force. Heavier seeds, if not assisted in some way, simply fall down towards the ground. Such dispersal by gravity is known as barochory and isn't the best strategy if you're growing on a wall. Thankfully, plants employ several effective mechanisms to help them disperse seeds and spores far and wide to reach every nook and cranny of a wall's surface.

The most important of these is wind dispersal (anemochory), and it's no surprise that many common, pioneer wall species rely on this method to get around. Fern and bryophyte spores are extremely small and lightweight, carrying long distances on the wind. While some are simply dropped from fronds and sporophytes into the wind, others are given a helping hand. The spore-bearing sporangia of the polypody ferns *Polypodium* spp., for example, have a band of thickened cells (an **annulus**) around them, the outer edge of which dries out when the spores are ripe. Eventually, the cells of the annulus suddenly

RIGHT: The yellow spores of this Common Polypody *Polypodium vulgare* have been flung explosively from their sporangia. Although many are scattered around the frond surface, most will have been launched into the air.

ABOVE: Mexican Fleabane growing on the top of a wall after seed was carried there by the wind. This species is spreading rapidly, with a three-fold increase in 10-km square occurrences since 1999.

rupture, and the band flicks back on itself, ripping the sporangia open and flinging the spores into the air.

Plants in the daisy family (Asteraceae), such as Mexican Fleabane, are particularly common on walls and rely on seeds with parachutes or plumes of hairs to carry their seed in the wind, as do the willowherbs *Epilobium* spp. and Red Valerian. The seeds of this latter species are adorned with a remarkable, branched umbrella-like structure that means they can travel at least 20 metres (66ft) from the parent plant, and probably much more when assisted by passing traffic (Geerts *et al.* 2017). The tiny seeds of Buddleja *Buddleja davidii* weigh only around 0.1mg each and have two small wings that help them stay airborne. Of course, as well as turbulence from vehicles, walls present a solid barrier to the wind and create their own vortices. The intense updraughts they produce readily dislodge seeds from their seedheads and carry them aloft. Such turbulence can be especially important in getting seeds high enough for long-distance dispersal (Tackenberg *et al.* 2003).

BELOW: A seed of Red Valerian with its delicate parachute-like pappus.

Walls provide perfect places for birds to perch, and while there they'll often preen their feathers for a while and then defecate before flying off. Any seeds they've been eating will be deposited on the top of the wall, a mechanism of dispersal known as **endozoochory**. This is particularly true of trees and shrubs with attractive berries, such as Bramble

Urban Plants

ABOVE: Yellow Corydalis is one of many wall plants whose seeds are dispersed by ants that nest in the dry and warm conditions between the stones.

Rubus fruticosus agg., Elder *Sambucus nigra*, Hawthorn *Crataegus monogyna*, Yew *Taxus baccata* and especially the many species of alien cotoneasters *Cotoneaster* spp. that are very popular in gardens. These are readily consumed by birds in autumn and winter and their occurrence on walls is often down to birds perching. Indeed, many such shrubs occur on the upper parts of the wall where birds alight (Gilbert 1992a).

As with pavements (see Chapter 7), many plants growing on walls are dispersed by ants (myrmecochory), which carry seeds with lipid-rich elaiosomes back to their colonies. Walls offer dry and warm nesting sites for ants, and Arthur Chater (former BSBI County Recorder for Cardiganshire) has observed seeds of Ivy-leaved Toadflax and Pellitory-of-the-wall being carried by Black Ants *Lasius niger* in Aberystwyth (Chater *et al.* 2000). Quite a few other common wall species are dispersed by ants, including Snapdragon *Antirrhinum majus*, Wallflower, Yellow Corydalis *Pseudofumaria lutea*, Herb-Robert *Geranium robertianum* and Ivy-leaved Speedwell *Veronica hederifolia*.

Nutrients and air pollution

Walls are unusual habitats because they can remain infertile for many decades. Debris and humus tend not to accumulate on vertical surfaces and the continual washing of rain removes any scant nutrients there might be. This favours plants of very low-nutrient habitats that can't tolerate much competition from more vigorous species. Many wall plants, especially those that grow on the tops of walls, have very low Ellenburg N values (a measure of nutrient requirements). These include common succulents such as Rock Stonecrop, Biting Stonecrop and White Stonecrop, ferns like Rustyback *Asplenium ceterach*, Wall-rue and Maidenhair Spleenwort, and even non-native plants such as Mexican Fleabane, Fairy Foxglove and House-leek *Sempervivum tectorum*.

Against this background of extreme infertility, air pollution is a rather bittersweet pill. Vehicle exhausts are a major source of oxides of nitrogen and ammonia, both of which provide a source of nitrogen for wall plants. Just two metres away from the edge of a busy dual carriageway, vehicle exhausts have been found to deposit an extra 5.5kg of nitrogen above background levels (Cape *et al.* 2004, see Chapter 5). That's enough to make a significant difference to plant communities, especially towards the base of a wall where pollution is concentrated by rainwater washing down the surface. Here, you're more likely to encounter vigorous nitrogen-demanding species such as Common Chickweed *Stellaria media*, Cleavers *Galium aparine* and Smooth Sow-thistle *Sonchus oleraceus*, as well as various species of green and blue-green algae (see 'Succession on walls', page 196).

The massive reduction in the deposition of sulphur dioxide as acid rain since the 1950s (see Chapter 5) has had a major impact on the flora of walls, with the return of many plants that had declined or disappeared from urban areas. In Cambridge, for example, two bryophytes, Thickpoint Grimmia and Intermediate Screw-moss, have increased enormously, with 14 times as many 1-km square records for the former and 10 times as many for the latter from 2010–2019 compared to 1950–1989 (Hill 2022). Lime-loving wall ferns such as Polypody, Maidenhair Spleenwort and Black Spleenwort are also now being seen more frequently in cities like Cambridge and London, and there has been an appreciable increase in plants such as Wallflower, especially in northern industrial towns that were once heavily polluted (Gilbert 1992a).

BELOW: House-leek has a small, fibrous root system allowing it to grow in very thin substrates on walls. It was also often planted on roofs following a Roman belief that it protected houses from lightning strikes.

Urban Plants

The rise of the rue

Few plants have made such a spectacular spread into urban areas following the fall in SO_2 than Rue-leaved Saxifrage *Saxifraga tridactylites*. This tiny winter annual, rarely growing more than a few centimetres tall, has recently become quite the unexpected star of the urban environment.

In fact, although wild habitats include limestone cliffs, scree slopes and limestone pavement, Rue-leaved Saxifrage has long been associated with human habitation. More than 420 years ago, the herbalist John Gerard described it as growing 'vpon bricke and ftone wals, vpon olde tiled houfes, which are growen to haue much moffe vpon them… It groweth plentifully vpon the bricke wall in Chauncerie lane, belonging to the Earle of Southampton, in the fuburbes of London, and fundrie other places' (Gerard 1597).

Between 1950 and 1990, Rue-leaved Saxifrage wasn't doing particularly well in rural settings, with widespread declines reported (Preston *et al.* 2002). But from around 2000, it suddenly began to increase rapidly in towns and cities, appearing in many where it had never been seen before, including Glasgow, Belfast and Stoke-on-Trent (Stroh *et al.* 2023). It's now popping up in all sorts of locations, from a builders' yard in the village of Annan (Dumfries and Galloway, Grace 2022) to the railway station of the small market town of Llanrwst (Denbighshire). In towns and cities from Bangor (Caernarfonshire)

Rue-leaved Saxifrage on the old wall of St Mary's Church, East Molesey, Surrey.

Rue-leaved Saxifrage with its characteristic deep red colour from anthocyanin produced to help protect its chloroplasts from strong sunlight.

to Salisbury (Wiltshire) it has spread across pavements, cobbles, roofs and along walls and railways. In some spots the species has become spectacularly successful, such as the many thousands of plants carpeting an old steel works in Port Talbot, South Wales. In one survey in Cambridge, it formed the largest population of any wall species with 500 plants on a 10m stretch of wall alongside Queens' College, but has since been eliminated by repointing (Hill 2022, Chris Preston pers. comm.).

Being a calcicole, the dramatic decline in SO_2 emissions is certainly important in this spectacular rise. It's difficult to judge how abundant it was as an urban plant in the past, although Gerard's observations suggest it was plentiful, and it appears to be coming back now that surfaces are reverting to their base-rich nature. The spread might also have been aided by the return of various bryophytes to these habitats, as cushions of moss provide nursery beds for Rue-leaved Saxifrage seedlings to get established.

There may be an important genetic factor too. Across Europe, the species has also increased in urban habitats since the 1980s and, in a study comparing plants from anthropogenic and natural habitats in Germany, Reisch (2007) found significant genetic differences. He suggests urban populations could have originated outside Germany, probably arriving through the railway network, and that these plants remain isolated, having little contact with natural populations. He also speculates that the warming climate and urban heat island, and the use of herbicides, may have selected urban-adapted ecotypes that are spreading rapidly.

Succession on walls

Any new vertical surface in an urban environment provides an opportunity for colonisation, with one group of species paving the way for others. Many of the early stages of succession are dominated by micro-organisms, and the diversity and importance of these pioneers are often overlooked. In a remarkable study of modern building façades in Germany, Hofbauer & Gärtner (2021) identified more than 220 species, including 80 species of ascomycete fungi, 75 species of green algae, 20 species of blue-green algae and 20 species of lichens. Rather than simply forming a thin biofilm on the wall surface, these organisms form complex biocrusts, interacting with the wall material as well as each other. They may even modify the physical properties of the wall surface, making it harder or more water repellent. Some of these organisms were very unusual, including *Porphyridium purpureum*, a marine red alga that colonises walls splashed with road salt, and *Excentrochloris fraunhoferiana*, a very large single-celled green alga discovered new to science during the study and known only from walls. The bases of urban walls are often rich in algae, and around 17 species of green and blue-green algae regularly form two different communities. The Prasiolales assemblage (dominated by *Rosenvingiella* spp. and *Prasiola calophylla*) is more common in cities with cooler, wetter, oceanic climates, while the Klebsormidium assemblage (mainly with species of *Klebsormidium*) is more prevalent in warmer and drier places (Rindi & Guiry 2004).

Several species of algae form distinctive red patches on walls. *Trentepohlia aurea* and especially *T. iolithus* are common on old concrete

LEFT: This damp wall in Llanrwst, North Wales, has been colonised by several species of algae, staining the surface black, red and green.

RIGHT: When the green alga *Haematococcus pluvialis* dries out on walls, it produces large red cysts rich in astaxanthin, a protective antioxidant. Astaxanthin is widely used in the aquaculture industry, fed to salmon and shrimp to intensify the colour of their flesh.

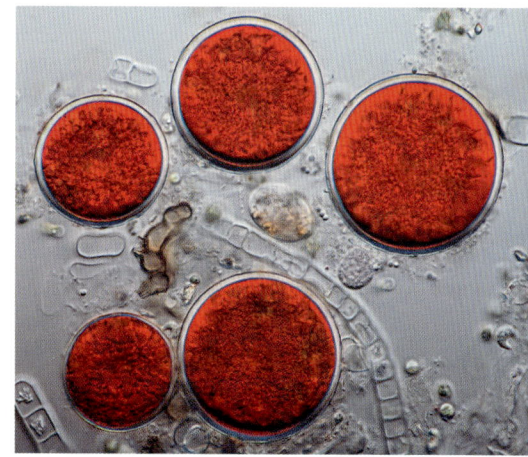

LEFT: *Xanthoria parietina*, variously known as Golden Shield Lichen, Yellow Lichen or Yellow Scale, is a nitrogen-loving species that often colonises bare brick and stone walls. Colonies commonly start growing where bird droppings have landed.

and cement walls, particularly in the milder, damper climates of western Britain and Ireland (Rindi & Guiry 2002). On walls that are subject to regular wetting and drying, a red stain is often created by a common green alga known as *Haematococcus pluvialis* (you might also have met this species on the bottom of dried-out birdbaths). Under conditions of drying stress, this alga produces deep red cysts that are rich in astaxanthin, an antioxidant that protects the cells from UV light.

Once a biocrust of micro-organisms has become established, other species follow. Most commonly, various species of algae and fungi on the wall come together to form lichens. Because they thrive on high levels of nitrogen, the familiar golden-yellow *Xanthoria parietina*

BELOW; LEFT: Wall Screw-moss is a strict calcicole, often completely covering the lines of lime-rich mortar on walls.

RIGHT: Mosses often act as nursery beds for vascular plants. This patch of Silky Wall Feather-moss in Llanrwst (Denbighshire) is supporting seedlings of Snapdragon and a bitter-cress *Cardamine* sp.

and dull grey *Physcia* species are often among the first. *Xanthoria* is particularly conspicuous, forming bright yellow dots and circles visible from afar. Bryophytes soon follow, with a handful of pioneer species including Wall Screw-moss and Anomalous Bristle-moss leading the way. When the spores of this latter species germinate, they have been seen to produce long-lasting mats of protonema (algae-like filaments) covering the wall, from which the familiar leafy moss (the gametophyte) eventually appears.

As lichens and bryophytes grow, more and more organic matter begins to accumulate and vascular plants start to appear, often germinating in clumps or carpets of moss. Among the first are species like Ivy-leaved Toadflax and Procumbent Pearlwort *Sagina procumbens*, as well as pioneer winter annuals such as Thale Cress and Rue-leaved Saxifrage. Germinating in moss doesn't guarantee survival, though, and indeed they can be carpets of death. A close examination of a 40cm patch of Wall Screw-moss on a Cambridge wall by Rishbeth (1948) showed that seedlings first appeared in early March followed by a large wave of germination in mid-April. By early May, 39 seedlings of six species had appeared, but all were killed with the arrival of dry weather in mid-May. Of course, not all seedlings on walls germinate in moss – many root directly into the cracks and crevices of the wall – but those that do have a high rate of mortality if they cannot find their own source of moisture.

As the wall ages and more vegetation develops, distinct communities of species evolve, finding and exploiting different micro-niches as they become available. Among the ferns, Maidenhair Spleenwort and Wall-rue are often the first to appear, followed by a variety of plants that are initially drawn from the pool of species in the immediate area. This gives many walls their own distinctive character, with those in neighbourhoods with large gardens, for instance, tending to have more alien escapes than those in large industrial estates, which might have a higher proportion of native species. It can, however, take many years for such communities to reach their maximum extent, a process that tends to be faster in the wetter climate of western and northern Britain and Ireland. In the drier parts of south-east England, it can take several decades for communities of plants to appear on cement-mortared walls (Gilbert 1992a).

The process of succession on walls is very different to that in less vertical habitats. Generally speaking, succession quite rapidly leads to diverse communities of tightly interwoven plants, all with complex interdependences. On walls, however, climax communities tend to be much simpler, often with just a few species that largely do not interact with each other (Darlington 1981). Very old walls of churches or Roman forts, for example, may be dominated by clumps of Pellitory-of-the-wall or Yellow Corydalis, with just a handful of other small species scattered over the masonry. This is because, even after many decades, the available substrate for growth is so thin and infertile it can't support dense and diverse communities of large plants. Once it develops to any depth, it tends to get washed off by the rain. This is why any available ledges in a wall will often support more vegetation, narrow shelves of opportunity on the otherwise depauperate surface.

ABOVE: The roots of this small birch *Betula* sp. tree have penetrated a wall, finding their way between the mortar and bricks and forcing them apart. To prevent more damage, the tree has already been killed with herbicide.

If the wall vegetation does become luxuriant, people often begin to react negatively towards it. This is especially true when woody trees and shrubs such as Ash *Fraxinus excelsior* and Buddleja start to appear, as their rapidly growing roots are so damaging to the masonry. The hydrostatic pressure inside root cells to keep them turgid can be extraordinarily high – generally around 0.5–1.0 megapascals, or around 2.5 to 5.0 times the pressure of the average car tyre. For a root in open ground this pressure is borne by the cell walls, but when pressing against a solid masonry surface the force is transferred to that surface and presses against it. This pressure is how plants move solid structures: a root cell pressure of 1.0 megapascals applied across 100 cm^2 is equivalent to a weight of one tonne (about the weight of a Black Rhinoceros), or about 10kg per cm^2 (Plants in Action 2018). Some herbaceous plants also damage walls; the swollen rootstock of Red Valerian, for instance, can easily dislodge bricks, stone and cement. But trees and shrubs do more damage than most because their long woody roots find their way down through the cracks and crevices in the wall, continually growing in length and width and gradually forcing apart the masonry. It's important to note that roots can't actually crack concrete or mortar, but instead find their way into the finest of pre-existing cracks between the bricks and mortar, quickly opening them up. Even young trees can have roots several metres in length and a few centimetres in diameter, enough to damage any wall.

As with pavements, the cleaning of herbaceous and woody wall vegetation using herbicides, mechanical removal or hand-weeding always resets the ecological clock, sometimes putting it back decades or even hundreds of years. In his survey of ancient town ramparts, Gilbert (1992) noted that Conwy in North Wales possessed some of the finest ancient wall vegetation he'd encountered in Great Britain, with large and colourful populations of Snapdragon, Red Valerian and Wallflower as well as Thick-leaved Stonecrop and luxuriant spleenworts *Asplenium* spp. The town was also well known for Southern Polypody *Polypodium cambricum*, an uncommon fern that formed substantial clumps on the 740-year-old town and castle walls. A few years ago, though, the world-heritage site was rather enthusiastically cleaned, and the wall vegetation is now much less impressive. Many of the castle's walls and ramparts are still rather bare, and you'll struggle to find many large plants of Southern Polypody. The only walls that still sustain abundant vegetation are those well out of reach of the maintenance crews.

Over the passage of time, any walls exposed to weathering will eventually crumble and succumb to the forces of gravity. Others sustain knocks and collisions that damage the bricks or stonework. Usually, once a few bricks or stones become loose, the masonry loses its integrity and will eventually tumble down. Sadly, this is an all-too-common experience for the urban botanist. In his three-year survey of wall vegetation in Middlesex, Douglas Kent noted that 'it was a common experience on a second visit to find that a particularly productive old wall had been repointed or rebuilt' (Kent 1961). In a more recent survey of 750 walls in the Isle of Ely, Cambridgeshire, Ron Payne comments that 'it was not unusual to find, on a second or later visit, that the structure had been repaired or even demolished, with the partial or total loss of its botanical interest' (Payne 2005). Such is the life of the mural botanist, constantly despairing in the face of fresh bricks, stone and mortar.

BELOW: Once abundant on Conwy Castle, the uncommon Southern Polypody is now much reduced thanks to over-enthusiastic cleaning. It's very much a species of western areas with a mild climate.

LEFT: The lower half of this old wall in Bangor (Gwynedd) was repointed a year ago, but has already been recolonised with Ivy-leaved Toadflax, Pellitory-of-the-wall and even Maidenhair Spleenwort from the original upper section that was left vegetated.

Although rebuilding and repointing inevitably impacts wall vegetation, it's often done to just part of the structure, creating a patchwork of new, clean, repointed sections among older areas of wall. If these older bits retain their original vegetation they can act as sources of seeds, spores and propagules that quickly repopulate the new sections of wall.

What grows on walls?

The number of species that can grow on walls is astonishing. Ron Payne, who has surveyed walls in south-east England for 25 years and probably studied more walls than any other botanist, estimates that more than 850 species have been recorded on walls in Great Britain. Indeed, he also suggests that, apart from aquatics, almost every species in our flora could potentially grow on a wall somewhere (Payne 2005). Even the species accounts in *Plant Atlas 2020* (Stroh *et al.* 2023) suggest that at least 360 vascular plant species, or 10% of our total flora, are regularly recorded growing on walls. Half of these regular wall plants (182 species) are aliens, mainly neophytes but also a handful of archaeophytes such as Wall Barley *Hordeum murinum* and Ivy-leaved Speedwell.

These numbers, however, include both rural and urban walls, and the number of species found in any single town or city will be much lower. Getting a handle on such figures isn't easy, as only a few detailed studies of urban wall flora have been published. This is a great shame, given the presumably large number of botanists that live in towns and cities. What could be of more interest to any botanist than observing the comings and goings of plants on the walls of their own homes, gardens and streets? Those studies that have been published are summarised in the table opposite. Of these, the walls of Cambridge and Durham are probably the most comprehensively studied, both of which have been resurveyed after considerable periods and provide valuable insights into how our wall flora might be changing.

In Cambridgeshire, a pioneering study of walls by Rishbeth (1948) found 186 different species, including all manner of ferns, shrubs, trees and grasses as well as both native and exotic flowering plants. Sadly, the number of walls surveyed was not mentioned, so we don't know the extent of the survey. A more systematic survey of 85 Cambridge walls in 2020 by Chris Preston and Jonathan Shanklin found 202 species (Hill 2022). Their richest individual walls, all beside rivers, brooks and ditches, supported 26–29 species within 10m lengths.

A little to the north of Cambridge, Ron Payne carried out a mammoth survey of 608 walls in the Isle of Ely from 1999 to 2004, recording an impressive 289 different species (Payne 2005). Of these, 31% were alien. This survey included both rural and urban walls, taking in villages and fenland countryside (43% of walls) as well as six towns (57% of walls), so the number of species is higher than a purely urban survey would be. To illustrate this, we can look at an even larger survey by Ron in south-eastern Essex. From 1973 to 1976 he surveyed the flora of 650 walls, recording 268 species in all, 29% of which were alien. Many of the walls were also in rural settings, including churchyards and railway bridges. However, if we take his only purely urban category – 278 urban garden walls – he recorded 150 different species (Payne 1978).

Staying in south-east England, Douglas Kent undertook a similarly comprehensive survey of 500 walls in Middlesex, a county dominated by north-west London but also including the surrounding rural countryside. In his four-year survey of walls of gardens, parks, private estates, cemeteries, bridges and buildings, 204 species were recorded, of which 51 (25%) were alien (Kent 1961).

Number of species recorded in various published surveys of walls

Town or city	Year(s)	What surveyed	Number of species	Proportion alien	Reference
Middlesex	1957–1960	500 rural and urban walls	204	25%	Kent (1961)
London area		72 walls	83		Kent (1961)
South-east Essex	1973–1976	278 urban garden walls (650 walls in total)	150 (268 in total)	(29%)	Payne (1978)
Cambridge	1937–1940	Numerous walls	186	19%	Rishbeth (1948)
Cambridge	2020	85 walls	202		Hill (2022)
Isle of Ely	1999–2004	608 rural and urban walls	289	31%	Payne (2005)
Durham	1953–1955	66 walls	159	33%	Woodell & Rossiter (1959)
Durham	2007–2008	68 walls	226	29%	Shimwell (2009)
Chichester	1992	2.4km ramparts	40		Gilbert (1992)
Southampton	"	1.2km ramparts	22		"
Chepstow	"	0.75km ramparts	42		"
Tenby	"	0.6km ramparts	25		"
Norwich	"	1.0km ramparts	26		"
Caernarfon	"	0.7km ramparts	14		"
Chester	"	3.0km ramparts	43		"
Denbigh	"	0.6km ramparts	48		"
Conwy	"	1.3km ramparts	37		"
York	"	2.5km ramparts	45		"
Berwick-upon-Tweed	"	2.5km ramparts	53		"

Survey dates, proportion of aliens and number or lengths of walls surveyed are given where known. Surveys are listed geographically from south to north, with Gilbert's survey of town ramparts treated separately to aid comparison.

Unfortunately, a list from purely urban settings is not provided but, in the same paper, Kent refers to another of his own surveys of 72 walls in 'the London area', taking in West Kent and Surrey, as well as Hertfordshire and Buckinghamshire. On these walls, he recorded 83 different species.

In the north of England, a three-year study of 66 walls in Durham by Woodell & Rossiter (1959) surveyed 15-metre (50ft) lengths of wall that had at least eight plant species. They found 159 species in all, many more than the authors expected, and again a rich mix of flowering plants, ferns, trees and shrubs, 33% of which were alien. Nearly half the species had also been found on Cambridge walls by Rishbeth (1948), showing the similarities – but also the differences – between wall floras of different cities. In 2007–8, the Woodell and

Rossiter survey was repeated by David Shimwell. He found that plant diversity had increased significantly, with 226 species recorded, and was surprised to find that most of the increase was down to an influx of 54 native species, with the proportion of alien taxa falling to 29% (Shimwell 2009).

A slightly different approach to surveying was taken by Gilbert in *Rooted in Stone* (1992). Rather than looking at different wall types in one city or area, he studied 11 towns and cities that still had an almost intact circle of ancient town walls and ramparts, including Conwy, York, Berwick-upon-Tweed and Chichester. The vegetation of each was surveyed and the number and abundance of species calculated. The results give us a good comparison of similar walls between the towns. On average, 21 species were found growing per 1km of town walls, the poorest flora being Caernarfon (10 species/km), while the richest was Chepstow (32 species/km). Apart from Caernarfon, walls in the oceanic climate of the north and west of Great Britain were generally richer than those in more continental climates further south and east.

Since all these studies span such a long period of time and are so different in their methodologies, it's difficult to make direct comparisons between them. However, we can bring them together to see which species occur most often and tease out some common themes about how plants behave on walls.

Top 12 wall plants

Considering the frequency and abundance of species among the different surveys (apart from Gilbert's survey of town wall ramparts, which we'll examine separately), we begin to see the same species occurring again and again. The top 12 wall species are shown in the table opposite.

All these species will be familiar to anyone that has looked at urban walls, but several things stand out as striking. The first is the sheer frequency of Annual Meadow-grass. This matches its abundance on pavements (see Chapter 5) and cements its title as the single-most frequent plant in our built environment. This isn't surprising, given its prodigious production of seed and ability to grow, flower and set seed in as little as six weeks. These characteristics give it a serious competitive advantage in the droughted environments of walls, where conditions for growth can be transient. The second striking feature

Top 12 wall plants

Species		Frequency (%)	Status	Life form
Annual Meadow-grass	*Poa annua*	41	Native	Annual
Dandelion	*Taraxacum* agg.	35	Native	Perennial
Ivy-leaved Toadflax	*Cymbalaria muralis*	24	Neophyte	Perennial
American & Broad-leaved Willowherbs	*Epilobium ciliatum* & *E. montanum*	22	Neophyte	Perennial
Smooth Sow-thistle	*Sonchus oleraceus*	22	Native	Annual
Rosebay Willowherb	*Chamaenerion angustifolium*	22	Native	Perennial
Ivy	*Hedera helix*	19	Native	Perennial
Groundsel	*Senecio vulgaris*	19	Native	Annual
Elder	*Sambucus nigra*	16	Native	Perennial
Male Fern	*Dryopteris filix-mas*	15	Native	Perennial
Oxford Ragwort	*Senecio squalidus*	13	Neophyte	Annual
Sycamore	*Acer pseudoplatanus*	12	Archaeophyte	Perennial

Frequency is the average percentage occurrence on walls in surveys of Middlesex, south-east Essex, Cambridge, Isle of Ely and Durham. Note the high proportion of native species.

is just how many of these species are also top 12 pavement plants, namely Dandelion, Groundsel, Smooth Sow-thistle and American Willowherb. The third is the appearance of Male Fern on the list, well ahead of more celebrated wall ferns such as the spleenworts. This might, however, reflect a bias in the published surveys, the majority of which have been based in south-east England where these smaller wall ferns tend to be much less frequent.

Most of the species on the list are not obligatory wall plants, but opportunistic species that will grow in any well-drained, disturbed urban habitat given half a chance. Indeed, they often colonise walls from adjacent habitats, such as grassland, gardens and wasteland. Again, in *Rooted in Stone*, Oliver Gilbert (1992) gives a vivid example of this recruitment from the local surroundings. Taking the circular thirteenth-century ramparts around York, he notes that the town wall is colonised by Water Figwort *Scrophularia auriculata* where it comes close to the River Ouse, by Harebell *Campanula rotundifolia* and Greater Burnet-saxifrage *Pimpinella major* where it runs beside open semi-natural grassland, and by Adria Bellflower *Campanula portenschlagiana* and Snapdragon where it's backed by gardens. Even a nitrogen-rich chicken run had an effect, encouraging the growth of

Urban Plants

ABOVE: Greater Celandine often grows on walls in nutrient-rich sites. An ancient belief held that placing the plant on the head of an ill person would foretell their fate; if they sang with a loud voice they would die, but if they wept, they'd live.

nitrogen-loving Greater Celandine *Chelidonium majus* on the adjacent wall. This is partly why urban walls are so fascinating, as their flora is derived from the pool of species in the immediate catchment, so no two towns have the same range of plants.

Gilbert (1992) divides wall species into three groups. First are accidental species, those that occasionally appear from the surrounding environment, but rarely persist for long. Examples include Lobelia, which often arises from plants in hanging baskets above, and Common Poppy *Papaver rhoeas*, which today comes mainly from patches of wildflower seed mixtures sown in parks and gardens. It's worth noting that Common Poppy was once much more frequent on walls; in the 1860s it was described as 'locally abundant on wall tops' in Middlesex but became much rarer as the rising use of herbicides eradicated it from cornfields (Kent 1961). Once the plant was no longer growing in the wider environment, it disappeared from walls.

The second group of wall plants are companion species. These appear more regularly on walls and tend to persist but, because they're habitat generalists, they're equally common on pavements, waste ground and other urban habitats. Most of the species in the top 12 list above are companion species, including Oxford Ragwort *Senecio squalidus*, Annual Meadow-grass, Smooth Sow-thistle and Rosebay Willowherb *Chamaenerion angustifolium*. To this list we can add many other regular wall species that fall just outside the top 12,

ABOVE: Wall Speedwell *Veronica arvensis* is one of many companion plants that grow on walls, as well as many other disturbed urban habitats like pavements and waste ground.

such as Ragwort *Senecio jacobaea*, Bramble, Procumbent Pearlwort, Red Fescue *Festuca rubra*, Wall Speedwell and Canadian and Bilbao Fleabanes *Erigeron canadensis* and *E. floribundus*.

Gilbert calls the third group selective species, but I prefer the term specialist species. These form a core group of around 20 species that tend to be largely restricted to walls. Although often outnumbered by other species, they regularly form the bulk of wall vegetation, giving it its distinctive character and identity (Gilbert 1992a). Most of them are chasmophytes (plants that grow in the crevices and fissures of rock faces) and are well adapted to growing on our artificial urban cliffs. While they almost exclusively grow on walls, especially in lowland areas, they can occur in other stony, well-drained habitats like pavements and rubble.

Some of these specialist species are now much more frequent on urban walls than they are in wilder, more natural settings. The small fern Wall-rue, for instance, grows naturally on steep rock faces and in the cracks and crevices of lime-rich rocks. Although it can be common in areas where such rocks outcrop at the surface, in much of lowland Britain and Ireland it is much more frequent as a plant of walls. The same is true of Maidenhair Spleenwort and Black Spleenwort. By exploiting the mortar in this way, these ferns can even get a foothold on walls made entirely of acidic rocks such as granite and slate, which they otherwise couldn't colonise.

Gilbert admits that his list of specialist species is rather subjective and open to interpretation, as deciding which species grow 'almost exclusively' on walls is difficult. His original list, for example, included Mind-your-own-business *Soleirolia soleirolii* and Purple Toadflax *Linaria purpurea*; the former of which is more abundant in damp lawns and shaded banks, while the latter is just as common on pavements and waste ground. I've therefore taken the liberty to revise and update the list of selective wall species below, including most of Gilbert's original suggestions but with others added (informed by published surveys and my own observations), and with them shown in decreasing frequency (Stroh 2023).

Again, the species on this list will be very familiar to anyone who regularly looks at walls, especially ancient examples such as castle ramparts, forts, town walls, churches and abbeys where the vegetation is well developed. Many of them are native wall ferns, which often

List of specialist wall species

	Species	Status	GB 10-km squares
Maidenhair Spleenwort	*Asplenium trichomanes*	Native	2,309
Wall-rue	*Asplenium ruta-muraria*	Native	2,197
Black Spleenwort	*Asplenium adiantum-nigrum*	Native	2,037
Ivy-leaved Toadflax	*Cymbalaria muralis*	Neophyte	2,024
White Stonecrop	*Sedum album*	Archaeophyte	1,743
Red Valerian	*Centranthus ruber*	Neophyte	1,658
Yellow Corydalis	*Pseudofumaria lutea*	Neophyte	1,383
Pellitory-of-the-wall	*Parietaria judaica*	Native	1,326
Reflexed Stonecrop	*Petrosedum rupestre*	Neophyte	1,263
Snapdragon	*Antirrhinum majus*	Neophyte	1,178
Trailing Bellflower	*Campanula poscharskyana*	Neophyte	1,101
Rustyback	*Asplenium ceterach*	Native	932
Mexican Fleabane	*Erigeron karvinskianus*	Neophyte	926
Wallflower	*Erysimum cheiri*	Archaeophyte	887
Navelwort	*Umbilicus rupestris*	Native	802
Flattened Meadow-grass	*Poa compressa*	Native	792
Adria Bellflower	*Campanula portenschlagiana*	Neophyte	787
Fairy Foxglove	*Erinus alpinus*	Neophyte	357

Original list from Gilbert (1992) but revised with additions from published surveys and my own observations. Listed in order of decreasing frequency in Great Britain 10-km squares according to Stroh *et al.* (2023).

It can be difficult to tell the two wall bellflowers apart, but it's easy when they're seen together.

LEFT: Adria Bellflower *Campanula portenschlagiana* has darker blue or violet, bell-shaped flowers and hairless stems.

BELOW: Trailing Bellflower *C. poscharskyana* has paler star-shaped flowers and hairy stems.

grow as distinct communities on walls. As well as the four species listed, we could add polypody *Polypodium* species as these are often restricted to walls, especially in the south and east of England.

As can be seen from the revised list of specialist wall species, just over half are garden escapes. These include traditional wall species such as Ivy-leaved Toadflax (see box on pages 214–215) and Snapdragon, as well as plants that have recently started to spread more rapidly, like Mexican Fleabane.

Wall ferns

Cities can be surprisingly rich in ferns. After a decade of hunting, a group of enthusiasts from the British Pteridological Society has found 30 different species in London alone, half of which are aliens (Edgington 2008). As well as this diversity, wall ferns are undergoing a boom in numbers thanks to the drop in sulphur dioxide emissions since the 1960s (Edgington 2003). As recently as the 1970s, Maidenhair Spleenwort and Black Spleenwort were absent from London, and there were only a few stunted plants of Hart's-tongue. Today, now that wall surfaces have become less acidic, robust and thriving colonies of these species are widespread. The two spleenworts have been recorded from more than a quarter of London's 1-km squares, a process of colonisation aided by long-distance dispersal events (Edgington 2007). Many other lime-loving species have appeared, such as Intermediate Polypody *Polypodium interjectum* in 1992 and the endearing little Rustyback in 1997 (Edgington 2008). Most extraordinary, though, is a single plant of Green Spleenwort *Asplenium viride*, a very rare fern of remote mountain cliffs and limestone pavement, which has appeared on the thoroughly incongruous wall of Ravenscourt Park Underground Station. Known here for the last 25 years, it's at the far end of the platform, so if you want to see it, you have to sit in the very last carriage of the trains.

And it's not just in London that ferns are thriving. In Bath (Somerset), 20 native species have been recorded since 2000, including surprising plants like Sea Spleenwort, normally restricted to coastal rocks but discovered growing on a basement wall in 2018 and doing well until the colony was 'blasted clean' in 2020. Nine alien species of fern have also been encountered in Bath, including a remarkable tally of five different species of brake ferns (*Pteris* spp., see Chapter 4), although sadly many of these have also been cleaned away or died out (Crouch 2020).

Ferns are regularly among the first species to colonise walls and can go on to become the most abundant wall plants. Their spores are so light and readily dispersed they spread quickly onto new surfaces, and the tiny micro-niches provided by porous bricks and mortar are ideal sites for germination. In fact, this substrate is so effective in germinating ferns that an old horticultural trick for growing spores is to sow them on damp trays of crushed bricks and mortar.

The tiny clump of Green Spleenwort on the wall of Ravenscourt Park Underground Station, London.

A clump of Common Polypody perched on the bracket of a downpipe.

Below are some of the common ferns you're likely to meet on urban walls. They're all lime-loving and often grow intermingled together, so if you find one, you'll probably encounter others.

Wall-rue *Asplenium ruta-muraria*
A fern with very distinctive small dark green fronds, each with rounded leaflets (pinnae). It's perhaps our single-most common wall fern, thriving especially on old mortar. Plants are often small and diminutive but can become quite luxuriant in northern and western areas.

Maidenhair Spleenwort *Asplenium trichomanes*
A delicate and distinctive fern, producing tufts of fronds. Each of these has a very dark midrib with a series of small, rounded leaflets on each side. This species can be abundant on mortared walls, often picking out the lines of cement (pictured on page 101).

Hart's-tongue *Asplenium scolopendrium*
A small to medium-sized fern, this one is distinctive because its long, lance-shaped fronds are undivided, like a tongue, hence the common name. The spore-bearing sporangia are arranged in characteristic parallel lines on the undersides of the fronds.

Polypodies *Polypodium* spp.
These attractive medium-sized ferns have lance-shaped, leathery fronds that are deeply dissected into two rows of long pinnae. The orange-brown spore-bearing sporangia are arranged in beautiful dots on the underside of the fronds. Common Polypody *P. vulgare* and Intermediate Polypody *P. interjectum* are widespread, with the latter often more common in parts of south-east England (Barden & Preston 2009). Southern Polypody *P. cambricum* is more frequent in south-west England, Wales and Ireland.

Rustyback *Asplenium ceterach*
A very distinctive and attractive little fern with neat, wavy-edged fronds that are covered in dense orange-brown felt on their undersides, hence the common name. It grows in compact tufts and on mortared walls and appears to be increasing.

Black Spleenwort *Asplenium adiantum-nigrum*
Another small to medium-sized fern, this species has lovely feathery fronds carried on stems that are black at the base. It seems to prefer more moisture at the root than other wall ferns and is most often found towards the bottom of walls or on retaining earth walls.

Wall-rue.

Rustyback.

Black Spleenwort.

Snapdragon is native to the Iberian Peninsula, where it grows on rocky cliffs and scree slopes, or similar habitats with bare, often disturbed soil such as roadside banks, railway embankments, path sides and sand dunes. Grown in gardens here since Elizabethan times, it's available in a wide range of often gaudy colours. The flowers, which famously snap open and closed when pressed on their sides, can only be pollinated by bees large enough to force open the 'mouth' of the flower, such as bumblebees *Bombus* spp. To help them do this, the keel of the lip where the bees land is covered with special cone-shaped cells. These provide a grip to the bees so they can push against the mouth of the flower and force their way in (Whitney *et al.* 2011). Snapdragon seeds are dispersed by gravity, which is why many plants also grow at the base of walls, and by ants, which relish nesting in the dry, warm conditions of walls. Although it's been naturalised in the wild here for at least 260 years, records have increased substantially since the 1950s thanks to better recording of alien species and a genuine spread, possibly fuelled by climate change. It's now one of the most frequent garden escapes in urban habitats (Stroh 2023).

In contrast to Snapdragon, Mexican Fleabane has only recently started to spread rapidly. It's been cultivated in British gardens since 1856, but mainly in southern areas due to a reputation for not being

RIGHT: The colourful flowers of Snapdragon *Antirrhinum majus* not only attract pollinating bees, but also children, who love 'snapping' the flowers open and closed by squeezing their sides together.

BELOW: Cone-shaped epidermal cells on the keel of the lip of Snapdragon flowers provide grip to visiting pollinating bees, and also scatter light, producing a sparkling effect that attracts and guides pollinators.

0.02mm

ABOVE: Mexican Fleabane can become invasive and eradicate other wall species. Note how the flowers open white but change to pink as they age, which may be a signal to pollinators.

entirely hardy, despite being able to survive frosts down to -15°C. It's a native of Mexico, Honduras, El Salvador and Guatemala where it's found in mountainous regions from 900 to 3,500m high. It grows on cliffs and in rock crevices, as well as steep, open banks and hillsides, but is also abundant in damp, open pine-oak forest (Nash 1976). The plant produces a woody taproot that allows it to penetrate cracks and fissures in rocks, hence its ability to thrive on walls. It is widely naturalised in North America, Europe, New Zealand, Japan and Hawaii (where it's a serious threat to native vegetation) and its spread is controlled in some countries such as Portugal, where growing it in gardens, selling it, or releasing it into the wild has been prohibited since 1999 (Barthelat 2019). In Britain, it spread locally following its escape into the wild in 1891 and was largely confined to southern England until around 1990, when it suddenly began to increase and expand northwards. It's now found widely in southern England and the English Midlands, at scattered sites in Wales, northern England, and Ireland, and has recently appeared at a handful of sites in Scotland, including Edinburgh and Glasgow (75 of the 79 records from Scotland date from 2007 onwards). It can come to dominate and behave invasively, eliminating almost all the other vegetation on old walls (Stroh *et al.* 2023).

Ivy-leaved Toadflax: the master of the masonry

Cascading down the bricks and stones, Ivy-leaved Toadflax *Cymbalaria muralis* is one of our most frequent wall plants, growing on nearly a quarter of walls in Great Britain. It's especially abundant in southern and western areas, where it relishes old walls with crumbling mortar and stonework.

It has small, glossy leaves, reminiscent of ivy, on wandering reddish stems that root into cracks and crevices, forming densely tangled mats. This spreading nature has led to other common names such as Wandering Sailor. Each flower is carried on a single stem and can be produced in such abundance that they colour the mats lilac. Indeed, without this plant many urban walls would be considerably duller in their stony nakedness. Occasionally, white- or pink-flowered forms occur, forming locally distinct populations.

Each flower resembles a tiny snapdragon and in the past the plant has been classified as both a snapdragon *Antirrhinum* and a toadflax *Linaria*. The relatively large lower petals are held out flat, a landing platform for pollinating insects, especially small solitary bees. Guided to the centre of the flower by a pair of yellow keels, they force these apart to reach nectar at the base of a spur at the back of the flower. In doing so, pollen is removed and deposited on the next flower visited.

After pollination, though, something quite remarkable happens, something that has helped Ivy-leaved Toadflax become a true master of the masonry. When the flower stalks (the **pedicels**) first appear, they hold the flowers upwards towards the light. Controlled by growth hormones (**auxins**), this **positive phototropism** places the flowers in view of passing bees. But after pollination, the mechanism is reversed. Now, **negative phototropism** means the pedicels grow *away* from the light. As the seedpods develop, their stalks bend backwards towards the dark, and on a wall, that's the cracks and crevices between the bricks and stones. Ivy-leaved Toadflax quite literally plants its own seeds into the wall, pushing them into dark recesses ready for germination. It's a beautiful mechanism that ensures seeds don't simply fall to the bottom of the wall, but are planted in its surface.

This 'self-planting' isn't, however, the plant's only mechanism of dispersal. As well as localised dispersal by gravity (barochory) and wind (anemochory), longer-distance dispersal is achieved by employing the services of ants (myrmecochory) that take up residence in walls. These collect the seeds for the lipid-rich elaiosome and carry them back to their nests to feed their larvae (see Chapter 7). In this way, they both disperse the seeds and plant them in one go.

Ivy-leaved Toadflax is native to the mountains of southern central and south-eastern Europe, particularly Switzerland,

Ivy-leaved Toadflax on a wall in Bangor, Gwynedd.

Slovenia, Croatia, Montenegro, and Bosnia and Herzegovina, as well as southern Italy and Sicily. Here, it thrives in rocky habitats such as cliff faces, scree slopes and rocky ground. William Baxter, Scottish botanist and curator at Oxford Botanic Garden (1813–54), suggested that some Ivy-leaved Toadflax seeds were introduced to Oxford by accident in a consignment of marble sculptures from Italy. After escaping into the gardens in 1648, plants became established on the walls of Oxford colleges, and soon became known as Oxford Weed, Oxford Ivy or Colosseum Ivy.

However, Ivy-leaved Toadflax was actually being grown here by at least 1617 as a rock-garden plant, and it was recorded as an escape soon after in 1640, when herbalist and botanist John Parkinson noted it growing 'in diverse places' and 'upon the thatched houses' in Hatfield, Hertfordshire (Harris 2024). The truth rarely gets in the way of a good story, though, and even today the tale of the sculptures is often retold.

These days, Ivy-leaved Toadflax is flowering much earlier than it used to. In a study of 385 British plants, Fitter & Fitter (2002) found that between 1991 and 2000, Ivy-leaved Toadflax flowered 35 days earlier than in the previous four decades. This is an 'extreme and significant' advancement in flowering time compared to the average advancement of 4.5 days. It may be that this southern European species, living as it so often does in the embrace of the urban heat island, is responding to our warming climate more than many other species.

Several other *Cymbalaria* species are found in Great Britain. Corsican Toadflax *C. hepaticifolia* is a rare garden escape, but Italian Toadflax *C. pallida*, with more rounded leaves and larger flowers, is more frequent. A fairly recent arrival, it's not spreading as quickly but is increasing, especially in northern England and southern Scotland.

Seedpods of Ivy-leaved Toadflax showing negative phototropism, turning away from the light and growing back towards the wall.

The white-flowered form of Ivy-leaved Toadflax growing in Russell Avenue, Dublin.

Italian Toadflax on a wall in Colwyn Bay, Conwy.

A recurring theme of urban botany also applies to walls, namely that their flora is dominated by a small number of common species, but these are joined by a huge range of transient (accidental) species. In south-east Essex, for example, Ron Payne found that just eight species occurred on 20% or more of walls surveyed, but 70% of species grew on fewer than ten of the 650 walls surveyed (Payne 1978). Similarly, in Durham, just 14 species occurred on 25% or more of walls surveyed, but 87% on fewer than ten of the 66 walls surveyed (Woodell & Rossiter 1959).

To emphasise the rarity of these transient, accidental species, many appear on single walls in an area and often as single plants. Both Douglas Kent and Ron Payne found that around 30% of species were seen on single walls in their surveys of Middlesex and the Isle of Ely (Kent 1961, Payne 2005). Similarly, in Cambridge, Chris Preston and Jonathan Shanklin discovered that 40% of the 876 species records they made were of single individual plants, or singletons as they call them (Hill 2022). Ivy-leaved Speedwell, for instance, was found on six walls in their survey but only ever as single plants. Many species therefore exist in very small, vulnerable populations.

Against the high turnover of plants on walls, though, some plants are remarkably resilient and can persist for a long time. An outstanding example is Clove Pink *Dianthus caryophyllus*, which was known to be growing on the walls of Rochester Castle (East Kent) for around 330 years from its discovery in 1666 until 1996, shortly after which some 'tidying up' of the walls destroyed the plant (Geoffrey Kitchener pers. comm.). Also just about scraping into the '300 club' is Tower Cress *Pseudoturritis turrita*, recorded on the walls of Trinity College, Cambridge, in 1722 and which was still present at the neighbouring St John's College in 2022, despite several recent efforts to clean the walls. Sadly, the Common Polypody on the wall of Garret Hostel Lane, Cambridge, didn't quite make it, as it only survived for 289 years from 1660 until the wall was demolished in 1949 (Bardon & Preston 2009). These long-lived populations, however, are very much the exception. Indeed, the life of many wall plants is extremely short, and the urban botanist soon learns not to hang around if they want to identify or photograph a particular species, as the subject might not be there next week.

Another recurring observation from the studies of walls is that because conditions are so harsh, many plants fail to reach maturity and flower. This can make identification difficult, especially for groups like grasses and willowherbs. On the other hand, plants that are distinctive when young, such as Buddleja, can be readily identified even as seedlings, even if they don't always survive. This can lead to under-representation of the former group in surveys, and over-representation of the latter. Ron Payne suggests this is why he found Buddleja to be the most frequent shrub in his survey, on a quarter of the 608 walls he looked at in the Isle of Ely (Payne 2005). It also reminds us that the urban botanist often needs a pair of binoculars to help record wall plants, although this naturally runs the terrible risk of being mistaken for a twitcher.

Woody plants on walls

Walls are perfect places for trees and shrubs to become established. Being open, sunny and well drained, they're ideal habitats for pioneer woody species like Birch, Ash, Sycamore *Acer pseudoplatanus* and Hawthorn to get a foothold. Indeed, large numbers of seedlings of such species can sometimes be observed germinating on walls in spring, although most of these will perish in the first period of dry weather. As far as trees and shrubs are concerned, walls are great nurseries, but poor mothers. Those plants that do manage to grow to any size invariably attract unwanted attention and are usually removed before they cause damage to the masonry. It's therefore rare to see sizeable trees and shrubs growing on walls, unless they're well out of reach or growing on a neglected wall. Very occasionally, a tree will survive for many years on top of a wall, almost becoming a bonsai with restricted root-growth. I well remember my PhD tutor, the plant morphologist Dr Adrian Bell, collecting an ancient but tiny, gnarled Hawthorn from a wall that was being demolished in Bangor, and growing it in a bonsai pot for years.

From the various surveys of walls, Elder and Sycamore emerge as the most frequent woody plants, but there are many others. Among the most common species are Ivy, Bramble and Buddleja, as well as the appropriately named Wall Cotoneaster *Cotoneaster horizontalis* agg. Almost any species of woody plant occasionally can put in an appearance on walls, including everything from native Rusty Willow *Salix cinerea* subsp. *oleifolia*, Rowan *Sorbus aucuparia* and Beech *Fagus sylvatica* to aliens like Fuchsia *Fuchsia magellanica*, Oregon-grape *Mahonia aquifolium*, Gooseberry *Ribes uva-crispa* and Lawson's Cypress *Cupressus lawsoniana*. These introductions are especially common on garden walls, which are often overhung by planted trees and shrubs and readily shower them with seed.

Yew is a particularly frequent wall tree, for three reasons. Firstly, it naturally favours very well-drained, lime-rich substrates; it's generally a plant of chalk and limestone landscapes, so mortar-rich walls are very much to its liking. Secondly, it's very popular horticulturally and is widely planted in gardens, parks and amenity areas and, of course, it graces almost every churchyard in the land. And thirdly, its berries are very attractive to birds, which perch on walls and deposit the seeds in their droppings. Yew can sometimes get established very high up on walls and out of reach of human hands. Perhaps the most famous is 'the Taxus on the Tower', a remarkably sturdy bush growing atop the 21m (68ft) tower of Culmstock Church in Devon. The plant is thought to date back to 1750, making it more than 270 years old, and has inspired quite a bit of folklore and rather a lot of rather bad poetry; here, for example, are several stanzas of an anonymous 34-verse poem from around 1900:

> *Some bird flew o'er, a seed let fall,*
> *Which found a dusty bed*
> *Within a crack of the old stone wall,*
> *And a twig shot up its head.*
>
> *That yew tree is a novel sight*
> *As jackdaws on it perch,*
> *Grown from the stones toward the light,*
> *The south side of the Church.*
>
> *A sight more strange cannot be seen,*
> *Though you the country scour,*
> *Than that queer nodding yew tree green*
> *Upon the old Church tower.*

Darlington (1981) says the Culmstock Yew was indeed bird-sown, but other theories suggest seeds were incorporated into mortar when four weathervanes were added to the tower in 1776, or that it was planted on the tower as part of a medieval topping-out ceremony when the tower was completed in the 1300s in the belief the Yew would displace evil spirits before the roof was sealed (Bromwich 2006). Thankfully, the tree is a much-loved feature of the church and in no danger of being removed.

ABOVE: The Culmstock Church Yew *Taxus baccata*, Devon, known as the 'Taxus on the Tower', may be more than 270 years old and was probably bird-sown. In the 1830s, a lad of fifteen, named Jones, tested the strength of the tree by sitting out among the branches.

LEFT: Wall Cotoneaster colonising the top of a wall in Caernarfon, Gwynedd. A highly confusing genus with many difficult-to-identify species, this group alone includes *C. adpressus*, *C. ascendens*, *C. hjelmqvistii*, *C. perpusillus* and *C. horizontalis*.

Birds, particularly Mistle Thrushes *Turdus viscivorus*, Blackbirds *T. merula* and Fieldfares *T. pilaris*, are naturally attracted to solid high towers and walls, where they'll perch and strip Yew berries of their edible, fleshy, outer aril and discard the inedible hard seeds over the edge. Other berries, such as blackberries, hollies, haws and elderberries, are eaten whole and the seeds defecated onto the wall top, where they germinate with a handy dose of fertiliser. This is an extraordinarily effective method of dispersal; Payne (2005) found that 89% of Cotoneasters and 71% of Elders growing on walls in the Isle of Ely were found on their tops.

Waterside walls

A very particular type of vegetation develops on walls that are constantly in contact with water, such as alongside urban canals, rivers, ponds, lakes, ditches and drains. In such situations, water is constantly drawn up into the masonry through porous mortar and brickwork, and the whole structure can be kept more-or-less permanently damp.

In Cambridge, Preston and Shanklin (Hill 2022) found a distinct community of plants on such walls featuring wetland species like Gypsywort *Lycopus europaeus*, Hemp-agrimony, Meadowsweet *Filipendula ulmaria* and Purple-loosestrife, as well as more generalist plants like Wood Avens *Geum urbanum*, Wood Dock *Rumex sanguineus* and Common Nettle *Urtica dioica*.

In London, a detailed survey of 92 walls at 16 sites beside the River Thames from Mortlake down to Woolwich recorded 90 different species, the majority of which were plants of disturbed and riparian habitats (Francis & Hoggart 2012). Brick walls were found to carry

RIGHT: Skullcap *Scutellaria galericulata* growing on a brick wall beside Regent's Canal, central London.

the most vegetation, with the most frequent species (in order of occurrence) being Buddleja, Guernsey Fleabane, Pellitory-of-the-wall, Gypsywort, Water Dock *Rumex hydrolapathum*, Procumbent Pearlwort and Hemlock Water-dropwort *Oenanthe crocata*. Alongside these were many other riparian species, including Marsh Yellow-cress *Rorippa palustris*, Water Mint *Mentha aquatica*, Water-pepper *Persicaria hydropiper*, Alder *Alnus glutinosa*, as well as many more typical wall species. This suggests that the normal wall flora is being augmented with a few riparian specialists, the seeds of which can be dispersed by floating in water (hydrochory).

Change in the flora of walls

As we're beginning to appreciate with urban floras, nothing stays static for long, and walls are no exception. We're lucky that wall-plant surveys of three towns have been repeated after a period of several years, allowing us to see how the flora is changing. These glimpses into the dynamic nature of wall vegetation are fascinating and, against the wider narrative of species loss in semi-natural habitats and the general negativity around the state of urban habitats, suggest that the flora of urban walls is doing well and in rather rude health.

In Durham, Shimwell (2009) repeated the survey undertaken 50 years earlier by Woodell & Rossiter (1959). Far from a story of decline, he found that plant diversity had increased by around 39–42%. It would be tempting to assume this was just through the arrival of more aliens, but in fact it was mostly due to an influx of 54 native species, compared to just 10 extra neophytes. As Shimwell put it, the wall vegetation had 'become more prominent, better developed and that the likelihood of encountering a species-rich community was far greater in 2008 than in 1958'. He suggests that the primary driver for this is the reduction in atmospheric sulphur dioxide and resulting de-acidification of surfaces since the 1950s.

Some of the biggest increases in the Durham survey were seen with Ivy (+41%), Ivy-leaved Toadflax (+36%), Nettle (+32%), Cleavers (+30%), Wood Avens (+30%), Ragwort (+28%), Ash (+27%) and Nipplewort *Lapsana communis* (+26%). Although this might indicate a general increase in nutrient-demanding, rather weedy species, the biggest declines were of Cock's-foot *Dactylis glomerata* (-18%), Groundsel (-18%), Annual Meadow-grass (-15%), Broad-leaved Dock

Rumex obtusifolius (-10%) and Sycamore (-10%). Of the new arrivals, the most successful were American Willowherb (62% of walls), Yorkshire Fog *Holcus lanatus* (41% of walls), Wall Cotoneaster (35% of walls), Red Valerian (28% of walls) and Oxford Ragwort (25% of walls). All of these newcomers will be very familiar to anyone looking at urban walls today.

In Cambridge, John Rishbeth listed the top 12 species and the number of walls they grew on in the 1940s. Unfortunately, these can't be converted to percentages as he didn't note the total number of walls he surveyed, but some comparison can be made with the top 12 from Preston and Shanklin's survey in 2020 (Hill 2022). Not surprisingly, Annual Meadow-grass takes the top spot in both surveys, while Dandelion moved down from second to third place. Ivy-leaved Toadflax moved from fifth up to fourth, and Groundsel from eighth place down to last. But that's it. No other species match on the two lists and it's all change on the walls, with 14 different species appearing and disappearing in the 80 years between surveys. The most frequent new arrivals include fleabanes (31% of walls), Hairy Bitter-cress *Cardamine hirsuta* (26% of walls), Wall Speedwell (25% of walls) and willowherbs (24% of walls), while Snapdragon, Feverfew *Tanacetum parthenium* and Rosebay Willowherb all fell out of the top 12. In particular, there has been a decline of woody plants on walls but an increase in annuals, implying a move towards more open, ruderal habitats. Preston and Shanklin suggest these changes might be down to a complex interaction of factors, probably including milder winters and warmer summers, less pollution from coal-burning fires, changes in the surrounding land in the city that acts as a catchment area from which the wall flora is drawn, and our own general intolerance of large and woody species on walls such as Elder and Rosebay Willowherb. Despite this high turnover of species, though, Cambridge hasn't seen the huge influx of new wall species that Durham experienced; the number of species only increased by 7% between the two surveys (just 16 new species), far behind the 39–42% found in Durham.

In 2023, Arthur Chater repeated his survey of 54 streets in Aberystwyth last examined in 1998 and 1973. Looking at species predominantly found on walls, it's clear that some have undergone quite remarkable changes over the previous 50 years (Arthur Chater pers. comm.). Again, the greatest change was of Ivy-leaved Toadflax, which increased by 46%, from 35% to 81% of streets. Two species

LEFT: Consolidating its position as master of the masonry, Ivy-leaved Toadflax has increased by 36% in Durham since the 1950s and moved from fifth to fourth place in the list of the top 12 wall plants in Cambridge since the 1940s.

less restricted to walls showed similar increases: Red Valerian (a 50% increase) and White Stonecrop (a 43% increase). Both these alien species are known to be increasing in many areas. Two native species, Pellitory-of-the-wall and Navelwort, both increased by 13%. The fern flora changed in different ways, with Maidenhair Spleenwort increasing by 17% and Intermediate Polypody by 13%, but Black Spleenwort decreasing by 6%, Wall-rue by 7%, and Hart's-tongue decreasing by an alarming 33%. Given the reported recovery of many ferns in light of falling SO_2 levels, these results are difficult to account for and need more work to understand.

These surveys illustrate just how distinct the wall floras are in different towns and cities, and how differently they're responding to changing environmental conditions. Despite a small handful of headline species that appear again and again, walls are remarkably diverse and dynamic habitats that can host a vast range of species, even if the majority are of fleeting appearance. But this is precisely what makes these urban cliffs such tantalising habitats to explore.

Urban fallow: waste ground and derelict land

chapter nine

Few buildings last forever, and the urban landscape is anything but static. It grows, it sprawls, it decays and it's reborn. This constant flux adds dynamism and diversity into urban habitats, a continual cycle of development and redevelopment. And, because urban land-ownership is generally focused down to the scale of individual buildings or small plots of land (rather than the vast acreages of fields and farms), these become the units of change. Explore any urban landscape and, after passing many intact buildings, you'll soon come across a gap: a building demolished or being refurbished, a disused parking area, a factory falling derelict, or just a patch of land that has – for the moment at least – escaped the relentless tide of development.

Traditionally, these undeveloped fragments have been called 'waste ground', 'derelict land' or, for larger post-industrial areas, 'brownfield sites'. All these terms are deeply rooted and very well established, part of our everyday lexicon. All of them, though, carry wholly negative connotations. They reinforce the idea that the land is quite literally wasted and derelict, it has no purpose, it's brown and lifeless and has no value. As a result, such land becomes viewed as undesirable, unsightly and even depressing. It's a sign of urban failure and decay.

In an attempt to change this narrative, Oliver Gilbert coined the term 'urban commons' for waste ground and derelict land (Gilbert 1989, 1992b). This is a great analogy, especially for larger brownfield sites. Commons in the countryside are areas of communal grazing, usually grasslands and heathlands that have escaped the worst ravages of agricultural intensification and often retain much of their biodiversity. But – and here's where we perhaps run into a difficulty

OPPOSITE:
Mugwort *Artemisia vulgaris* growing on disused fallow land opposite Canary Wharf, London.

with the term – they are subject to continual management to keep them in good condition. This usually takes the form of grazing with horses or sheep or sometimes cattle, and occasionally an annual hay-cut. In contrast, urban waste ground, derelict land and brownfield sites lack any management. Indeed, the very hallmark of such land is that it's abandoned and left to its own devices.

So, to draw on a slightly different term with agricultural roots, I prefer '**urban fallow**' to describe such habitats. Agricultural fallow land is left to lie dormant for a few years before being reworked, temporarily left uncultivated and uncropped before becoming productive again. And this is exactly the same situation with most urban fallow. It usually isn't abandoned for long, but is redeveloped, cleared and built upon again. For a developer, urban fallow is an opportunity in waiting; it lies dormant for a spell before becoming productive again. Urban fallow land makes no money, and that's a predicament which attracts attention from developers. It rarely survives for long.

Urban fallow, then, is where plants can get a foothold, at least for a few years. In many ways, the habitat mirrors street pavements, car parks and town squares – it's often sealed by areas of concrete or asphalt, it lies over poorly developed, infertile soils, and it can be subject to intense heat and drought in summer. But, unlike pavements, urban fallow has been unleashed from the intense footfall and

BELOW: An area of urban fallow between houses in Llandudno Junction, Conwy, with Buddleja *Buddleja davidii*, Bramble *Rubus fruticosus* agg., Red Valerian *Centranthus ruber* and the signature abandoned supermarket trolley.

Urban fallow: waste ground and derelict land

ABOVE: A derelict textile mill in Bradford (Yorkshire), with abundant growth of Rosebay Willowherb *Chamaenerion angustifolium*, Great Willowherb *Epilobium hirsutum* and Buddleja. Many such sites are now targeted for redevelopment as housing.

pressure of constant trampling. Here, at last, succession is allowed to proceed, especially on land that's been worked over and left bare except for patches of rubble, crumbling concrete and asphalt. Finally able to get their roots into the soil below, plants can encroach and spread, seed around and begin to take over.

These days, some would enthusiastically call this process 'rewilding', an opportunity for nature to take control and reclaim the land without the touch of human hand. However, rewilding has become a horribly confused term, applied to anything and everything from traditional highly managed species-restoration projects to sowing wildflowers in a garden. Unfortunately, many people now equate rewilding with complete land abandonment, which it most certainly is not. As a result, the term rewilding has effectively become obsolete (Hayward *et al.* 2019). Urban fallow is not rewilding, but it does allow the natural processes of succession to take place unhindered, if only for a few years.

Areas of urban fallow can be wildly exciting, even bordering on the romantic. It's where the most adaptable native plants and a host of opportunistic alien species are finally unleashed to create entirely new and novel communities. Some of these, such as Birch *Betula* spp. and Buddleja *Buddleja davidii* scrub, have become emblematic of waste

Urban Plants

RIGHT: The glamorous side of urban botany. These dilapidated buildings were photographed just off the much more salubrious tourist hotspot of the Royal Mile, Edinburgh, in 2006. Such juxtaposition of buildings in different states of urban decay adds to the diversity of plants that can be found in city centres.

ABOVE: Although tantalising for the botanist, sites such as this derelict mill in Bradford can be dangerous and are often fenced off to prevent access. Frustratingly, plant identification has to be done through a wire fence, sometimes with binoculars in hand.

ground and post-industrial sites. Here, we truly begin to get a glimpse of what urbanised land might look like if we weren't around. And alongside the typical plants we'd expect to find, we even get a few surprises, with orchids, rare ferns like Moonwort *Botrychium lunaria* and even parasitic species such as Toothwort *Lathraea squamaria* putting in unexpected and thrilling appearances. With mosaics of very different soil conditions and vegetation of different ages and structures, urban fallow can be home to more species than any other urban habitat (Bonthoux 2014). When human pressure is finally relaxed, the plants move in.

Urban fallow: waste ground and derelict land

LEFT: Urban fallow sites are often highly heterogeneous in nature. Here, a mixture of derelict buildings and redevelopment in Stourbridge (Worcestershire) creates a mosaic of habitats.

For botanists there are, however, three big frustrations with urban fallow. The first is that the land is difficult to get into and explore. Usually, you can't just wander in and have a poke around to see what's there. Because the land is private, it's almost always completely fenced off. This is entirely understandable, as no landowner wants to be responsible for a botanist falling into a hidden underground basement, injuring themselves on some abandoned machinery, or exposing themselves to hazardous material while looking for interesting plants. Some sites have security cameras or even guards monitoring them round the clock. Access is denied, leaving us to peer in from the edges through the wire, binoculars in hand, trying to work out what's growing inside. Fleabanes are difficult enough to identify close-up, but even harder when they're far away behind a fence.

The second challenge is that, in some areas at least, urban fallow is a precious and diminishing resource. The pressure to develop every square metre of urban land has become so intense that nothing escapes the developers' attention. London's former docklands, for example, once supported much of the capital's urban fallow, but have now been redeveloped to accommodate the multitude of companies that are part of the booming service sector, while other large areas have been lost to housing. Urban fallow now tends to occupy smaller, more widely dispersed sites created through abandonment of individual buildings (London Biodiversity Partnership 2001). Similarly, Cambridge is a member of the Fast Growth Cities (FGC) group, which also includes

Oxford, Norwich, Peterborough, Milton Keynes and Swindon. Current government ambition is to turn Cambridge into 'the Silicon Valley of Europe', with up to 250,000 new homes alongside new business parks, laboratories and science centres. Such ambitions leave little room for fragments of fallow, and today, in the wake of decades of expansion, precious few remnants remain and those that do are inevitably targeted for development (Hill 2022). As always, growth and regeneration are continual themes, making urban fallow a highly dynamic and ever-changing habitat.

And it's not just redevelopment for a few houses or commercial units. Larger areas of urban fallow often get identified as potential new 'green spaces' that should be 'improved', transformed into soft-end-uses such as public parks and recreational spaces. The fascinating spontaneous vegetation that has evolved by itself is swept away and replaced with an amenity landscape of planted trees, flowerbeds and grassy lawns, perhaps with the odd identikit wildflower meadow and pond which are installed, ironically, to enhance biodiversity. Underpinning these developments is a complete ignorance of the value of the original habitat, of its own biological, cultural and historical value. The Old Brickworks might once have been exceptionally rich in post-industrial archaeology, plants, invertebrates and stories of the communities it supported, but far better we have 'active-travel routes' through manicured lawns to a café beside a eutrophic duck pond. Developers benefit by spending

RIGHT: A small plot of urban fallow in Cambridge, with Sycamore *Acer pseudoplatanus*, Great Willowherb and Common Mallow *Malva sylvestris* as well as a carpet of mosses. Such sites are increasingly rare in the city due to intense pressure for development.

Urban fallow: waste ground and derelict land

ABOVE: Construction of the Olympic Park for the 2012 London Games led to one of the biggest losses of urban fallow habitat in the capital, including post-industrial land, gas works, tanneries and old munitions factories. In all, 45ha (111 acres) of Sites Important for Nature Conservation were lost.

thousands or even millions of pounds on such schemes, so these 'improvements' to urban fallow always get approved.

The final frustration with urban fallow is that sites are invariably doomed, and often get redeveloped just as they begin to flourish. This transience is, of course, an intrinsic part of the habitat. But it's still deeply annoying when that wonderful patch of abandoned land between the station and the corner shop where Wild Teasel *Dipsacus fullonum* grows tall among a sea of Purple Toadflax *Linaria purpurea*, and where you saw your first Bee Orchid *Ophrys apifera* last year, is suddenly swept away overnight as the bulldozers move in. There's nothing you can do, and you knew it would happen one day, but now it's all gone you're just left feeling empty and, well… rather sad.

Defining urban fallow

Many different habitats fall into the definition of urban fallow, but fundamentally they all occur on land that has previously been developed but is no longer being used. This is, however, a very wide definition generally employed to describe brownfield land. Instead, urban fallow is perhaps more closely aligned with urban wasteland, which is usually defined as semi-natural vegetation that has developed on artificial substrates. These substrates can include the old foundations and remnants of buildings and factories, imported anthropogenic soils, and abandoned car parks and railway sidings. This slightly narrower definition is important, because the single-most influential factor that contributes to the development of urban fallow is the nature of the substrate. The depth and age of the soil, its chemistry and water relations, the amount of disturbance and the materials it includes all determine which species it can support.

This means that quite a lot of brownfield falls outside the definition of urban fallow, as these sprawling sites develop on a much wider range of disturbed soils, including old quarries and mine spoil heaps and **bings**, silt lagoons, brick pits, disused airfields, former munitions depots and large post-industrial sites (Buglife 2023). Although these sites can be spectacularly important for plants and invertebrates, their vegetation is essentially composed of semi-natural habitats like grasslands, woodlands and wetlands. Whole books, papers, PhD theses and websites are dedicated to their ecology, value, loss and conservation but, because they're often located towards the periphery of urban settlements, they fall slightly outside the remit of the urban core considered here. Instead, thinking of the abandoned steelworks, coal-fired power plants and old gravel quarries on the edge of major industrial cities like Sheffield, Swansea and Glasgow, these peri-urban sites tend to lie on the outer edges of the urban–rural gradient, helping to soften the interface between urban and rural and between industrial and agricultural.

For our purposes, then, urban fallow tends to apply to smaller inner-city sites that are more heavily urbanised and more directly influenced by their substrate. These plots of land litter the urban landscape and in planning terms are often classed as 'vacant or derelict land' (VDL). Prioritised as potential land for rebuilding, especially housing, there's a subtle difference between the two; vacant land can be built on again more or less straight away, while derelict land requires initial work to clear hazards or contaminated materials. In Great Britain, around 10% of the urban land area comprises derelict plots, usually less than one hectare in size (Austin 2002). This probably varies quite a bit from place to place; more up-to-date figures are difficult to obtain or put into context, but in Scotland the area of derelict and urban vacant land in 2022 was 9,236 ha (22,823 acres), or 5% of the total urban area, a decrease of 27% since 2016 (Gov.Scot 2023).

Urban fallow: waste ground and derelict land

As well as empty inner-city building and factory plots, urban fallow also includes other classic waste ground habitats, such as:

- odd-shaped fragments of unusable land between streets and buildings;
- unused strips of land or access tracks between industrial and commercial units, and alongside railways;
- old forecourts of abandoned garages and shops that open onto streets;
- unmanaged edges of rough car parking areas;
- old inner-city gas works and railway sidings;
- dumping grounds for landfill, building waste and fly-tipping;
- areas underneath flyovers and railway bridges;
- areas around city docks.

More than any other habitat, urban fallow encompasses a huge variety of sites and socio-economic situations, from derelict urban housing plots to areas earmarked for grand new infrastructure projects. They vary in size from just a few square metres to many hectares, and they range in age from just a year to several decades. But, despite this diversity, there are common threads to their ecology that tie these fragments of land together.

BELOW: Once the centre of a busy fishing industry, the old Lord Line dock offices at St Andrews Quay, Kingston upon Hull, were abandoned in the 1970s. The surrounding land now supports species-rich grasslands, wetlands and scrub.

Ecology of urban fallow

Urban fallow land can be exceptionally diverse, with a mosaic of disturbed ruderal habitats, dry and wet grassland and transitions to scrub and pioneer woodland. Four factors come together to encourage this unique richness (Salisbury *et al.* 2021, Woźniak *et al.* 2018). Firstly, urban fallow sites are usually **open and sparsely vegetated**, at least to begin with. Open ground is prime for colonisation, especially with ruderal and early-succession species as well as invasive non-native plants, so many different species can move in to occupy the land quickly. Secondly, **soils are often thin and nutrient poor**, and frequently contaminated with heavy metals. This helps smaller, less-competitive species get a foothold and the low fertility stunts the growth of more vigorous, dominant plants. Thirdly, urban fallow sites often have a **complex topography**, with dry ridges of earth, wet ditches, low areas prone to flooding and steep banks. This creates a lot of different microhabitats for plants to grow. Finally, the **lack of active management** means that succession is left to do its own thing, creating wonderfully varied mosaics of habitats over the years. In many ways, these are the sites where nature has had most opportunity to reclaim the former urban landscape, but you don't have to scratch far beneath the surface to see the rubble of their urban roots.

In an attempt to understand the relative importance of factors influencing urban fallow plant diversity, Bonthoux *et al.* (2014) reviewed the findings of 37 different studies into wasteland diversity, most of which were undertaken in cities across Europe, especially Germany, France and Great Britain. They found that the most important factors operated locally at the site level, while others acted at the landscape scale across many sites. Let's take a look at these in turn to see how they impact urban fallow.

Local site factors

It might seem a little obvious, but the size of the patch has a big effect on its diversity: the bigger the site, the more species it can support. In a study of 50 derelict urban sites in the West Midlands, Angold *et al.* (2006) found a very close correlation between patch size and diversity. In the Paris area, Muratet *et al.* (2007) found that as sites double in size, the number of species also nearly doubles. Of course, more species can occupy a site if more land is available. But, because of the heterogeneity of urban fallow land, larger sites also tend to have more micro-niches in close juxtaposition; a thin, droughted soil over an old cement floor may lie beside a deep, moist soil in a land drain, each supporting very different plants.

Perhaps more than anything, urban fallow is all about time. It represents a transition between the abandonment of our urban infrastructure and the establishment of recognisable semi-natural habitats like grasslands and woodlands (which are more characteristic of brownfield sites). The process of succession is similar to that seen on pavements, but here it is allowed to proceed for longer. A freshly cleared or recently abandoned site presents a golden opportunity for pioneer annuals to colonise the open substrate. If seeds are not already present in the soil seed bank, they need to arrive as quickly as possible. The plants that do arrive tend to produce lots of small, readily dispersed and long-lived seeds, all characteristics of pioneer species (Westermann et al. 2011). Plants of the daisy family (Asteraceae) and willowherbs *Epilobium* spp. are particularly common in young urban fallow habitats as their seeds have a pappus or parachute to aid wind dispersal (Austin 2002).

The first pioneering annuals are quickly joined by a few perennial species, which gradually come to dominate after several years. At the same time, woody species begin to get established, eventually creating dense scrub communities after a period of around 5–10 years. These later-successional species tend to produce larger, less readily dispersed seed, although some pioneer tree species are wind dispersed (Westermann et al. 2011). In Paris, a classic feature of vegetation succession was observed on urban fallow, whereby most species are seen in intermediate stages rather than at the beginning or end. Highest plant diversity (around 51 species) was noted on sites 4–13 years old. Younger sites had slightly fewer species (approx. 47), but older sites were markedly less diverse, with just 34–35 species. This decline in diversity over time occurs as dense stands of trees and shrubs become established, shading out the more diverse vegetation of open habitats (Muratet et al. 2007).

This process of succession rarely proceeds evenly across an urban fallow site. Thanks again to the heterogeneity of the substrate, it can be held back on thinner, less fertile and drier patches of soil, and on heavily contaminated soils or waterlogged soils. Ongoing disturbance from events such as fires, burrowing mammals and human activity also resets the ecological clock in places, creating new patches of bare open ground ready for colonisation (Angold *et al.* 2006). Complex mosaics of vegetation therefore often develop, with mixtures of annual communities developing in and around patches of perennials and interspersed with areas of scrub.

This mosaic is why many urban fallow sites are so fantastic for invertebrates. The diversity of plant species is matched with a diversity of vegetation structure, everything from carpets of tiny annuals to areas of tall grass and dense scrub, creating ideal conditions to support different life-stages of insects. Brownfield sites in the Thames Estuary alone, for example, support at least 100 Red Data Book and 400 Nationally Scarce species (Falk 2020). Plants characteristic of urban fallow often host many interesting invertebrates. The larvae of the widespread Mullein Moth *Cucullia verbasci*, for instance, feed on species of Mullein *Verbascum* spp. as well as Buddleja, while adults of the Nationally Scarce Large Yellow-face Bee *Hylaeus signatus* forage mainly from Weld *Reseda luteola* and Wild Mignonette *R. lutea*. Two other common urban fallow plants, Mugwort *Artemisia vulgaris* and Wormwood *A. absinthium*, support several Red Data Book species of Tumbling Flower Beetles *Mordellistena* spp., which are known to nest in their stems (Bodsworth *et al.* 2005).

The soil, then, is critical to the development of urban fallow, and can be rather complex in nature. Repeatedly modified and disturbed, it's usually a mixture of native and imported soil, along with anthropogenic admixtures including bricks, concrete, aggregates, sand, asphalt, flagstones and compacted ballast, as well as many other building and construction materials such as plastic water and drainpipes, electrical cables and conduits, waste insulation material, chipboard, metal fragments and ceramic tiles. These inclusions can influence the physical properties of the soil, its moisture levels, permeability, drainage, pH, fertility and mineral content. In all the studies of wasteland vegetation reviewed by Bonthoux *et al.* (2014), soil properties had the greatest influence on plant communities. In Brussels, for example, Godefroid *et al.* (2007) found that higher pH caused by the inclusion of concrete favoured Buddleja, Annual Mercury *Mercurialis annua*, Bittersweet *Solanum dulcamara* and Narrow-leaved Ragwort *Senecio inaequidens*. Higher soil moisture encouraged Ivy *Hedera helix*, Hedge Bindweed *Calystegia sepium* and Creeping Bent *Agrostis stolonifera*, while higher soil nutrients favoured Knotgrass *Polygonum aviculare*, Annual Meadow-grass *Poa annua*, Greater Plantain

Urban fallow: waste ground and derelict land

LEFT: The Large Yellow-face Bee is a striking solitary bee with a dark body and a pale yellow 'mask' on its face. It is mainly found scattered throughout southern and central England. Here it is foraging on Weld.

Plantago major and Common Nettle *Urtica dioica*. On rubble soils, though, Common Mallow, Hoary Willowherb *Epilobium parviflorum* and Meadow Fescue *Schedonorus pratensis* were more frequent. Overall, they discovered that rubble and sand created a distinct vegetation community, which was very different to the one that developed on concrete and stone. Generally, urban fallow soils are highly diverse and variable across sites, sometimes varying in pH from as acidic as 2.2 to as alkaline as 7.7 (Godefroid *et al.* 2007).

Another feature of many urban fallows is that they're generally rather flat. Unlike large areas of brownfield, these smaller sites are often graded with bulldozers after being cleared, excising topographic features and levelling them ready for future building work. This can affect microclimate and micro-niche availability by removing slopes and banks that might face the sun or create shade, changing the local temperature and humidity. Such factors might not sound very important, but in Brussels, Godefroid *et al.* (2007) found these were remarkably significant, affecting the distribution of plants like Common Poppy *Papaver rhoeas*, Fat Hen *Chenopodium album* and Shepherd's-purse *Capsella bursa-pastoris*, which preferred to grow in sunnier spots with marginally higher temperatures.

Wider landscape factors

Because local site conditions are so instrumental in the development of urban fallow, wider landscape factors have less of an influence, but they do play a role. The most important of these is the degree of habitat fragmentation, which affects the movement of species between sites. In the West Midlands, 25 species were found to be significantly more frequent on urban fallow sites if other similar sites were close by (Austin 2002). These included plants like Wormwood and Fennel *Foeniculum vulgare* that are real signatures of urban fallow. In Berlin, Westermann *et al.* (2011) found that which species grew on abandoned railway sites was largely determined by the proportion of ruderal and woodland habitats in the immediate vicinity, suggesting that longer-range dispersal was limited.

Urban fallow sites are particularly prone to being isolated within landscapes of tall buildings and broad expanses of pavement, concrete or tarmac. These potentially reduce the movement of seeds and other propagules between sites. This 'hemming-in' of urban fallow was seen in Paris, where Muratet *et al.* (2007) found that if a site was within 200m of a building, the proportion of infrequent species declined, so small sites surrounded by buildings were instead dominated by common species. Similarly, Godefroid *et al.* (2007) found that in Brussels, urban fallow sites completely surrounded by walls had a lower plant diversity than open sites.

Buildings, then, act as barriers to dispersal. But plants do get around and colonise small patches of urban fallow. It's likely that the early stages of succession are assisted by wind dispersal and the movement of small, lightweight seeds in soil carried around on people's footwear and by traffic. In a fascinating study in Paris, Muratet *et al.* (2013) found that the number of footpaths between patches of urban fallow accounted for the similarity between plant communities better than the straightforward distance between them. This suggests that the 'flow' between sites – traffic from direct on-the-ground connections like walking, driving and the

BELOW: Fennel is often seen by roadsides, where its spread may be assisted by vehicles.

ABOVE: Paths such as these through a wildflower area in Burgess Park, London, are ideal places where seeds can be picked up on our footwear and carried to other sites. This flow of seeds connects the sites and helps the rapid colonisation of new areas nearby.

LEFT: Small patches of urban fallow are often isolated by buildings and broad expanses of tarmac, such as here in Llandudno Junction, Conwy. These highly fragmented sites are most readily colonised by common plants with light, wind-dispersed seeds, like Common Ragwort *Jacobaea vulgaris* and Spear Thistle *Cirsium vulgare*.

movement of mammals – might be more important in spreading urban species around than we realise. These routes through the landscape are very different to intentional 'urban green corridors' (strips of semi-natural habitats such as grasslands and woodlands alongside rivers, roads and railways), which have been rather comprehensively dismissed as conduits of plant diversity between urban fallow patches (Angold *et al.* 2006, Austin 2002). In the urban landscape, plants move around readily in the wake of our footsteps and our vehicles, not through green corridors we might construct for them.

What grows on urban fallow?

The short answer is, almost anything! Given the huge diversity of urban fallow soils and the range in age of sites, it's no surprise such places support more plant species than any other urban habitats. This is why exploring them can be so thrilling. In the *New Atlas*, more than 700 species are mentioned as growing on 'waste ground' or in 'waste places' (Preston *et al.* 2002). This huge number reflects the sheer diversity of vegetation communities that develop over time, from carpets of tiny ruderal annuals to dense stands of scrub and trees.

Several surveys of urban fallow sites in Great Britain and Europe reveal just how rich they can be, which species predominate, and the unusual communities they form. Some of the earliest studies examined the regrowth that occurred on Second World War bomb sites and provide a fascinating insight into the flora that colonised and how they arose. The most famous study, by Jones (1957), looked at 85 sites in six areas of London during 1952, 1953 and 1955, around 11 to 15 years after the last air raids. The largest of these sites, the Cripplegate area, gives an idea of the scale of destruction: it was a 39-acre scar half a mile long by a quarter of a mile wide with almost nothing standing. Importantly, it was noted that much of the rubble had been removed, leaving only basement floors and walls up to ground level. Habitats

BELOW: A decade after the Blitz, the bombed remains of Noble Street in Cripplegate, London, had developed a varied flora. The first trees and shrubs are getting established between well-worn paths, and rough grassland covers much of the ground.

were varied and included brick scree, paths and roads, tips, former gardens and walls. Many sites became oases of green among the destruction, and some were even enhanced with paths and plantings to make them more attractive and to grow vegetables.

The flora of these sites gives a valuable insight into the evolution of urban fallow, and the social, cultural and historical influences behind the origins of different plants. Although the surveys were undertaken around 70 years ago, many of the species remain dominant features of our cities, while others have declined. Some plants that were rare back then have since surged in abundance. An impressive 342 species were found on the bomb sites. Jones categorised these by their different modes of dispersal. Not surprisingly on such open sites, **wind-dispersed (amenochorus) plants** were the most frequent, especially Rosebay Willowherb *Chamaenerion angustifolium* (99% of sites; see Chapter 2). Other abundant wind-dispersed plants included Oxford Ragwort *Senecio squalidus* (100% of sites), Canadian Fleabane *Erigeron canadensis* (99%), Creeping and Spear Thistles *Cirsium arvense* and *C. vulgare* (both 100%) and Coltsfoot *Tussilago farfara* (98%). It's interesting to note the presence of some rapidly expanding plants that we might think of as more recent arrivals, including Tree-of-heaven *Ailanthus altissima* on four sites and Great Lettuce *Lactuca virosa* on five.

Perhaps the most unexpected mode of dispersal on the bomb sites was **horses**, or rather the seeds carried in their hay, food nosebags and dung. There were still quite a few horses in London streets in the 1940s and when roads were swept, their dung was thrown against the base of walls. The hay usually came from two types of meadow. Traditional lowland

ABOVE: Rosebay Willowherb growing in the bombed ruins of St Andrew's Church, Holborn, London, 1946.

BELOW: Chicory was commonly grown for horse fodder in the 1940s and 1950s. Today, it's increasing again thanks to a renewed interest in its use in forage crops and its popularity in wildflower seed mixes.

LEFT: Lady's-bedstraw often grew on London bomb sites after being brought into the city with hay for horses, or from seed in their dung. The flowers were once used to give Double Gloucester cheese its colour.

RIGHT: Wall vegetation on London's Second World War bomb sites was often rather sparse, with Perennial Wall-rocket being the most frequent species. Even today, the British headquarters of this species is in and around London.

neutral hay meadows gave rise to 42 species including Red Clover *Trifolium pratense*, Oxeye Daisy *Leucanthemum vulgare*, Lady's Bedstraw *Galium verum* and Meadow Vetchling *Lathyrus pratensis*, as well as 19 different grasses such as Sweet Vernal-grass *Anthoxanthum odoratum*, Meadow Foxtail *Alopecurus pratensis* and Yellow Oat-grass *Trisetum flavescens*. Several species once commonly grown in meadows as fodder plants, like Sainfoin *Onobrychis viciifolia*, Chicory *Cichorium intybus* and Lucerne *Medicago sativa* subsp. *sativa*, were also found. Hay also came from annually cultivated leys composed of various mixed crops, and 30 species originated from these including annual cornfield weeds such as Common Poppy, Sun Spurge *Euphorbia helioscopia*, Fool's Parsley *Aethusa cynapium* and Scarlet Pimpernel *Lysimachia arvensis*. Bomb sites in Finsbury and Cripplegate even yielded Shepherd's-needle *Scandix pecten-veneris*, an arable species which today is very rare and declining.

Among these was a wide range of other species. Annual Meadow-grass was once again near the top of the list, found on 99% of sites, along with Mugwort (98%), Procumbent Pearlwort (84%) and Wall Barley *Hordeum murinum* (82%). Bracken *Pteridium aquilinum* was surprisingly common, found at 98% of sites, mainly because its spores germinated so readily on screes of broken bricks. It became customary for city workers to eat their sandwiches and fruit on the open sites at midday, so **edible plants** like Cherry *Prunus avium*, Apple

Malus sylvestris and Plum *Prunus domestica* were common, and even single plants of Orange *Citrus aurantium* and Peach *Prunus persica*. Eighteen sites were home to Tomato *Solanum lycopersicum* and one plant of Hop *Humulus lupulus* was, appropriately, found near the Whitbread Brewery. **Wall vegetation** was noted as being rather sparse, possibly through the effects of fire and demolition of the walls, and the fact that many walls were remnants of basements. Just five species occurred regularly, the most common of which was Perennial Wall-rocket *Diplotaxis tenuifolia*, found at 67% of sites. Ivy-leaved Toadflax *Cymbalaria muralis* was remarkably rare, occurring at just six sites.

The final large group of plants that Jones found on bomb sites were those arising from **horticulture**. This group of 68 species included escapes from gardens, throw-outs from office window-boxes, and seed that was deliberately scattered on the sites to make them more attractive, an understandable practice that was especially prevalent shortly after the war. Evening-primrose *Oenothera* spp. was the most abundant of these, found on 58% of sites, followed by Purple Toadflax (40%), Pot Marigold *Calendula officinalis* (39%) and Hollyhock *Alcea rosea* (35%). At this time, Buddleja was still relatively uncommon, found on just 34% of sites. Even more surprisingly, both Red Valerian *Centranthus ruber* and Yellow Corydalis *Pseudofumaria lutea* were particularly rare, each occurring on just two sites. Other rare escapes included Chinese-lantern *Alkekengi officinarum*, Mexican Aster *Cosmos bipinnatus* and Goat's-rue *Galega officinalis*.

Many of the processes and patterns of colonisation described by Jones (1957) would

ABOVE: Evening-primroses were often sown on bomb sites to make the rubble scars more attractive. They are still common today; this Large-flowered Evening-primrose *O. glazioviana* is flowering near St Pancras Station, London.

BELOW: Colt's-foot can form large patches on urban fallow land. Its flowers appear in March and April before the leaves emerge, making it an important early source of food for pollinators.

ABOVE: A large area of urban fallow at Balsall Heath, Birmingham, with developing scrub of birch *Betula* sp., Buddleja and Sea-buckthorn *Hippophae rhamnoides*. Highlighting the transient nature of such habitats, the area is earmarked for redevelopment by 2040 as part of Birmingham's Big City Plan.

have occurred in other British cities bombed during the Blitz, the echoes of which are still felt today. Jones's survey is one of many similar studies across European cities, especially Berlin, that stimulated a wider interest in urban floras (Sukopp 2002, 2003). People began to take a serious interest in the plants growing in anthropogenic habitats, often for the first time, and urban ecology started to emerge as a new and exciting discipline.

In the early 1980s, two studies examined the vegetation of urban fallow habitats in Great Britain. In Birmingham, Haigh (1980) looked at 30 different 'weed patch sites' on derelict building plots. He found 61 species, of which 15 occurred on more than half the sites. Top of his list were meadow-grasses *Poa* spp. (found on 90% of sites), followed by Colt's-foot (86%), Oxford Ragwort (80%), Dandelion *Taraxacum* agg. (72%), Curled Dock *Rumex crispus* (70%), Groundsel *Senecio vulgaris* (70%), White Clover *Trifolium repens* (70%), Rosebay Willowherb (67%), Creeping Thistle (67%) and Mugwort (60%). Meanwhile, in Sheffield, Clemens *et al.* (1983) surveyed 47 urban demolition sites – mostly former terraced housing with small gardens – that had been bulldozed and abandoned for five years or more. The most frequent species they encountered show many similarities with the Birmingham survey, with Colt's-foot (76% of quadrats), Dandelion (74%), Oxford Ragwort (56%), Creeping Thistle (54%), Rosebay Willowherb (53%) and White Clover (32%) topping the list.

Urban fallow: waste ground and derelict land

Mugwort was less common at 24%, while grasses were more frequent, especially Creeping Bent (60%), Perennial Rye-grass *Lolium perenne* (60%) and Yorkshire-fog *Holcus lanatus* (58%).

More recently, a detailed survey of urban fallow was undertaken by Kevin Austin, who surveyed 50 urban derelict sites in and around Birmingham, Sutton Coldfield, Wolverhampton and Dudley in the West Midlands in 1998–99 (Austin 2002). These included city-centre, suburban and urban-fringe habitats, mostly bulldozed houses and factories but also abandoned railway tracks and embankments, disturbed road edges, filled-in refuse tips and quarries and some former farmland and arable. The youngest site had been bulldozed two years before the study, while the oldest had lain derelict for 20 years – long enough to develop quite mature stands of vegetation. In total, he recorded an extraordinary 378 species. Of these, 67% were native, 20% were neophytes and 13% were archaeophytes, perhaps a lower proportion of aliens than expected given their apparent abundance in urban fallow.

In a pattern we've also witnessed on pavements and walls, a few of these plants (27 species) formed the core of an urban fallow community found repeatedly on many sites (more than three quarters of them in this case), while the vast majority of species occurred sporadically on just a handful; 225 species (60%) occurred on just five or fewer sites. These latter were a truly eclectic mix of species, making them perhaps the most unexpected and thrilling element of the urban fallow flora. They included everything from Common Spotted-orchid *Dactylorhiza fuchsii* in an old brickworks used for landfill, to Wild Onion *Allium vineale* on an abandoned rubbish tip and even Marsh Hawk's-beard *Crepis paludosa*, a plant normally found on damp riverbanks in northern Britain, growing in the garden of a demolished house.

Brick rubble from demolished buildings was home to an especially rich flora. Different sites on this substrate supported aliens as diverse as Stag's-horn Sumach *Rhus typhina*, an invasive shrub from eastern North America, the popular border perennial Russell Lupin *Lupinus × regalis* and French Marigold *Tagetes patula*, a familiar bedding annual originally from Mexico.

BELOW: Wild Onion, a native species of rough grassland, hedges, verges and disturbed ground. Some forms produce bulbils in the flowerheads that drop and grow straight away, allowing it to increase rapidly.

Urban peas

With more than 19,600 species, the pea family (Fabaceae) is the third-largest flowering-plant family in the world, after daisies (Asteraceae) and orchids (Orchidaceae). Many seem to have a particular penchant for urban habitats, especially urban fallow. In Britain and Ireland, these include a wide range of native and alien clovers, vetches, medicks, tares and melilots, as well as peas and beans and even a few trees. Many do well on urban sites thanks to symbiotic bacteria in their root nodules that fix nitrogen, giving them an advantage on infertile, skeletal soils. The species below are worth looking out for and give an idea of the range of plants in the family.

Goat's-rue *Galegea officinalis*
This perennial herb can form large clumps of arching stems clothed with spikes of lilac-pink flowers. Originally from central and southern Europe east to Pakistan, it's popular in gardens and was first recorded in the wild on ballast in Hartlepool (Co. Durham) in 1866. Recently, it has started to spread rapidly, with a big increase in records since 1990, especially in the London area where it's become widespread (Stroh *et al.* 2023). It seeds itself along path sides, road verges and railway embankments, and in some urban fallow sites has become an aggressive invasive that's difficult to control.

False-acacia *Robinia pseudoacacia*
Very popular in gardens and widely planted as a street tree and as part of amenity plantings, this fast-growing deciduous tree can eventually reach 25m in height. It bears drooping clusters of lightly scented white flowers. Originally from eastern North America, it was first noted in the wild in 1888 and has steadily increased since then, mainly in lowland England. In mainland Europe, it's an extremely invasive species in both urban and rural settings, reproducing by both seed and vigorous suckering from the roots. Although it's not behaving in the same way here yet, it has become problematic on pavements and urban fallow in London and may turn more aggressive as our climate warms.

Broad-leaved Everlasting-pea *Lathyrus latifolius*
This is one of several similar, large herbaceous climbers that tend to scramble up and flop over surrounding vegetation, fences and other supports. Originally from southern Europe,

Goat's-rue.

False-acacia.

it is popular for its intense pink flowers and frequently escapes, forming long-lived colonies on railway embankments, road verges and urban fallow. It appears to be increasing, becoming particularly frequent in London and in towns and cities in the English West Midlands. Similar species include Two-flowered Everlasting-pea *Lathyrus grandiflorus* and our native Narrow-leaved Everlasting-pea *L. sylvestris*.

Lucerne *Medicago sativa* subsp. *sativa*
With its long and rather obscure history as a fodder crop for livestock, this perennial herb was once very widely cultivated for hay or as a green manure. It thrives particularly well on dry, sandy soils where its deep roots can reach moisture. Although less frequently grown now, there is renewed interest in the species as a component of herbal leys, and it's also sometimes sown in wildflower mixtures. It's found on path sides, pavements and waste ground, especially in the London area and the English West Midlands north to Newcastle upon Tyne.

Hare's-foot Clover *Trifolium arvense*
This adorable and distinctive little clover is a native annual, usually found by the coast on sand dunes, heaths and sea cliffs. However, it's now become frequent in urban areas inland, often appearing on railway ballast, waste ground and, occasionally, pavements, where it relishes the open conditions and free-draining, sandy soil. It's particularly common in and around Birmingham, Nottingham, Sheffield and Liverpool. It sometimes makes surprise appearances on green roofs, where it's introduced in wildflower seed mixtures, and is also spread around in excavated sands and gravels used for construction.

Broad-leaved Everlasting-pea.

Lucerne.

Hare's-foot Clover.

This substrate also produced some surprising natives, including Harebell *Campanula rotundifolia*, a declining species in England, and – astonishingly – several sites for Allseed *Linum radiola*, a rare annual normally found growing in the damp, peaty hollows of acid heathland. Brick rubble seems to be a particularly good substrate for urban fallow vegetation; a survey of brownfield sites in Berlin and Bremen, Germany, showed that plots with brick rubble had more species, higher plant cover and higher plant density than those without. They were also less acidic and richer in nutrients such as potassium and phosphorus (Schadek *et al.* 2009).

All the common urban fallow species in Austin's survey are familiar native perennials of rough, disturbed and relatively fertile soil. Top of the list, and found in more than 90% of the sites, were Creeping Bent, Rosebay Willowherb, Creeping Thistle, Yorkshire-fog, Perennial Ryegrass, Ribwort Plantain *Plantago lanceolata*, Dandelion, Cock's-foot *Dactylis glomerata*, White Clover, Common Nettle and Black Medick *Medicago lupulina*. These tend to form rather weedy communities dominated by vigorous, highly competitive species with fewer associates.

Surprisingly, some of the aliens we might think of as emblematic of urban fallow habitats today were less frequent, for example Oxford Ragwort (60% of sites), Mugwort (54%), Buddleja (50%), Prickly Lettuce (44%), Purple Toadflax (38%), Canadian Goldenrod *Solidago canadensis* (38%) and Canadian Fleabane (43%). This could reflect the inclusion of some urban-fringe sites in the survey, which included grassy disturbed road verges and even fallow arable land on the outskirts of town. Generally, more neophytes were found in sites that were larger, more urban, and closer to gardens, although some species, such as Michaelmas-daisies *Symphyotrichum*, Beaked Hawk's-beard *Crepis vesicaria* and Broad-leaved Everlasting-pea *Lathyrus latifolius*, were more closely associated with abandoned railways.

A survey of 98 wasteland sites in the Hauts-de-Seine district of Paris, one of the most densely inhabited parts of France, revealed similar results to those from the West Midlands (Muratet *et al.* 2007). Again, the sites were rather broadly defined; as well as abandoned building sites and housing and industrial plots, they included irregularly managed gardens, parks, golf courses and sport fields as well as disturbed woodland edges or riverbanks. In total, 365 species were found, just 13 fewer than the West Midlands survey. The poorest sites were home to as few as five species, but the richest had 92 and

ABOVE: Stag's-horn Sumach *Rhus typhina*, a popular, if invasive, shrub or small tree grown in gardens. It spreads by suckers and most occurrences are relicts of old gardens, but the species does occasionally set seed if male and female plants are present.

the average was 39 species per site. The Paris sites had a slightly lower proportion of aliens, at 20% of species compared to 33%.

Again, the familiar urban pattern of 'few-species-in-lots-of-sites and lots-of-species-in-few-sites' was seen. Nine species were found in more than half the sites, namely Mugwort, Creeping Thistle, Ribwort Plantain, Hawkweed Oxtongue *Picris hieracioides*, Common Nettle, Dandelion, Hedge Bindweed, Broad-leaved Dock *Rumex obtusifolius* and Buddleja. Again, all these are perennials that prefer fertile soils in urban areas and produce copious seed that's easily dispersed. On the other hand, 109 species (30%) were only recorded once, including unusual plants like Grass-poly *Lythrum hyssopifolia*, White Mullein *Verbascum lychnitis* and Cypress Spurge *Euphorbia cyparissias*.

As with the West Midlands survey, emblematic aliens of urban fallow were perhaps less common than might have been expected. Five of the most invasive species of the Paris area were surprisingly infrequent: Buddleja (50% of sites), Canadian Goldenrod (21%), Tree-of-heaven (20%), False-acacia (20%) and Japanese Knotweed *Reynoutria japonica* (18%), while Narrow-leaved Ragwort, considered by some to be invasive and almost exclusive to wasteland, occurred in just 6% of sites. Again, this is probably down to the broader definition of waste ground in the study, which included occasionally mown grasslands and disturbed semi-natural sites. On the other hand, it might be that the showy garden escapes tend to catch our attention in these habitats, making them seem more frequent than they actually are.

Buddleja: the beautiful beast

Few plants are more emblematic of the urban landscape than Buddleja *Buddleja davidii*. Springing up in endless profusion on walls, pavements, railways and waste ground, it elicits strong reactions. Loved and loathed in equal measure, it's the association with dereliction and decay that irked TV and radio presenter, Adrian Chiles, when he wrote in the *Guardian*: 'It's not a bad-looking thing with its slender purple flowers; a splash of colour swaying in the monochrome of unloved, uncared for, unproductive land and property; but how much better it would be if we lived in a country where it had nowhere to grow … send the buddleia back to China, I say' (Chiles 2019). Of course, some people (including me) – and a vast horde of pollinating insects – might beg to differ.

Buddleja was first brought to European attention by Père Armand David (1826–1900), a gifted teacher and Catholic missionary who travelled extensively in China, Tibet and Mongolia in three expeditions from 1862 to 1873. A gentle man with a deep respect for the cultures in which he lived and travelled, he was an exceptional all-round naturalist with an interest in geology, ornithology, zoology and botany. As well as Buddleja (which bears his name, *davidii*), he was the first Westerner to see one of the world's most beautiful trees, the Dove Tree or Handkerchief Tree *Davidia involucrata*, and a creature he described as 'a most excellent black and white bear', the Panda *Ailuropoda melanoleuca*. There is, perhaps, a rather beautiful irony in his connection with both Buddleja, one of the world's most unpopular invasives, and the Panda, a much-loved global symbol for nature conservation.

In its native range, Buddleja is an opportunist shrub that makes the most of a wide variety of disturbed habitats. It's as happy with a precarious life clinging to rocky mountain cliffs up to 3,500m as it is on the shingle banks of lowland rivers, where thickets were described by one early visitor to China as providing 'famous harbourage to tigers' (Gilbert 1992b). Importantly, it also grows in disturbed anthropogenic habitats in China, including walls, roadsides and abandoned cultivated land (Tallent-Halsell & Watt 2009).

Following its discovery, it didn't simply arrive in Europe and take off, but suffered a rather stuttering start. Several early introductions of seed produced rather weak and straggly plants with insipid flowers. Then, in 1893, seeds from near the spectacular mountainous Tibetan border town of Kanding (then called Tatsienlu) were sent to Louis de Vilmorin in France, a horticulturalist specialising in breeding and selecting new forms of plants. These produced much stronger, more upright shrubs with strongly coloured flowers, giving them huge horticultural potential. Three years later, in 1896, seeds from these Kanding plants were sent on to Kew Gardens in London (Ebeling & Tallent-Halsell 2009, Tallent-Halsell & Watt 2009).

Buddleja quickly became extremely popular with British gardeners, and it wasn't too long before it jumped over the garden wall. Rather

Seeds of Buddleja ripen three weeks after flowering and a large specimen can produce three million seeds, 95% of which are carried at least 10m from the bush.

than spreading outwards from one point of escape, it launched its invasion on many fronts. The seaside town of Harlech in Merionethshire takes the honour of the first record in the wild, when renowned botanist George Claridge Druce discovered it there in 1922. Other sites followed quickly, including the base of a cliff near St Lawrence on the Isle of Wight in 1923 and, in an early foray into the habitat it would come to dominate, fallow land in Cardiff Docks in 1924. Today, it's recorded from nearly 70% of 10-km squares in Britain and Ireland and is continuing to spread, especially in the north and west.

Of course, the purple spikes of exceptionally fragrant flowers that we find so attractive are designed purely for one thing – pollination. In *Flora Britannica*, Richard Mabey (1996) reports seeing more than 50 butterflies and moths of 10 different species on a single bush in his garden at once. The heady scent is formed from a unique and complex cocktail of 41 different compounds, each of which produces a different fragrance 'note' (Andersson *et al.* 2002). Each compound will trigger various detection and feeding responses in different pollinating invertebrates, including bees, beetles and flies, and the scent even attracts some insect pests that feed on Buddleja (Guédot *et al.* 2008). Some of the compounds produced by the flowers and their associated fragrance notes include:

- 4-oxoisophorone – honey, tea, woody-musty smells, tobacco and saffron
- benzaldehyde – bitter almonds and cherry
- 6-methyl-5-hepten-2-one – citronella and lemongrass
- hexyl acetate – fresh green apple and pear
- (Z)-cinnamaldehyde – cinnamon
- ß-cyclocitral – saffron, sweet-tobacco, grape and rose

Of these, 4-oxoisophorone is particularly strong and characteristic of Buddleja, which is why many people liken the smell to honey with musty undertones. As well as scent, pollinators are attracted to the flowers by visual cues (Lehner *et al.* 2022). The purple colour is a strong overall

The flowers of Buddleja produce a scent of honey with woody-musty and tobacco undertones.

signal, but the bright orange blotch at the centre of each flower helps direct pollinators to the corolla tube where the nectar is located. This colour comes from crocin, a compound that also gives the stamens of Saffron Crocus *Crocus sativus* their strong orange colour and which is also used as a yellow food colouring (Ahrazem *et al.* 2017).

Buddleja on old pavement cobbles in Dublin Docklands.

Using a more precise definition of urban fallow that's perhaps closer to ours, Godefroid *et al.* (2007) surveyed 22 wasteland sites in Brussels. All the sites were unused or vacant plots of land, including former industrial sites and large building areas such as demolished houses where the vegetation had developed spontaneously. They found far fewer species, just 74 in all, but this may be because they only surveyed an average of two 4m^2 plots at each site rather than listing all the species to be found. Most frequent were Buddleja (37% of sites), Creeping Thistle (37%), Wall Barley (26%), Greater Plantain (26%), Common Couch *Elymus repens* (24%), Broad-leaved Dock (21%) and Canadian Fleabane (21%). Again, these are all species that produce large quantities of seed and that thrive on fertile, disturbed soils.

Urban fallow communities and succession

Given the wide diversity of soils, huge range of species, and the rapid development and turnover of habitats over time, it's not surprising that getting to grips with urban fallow vegetation communities is a challenge. In addition, most of the research focus has been in Europe, particularly Eastern European countries such as Poland, the Czech Republic, Hungary and Bulgaria (Mucina 1990), the majority of which use the Braun-Blanquet system of vegetation classification which is unfamiliar to most British botanists. Another stumbling block is that our own National Vegetation Classification (NVC) doesn't cover urban habitats, although some of the arable-weed communities of 'vegetation of open habitats' are found in urban settings (Rodwell 2006). However, surveying plants on derelict land in the English Midlands, Shepherd (1992) identified 17 different vegetation communities and matched them to the European classification. Austin (2002) developed this further with his own English Midlands survey, matching Shepherd's classification with the NVC. He found the match was generally rather poor, especially for early-pioneer communities, of which only 19% could be matched. Indeed, five of these, including one characterised by Oxford Ragwort and Canadian Fleabane, were particularly distinct and didn't match any NVC community, suggesting that they're unique signatures of urban fallow habitats.

Once a site has been demolished and cleared, the process of succession begins more or less straight away as pioneer annuals colonise the ground. It continues through taller perennial herb and grass communities and on through scrub until either the climax scrub woodland vegetation is reached or – and this is a much more likely scenario in urban fallow – until the site is disturbed again or redeveloped.

Various successional stages can be recognised, each with their own suite of communities depending on local site conditions. Borrowing the terminology of Gilbert (1989), these can be described as the **Oxford Ragwort Pioneer Stage**, the **Rosebay Willowherb Tall-herb Stage**, the **Coarse Grassland Stage** and the **Buddleja Scrub-woodland Stage**. Each of these is described in more detail below. Both Shepherd (1992) and Austin (2002) build on these stages, adding considerable detail to the different communities that can be found in them and relating them to different vegetation classifications. Local variations are enormous, but the type and style of the vegetation usually remains similar and can be recognised wherever you are. One important point is that most plants aren't exclusive to individual stages but tend to appear in different quantities at different times. So, Buddleja, for example, will often arrive in the first pioneer stage and persist through all stages of the succession, but not develop into dominant stands of Buddleja scrub for quite a few years.

The Oxford Ragwort Pioneer Stage

The first stage of colonisation is dominated by annuals, along with a few short-lived perennials, usually arriving from wind-borne seed or from the soil seed bank. Many of the annuals commonly seen on pavements, such as Rue-leaved Saxifrage *Saxifraga tridactylites*, Annual Meadow-grass, Groundsel and willowherbs *Epilobium* spp., can predominate, sometimes in breathtaking quantities. Colonisation of the bare ground can be rapid: one site in Sheffield cleared in January 1981 was home to 41 different species by the following August, with only 13 additional species arriving over the next four years (Gilbert 1989). Pioneer bryophytes also make the most of the open soil, particularly acrocarpous species such as Bonfire-moss *Funaria hygrometrica*, Lesser Bird's-claw Beard-moss *Streblotrichum convolutum*, Silver-moss *Bryum argenteum* and Bicoloured Bryum *Bryum dichotomum*. More acidic locations can be colonised with dense stands of Redshank *Ceratodon purpureus*, while wetter sites are sometimes colonised with the almost white shoots of Pale Glaucous Thread-moss *Pohlia wahlenbergii*.

As well as annuals, biennials can be frequent in the first few years, particularly species like Wild Carrot *Daucus carota* subsp. *carota*,

ABOVE: The first stage of urban fallow is dominated by annuals and biennials, such as in this fenced-off patch of building land with Hoary Mustard *Hirschfeldia incana* and Wild Teasel, and the first few perennials like Purple Toadflax and Mugwort.

Weld *Reseda luteola*, Viper's-bugloss *Echium vulgare*, Great Mullein *Verbascum thapsus*, Common Evening-primrose *Oenothera biennis* and Wild Teasel *Dipsacus fullonum* growing in great abundance on the bare soil. Most of these prefer more lime-rich soils; on more acidic sites, Foxglove *Digitalis purpurea* can spread rapidly. Wind-dispersed shrubs such as Buddleja and Goat Willow *Salix caprea* also usually appear now, along with a wide range of perennials such as Rosebay Willowherb which can come to dominate. New species arrive over the following few years and the diversity of the site usually reaches its highest at this point, sometimes with nearly twice as many species as later stages (Austin 2002). The edges of the site are often the richest, especially if bounded by roads or paths where new species can be introduced by vehicles and people.

As the name of this vegetation stage implies, Oxford Ragwort often becomes a dominant pioneer species. It's helped by its exceptionally long flowering period, which lasts from March through to December thanks to the successive flowering of axillary flowerheads as the plants grow. Plants will often carry budding, flowering and seeding inflorescences all at the same time. Its huge seed production (around 10,000 seeds per plant) and ability to germinate year-round mean it can quickly form dense stands, colouring urban fallow land bright yellow for many months. This species is often encountered in association with Canadian Fleabane, and other alien fleabanes such as Guernsey Fleabane *Erigeron sumatrensis* and Bilbao Fleabane *E. floribundus*, forming a distinct community that's especially frequent on thin, dry soils over brick rubble, concrete, gravel and abandoned railways (Austin 2002). This community, which will be familiar to anyone who has botanised urban streets, railway stations and waste ground, is not covered by the NVC and seems to be uniquely urban.

Another very common pioneer community developing at this stage is characterised by Hedge Mustard *Sisymbrium officinale* and Scentless Mayweed *Tripleurospermum inodorum*, along with Smooth Sow-thistle *Sonchus oleraceus*, Yorkshire-fog *Holcus lanatus* and Barren Brome *Anisantha sterilis*. This community is particularly frequent on brick rubble and mounds of earth around the edges of sites with well-drained, dry soils. On more fertile soils, such as old gardens or where topsoil has been spread or dumped, different communities form. One is characterised by Common Fumitory *Fumaria officinalis* and Common Field-speedwell *Veronica persica*, while even more nutrient-rich sites have another characterised by Common Chickweed *Stellaria media* and Shepherd's-purse. Of course, other common weeds of cultivation will join these, such as Petty Spurge *Euphorbia peplus*, Common Poppy and Small Nettle *Urtica urens*.

Several other pioneer communities appear to be unique to urban habitats. One is characterised by Wall Barley, which can form dense stands on open waste ground, but is perhaps more commonly associated with the bases of walls, the edges of paths, car parks and roadsides. In contrast, a community characterised by Rat's-tail Fescue *Vulpia myuros* and another characterised by Mouse-ear-hawkweed *Pilosella officinarum* are both almost exclusively found on the dry, nutrient-poor clinker and cinders of disused railway lines.

ABOVE: Two biennials together. Native Viper's-bugloss is joined by an alien Evening-primrose, some species of which arrived on ship's ballast through ports such as Liverpool.

BELOW: Weld often grows in abundance in the first few years of urban fallow, especially on lime-rich soil. Known in Great Britain since the Iron Age, it has long been cultivated for making a yellow dye.

From Sicily to city slicker: why is Oxford Ragwort such an urban success?

Oxford Ragwort *Senecio squalidus* has to be one of our most familiar urban flowers. It's often so joyously abundant on pavements, walls, waste ground, railways and road verges that it's difficult to believe it only appeared after escaping from Oxford Botanic Garden in 1794. But understanding how it got here in the first place has required some remarkable detective work and genetic analysis, the details of which have only recently been resolved.

The original story relates that seeds of the species were brought to Oxford from Sicily, where the plant grows on the flanks of Mt Etna, Europe's most active volcano. However, it soon became clear the plant is actually a hybrid between two other species growing on the mountain. The first of these, *Senecio aethnensis*, is a high-altitude plant, growing in the barren landscape of old lava flows above 2,500m. Flowering for just a short period during July and August, it's adapted to cope with high UV light and high levels of sulphur pollution, always helpful if you live on an active volcano. It's also cold tolerant, being regularly covered by snow in spring. By contrast the other parent, *S. chrysanthemifolius*, grows at the base of the mountain, below 700m. Thriving on disturbed agricultural ground and roadsides, it's a ruderal species adapted to intense heat and summer drought, flowering early in the year and often dying by June.

On the slopes of Mt Etna between these two species, a whole range of hybrid intermediates is found, the higher ones more like *S. aethnensis*, the lower ones more like *S. chrysanthemifolius*. It was assumed that seeds from these intermediate plants were sent to Oxford Botanic Garden sometime before 1699. There, it was said they grew in the garden and, through successive generations over a 100-year period, became adapted to our own climate and conditions, eventually evolving into the new species *Senecio squalidus*.

However, recent research suggests that something a little more interesting happened. Rather than the original hybrid coming directly from Mt Etna, it seems that seeds of both parents were sent to Mary Somerset, the Duchess of Beaufort, who grew them in her garden at Badminton, Gloucestershire (Harris 2002). Mary, a distinguished botanist and gardener, was a formidable woman who, it was said, would strike terror into the hearts of her servants and instantly dismiss any she found to be not working hard enough (Fraser 1993). As well as compiling a 12-volume herbarium, she is credited with introducing 1,500 plants to horticulture including Geranium *Pelargonium zonale* and Blue Passionflower *Passiflora caerulea*.

Back to Oxford Ragwort. Through an 'ABC analysis using genome-wide polymorphism

Senecio aethnensis growing high on the lava fields of Mt Etna, Sicily.

Mary Somerset, Duchess of Beaufort (1630–1715).

Senecio chrysanthemifolius growing in abandoned fields near the base of Mt Etna, Sicily.

Oxford Ragwort *Senecio squalidus* growing beside a wall in Conwy, North Wales.

data obtained from RNA sequences' (modern genetics is full of such arcane language), it's been shown that the hybrid sent to Oxford Botanic Garden actually came from a cross of the original parents in Lady Beaufort's garden at Badminton, not the slopes of Mt Etna. Once in Oxford, the plants underwent rapid speciation within about 50 generations, probably involving additional backcrosses with plants of *S. chrysanthemifolius* that were also growing there. For this reason, the genome of *S. squalidus* is about 72% *S. chrysanthemifolius* and 28% *S. aethnensis* (Nevado et al. 2020).

To understand why Oxford Ragwort has been so successful, we just need to look back at its original parents. One flowers in late summer, the other in early spring; one grows on infertile rocky lava, the other on disturbed, fertile soil; one is adapted to cold and snow, the other to summer heat and drought. The hybrid has combined all these qualities. It can grow and flower all year round, in cold or heat, and it thrives on disturbed rocky soils (just think of the clinker of railway tracks, the brick rubble of waste ground or the gap between pavement and wall). Add the production of prodigious quantities of wind-dispersed seed and a dash of pollution tolerance, and you have a plant primed to colonise urban habitats.

Once the plant escaped Oxford Botanic Garden in 1794 it spread quickly, becoming 'very plentiful on almost every wall' in Oxford by 1825 (Harris 2002). Soon, the wind-borne seed found its way to the new railway station, built in 1844 to serve the rapidly expanding railway network. In one of the most vivid observations in British botany, Druce (1927) described what happened next: 'the vortex of air following the express train carries the fruits in its wake. I have seen them enter a railway-carriage window near Oxford and remain suspended in the air in the compartment until they found an exit at Tilehurst.' This little journey of around 32km (20 miles) set the scene for the rapid spread of the new species through Great Britain, exploiting the bare rocky clinker of the railway lines, 'a replica of the lava-soils of its native home in Sicily', as Druce put it (Harris 2002).

Today, Oxford Ragwort is found through almost all lowland England and Wales, although it remains strangely scarce in Ireland and much of Scotland. However, even in England it has recently started to show signs of a decline, particularly since 2000. This might be down to more overzealous tidying up of streets and redevelopment of urban fallow sites, but is also typical of the 'boom–bust' cycle that's exhibited by many invasive alien species (Stroh et al. 2023). It's unlikely to disappear from our cities, but maybe its heyday is coming to an end.

This riotous pioneer stage of urban fallow, full of interest with different species jostling for space, is one of the most exhilarating communities of urban plants. Gilbert (1989) makes the fascinating point that, with little grazing, disturbance or competition, and a rocky substrate that's been ground up, is full of nutrients and is often lime-rich, conditions on these sites might be similar to those when the glaciers retreated at the end of the last ice age. It's an interesting comparison. Unfettered and free to spread over the ground as they like, some urban fallow plants might, as Gilbert puts it, 'have never had it so good since'. In this light, you might never look at a bit of waste ground or derelict urban ground in the same way again.

The Rosebay Willowherb Tall-herb Stage

The pioneer stage sees the arrival of some larger annuals and perennials and, after a period of around three to six years, these begin to dominate, shouldering aside the smaller annuals and biennials that went before. These 'tall-herb' communities considerably increase the sheer quantity of vegetation that's growing at the site (the biomass), and this organic material in turn contributes to the development of deeper more fertile soils and, therefore, ever larger plants.

The transition from pioneer to tall-herb communities is gradual, and its early stages are sometimes marked by another community that appears to be unique to urban fallow. This is characterised by dense stands of White Melilot *Melilotus albus* and Ribbed Melilot

BELOW: Dense stands of yellow Ribbed Melilot, left, and White Melilot, right, can form in the early stages of the tall-herb succession, sometimes even growing together. This community seems to be unique to urban fallow.

Urban fallow: waste ground and derelict land

LEFT: Wormwood is particularly frequent on urban fallow sites in the English Midlands. Its distinctive silvery-grey leaves are highly pungent and the plant is used as a key flavouring of the potent alcoholic drink absinthe.

M. officinalis that are particularly frequent on clay soils and abandoned clay pits, but also over brick rubble. These plants, both originally from southern Europe and Asia, are large annuals or biennials with long spires of small white or yellow pea-like flowers. White Melilot was first recorded here in 1822, arriving as a contaminant of grain and birdseed. Ribbed Melilot arrived a little later, in 1848, having been introduced with clover seed that came in from North America. The two species are sometimes found growing together, often with Mugwort and Wormwood *Artemisia absinthium*. This latter species – a tall, impressive and very strong-smelling archaeophyte – is particularly frequent in the English Midlands, stretching from Birmingham through Nottingham, Sheffield and on up to Leeds.

Of course, the iconic star-of-the-show of tall-herb communities is Rosebay Willowherb. In his *Herbal* of 1597, Gerard described it rather wonderfully: 'The branches come out of the ground in great numbers, growing to the height of six foot, garnished with brave flowers of great beauty ... of an orient purple colour.' Today, we probably take it a little bit for granted; it's so ubiquitous that few urban fallow sites (or indeed, any urban site!) will be without it. Much of this success is down to its wind-borne seeds, each of which is adorned with a little parachute of fine hairs, and which can be blown onto any patch of land in impressive quantities. In his study of derelict urban waste ground in the West Midlands, Austin (2002) placed 120 seed traps

ABOVE: Rosebay Willowherb colonising urban fallow land and flowering profusely in front of a shipping container.

BELOW: Each Rosebay Willowherb seedpod produces from 250 to 500 seeds, and a whole plant can release 70,000 seeds into the air. Their very low rate of fall means they can travel large distances to colonise new sites.

across three sites for ten weeks to assess which species arrived in the airborne 'seed rain'. Rosebay Willowherb was the most widespread species encountered by a considerable margin, with viable seed collected at 56% of all traps (way ahead of Yorkshire-fog at 33% of sites). It was also the third most abundant species (behind Common Nettle and goldenrods *Solidago* spp.), with 211 seeds collected across the three sites. This rain of seeds is a very gentle one, though. In one endearing experiment, Sir Edward Salisbury dropped seeds of various species from a height of about 3m in still air. Rosebay Willowherb was the slowest to reach the ground, taking 33 seconds (Salisbury 1961). Such lightweight seeds with high drag will be carried very long distances in turbulent air.

Once Rosebay Willowherb plants arrive and become established at a site, they also reproduce vegetatively by underground rhizomes that can spread outwards up to one metre (40in) a year. In this way, very wide clumps of tightly packed stems can develop, putting on spectacular displays when they flower in summer. Few other plants can cope with this density of growth. Of those that can, grasses are the most common, especially Yorkshire-fog, False Oat-grass *Arrhenatherum elatius* and Cock's-foot, along with other tall, robust herbs like Common Nettle, Hogweed *Heracleum sphondylium* and Creeping Thistle.

The exact origin of our urban Rosebay Willowherb is a little uncertain. Up until the nineteenth century, the plant was rather scarce and restricted to rocky places, often upland mountain cliffs and screes. Then, it underwent a sudden expansion, moving into all sorts of disturbed habitats, including urban waste ground, burnt areas of heathland, cleared woodland, cultivated and fallow fields, roadsides and railways. By the end of the 1950s, it had occupied 78% of 10-km squares in Great Britain (today, it occupies an impressive 93%). All sorts of theories have been suggested for its spread through the lowlands, including the rise in cigarette smoking and picnic campfires causing more heathland fires, its occupation of fire-damaged bomb sites in the Second World War, the spread of seed through the railway and road network, our warmer and wetter winters, and the introduction of robust forms from North America to grow in gardens. As yet, we don't really know the answer, and it's probably a combination of several of these factors – although Salisbury's suggestion of a link to cigarette smoking seems rather unlikely (Salisbury 1961). Gilbert (1989) makes the point that the second British record, in 1666, was in Greenwich, London, 'in the place where the ballast is taken up', and notes that it was a popular garden plant, known as French Willowherb. It's possible,

BELOW: The edges of this car park are at the tall-herb stage of urban fallow, with abundant Common Mallow, Weld, False Oat-grass and Barren Brome. On the far side, tall plants of invasive Giant Hogweed are flowering.

therefore, that the Rosebay Willowherb we see in the lowlands could well be an introduced plant that spread rapidly as our transport networks developed.

As dominant as Rosebay Willowherb can be, many other tall herbs are also characteristic of this stage of urban fallow. The habitat is still relatively open at this stage of succession and, with competition quite low, species still jostle for space. These conditions can create an extremely rich flora, with both native and alien species coming together to create distinct communities. Mugwort and Common Nettle, for instance, form a community on sandy soils mixed with brick, concrete and rubbish, often colonising mounds of earth on derelict plots (Austin 2002). Other large, native tall-herb species that are typical of disturbed ground include Common Mallow *Malva sylvestris*, Great Willowherb, Goat's-beard *Tragopogon pratensis*, Hemlock *Conium maculatum* and both Creeping and Spear Thistle. Plants of shaded hedgerow and woodland margin communities, such as Hedge Woundwort *Stachys sylvatica*, Common Figwort *Scrophularia nodosa* and Bittersweet, often appear along with plants of damper ground like Hemp-agrimony *Eupatorium cannabinum* and Reed Canary-grass *Phalaris arundinacea*, while some of the more robust grassland and meadow species such as Common Knapweed *Centaurea nigra*, Oxeye Daisy *Leucanthemum vulgare*, False Oat-grass and Cat's-ear *Hypochaeris radicata* can also thrive (Gilbert 1989).

As for alien tall-herb plants, almost anything we grow in our herbaceous borders can make an appearance. The list is long, but some of the more common species are Canadian Goldenrod and Early Goldenrod *Solidago gigantea*, Green Alkanet *Pentaglottis sempervirens*, Dotted Loosestrife *Lysimachia punctata*, Russell Lupin, Garden Columbine *Aquilegia vulgaris*, Garden Lady's-mantle *Alchemilla mollis*, Rose Campion *Silene coronaria*, Peach-leaved Bellflower *Campanula persicifolia*, Perennial Cornflower *Centaurea montana*, Russian Comfrey *Symphytum × uplandicum*, Michaelmas-daisies and Soapwort *Saponaria officinalis*. Others, such as Silver Ragwort *Jacobaea maritima*, Garden Cat-mint *Nepeta × faassenii* and Bearded Iris *Iris germanica*, are extraordinarily common in gardens but, for various reasons, only rarely escape.

Quite a few of the more robust perennial garden herbs regularly escape onto fallow ground, especially Feverfew *Tanacetum parthenium*, Spear Mint *Mentha spicata*, Horseradish *Armoracia rusticana*, Tansy *Tanacetum vulgare*, Fennel *Foeniculum vulgare* and Lemon Balm *Melissa officinalis*, creating rich pickings for urban foragers. Many of these plants originate as relicts of cultivation where houses have been demolished and garden plants have survived the levelling and grading of derelict sites, or they spread into fallow areas from neighbouring properties. Selected by gardeners for their robustness and flamboyance, these species can often be a conspicuous element of the tall-herb flora.

Several species that have recently become very popular garden perennials are also moving into urban fallow thanks to their prodigious seeding habits. The best example is probably Argentinian Vervain *Verbena bonariensis* which seeds abundantly, as anyone who's planted it in their garden will know. Originally from eastern South America, it was first recorded in the wild here in 1949 but since 2000 has spread rapidly in England, with scattered records in Wales, Scotland and Ireland (Stroh *et al*. 2023). Hot on its heels is Argentine Needle-grass *Nassella tenuissima* (formerly *Stipa tenuissima*), another native of South America that's beginning to take off on waste ground, especially in and around London. More species will undoubtedly follow, particularly as climate change is encouraging people to grow different plants adapted to droughts and heat, and some might become dominant and alter the face of urban fallow. It's impossible to predict which species might behave this way; the important thing is to continually record and map our urban flora to see how different species are behaving.

BELOW: A very well-established colony of Bearded Iris *Iris germanica* flowering happily on heaps of slag waste near the Redcar steelworks, north-east Yorkshire.

Urban Plants

The Coarse Grassland Stage

After a period of around 7–12 years, the vegetation begins to change again and becomes much grassier in nature. Small, annual grasses give way to larger, perennial species, and this is where Gilbert's epithet of 'urban commons' perhaps becomes most appropriate. These open spaces, now long abandoned and unmanaged, begin to look like meadows and grasslands, with patches of flowering herbs scattered through the grass. At this point, as the sward becomes denser and closes up, plant diversity begins to drop and urban fallow sites begin to look more similar to each other, with less variation in the species present.

In the absence of regular management, coarse grasses like False Oat-grass, Cock's-foot, Common Couch, Red Fescue *Festuca rubra* and Yorkshire-fog become particularly frequent. Some finer grasses such as Common Bent *Agrostis capillaris*, Crested Dog's-tail *Cynosurus cristatus* and Yellow Oat-grass can survive where lower soil fertility checks the growth of other species. All these are accompanied by the usual coarse-grass associates like Ribwort Plantain, White Clover, Common Bird's-foot-trefoil *Lotus corniculatus*, Dandelion, Broad-leaved Dock and Ragwort *Jacobaea vulgaris*. Also present are plants that prefer to grow in disturbed grassland, where they can get a foothold in patches of more open soil, such as Smooth Hawk's-beard *Crepis capillaris* and Black Medick. Some communities, especially on damper ground, are dominated by Creeping Bent, often with Silverweed *Potentilla anserina*, Greater Bird's-foot-trefoil *Lotus pedunculatus* and Greater Plantain.

One of the characteristics of this stage is the formation of distinct stands of perennial herbs, and indeed patches of developing scrub, through the site as the grassland matures. Rosebay Willowherb is particularly prone to doing this as it begins to decline from its heydays of earlier years. Alongside it, Common Ragwort often grows, the two creating a colourful contrast that's highly attractive to pollinators. Other more invasive species may begin to spread, and Giant Hogweed *Heracleum mantegazzianum* can often be found towering above the vegetation. Originally from south-western Asia, this colossal species

BELOW: Giant Hogweed invading a tall-grass community by a river in Manchester. At one time, children used to make pea-shooters and musical pipes from its hollow stems, until its potential to blister the skin in sunlight was more widely appreciated.

ABOVE: A classic area of urban fallow in the coarse grassland stage, dominated by vigorous grasses and stands of robust perennials including Common Ragwort *Jacobaea vulgaris* and Rosebay Willowherb.

was first introduced to Great Britain as a horticultural curiosity around 1817. It was recorded in the wild just 11 years later, and from the 1960s onwards it spread rapidly, particularly along riverbanks, ditches and roadsides. Famously causing severe blisters if the sap gets on your skin and is exposed to sunlight (photodermatitis), it's now regarded as one of the most invasive species in Europe, modifying vegetation structure and shading out smaller species. Ruderal tall-herb grasslands are particularly impacted by its arrival, with every 50% increase in Giant Hogweed cover eliminating 2.4 of the species that were originally present. However, before we get too hot-under-the-collar about this, several studies have shown that this reduction in species diversity is actually part of the normal course of succession from low-growing, open grassland to tall-herb communities and, ultimately, the development of scrub and woodland. It also occurs with the arrival and spread of larger native species as well as other neophytes, and isn't necessarily just down to the appearance of Giant Hogweed (Thiele & Otte 2007).

As the grassland matures, more plant detritus builds up like a mulch on the soil surface, increasing its fertility and moisture levels, with the tall herbs also acting almost like a mini-forest, trapping moisture around the base of the stems. The bryophyte flora changes in response to this, with the arrival of larger pleurocarp species like Creeping Feather-moss *Amblystegium serpens*, Pointed

Spear-moss *Calliergonella cuspidata*, Rough-stalked Feather-moss *Brachythecium rutabulum*, Common Feather-moss *Kindbergia praelonga* and Clustered Feather-moss *Rhynchostegium confertum*. Some of these are also common in woodlands, relishing the higher fertility and humidity of the taller vegetation, and often persist into the next stage of the succession (Gilbert 1989).

ABOVE: Common Feather-moss is a ubiquitous species in shaded sites on fertile soils. It often develops in the later stages of urban fallow and persists into the scrub stage.

The Buddleja Scrub-woodland Stage

The final stages of the urban fallow succession are fascinating but, because of the inherently transient nature of the sites, are not always reached. The high value of urban land and pressure for redevelopment are so strong that many sites don't last long enough for scrub and woodland to develop. In the West Midlands, Austin (2002) found that the average age of derelict and vacant sites was nine years. Moreover, only 23% of sites were aged 10–20 years and only four sites (9%) were older than 20 years. Clearly, very few sites survive long enough to progress all the way through to mature woodland.

Because most sites are abandoned and receive no regular management, succession can take place unhindered and quite quickly. However, because they also tend to be isolated within the built environment and aren't in close proximity to other blocks of existing woodland habitat, there's a restriction on which species can arrive. These two conditions create a rather odd situation that's rarely seen elsewhere. In the early pioneer stages of the succession, the bare ground is usually colonised by trees and shrubs with small, wind-dispersed seed. These include Buddleja, Silver Birch *Betula pendula*, Downy Birch *Betula pubescens* and several willows, especially Goat Willow *Salix caprea*, Rusty Willow *S. cinerea* subsp. *oleifolia* and, in more northern and western areas, Eared Willow *S. aurita*. These initially grow quickly and, after three or four years, become quite conspicuous among the flowering plants. However, at this point the grasses and other herbaceous vegetation become quite thick, making it difficult for more of these pioneer shrubs and trees to get established. As Gilbert (1989) puts it, their 'window of opportunity' lasts just a few years, so after around ten years sites tend to be dominated by stands of even-aged shrubs and trees.

Urban fallow: waste ground and derelict land

On sites with very infertile, stony substrates, particularly abandoned railway tracks and sidings with their thick beds of clinker and cinders, the herbaceous vegetation may remain thin and open for many years. So here, development of scrub tends to carry on unhindered. This is why such sites are often swamped with very dense thickets of Buddleja, birch and willow scrub. This type of vegetation, where Buddleja predominates, is another community that seems to be unique to urban areas.

Trees and shrubs with small, lightweight seeds can readily become established on open sites. But those with larger seeds, if they arrive, can become established in much thicker swards and go on to form mixed-aged populations over time (Gilbert 1989). Many of these plants have edible berries that are brought in by birds, including native species such as Hawthorn *Crataegus monogyna*, Bird Cherry *Prunus padus*, Blackthorn *P. spinosa*, Elder *Sambucus niger*, Rowan *Sorbus aucuparia*, Holly *Ilex aquifolium* and Yew *Taxus baccata*, while Hazel *Corylus avellana* will often appear thanks to the activity of small mammals. If they've been planted in gardens and amenity areas nearby, alien species like Swedish Whitebeam *Sorbus intermedia*, Garden Privet *Ligustrum ovalifolium*, Thunberg's Barberry *Berberis thunbergii*, Duke of Argyll's Teaplant *Lycium barbarum*, Snowberry *Symphoricarpos albus* and a plethora of confusing Cotoneasters *Cotoneaster* spp. can also become established from bird-dispersed fruit, as can Sea-buckthorn *Hippophae rhamnoides*.

Bird dispersal is also the main way that Bramble *Rubus fruticosus* agg. arrives. It can appear in the very earliest pioneer stages of succession and often persists through to later stages thanks to its unusual pattern of growth. New, vigorous shoots (known as **primocanes**) emerge from the base of the plant each year, growing bolt upright at first. Then, during late summer and autumn, they arch over and head towards the ground, often reaching several metres away from the main plant. When the tips touch the soil, they become narrow and bury themselves into the ground, easily pushing down between lumps of rubble or gaps in the concrete. Once buried, they root and produce buds that grow as new plants the next

BELOW: Although native to the east coasts of England and southern Scotland, Sea-buckthorn is widely used in amenity and landscape planting, where it can spread and become highly invasive. Its sour orange berries are rich in vitamin C and increasingly foraged as a wild food.

year. In this way, Bramble forms spreading patches that 'leapfrog' over surrounding vegetation, as the shoots can penetrate and grow through thick grassy swards that would otherwise prevent seedlings from establishing. The blackberries we enjoy eating appear on much shorter flowering lateral shoots (known as **floricanes**) that grow off the primocanes the following year. It's worth noting that what we know as 'blackberry' is actually a collection of more than 320 different apomictic microspecies. Each of these has its own variations in leaves, thorns, glands, flowers and berries, making them virtually impossible for most people to identify unless you're a batologist (a specialist in *Rubus* identification). A few of these microspecies produce particularly heavy crops of large, sweet fruit and have been selected for gardens. Of these, Giant Blackberry *Rubus armeniacus*, a huge plant that can reach 3m high with spreading canes 12m long, is probably the most common and regularly appears on urban fallow sites, as does Parsley-leaved Bramble *Rubus laciniatus* which, as the name suggests, is one of the most easily identified microspecies with its finely divided leaves.

Other large-seeded shrubs and trees turn up under their own steam. Ash *Fraxinus excelsior* and Sycamore *Acer pseudoplatanus* are perhaps the most prominent, arriving if mature trees are nearby and their winged seeds travel far enough by air. Several woody plants of the pea-family (Fabaceae) can spread through seed exploded from their seedpods, including native Broom *Cytisus scoparius*, Gorse *Ulex europaeus* and alien species such as Laburnum *Laburnum anagyroides* and, increasingly, False-acacia. Both Apple *Malus domestica* and Crab Apple *M. sylvestris* can appear too, the former usually from fruit discarded by people, the latter through bird or animal dispersal.

If you're familiar with urban fallow sites, you'll appreciate the wide range of woody plants that can become established. In the West Midlands, Austin (2002) recorded 61 different species across 50 sites, half of which were native and half alien (a higher proportion of aliens than the total flora recorded, at 33%). Most of the less frequently recorded species were aliens such as Turkey Oak *Quercus cerris*, Fuchsia *Fuchsia magellanica*, Lilac *Syringa vulgaris*, Red-osier Dogwood *Cornus sericea* and Steeple-bush *Spiraea douglasii*, indicating the diversity of species that escape from gardens or from amenity planting.

These infrequent escapes, though, usually just occur as occasional individuals or spreading clumps, and rarely form the bulk of the woody vegetation. The final transition to mature woodland is

ABOVE: The final stage of urban fallow, as scrub develops into woodland, has developed here on the Clune Park Estate, Inverclyde, Scotland, after being abandoned for 25 years.

extremely uncommon, as sites rarely survive long enough, so urban fallow woodland tends to be dominated by species that live fast and die young, particularly birches *Betula* spp. and willows *Salix* spp., as well as a few longer-lived pioneer species like Sycamore, Aspen *Populus tremula* and Ash. The lifespan of these trees can also be restricted by soil conditions. In many years of urban botanising, Gilbert (1989) never saw a native oak *Quercus* spp. thriving on a rubble substrate, despite many seedlings appearing from acorns buried by Magpies *Pica pica*. Indeed, few of these oaks survived more than four years.

One final point to make is that, unlike the early pioneer stages of succession, these fascinating scrub–woodland transitions seem to have been rather ignored by ecologists. Their value as wildlife habitats is of course appreciated by many people, but there's very little research literature on their development and diversity and the important contribution they make to supporting a wide range of other urban wildlife, especially populations of invertebrates, birds and mammals. This is a shame, as they represent the last stages of urban succession, the ultimate reclaiming of the urban landscape after it's been abandoned. A better understanding of how such scrub woodlands form, and become diverse in both native and alien species, can only help us encourage and manage the regeneration of these uniquely urban habitats.

The grassy bits

chapter ten

Urban landscapes are patchworked with pockets of grass. But, while we lie on the soft sward eating sandwiches at lunchtime, kick a ball around a football field at the weekend, or let our dogs run free across the wide-open park every morning, most people probably give the green carpet under our feet very little thought. It is, after all, just grass. Regularly mown lawns, perfectly even in height and replete with parallel stripes, can come in for particular scorn, especially from those that take an interest in wildlife.

But lawns and other grassy habitats sometimes pack a staggering floral punch. One square metre of lawn can easily be home to more than a hundred flowers of Daisy *Bellis perennis*, as well as dozens of Dandelions *Taraxacum* agg., White Clover *Trifolium repens* and Creeping Buttercup *Ranunculus repens*. Multiply these numbers across a whole lawn, playing field or park and you can have millions of flowers at your feet, a floral feast that's unmatched anywhere else in the urban landscape.

Towns and cities take in a very wide range of grassland habitats. There are parks, sports fields and pitches, lawns in domestic gardens, road verges, rough banks, roundabouts, river edges, canal towpaths, churchyards and cemeteries, and a multitude of small grassy fragments – those bits of grass around road junctions, buildings and car parks, pavements, industrial estates, retail parks and undeveloped patches of land. Collectively, these make grassland one of the largest of urban habitats, covering a total of 23,865 hectares (roughly equivalent to the area of Liverpool) or 1.2% of the urban area in the UK (ONS 2023).

Many of these are basically semi-natural grasslands that behave very similarly to those found in rural landscapes. As with all things urban,

OPPOSITE:
Daisy and Creeping Buttercup carpeting a grassy verge in an industrial estate near Conwy. These species attract a wide range of pollinators, mainly hoverflies and solitary bees but also flies, beetles and ants.

though, they do follow a gradient of increasing human modification as you move towards the city centre. On the outskirts of town there might be grazing pastures, silage fields and even, occasionally, hay meadows – fields that are still used by farmers, smallholders or horse-keepers to graze and feed their livestock. These will be typical agricultural grasslands with many of the usual meadow species, depending on soil conditions, the intensity of management and the age of the sward. As you move into the suburbs, the density of houses and gardens increases and open fields are gradually replaced by domestic lawns, playing fields and sports grounds, large cemeteries and parks. Although the urban boundary can sometimes appear to be quite abrupt, when modern housing estates, industrial and retail parks border farmers' fields, in the wider landscape the transition is usually gradual. Further towards the city centre, housing, retail and industry all increase and the grassland area decreases, with ever-smaller gardens, churchyards instead of cemeteries, and fewer parks and playgrounds. In the heart of the city, small surviving fragments of grassland become disproportionately more important, with narrow strips of road verge and patches of grass around roundabouts, road junctions and buildings and small parks providing a few scant grassy habitats.

The majority of these grasslands will be fairly recent creations, sown or re-seeded within the last few decades. But some can be much older. Occasionally, fragments of former meadows or pastures can become encapsulated by the urban sprawl as it grows around them. These echoes of the pre-urban landscape might retain their diversity and are sometimes home to important grassland species. The grounds of Salisbury Cathedral, for example, support a population of Fiddle Dock *Rumex pulcher*. This species, an indicator of ancient grasslands, might be just one such echo. Several nineteenth-century paintings show cattle grazing around the cathedral and it's likely that some species growing in the grounds today survive from those original pastures. Similarly, a bank of mown grass in Crookes Valley Park, Sheffield, supports populations of acid grassland species including Harebell *Campanula rotundifolia*, Mat-grass *Nardus stricta* and Heath-grass *Danthonia decumbens*. Few of the sunbathers using the bank are probably aware they're lying on a remnant of the original ancient acid grassland of Crookesmoor from which the park is named (Gilbert 1989).

Most patches of urban grassland are much more recent in origin, and the majority tend to be rather species poor when compared to

The grassy bits

LEFT: *Salisbury Cathedral from the Bishop's Grounds*, John Constable (1823). Surrounded by water meadows beside the River Avon, cattle once grazed right up to the cathedral walls.

LEFT: Fiddle Dock growing in the lawns around Salisbury Cathedral. After being pointed out to the ground staff, the plants are now left unmown and allowed to flower and set seed.

ancient, rural grasslands. Although the soils can be quite fertile, they're often rather dry and suffer from high levels of disturbance and pollution, especially nitrogen, ammonia and particulates. These conditions tend to encourage coarser, more vigorous grassland species. In the most extreme cases, one or two species of grass predominate, the uniform sward broken up by just a few broad-leaved herbs. In the

Urban Plants

RIGHT: City-centre amenity grasslands can be extremely dull and species poor. Although St Andrew Square is one of the most prestigious addresses in Edinburgh, the 15-year-old lawn at its heart is a monotonous expanse of Perennial Rye-grass and very little else.

very centre of Edinburgh, for instance, the grass in St Andrew Square is regularly mown to keep it extremely short. Although 15 years old, the sward is dominated by Perennial Rye-grass *Lolium perenne* with just a few patches of White Clover *Trifolium repens* and the occasional Dandelion. While Annual Meadow-grass *Poa annua* survives along the edges of the paths, the entire park contains just four species.

Having been involved with the creation and conservation of species-rich meadows for over 20 years, I find their establishment and development fascinating. Three factors are particularly important in determining the species found in urban grasslands: the history of the site (its age and origin), the nature of the soil and its fertility, and how the grass is managed. The evolution of urban grassland over time follows a marked pattern. As well as vigorous grasses, newly sown swards include ruderal annuals that have arisen from disturbance of the soil seed bank, or have been introduced with topsoil. Shepherd's-purse *Capsella bursa-pastoris*, Groundsel *Senecio vulgaris*, Knotgrass *Polygonum aviculare* and Scentless Mayweed *Tripleurospermum inodorum* are particularly frequent at first, but are quickly eradicated by regular mowing. As these ruderal species go, common mowing-tolerant species arrive, especially White Clover, Daisy, Common Mouse-ear *Cerastium fontanum*, Dandelion, Creeping Buttercup and Selfheal *Prunella vulgaris*. Over the years, unless regularly fertilised, soil fertility drops and less competitive species arrive, including the likes of Field Wood-rush *Luzula campestris*, Common Bird's-foot-trefoil

ABOVE: The transition from agricultural fields to amenity grassland and then domestic garden lawns on the outskirts of Luton. Different grassy habitats develop in response to the type and intensity of management – everything from ungrazed pasture to tightly mown lawns.

Lotus corniculatus, Lady's Bedstraw *Galium verum* and Hop Trefoil *Trifolium campestre*. In the oldest mown grasslands, where fertility is lowest, species diversity may actually decline and swards become dominated by fewer species. This isn't always the case, though: one of the oldest lawns in Great Britain, established around 280 years ago at Chatsworth House in Derbyshire, is home to 56 species including wonderful ancient grassland flowers like Mountain Pansy *Viola lutea* and Tormentil *Potentilla erecta* (Gilbert 1989).

The grasses

While lawns and other urban grasslands often look like uniform carpets of green, they're usually composed of a handful of different grass species. Areas of long grass left unmown or only cut a few times each year are likely to be dominated by large, vigorous species including Perennial Rye-grass, Cock's-foot *Dactylis glomerata*, False Oat-grass *Arrhenatherum elatius*, Yorkshire-fog *Holcus lanatus* and Common Couch *Elymus repens*. Tall and dense, you'll often notice their seedheads in areas of unmown grass, especially the distinctive outline of Cock's-foot and the soft, pinkish haze created by swathes of Yorkshire-fog that give the grass its name.

Subjected to regular mowing and heavy trampling, amenity lawns in gardens, parks and sports fields need to be extremely hard-wearing. A small suite of tough and tolerant species are usually

RIGHT: Yorkshire-fog grows in a remarkably wide range of soil conditions and tolerates mowing, so is one of the most common urban grasses. Most plants are a soft pink colour, but pale white individuals aren't uncommon and stand out among the others.

sown together in specially formulated mixes, often sold in bags with 'Hard Wearing' emblazoned across the front, just to reinforce the point. These plants tolerate regular cutting by **tillering**, whereby many lateral shoots grow out sideways from the base of the plant when it's mown (or, indeed, grazed). In a study of domestic urban lawns in Sheffield, Thompson *et al.* (2004) found that just over 80% of the average lawn was covered by grasses, and most of that cover came from hard-wearing species like Common Bent *Agrostis capillaris*, Red Fescue *Festuca rubra* and Perennial Rye-grass. Other frequent species in such lawns include Creeping Bent *Agrostis stolonifera*, Yorkshire-fog, Rough Meadow-grass *Poa trivialis*, Smooth Meadow-grass *P. pratensis* and Annual Meadow-grass. This last species, which often arrives by itself, is particularly frequent where trampling is most intense, such as around the entrance to parks and along the edges of paths. The seed mixes used to create these lawns can be tailored for particular uses, and so in situations where harder-wearing lawns are needed, such as sports pitches and amenity grasslands, Chewing's Fescue *Festuca rubra* subsp. *commutata* and the non-native Hard Fescue *Festuca trachyphylla*, originally from central Europe, are sometimes sown. In wetter areas with damper soils, Meadow Foxtail *Alopecurus pratensis* and Creeping Bent can predominate,

The grassy bits

LEFT: Although rarely allowed to flower in such situations, Common Bent is one of the most commonly sown grasses in lawns. It has very fine leaves and branches freely from the base, giving the sward a soft but hard-wearing quality.

while Timothy *Phleum pratense*, Black Bent *Agrostis gigantea* and Tall Fescue *Schedonorus arundinaceus* prefer the fertile, disturbed soil of waste ground and road verges.

Many other grasses frequently found in rural grasslands are rather uncommon in urban settings. These include Crested Dog's-tail *Cynosurus cristatus*, Quaking Grass *Briza media* and Yellow Oat-grass *Trisetum flavescens*, as well as Sweet Vernal-grass *Anthoxanthum odoratum* with its characteristic scent of newly mown hay. If such species do occur, they tend to be found in fragments of older grassland that are managed like hay meadows, such as churchyards and grounds surrounding historical buildings and monuments, or in newly sown wildflower meadows using high-quality seed mixes.

One man went to mow

Grasslands are unique among most urban habitats because, unlike walls, pavements and urban fallow, they are usually regularly managed, sometimes on a weekly basis throughout spring and summer. Above all else, the frequency of mowing, strimming or – in a few cases – grazing and hay-cutting, governs which species are present. When mowing and cutting is regular or grazing is continuous, short-grass swards are created with species adapted to survive in these conditions. When management is relaxed and long grass is allowed to grow, different species come to the fore. Such grass is usually cut once a year, at the end of summer, in an attempt to replicate the traditional management of hay meadows.

Grazing with cattle and sheep is rarely practised within city boundaries but makes a real impression when it is, creating a tantalising juxtaposition of rural and urban cultures. This hasn't always been the case, however. For most of our urban history, grassy commons were frequent features of towns, used as places for the shared and communal grazing of livestock. This would have been granted to local farmers, townspeople and traders bringing their cattle and sheep to market. Beginning in the early 1600s, the Inclosure Acts began to place such land into private ownership, and urban commons came under huge pressure for development, squeezing out room for livestock grazing.

A few of these ancient urban grazing commons do survive, though, and nowhere more so than in the university city of Cambridge, where the early focus on scholarship placed relatively few demands on land for development. Today, cattle are allowed to graze five commons in the city (Coe Fen, Coldham's Common, Midsummer Common, Sheep's Green and Stourbridge Common) and are much loved by local residents, despite turning some paved footpaths 'slippery and excremental' as one person put it (Independent 2018). The low level of grazing employed helps keep the grass short but, since it takes place during spring and summer when most plants are in flower and setting seed, it tends to have a rather detrimental effect on species diversity. Most of the cattle-grazed commons, which are located on quite fertile former floodplains, are rather species poor and dominated by vigorous grasses and other competitive plants of grazed pastures, such as Creeping Thistle *Cirsium vulgare*, Common Nettle *Urtica dioica* and Creeping Buttercup.

Of course, the life of most urban grasslands is ruled by lawnmowers. Ever since their invention in 1830 by Edwin Beard Budding, an engineer from Stroud (Gloucestershire), British men have been peculiarly obsessed with creating expansive carpets of uniform grass monocultures, preferably with stripes and definitely without any 'weeds'. This fetish became more achievable with the invention of motorised mowers in the 1890s, some of the first of which were steam powered, but were quickly superseded by petrol engines.

The grassy bits

ABOVE: Around 120 cattle graze five urban commons in Cambridge, including these fine Red Poll cows on Coe Fen. This breed, originally from Norfolk and Suffolk, lacks horns (they're 'polled'), making them more acceptable in public places.

LEFT: A flail mower being pulled behind a tractor on Jesus Green, Cambridge. Such mowers can cut large areas, quickly producing a uniform short sward. The clippings are not normally collected but spread on the surface, creating a 'thatch' that inhibits the growth of broad-leaved lawn species.

Today, all manner of grass-cutting technology is available, from traditional domestic petrol mowers to tractor-drawn flail mowers and from hover mowers (first introduced by Flymo) to robotic, self-propelled mowers with rechargeable batteries and GPS guidance (Old Lawnmower Club 2024). As well as regular mowing, a cocktail of herbicides and fertilisers is also used to eradicate unwanted blemishes and help create that pristine bowling-green look.

#NoMowMay

We are deeply addicted to mowing. Large areas of grass in parks, sports grounds and amenity areas, as well as domestic garden lawns, are mown regularly, producing a uniform sward just a few centimetres in height. The frequency of mowing is surprisingly high; in a survey of domestic lawns by Plantlife in 2019, 47% of people reported mowing their lawns at least once a fortnight (Dines unpublished data).

Yet, lawns and areas of long grass have huge potential to support wildlife. In an attempt to change attitudes, I created the #NoMowMay campaign while at Plantlife with the aim of encouraging people to mow their lawns less often. The idea is rather simple: if people put their mowers away for a month and see what appears on their uncut lawns, they might be inspired to mow less often, or even not at all. Attitudes around mowing are so ingrained that for many people, asking them not to mow at all straight away would be a step too far. Instead, #NoMowMay offers them a way to try a different approach – namely, to leave their lawns alone for a month and see what happens. This softer step would then hopefully be the first in a journey to appreciating the multiple benefits of mowing less often, which include saving time, reducing petrol costs and CO_2 emissions, and providing habitat for wildlife. When the idea popped into my head one morning, #NoMowMay was one of those rare 'eureka' moments. I instinctively knew it had potential, but I could never have imagined quite how enthusiastically it would be adopted. As well as thousands of individuals taking part each year, many groups, organisations, communities, councils (e.g. Aberdeenshire and Cambridgeshire) and even entire cities (e.g. Bradford and Newcastle upon Tyne) have since adopted the #NoMowMay initiative. It has even gone global, with participation in Europe, the United States and Canada.

In Great Britain, our previously unshakable devotion to mowing seems to have been challenged, with a genuine change in lawn-mowing behaviour. The most recent Plantlife survey shows that just 16% of people mowed their lawns every week or two (a drop of 31%), but that 50% mowed them once a month or two (an increase of 24%). In addition to #NoMowMay, now #LetItBloomJune and #NoMowSummer have taken off, with the number of households leaving their lawns entirely unmown through spring and summer doubling from 10% to 21% (Dines unpublished data). Admittedly, these are people taking part in the lawn survey and are likely already willing to change their behaviour, but the popularity of #NoMowMay and the survey results do suggest a genuine shift in attitudes.

Not everyone sees #NoMowMay as positive, though. Strongly held attitudes towards 'weeds' are difficult to overcome and many people dislike long grass, feeling that it makes their neighbourhoods seem untidy and uncared for. This reaction is fascinating. As well as concerns on social media about areas looking a mess and even reducing house prices, some people have genuine anxiety about uncut grass; it can, for example, reduce access and may cause trips and falls, it can trap rubbish, and the seedheads of grasses can injure pets. One person who took part in #NoMowMay expressed fears that their garden had become so wild it might harbour snakes. As much as we might scoff at such concerns, genuine fears have to be accommodated and rationalised, with solutions including paths cut through long grass to ensure access and borders mown around the edges to give an impression of 'managed messiness'. We find the wild a deeply attractive notion, but we're much more comfortable with it when it's under control.

The general reaction to #NoMowMay, though, is one of sheer delight. Putting the mower away for a month, or indeed for the whole of spring and summer, allows plants to flower and people are thrilled to see what appears, often for the first time. From 2019 to 2021, Plantlife ran Every Flower Counts, a citizen science survey I designed in which people recorded the number of flowers within square metre quadrats on their lawns in May and again in July. More than 14,000 quadrats were surveyed all the way from the Isles of Scilly to Orkney, with around 500,000–650,000 individual flowers counted

BELOW: Verges in Dorchester, Dorset, have been left uncut by the council for #NoMowMay to allow flowers to bloom, creating attractive displays for residents and valuable resources for pollinators.

by participants each year. Bucking the preconception of botanical dullness, the diversity of the lawns in the survey was astonishing, with 281 species recorded in all (Dines unpublished data). This total includes both rural and urban locations, but it gives an idea of how diverse lawns actually are (by comparison, a survey of 52 urban lawns in Sheffield recorded 159 species, Thompson *et al.* 2004).

By a considerable margin, the most common and floriferous species in lawns was Daisy, found on 77% of lawns and producing an average of 39 flowers per square metre. The other species making up the top five were Creeping Buttercup (52% of lawns), Dandelion (38%), White Clover (33%) and Selfheal (20%; Dines unpublished data). Alongside these, many typical grassland and meadow species appear in uncut lawns, such as Common Bird's-foot-trefoil, Oxeye Daisy *Leucanthemum vulgare*, Cowslip *Primula veris* and Red Clover *Trifolium pratense*. Occasionally, more unusual grassland species pop up, including Meadow Saxifrage *Saxifraga granulata* and Grass Vetchling *Lathyrus nissolia*. Older lawns that have been under the same ownership, and therefore management, for many years can be especially rich. In Middlesbrough, for example, a patch of Adder's-tongue Fern *Ophioglossum vulgatum* appeared in the front garden of a suburban house dating from the 1950s. Unfortunately, the plant was killed in 2014 when the house was sold and the new owners herbicided the lawn (Allen 2023).

People are understandably most excited, though, by the appearance of orchids on their unmown lawns. Common Spotted-orchid *Dactylorhiza fuchsii* is by far the most frequent species, making up 25% of all orchid records in the Plantlife survey, followed by Early-purple Orchid *Orchis mascula*, Pyramidal Orchid *Anacamptis pyramidalis* and Southern Marsh-orchid *Dactylorhiza praetermissa*, each at around 15% of orchid records. All of these species seem to be moving northwards in response to climate change (Stroh *et al.* 2023, Walker *et al.* 2023), and Southern Marsh-orchid is particularly interesting as it appears to tolerate drier lawns and meadows than before. Another orchid that appears on urban lawns is Autumn Lady's-tresses *Spiranthes spiralis*, which can persist for many years as tiny rosettes in the sward, ducking under the mower blades. When mowing is finally relaxed, hundreds of flowering stems can appear, to the shock – and delight – of the homeowners. It's particularly frequent in towns and cities on the chalk along the south coast of England, especially from Bournemouth to Hastings.

The grassy bits

LEFT: One of the latest-flowering British orchids, Autumn Lady's-tresses can be common on old lawns overlying chalk, especially along the south coast of England. It's pollinated by bumblebees, which are attracted by the vanilla scent.

LEFT: Displays of Bee Orchids are increasingly common on urban lawns, such as this enviable example in Norfolk. The seed capsule behind each flower can produce 7,000–9,000 dust-like seeds, which disperse many hundreds of metres from the plant.

Bee Orchid *Ophrys apifera* is relatively infrequent (8% of orchid records), but perhaps creates the most excitement due to its extraordinary flowers. With their hairy brown lips, the flowers mimic female bees and even emit the pheromones needed to entice males into an act of pseudocopulation to pollinate them. Sadly, the species of bee responsible for this forlorn act of fornication doesn't occur in Great Britain, and so our Bee Orchids have to resort to self-pollination instead. However, this is proving be a very effective strategy as the range of this species is increasing rapidly, with many new records in the north of Britain and in Ireland. Climate change is likely to be driving this expansion, and lawns are a particular source of new sightings.

Extraordinary urban orchids

Orchids are the epitome of the rare, exotic and exacting, so it often comes as a surprise when they materialise in urban habitats. We've already met the only British population of Lesser Tongue-orchid *Serapias parviflora* living the high life on the green roof of a bank in central London (see Chapter 1), but there are many others.

Carefully managed lawns can mimic the natural grassland haunts of many orchids. Those on chalk in southern England sometimes support rarer species, including Man Orchid *Orchis anthropophora*, Fly Orchid *Ophrys insectifera* and Lady Orchid *Orchis purpurea*. Perhaps most remarkable and inexplicable, though, is the appearance of Heart-flowered Tongue-orchid *Serapias cordigera* – a species from the Mediterranean and southern Europe – in a small and otherwise rather dull suburban lawn in Sheffield, South Yorkshire. The plant sprang up in the unmown lawn alongside Common Spotted-orchid in 2021 and is still growing there. Exciting appearances like this generate much speculation as to whether such plants arrive naturally by themselves (the tiny seed carried long distances from continental Europe) or have been assisted by human hand (sowing seed, planting tubers or escaping from cultivation, see Bateman 2022 for a review). In this case, the orchid's appearance

Heart-flowered Tongue-orchid growing on an otherwise dull suburban lawn in Sheffield.

is a complete mystery, as the nearest wild plants grow 563km (350 miles) away in Brittany, France, and none of the neighbours in the area know of the plant being introduced or cultivated nearby (Sean Cole pers. comm.).

From around 2000 onwards, the imposing Lizard Orchid *Himantoglossum hircinum* has been popping up across England more frequently, perhaps assisted by climate change. Although often fleeting in appearance, sites include lawns (such as one in Sandwich, Kent) and road verges (e.g. in Northampton, Reading, Peterborough and Lewes). The verge sites are sometimes rather rank and species poor, not exactly the high-quality grassland habitat you'd expect for such a spectacular orchid. One former site behind a bus shelter on a busy, drab roadside in west London was, for example, described by Mark Spencer as 'surrounded by cock's-foot, cow parsley, dog poo, beer cans and crisp packets'. Sadly, some of these plants have succumbed to theft following publicity on social media, or suffered from poor habitat

Lizard Orchid flowering on the outskirts of Salisbury, Wiltshire.

management by councils. Here is a species receiving the full throttle of legal protection (it's listed on Schedule 8 of the Wildlife and Countryside Act 1981), but it seems that even this isn't enough to protect it.

Much more common and widespread, Broad-leaved Helleborine *Epipactis helleborine* is nonetheless another orchid inexplicably increasing in urban sites. Most famously, this woodland species has been spreading in the centre of Glasgow. One of the first records dates back to a Motherwell garden in the 1920s, but since the 1970s it has been appearing in gardens, churchyards, parks and urban fallow land, often growing along the base of fences and railings that afford some protection from weeding, disturbance and herbicide. It's also been found beside car parks, road gutters, on scrubby disused railway lines and even old coal spoil heaps (Dickson et al. 2000). Today, it's recorded from hundreds of sites within the city, which is now the stronghold of the species in Scotland, and it's even regarded by some as a weed. More recently, this orchid has started to appear in many other towns and cities, including pavements in Stirling, Belfast, Harrogate and Colwyn Bay, a verge in Tremorfa Park, Cardiff, and in the lawn of Trinity College, Dublin, after it was left unmown for #NoMowMay.

Another orchid on an extraordinary march is Dune Helleborine *Epipactis dunensis*. This rare species traditionally grows in dunes on Anglesey and the English coast from Liverpool to Blackpool and as far north as Barrow-in-Furness, Cumbria. In 2014, Joshua Styles discovered ten plants in a car park at Edge Hill University, Lancashire. By 2017, the population had grown to more than 200 individuals spread over other parts of the campus. In 2015, plants were found growing beside the Life Sciences Building at the University of Liverpool. Most unexpected, though, were the specimens Kevin Walker spotted in an amenity flowerbed in the centre of Harrogate in 2015. Unfortunately, these beds are scheduled for replanting, so the orchids will be translocated to an RHS garden nearby. Dune Helleborine has also appeared in various parts of Newcastle upon Tyne, including areas of woodland, shady grassy verges and along the banks of the River Tyne. In 2019, plants were encountered in various parts of Dublin, the first time the species had been confirmed in Ireland. Most were growing in suburban woodland alongside a river and all are vulnerable to disturbance and development (Santos & Sayers 2020). Like all orchids, Dune Helleborine is very mobile thanks to its tiny wind-borne seed, and this exciting new urban chapter of its story is still being written.

Broad-leaved Helleborine growing through a tree-pit grating on a Glasgow street.

Dune Helleborine in an amenity flowerbed in the centre of Harrogate among *Rosa* 'Pink Flower Carpet'.

Native plants make up the vast majority of lawn species. In both the Plantlife and Sheffield surveys, the top 25 lawn species were all natives, while in the Plantlife survey 78% of all species were native (Dines unpublished data, Thompson *et al.* 2004). A few aliens, however, have become very well established on urban lawns, often making themselves look so at home that many people mistake them as native. This is particularly true of Fox-and-Cubs *Pilosella aurantiaca* with its bright orange-red flowers, originally introduced from European mountains in 1629. Although it's been known in the wild here for more than 230 years, it is still increasing rapidly in grassy habitats, usually fitting in quite benignly amongst native species. A more recent arrival is Slender Speedwell *Veronica filiformis* from Turkey and the Caucasus, which escaped from cultivation in 1927 but has since become just as widespread on lawns. This remarkable colonisation has been helped by the plant's ability to resprout from small fragments of stem, something that's amply assisted by mowing, as well as reproduction by seed. Other aliens are escaping from cultivation and joining them. Both Lawn Lobelia *Pratia angulata* from New Zealand and Matted Pratia *P. pedunculata* from Australia seem to be increasing in lawns, where they can form very dense and extensive carpets with their small blue flowers. Other lawn invaders include Least Yellow-sorrel *Oxalis exilis* from Australasia and Leptinella *Cotula squalida* from New Zealand, a densely creeping plant with ferny foliage sometimes grown as a lawn-grass substitute.

RIGHT: Very few native British plants have orange flowers, so the fiery blooms of Fox-and-Cubs really stand out on lawns, verges and in rough grass.

LEFT: Originally from Australia, Matted Pratia is a newcomer to our lawns, with the first records dating from 1999. It's now sparsely but widely distributed throughout Great Britain.

The long and the short of it

Most urban lawns mown to within an inch of their life are regarded as dreadful habitats for broad-leaved plants. But in fact, a distinct community of species well adapted to short-grass swards can be abundant, especially when the frequency of mowing is reduced to around once a month and fertilisers and herbicides are avoided. The resulting sward can be exceptionally floriferous and valuable for invertebrates, especially hoverflies like Marmalade Hoverfly *Episyrphus balteatus* and solitary mining bee species such as Tawny Mining Bee *Andrena fulva* and Ashy Mining Bee *A. cineraria* that can burrow and nest in patches of bare soil. On the other hand, when areas of long grass are allowed to develop by not mowing through spring and summer, a different community of plants develops with a greater range of species. The higher diversity of flowers attracts a wider range of pollinators, especially butterflies such as Meadow Brown *Maniola jurtina*, moths like Six-spot Burnet *Zygaena filipendulae* and bumblebees including Buff-tailed Bumblebee *Bombus terrestris* and Common Carder Bee *B. pascuorum*. The ideal situation in any single site is a mixture of both, with areas of long grass and short grass in close proximity. This arrangement, which has been wittily referred to as the 'mowhican cut', maximises plant diversity and vegetation structure, both of which are vitally important for other wildlife.

Frequent mowing to create short grass keeps the sward under around 5cm (2 inches), often with quite a lot of bare ground. These conditions mimic tightly grazed semi-natural grasslands, including sand dunes, chalk downland and limestone grassland, which are rich in species highly adapted to regular decapitation. On lawns, plants like Daisy, Greater Plantain *Plantago major* and Dandelion grow as rosettes with prostrate leaves close to the ground, ducking under the mower blades. They can quickly produce seeds after flowering (in as little as nine days in the case of Dandelion), allowing them to seed abundantly between mowing cycles. Other plants dodge the blades by adopting a prostrate form of growth, spreading laterally. In particular, White Clover, Selfheal, Creeping Buttercup, Common Bird's-foot-trefoil, Germander Speedwell *Veronica chamaedrys* and Thyme-leaved Speedwell *Veronica serpyllifolia* grow with long prostrate shoots or stolons that lie close to the ground. Their flowers are often produced in abundance above the foliage and get chopped off by the mower. This, however, simply stimulates the production of yet more flowers because no seeds are set (ripening seeds produce hormones that suppress further flowering, which is why we dead-head our garden plants to produce more flowers). In Daisy, mowing can result in the production of more than three times as many seedheads, while mown plants of Greater Plantain produce prostrate (rather than erect) flower stalks that can generate more than 30,000 seeds, 50% more than normal (Warwick & Briggs 1980a,b).

Continual decapitation can, over time, select genetic forms of plants more adapted to growing in short grass. In a wonderful series of experiments investigating these ecotypes, Warwick & Briggs (1978a,b, 1979, 1980a,c) found that prostrate forms of Annual Meadow-grass collected from bowling greens retained their prostrate growth when cultivated in a greenhouse, suggesting an underlying genetic mechanism. They also responded better to clipping by growing smaller and more sideways (tillering) compared to more erect plants from nearby flowerbeds. Greater Plantain also retained its dwarf form in cultivation. However, although smaller forms of Daisy, Yarrow *Achillea millefolium*, Ribwort Plantain *Plantago lanceolata* and Selfheal were found to grow in lawns, they didn't retain this character when grown under glass.

A final tactic to survive regular mowing is shown by small annuals that grow quickly and simply remain close to the ground. These include charming small clovers like Lesser Trefoil *Trifolium dubium*, Black Medick *Medicago lupulina* and Hop Trefoil *Trifolium campestre*, as well as Wall Speedwell *Veronica arvensis* and Thyme-leaved Sandwort

Arenaria serpyllifolia. Lesser Trefoil can be particularly floriferous in lawns, producing an average of 130 flowerheads per metre square, each with around 5–20 tiny individual flowers (Dines unpublished data).

These short-grass plants are some of the most floriferous species on lawns, and the quantities of flower can be impressive. Results of Plantlife's citizen science survey Every Flower Counts show that at peak flowering in May, the average lawn will have around 39 Daisy flowers/m^2 and nine Creeping Buttercup flowers/m^2. Dandelions, although conspicuous, tend to be rather sparsely distributed, averaging seven flowers/m^2, while Germander Speedwell averages five flowers/m^2. As spring turns to summer, the pattern of flowering changes quite dramatically. By July, the average lawn is dominated by White Clover with 33 flowers/m^2 and Selfheal with 30 flowers/m^2. Other plants like Bird's-foot-trefoil also reach a peak with nine flowers/m^2, as does Cat's-ear *Hypochaeris radicata* with four flowers/m^2 (Dines unpublished data).

With so many flowers packed into such small areas of grass, even regularly mown lawns can produce prodigious quantities of nectar and pollen. Nectar sugar is collected by pollinators for fuel, while pollen is a source of proteins and amino acids to feed developing larvae. Different species create different proportions of nectar and pollen, depending on their pollination strategy. Selfheal, for example, puts its effort into producing nectar sugar but relatively little pollen, while Daisy does the opposite, making much more pollen than nectar

LEFT: Short-grass lawns can be extremely floriferous with a mixture of plants adapted to growing in tightly mown swards, including White Clover, Selfheal and Common Bird's-foot-trefoil.

sugar (Baude *et al.* 2016). On the average regularly mown lawn with a good diversity of such species, nectar production in May reaches 26,964 microgrammes nectar sugar/m², which is roughly enough to provide the energy requirements of 2.5 honeybees/day. This rises in July to 75,863 microgrammes/m², enough to sustain 6.9 honeybees/day. Most of this extra nectar comes from White Clover, which is especially nectiferous (Dines unpublished data).

Almost all these short-grass species will also be present where longer grass is allowed to grow, but they're joined by a wider range of other species. These long-grass plants are less tolerant of regular mowing, growing when grass is left uncut between early spring and late summer. They tend to be taller-growing species that can compete with the dense sward of grass as it comes into flower, and include many traditional hay-meadow plants such as Meadow Buttercup *Ranunculus acris*, Oxeye Daisy, Tufted Vetch *Vicia cracca*, Yellow-rattle *Rhinanthus minor*, Common Sorrel *Rumex acetosa*, Common Knapweed *Centaurea nigra* and Common Ragwort *Jacobaea vulgaris*. These often flower during one short period of the year, or later in the year, so cannot cope with repeated mowing. If they are cut down in spring (as may be the case on a road verge), they can regrow and flower again but take much longer to do so, sometimes well into late summer or autumn.

BELOW: Areas of long grass, left unmown from early spring to late summer, allow a wide range of hay-meadow species that cannot tolerate repeated mowing to grow.

Although long-grass habitats tend to produce slightly fewer flowers per square metre than lawns (an average of 97 flowers/m^2 compared to 117 flowers/m^2, Dines unpublished data), the diversity of species – and therefore different flower shapes to attract different pollinators – is greater. Long-grass areas, for instance, can support dense populations of Yellow-rattle, which is exclusively pollinated by large species of bumblebee, including Garden Bumblebee *Bombus hortorum* and Early Bumblebee *B. pratorum*. Long grass also provides a wider range of foodplants and shelter for adults and larvae for a huge range of invertebrates including ground beetles, leaf beetles, capsid bugs, thrips, weevils, aphids, flies, leafminer moths, leafhoppers, craneflies, gnats and midges. This is why long grass is such a valuable habitat for wildlife.

The strangely contentious issue of urban wildflower meadows

The creation of urban wildflower meadows has become a popular response to the loss of species-rich habitats from rural areas, where more than 97% of meadows were lost in England and Wales between 1932 and 1984 (Fuller 1987), with further losses of 50–59% from the 1960s up to 2013 (Ridding *et al.* 2015). You'd be forgiven for thinking that nothing could be more wonderful and rewarding than filling patches of land with flowers for pollinating insects. Indeed, what better way to bring nature back into the city than by sowing a wildflower meadow? But botanists are a peculiar bunch, and nothing provokes them more than calling something 'a wildflower meadow' when it's not. One recent case sparked particular scorn and serves to illustrate the issue.

It all kicked off when nearly 13km (8 miles) of urban road verges and roundabouts around Rotherham, South Yorkshire, were planted with flowers in 2013. In a bid to bring some colour into the borough and provide flowers for pollinators, the council used a mixture of annuals formulated by Pictorial Meadows, a supplier of horticultural mixtures for amenity landscape planting. The resulting 'river of flowers' caused quite a stir and the colourful 'wildflower meadows' captured headlines in local press and national media. For botanists, the problem was that the flowers were not 'wild' and they weren't 'meadow' species. Instead, the mix included annual garden flowers such as Californian Poppy *Eschscholzia californica*, Garden Tickseed

Urban Plants

Coreopsis tinctoria and Mexican Aster *Cosmos bipinnatus*, all from North America and Mexico, Bullwort *Ammi majus*, Rose-of-heaven *Silene coeli-rosa* and Pot Marigold *Calendula officinalis* from southern Europe, and Garden Orache *Atriplex hortensis* from Central Asia, as well as cornfield annuals such as Cornflower *Centaurea cyanus* and Common Poppy *Papaver rhoeas*. Like many other such mixes that are available, it didn't include any of the grasses that are a critical component of meadows (which is one reason why these mixes pack such a floral punch).

For many botanists, this was a red rag to a bull. Social media filled with pleas from exasperated botanists that these are 'NOT wildflowers', 'NOT meadow flowers', 'NOT native flowers' and 'NOT meadows' (and believe me, when botanists begin to type in block capitals you know they're *really* upset). On the other hand, many residents responded by saying how stunning the flowers looked, how much better they were than the rank vegetation that was there before, and how much they loved seeing them while driving through their streets. Being told that they were somehow wrong to feel this way because these weren't 'real meadow flowers' didn't go down well and, as is so often the case on social media, arguments became polarised, heated and even vitriolic (at one point, the alarming hashtag #MeadowNazi was being bandied around).

BELOW: Urban verge displays, such as this one in Birmingham, are a new form of amenity horticulture aimed at enhancing the urban environment. They bring a lot of colour into the city and a lot of joy to residents. Just don't call them wildflower meadows!

It's true that these aren't genuine native wildflower meadows, far from it. But, instead, it might help to see these plantings for what they actually are – an attempt by local councils and others to make their town roads look more attractive and cared for, to do their bit for pollinators, and to test the water around what is an acceptable look for town-centre verges. No, they're definitely not 'natural', they're not 'wild' and it's not wild plant conservation. They're 'designer meadows', a new form of amenity horticulture aimed at enhancing the urban environment. They're also spectacular and they give a lot of people a lot of pleasure.

However, while these colourful horticultural mixes do indeed help pollinators, genuine wildflower meadows – complete with their diversity of grasses and broad-leaved herbs – have the potential to support a much wider range of wildlife by providing foodplants for invertebrates. If we take 67 of the most common plant species in a lowland neutral grassland, they collectively have the potential to support more than 1,400 different insect species, including 297 macro-moths, 193 micro-moths, 106 aphids, 102 gall midges, 91 weevils, 87 leaf-miner flies, 57 leaf beetles, 29 sawflies and 23 thrips. In contrast, a typical pollinator mix with a dozen cornfield and garden annuals would provide food to just 50 species of invertebrate, mainly various flies and moths (Dines unpublished data). Once established, genuine meadows also require much less maintenance, needing just

ABOVE: This upland hay meadow in Muker, North Yorkshire, provides food plants and shelter to a huge range of invertebrates. Wood Crane's-bill *Geranium sylvaticum*, for example, is a food plant for the Meadow Crane's-bill Weevil *Zacladus geranii* and the Crane's-bill Mining Sawfly *Fenella monilicornis*, while Red Clover *Trifolium pratense* alone can support 85 different species.

Urban Plants

ABOVE: Transformation of Everton Park, Liverpool, from a cornfield annual mix (left) to a more authentic wildflower meadow (right) following eight years of careful seeding and habitat management.

one hay-cut at the end of summer and maybe one more cut before spring. In contrast, areas with pollinator mixes have to be sprayed with herbicide, cleared, cultivated and re-sown with expensive seed mixes each year. For this reason, some councils are now looking towards more sustainable solutions, including seed mixes harvested from genuine native wildflower meadows.

There is also a worry that these pollinator mixes raise expectations and people begin to think that all wildflower habitats should deliver similarly intense floral displays. Generally, our native species are more delicate and much less concentrated. This is their inherent beauty. But in town centres, parks and window boxes and on urban roads and roundabouts, pollinator mixes remind us all of the beauty and value of flowers. And today, when people are more disconnected from the natural world – and plants in particular – than ever before, perhaps we should seize every opportunity to celebrate and love all the flowers in our lives.

These dramatic riots of colour, injected into the heart of the urban landscape and beloved by many residents, are perhaps best seen as the start of a transition to more authentic wildflower meadows. With

The grassy bits

ABOVE: In the first year after being created, the King's College wildflower meadow was vibrant with annual cornfield flowers, sown specifically to provide colour until the perennial meadow species became established.

care and the right management over time this can be achieved. A spectacular example is Everton Park in Liverpool, where eight years of careful seeding and habitat management through Kew's Grow Wild project has seen a cornfield annual mix transform into a young lowland neutral hay meadow full of traditional grassland species.

Other urban meadows are embarking on the same journey. In 2019, a part of the 250-year-old lawn at King's College, Cambridge, was cultivated and sown with a carefully formulated seed mix. This aimed to replicate traditional East Anglian hay meadows, with 62 different meadow species including Field Scabious *Knautia arvensis*, Quaking-grass and Cowslip and rarer species of conservation value including Clustered Bellflower *Campanula glomerata*, Sulphur Clover *Trifolium ochroleucon* and Purple Milk-vetch *Astragalus danicus*. In addition to these, 12 species of cornfield annuals were included to provide a splash of colour in the first few years (Marshall *et al.* 2023). Cue outrage from some botanists when the so-called wildflower meadow was seen to be a swathe of Common Poppy, Corncockle *Agrostemma githago*, Corn Marigold *Glebionis segetum* and Austrian Chamomile *Cota austriaca*.

However, a few years later these cornfield species are now receding, and genuine meadow plants are coming to the fore. The former lawn is rapidly transforming into an authentic hay meadow, helped by traditional management techniques which even include using a magnificent pair of shire horses to cut the hay. It's remarkable to see these animals at work in the centre of the city, a real spectacle that provides a further talking point around the loss of hay meadows and their cultural and historical significance.

The benefits of the new Cambridge meadow have been studied in detail (Marshall *et al.* 2023). Plant species richness was found to be 3.6 times higher than the traditional lawn, with 84 species recorded in total. This had a considerable influence on invertebrates. Diversity of spiders and bugs was 3.7 times higher than the lawn, and the number of individuals was 3.8 times higher, while total invertebrate biomass in the meadow was 25 times higher than the lawn. Insectivorous bats responded to this abundance, with 100 visits over the meadow compared to 32 over the lawn. The study also showed that regular mowing and fertilising of the traditional lawn meant its annual CO_2 emissions were 112 times higher than the meadow, while its maintenance regime was 132 times more expensive.

There were social benefits too. Nearly 280 university staff and students were asked about the meadow, and the response was overwhelmingly positive. Almost 70% said they'd also like a mix of lawn and meadow on their campus, while just four people said they'd prefer traditional lawn. Two-thirds of people had no objections to the conversion of the lawn to meadow, and of those that did, the main concern was around the loss of recreational space. Perhaps most importantly, more than 84% of people said meadows supported their well-being; as one person put it, 'Meadows are great, they heal my soul' (Marshall *et al.* 2023). All in all, the huge environmental and societal benefits of creating urban wildflower meadows far outweigh any concerns about where the species come from or whether they're 'real' meadow plants or not.

OPPOSITE:

TOP: Two shire horses, Cosmo and Boy, help out with the traditional annual hay-cut at the King's College wildflower meadow, Cambridge.

BELOW: The meadow, here in 2022 awash with Oxeye Daisy and Common Sorrel, has been extremely well received by university staff and students.

The grassy bits

Street trees

chapter eleven

We are rather peculiarly obsessed with trees, and urban trees in particular. We're passionate about them, we celebrate them, we have emotional connections with them and we fight for them when they come under threat. They're landmarks in the concrete jungle, large sentinels that can even become old friends. While we tend to ignore almost all the other plants growing at our feet, we cherish the trees. Perhaps it's something to do with their sheer physical size and presence; they are plants we can relate to, living organisms on our own scale. In the urban landscape, trees take on an even greater significance, totems for the natural world we've lost.

Urban trees and woodlands are undeniably valuable and bring many benefits. They substantially reduce the urban heat island by shading surfaces and cooling the air through evapotranspiration. They help to alleviate flooding by intercepting rainfall and improving soil permeability. They improve air quality by filtering particulates and contributing to carbon capture. And they have a dramatic effect on the aesthetics of urban landscapes, screening and softening harsh surfaces, improving mental and physical health and social cohesion, and reducing noise pollution (Jeanjean 2017, Rogers *et al.* 2015). And, of course, their leaves, branches, pollen, nectar, wood and roots provide shelter and food for a vast and interconnected web of other wildlife. But perhaps the most important benefit is one that's rarely mentioned. As Mark Johnston puts it in his excellent *Street Trees in Britain: A History*, trees are 'simply the most beautiful and majestic natural objects in an often dirty and depressing urban landscape' (Johnston 2017).

There are, of course, many different types of urban woodlands. As settlements expand and grow, they surround and engulf patches of established woodland. From light and airy Ash *Fraxinus excelsior*

OPPOSITE:
A wonderful avenue of London Plane trees provide shade for pedestrians on a Dublin street.

woods on limestone, to floodplain carr of willow *Salix* spp. and Alder *Alnus glutinosa*, and ancient woodlands of oak *Quercus* spp., these fragments of semi-natural woodland encapsulated by urban sprawl are valuable hotspots of urban biodiversity. On the edges of town, such fragments can be large and still retain many of their original species. But as time goes on and they get more fragmented and embedded within the urban sprawl, they become diminished. Habitat specialists such as Moschatel *Adoxa moschatellina* and Sanicle *Sanicula europaea* disappear, invasive native and alien species like Common Nettle *Urtica dioica*, Bramble *Rubus fruticosus* agg., Variegated Yellow Archangel *Lamiastrum galeobdolon* subsp. *argentatum* and Spanish and Hybrid Bluebell *Hyacinthoides hispanica* agg. come to dominate, and they become modified by our daily activities, the disturbance from footpaths and the abandonment of traditional woodland management, like coppicing and grazing.

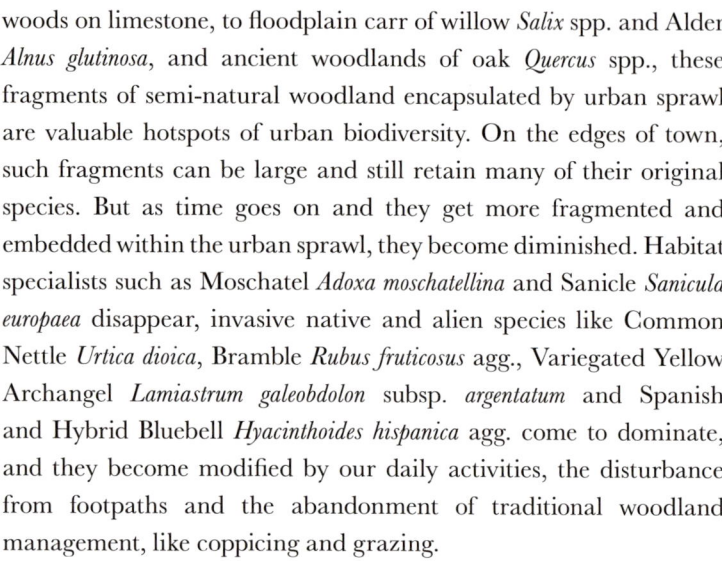

BELOW: A glorious specimen of our native Black Poplar on the junction of Pentonville Road and Rodney Street in central London.

Other urban woodlands arise from more recent planting or through natural regeneration. On patches of long-abandoned urban fallow land – especially around industrial sites and along railways and property boundaries – small woods occasionally develop, usually dominated by quick-growing species such as willow, birch *Betula* spp., Ash and Sycamore *Acer pseudoplatanus*. Small patches of woodland and groups of trees are also scattered across our parks and, especially, as corridors along the edges of roads and railways. These include trees that were originally planted but have since been augmented with other species by natural regeneration. In more open settings, like parks, gardens, business parks and industrial estates, lone trees can be found. As well as individuals planted to enhance the landscape, some of these are ancient trees of great character and cultural importance. Such sentinels are usually cherished relics of the pre-urban landscape, veteran specimens of oak, Black Poplar *Populus nigra* subsp. *betulifolia*, Sweet Chestnut *Castanea sativa*, elms *Ulmus* spp. and Yew *Taxus baccata* that were protected as they were swallowed up by the growing city. Fine examples include the 800-year-old Crouch Oak in Addlestone, Sussex, the 500-year-old Grantham Oak in Lincolnshire, and a magnificent veteran specimen of Black Poplar at Gorton Park, Manchester.

ABOVE: The Crouch Oak in the town of Addlestone, Surrey. This 800-year-old veteran Pedunculate Oak *Quercus robur* is famous for shading Queen Elizabeth I as she picnicked beneath its branches, presumably without the benefit of electric street lighting.

Then, of course, we have the trees planted along our streets. From splendid avenues of towering limes *Tilia* spp. lining Victorian suburbs to pretty flowering cherries *Prunus* spp. planted around modern housing estates, street trees are part of everyday urban life – the ones we encounter most frequently while walking around town. Street trees have, by their nature, been planted very deliberately, usually within the pavement or verge to provide a boundary alongside the road. Planting is normally done at regular intervals to create a continuous line or avenue, but individual trees are also common, especially around street junctions and bus stops. Street trees are particularly important in providing us with shade and shelter as we walk, and they make an enormous contribution to ameliorating the urban heat island and softening the urban landscape. This aesthetic enhancement has social and economic impacts too; streets lined with trees can increase house prices by as much as 15% and, given the choice, most urban residents say they'd prefer to live on streets that have trees (Rogers *et al.* 2015).

Before the 1950s, most street trees were very large-growing species. Victorians were particularly fond of the statuesque presence of limes, elms and London Plane *Platanus* × *hispanica*, and many of the biggest specimens were planted then, a living history now lining our streets. As new streets were built and others redesigned during the Industrial

ABOVE: Northumberland Avenue, London, with its particularly fine boulevard of London Plane trees shading the road and pavement. Planted in around 1886, they are very much a living history of Victorian street engineering.

Revolution, trees were planted with utmost care in newly constructed pavements, with large pits being dug and filled with 'proper soil' and drainage grates placed nearby to supply the roots with water (Johnstone 2017).

But, since then, we've come to favour smaller, more ornamental species that sit more comfortably within our streets and which require less maintenance (Gilbert 1989). The result is that streets today are overwhelmingly dominated by small, mainly non-native trees, many of which are planted with little care and which, sadly, suffer as a result.

For botanists, it's the spontaneous urban flora that provides the most interest, rather than trees that have been deliberately planted (anyone wanting to learn more about planted street trees should read the excellent and entertaining *London is a Forest* (2022) by Paul Wood). As well as the small range of native tree species that spring up around town, many of the alien trees planted along our streets and in front gardens, parks and amenity planting schemes also seed themselves around. A few of these go on to become well established in the urban landscape. They add a fascinating and often exotic component to the urban flora, but also include some very problematic invasive species.

You can't see the wood for the trees

Many urban areas are remarkably well endowed with trees and woodland. As of 2021, there were an estimated 94,385ha (233,230 acres) of **semi-natural woodland** within the urban boundary in the UK, 4.6% of the total urban area (ONS 2023). This is woodland that falls within the broad habitat definition, in other words patches of natural woodland more than 0.5ha in size and with 20% of the canopy more than 5m high. In addition to this there are estimated to be 73,700ha (182,116 acres) of **urban small woods** (which range in size from 0.1–0.5ha), 90,300ha (223,136 acres) of **groups of trees** (clusters of trees that are less than 0.1ha), and 15,000ha (37,066 acres) of **lone trees in open landscapes** (individual trees more than 2m high). That's an awful lot of woodland.

Getting a sense of the actual number of trees is much more difficult. Using a survey of 724 plots across London, the London iTree report estimates that there are 8.42 million trees in London (Rogers *et al.* 2015), nearly one tree for every person living in the city. Looking at street trees alone, the London Tree Map (2024) estimates there to be 880,000 individual trees in the England capital. So far, this project has collected data for 26 of the 33 London boroughs. The map also categorises each tree into one of 24 types, such as maple, cherry, lime, chestnut, birch and poplar, with London Plane not surprisingly being the most abundant. A similar map is being developed in Sheffield, where the number of street trees was estimated to be around 35,000 in 2006. This was, however, before the highly controversial programme of felling that saw more than 5,500 trees cut down between 2013 and 2015 (Lowcock 2023, see 'The future of the urban forest', page 329). In Cambridge, a council audit of trees in 2013 estimated that there were 240,000 trees in the city, although another survey in 2018 with different criteria upped this to 330,000 (Hill 2022). Clearly, counting trees isn't a straightforward business.

Many city councils have published tree action plans which estimate the number of their street trees – for example 80,000 in Manchester, 8,550 in Edinburgh (down from 11,000 in the 1990s), 30,000 in Plymouth and 9,000 in Belfast. It's been estimated that 84% of neighbourhoods in England have less than the government target of 20% tree coverage (Friends of the Earth 2023), so almost every town and city now appears to have its own ambitious tree-planting strategy, with targets to plant thousands more trees in the coming years.

Of course, trees and woodland aren't equally spread across the urban landscape, but are much more frequent in some areas than others. This inequality has a clear socio-economic link, with more affluent areas holding greater amounts of woodland cover. A recent study of 68 British urban settlements showed that the top five greenest urban centres were Exeter, Islington, Bristol, Bournemouth and Cambridge, while the bottom five were Glasgow, Leeds, Liverpool, Sheffield and Middlesbrough. It's notable that the top five are all in affluent parts of southern England, while the bottom five are ex-industrial areas in the North (Robinson *et al.* 2022).

Another recent survey in England has shown that the wealthiest urban areas have an average of 15% tree cover, while those with the highest rates of social deprivation have around 7% cover (Friends of the Earth 2023). Such differences often have historical roots. Large, detached Victorian houses, for instance, were often built on the outskirts of town, with large gardens that retained more trees from the previously rural landscape. Wealthier suburbs could also afford more street planting to recreate the tree-lined avenues that their residents enjoyed when visiting fashionable European cities like Paris and Brussels (Johnston 2017). In contrast, poorer Victorian neighbourhoods suffered from much denser terraced housing with little or no garden, and their residents had other priorities in life.

BELOW: 93% of street trees have been catalogued in the London Tree Map, including these impressive avenues of London Plane trees along Alma Grove and Balaclava Road in Bermondsey.

ABOVE: The socio-economics of street trees. Areas of dense, terraced housing in Liverpool have small gardens and few or no street trees. By contrast, wealthier roads with large detached and semi-detached houses have lines of mature trees on the street and large, well-wooded gardens.

The diversity of street trees

In order to understand which species are seeding into urban environments, we need to know which trees are being planted. The diversity involved is truly remarkable and might come as a surprise to many, as botanists tend not to record trees planted in streets, parks and gardens. However, data supplied by London borough councils show that they have 898 different species, cultivars and hybrids in their care, of which 91% are alien (Mick Crawley pers. comm.). In the pattern that's now familiar with other urban habitats, a few trees dominate the plantings but the vast majority are infrequent or rare. In this case, the top 14 species and cultivars make up 52% of trees in London, while 800 others make up just 10%. Some of the rarest include very unusual species such as the Chinese Lacquer-tree *Toxicodendron vernicifluum*, Tasmanian Alpine Yellow Gum *Eucalyptus subcrenulata* and Macedonian Oak *Quercus trojana*.

Of the trees on the list, at least 142 are regularly planted on London streets (Mick Crawley pers. comm.). As you might expect, London Plane takes the top spot by a considerable margin (9% of all trees), followed by Norway Maple *Acer platanoides* (5%), Lime *Tilia* × *europaea* (4%), Wild Cherry *Prunus avium* (3%), Hornbeam *Carpinus betulus* (3%) and Horse-chestnut *Aesculus hippocastanum* (2%). Surprising entries in the top 12 include Callery Pear *Pyrus calleryana* 'Chanticleer' (2%) and False-acacia *Robinia pseudoacacia* (1%), while some of London's wealthier boroughs seem to have a penchant for Maidenhair-tree *Ginkgo biloba*.

One important aspect of these plantings is that they are largely random, with little thought or planning over which species should go where and why (Oliver 1989). This leads to considerable variations in the types and proportions of trees in different towns and cities. In Sheffield, for example, Lime takes the top spot, followed by London Plane, Sycamore, Ash, Horse-chestnut and then elms. As well as these, Beech *Fagus sylvatica* and Alder are frequent, unlike in London (Oliver 1989).

Regional variations are also demonstrated by the biggest ever study of English street trees, a 1989 survey of 3,600 trees in 30 towns and cities from Exeter to Norwich and north to Durham (Hodge 1991). Unfortunately, the report only gives the genus of the trees, not the species, but the results show that maples *Acer* (22%), whitebeams *Sorbus* (18%), cherries *Prunus* (16%), birches *Betula* (8%) and limes *Tilia* (6%) were the most frequent street trees, with hawthorns *Crataegus*, ash *Fraxinus*, planes *Platanus*, False-acacia *Robinia* and apples *Malus* all a little way behind at 3%. In northern towns, however, birches, limes, rowans and Sycamore were more common, while maples were significantly more frequent in southern towns, along with False-acacia and whitebeams. Planting also significantly varies between town centres and the suburbs, perhaps reflecting the historical switch from large to small street trees. The biggest contrasts were between Plane trees, which are almost exclusively found in town and city centres, and hawthorns, which are virtually confined to the suburbs.

Horticultural fashions are notoriously fickle, and other species are now being planted more frequently. In Birmingham, a study of newly planted street trees found that Sweet Gum *Liquidambar styraciflua*, a small tree with flamboyant autumn foliage, was the third-most frequent species (9% of trees), while

BELOW: London Plane with its beautiful bark patterned like camouflage. The oldest and largest specimen is said to be the corpulent giant known as 'Barnie', planted around 1685 in Barn Elms, Richmond upon Thames.

Street trees

LEFT: A very fine specimen of Hawthorn 'Paul's Scarlet' *Crataegus* × *media*, in a London suburb. One of the most popular street trees, this is a hybrid between our two native species, Hawthorn *C. monogyna* and Midland Hawthorn *C. laevigata*.

Tulip-tree *Liriodendron tulipifera* was the eighth-most frequent (5% of trees) and Honey Locust *Gleditsia triacanthos* the twelfth (4% of trees). It's not known how well these species will fare in the urban landscape, but Sweet Gum and Honey Locust seemed to be performing well, with 93% of trees in the survey judged to be in good or fair condition six years after planting (Birmingham Tree People 2024).

LEFT: With its breathtaking autumn foliage, Sweet Gum has recently become a popular street tree. It's native to warmer parts of eastern North America and montane regions of Mexico and Central America, so may be benefiting from the warm embrace of the urban heat island.

The trees that seed

For the urban botanist, most interest lies with the trees that seed themselves spontaneously around the city. Many native species are prolific seeders, of course, especially those with small, lightweight seed, or winged seeds that can be carried on the wind. Perhaps the most commonly encountered are Sycamore, Ash, Silver Birch *Betula pendula* and Downy Birch *B. pubescens*, and willows such as Goat Willow *Salix caprea* and Rusty Willow *S. cinerea* subsp. *oleifolia*. Sometimes, many hundreds of such seedlings can be encountered along the edges of pavements, on walls, in disturbed ground, along gutters and on urban fallow land. Despite such impressive recruitment, the vast majority of these tiny trees are doomed to perish, and those on walls, pavements and road edges are especially vulnerable as they either become droughted or fail to reach a substrate that can sustain them. Chris Preston describes these as 'sink populations', with repeated annual germination of huge numbers of seedlings that almost never reach maturity (Preston & Chater in prep.). Those few that do survive are often removed when they get to a noticeable size.

Outside London, limes (also known as lindens) are perhaps the most frequent urban trees, forming magnificent, towering specimens with attractive heart-shaped leaves and flowers that scent the air in early summer. The majority are Lime *Tilia* × *europaea*, a fertile hybrid between our two native limes, Small-leaved Lime *T. cordata* and Large-leaved Lime *T. platyphyllos*, which are also commonly planted on streets. Gilbert (1989) takes a rather dim view of limes as urban trees since they have many shortcomings for the role. They're large and fast growing so need constant pruning to keep them in check, but the removal of dominant leader shoots stimulates the production of many small 'epicormic' shoots from the base of the truck, which also then need regular pruning, making specimens look untidy if they're not attended to. Trees also become covered with huge populations of Lime Aphid *Eucallipterus tiliae* in summer. These cover the undersides of leaves, extracting sugar and amino-acids from the sap of the phloem. However, the amino-acids are rather dilute, so

BELOW: Like the vast majority of similar seedlings, this birch is almost certainly doomed. Growing between a paving slab and a wall, there's little substrate for it to root into and so it will probably perish in the next drought.

the aphids take in large quantities of sugar-rich fluid, excreting the excess from their backsides. As anyone who has parked their car underneath a lime will know, everything below the canopy quickly gets covered with this sticky deposit. To make matters worse, the sugary coating then turns black as it's colonised by sooty moulds (*Fumago* and *Capnodium* spp.). On the plus side, of course, the aphids are a source of food for other wildlife and the trees are extremely important for pollinators, especially Honey Bee *Apis mellifera*, Buff-tailed Bumblebee *Bombus terrestris* and hoverflies. The size and growth rate of *Tilia* × *europaea* means Small-leaved Lime is becoming a more popular street tree these days as it's smaller and more easily managed. All these limes seed frequently in urban settings but, again, they almost never reach maturity.

The majority of alien trees only rarely reproduce from seed; most of those on the long list from the London boroughs have never been known to arise spontaneously. In some cases, this is due to barriers in seed production. One of the most common street trees,

ABOVE: Seedlings of limes *Tilia* spp. have unique, deeply divided seed-leaves (cotyledons) that are worth hunting for around the base of the trees in spring.

BELOW: The most common street tree in Great Britain is probably Lime *Tilia* × *europaea*, here forming an impressive avenue along Muirhouse Parkway, Edinburgh.

for example, is Kanzan Cherry *Prunus* 'Kanzan', a neat, spreading tree laden with pink double flowers in spring. It's rather too Barbara Cartland for me (I much prefer the white of *Prunus* 'Tai-haku'), but it's so popular it's become a real signature of suburbia. The flowers, though, are completely sterile, never producing fertile seed, and so spontaneous seedlings are unknown on our pavements.

Few alien trees are as beautiful or popular as the birches, particularly varieties of Himalayan Birch *Betula utilis*, Erman's Birch *B. ermanii* and Chinese Red Birch *B. albosinensis* with their extraordinary colourful bark ranging from white to tan, and salmon to reddish-orange. This is a really diverse genus and nearly 50 different species, varieties and hybrids are grown in London gardens (Mick Crawley pers. comm.). Many remain small and compact and are ideal for the urban environment. However, despite being so common along streets, outside offices and in amenity planting schemes, seedlings of the alien species and varieties have, for some reason, never been reported. A hybrid between Himalayan Birch and Silver Birch was discovered in Cambridge in 2001 (Leslie 2019), but so far regeneration of the alien species themselves remains elusive. Now, there's a challenge for someone!

BELOW: Many different birches are grown for their colourful bark, such as here with *Betula albosinensis* 'China Ruby' (top) and *Betula ermanii* 'Grayswood Hill' (below). The horizontal streaks are lenticels, where porous openings in the bark allow air into the tissues below.

A slightly different case is that of Maidenhair-tree, a very beautiful conifer from China that's enormously popular for its fan-shaped leaves that turn butter yellow in autumn. A 'living fossil', known to be over 200 million years old, plants are either male or female (the species is dioecious) and so both are needed for fruits to be produced. Unfortunately, though, the fleshy prune-sized fruits smell strongly of vomit because their skins contain butyric acid, a fatty acid which is also found in our intestines. Female trees are therefore rarely planted (after all, who wants their street to smell of sick?) and spontaneous seedlings of Maidenhair-tree are very uncommon.

Other alien trees, of course, have no such barriers and seed around freely. London Plane, for instance, is a fertile hybrid between American Sycamore *Platanus occidentalis* and the hardy but warmth-loving Oriental Plane

ABOVE: Maidenhair-tree *Ginkgo biloba* in autumn on Chipping Campden high street, Gloucestershire. It's remarkable to think that this and several other species of *Ginkgo* have inhabited Great Britain in the past, including *G. huttonii* in Yorkshire during the Jurassic, and *G. gardneri* on the Isle of Mull in the Palaeocene.

ABOVE: Star of the suburban retail car park, Swedish Whitebeam *Sorbus intermedia* is a magnet for berry-eating birds like thrushes and blackbirds, and often attracts small groups of winter-visiting Waxwings *Bombycilla garrulus*.

P. orientalis. It was first recorded as growing at Oxford Botanic Garden in 1666 and its qualities as an urban tree were quickly recognised; it grows fast, responds very well to pollarding (useful for when it has outgrown its space), is very tolerant of air pollution and does well with a restricted root-space in poor soil. It was widely planted on streets from the early 1800s, but it wasn't until 1939 that the first self-sown seedlings were noted growing on the Thames Path at Mortlake in central London (Stroh *et al.* 2023). Today, it seeds itself around very freely with dispersal aided by a tuft of stiff hairs on each seed that catch the wind. Although widely planted throughout England, the highest density of trees is still in the capital.

Urban Plants

ABOVE: One of our fastest-spreading urban trees, Grey Alder is very cold-tolerant and fixes nitrogen through symbiotic bacteria in its root nodules, helping it to survive on infertile soils.

Another alien tree that seeds freely is Swedish Whitebeam *Sorbus intermedia*. This is one of a select group that are very commonly planted in the car parks of supermarkets and edge-of-town retail parks, as well as on streets. They are generally small and compact with neat crowns and grow steadily into low-maintenance trees. Swedish Whitebeam is native to Finland, Sweden, Norway and the Baltic and was first grown in Great Britain in 1789, but has soared in popularity and records are increasing, especially in the last 20 years.

Two species of alder *Alnus* are regular components of the urban car-park planting pack, as well as being popular street trees. Originally from Corsica, southern Italy and Albania, both seed prolifically and are increasing. Grey Alder *A. incana* is the more common of the two and forms an elegant small tree with a grey trunk and greyish-green, corrugated leaves (*incana* means grey). It was first grown in Great Britain in 1780 and tolerates a wide range of wet and dry soils, which might explain why it's doing so well. Unlike other non-native trees, spontaneous seedlings of this species do reach maturity and often appear on urban fallow ground and railway embankments. It is, for example, one of the fastest-spreading species in Newcastle upon Tyne (James Common pers. comm.). Italian Alder *A. cordata* is similar in size and shape, but is slightly coarser with smooth, dark green, heart-shaped leaves. It does well on drier soils and seeds around just as enthusiastically as Grey Alder in many areas.

Another exceptionally common urban tree, although one that's often overlooked, is Lawson's Cypress *Cupressus lawsoniana*. Originally from California and Oregon in North America, its fast rate of growth and eventual size make it unsuitable as a street tree, but it's very commonly planted in gardens, parks and churchyards. It seeds prolifically and small plants can often be found on walls and along their bases. Most of these eventually perish, or they're removed when they get noticeable, but it does become established on railway embankments, urban fallow land and woodland margins. The number of records has increased significantly since the 1990s, and it's notably frequent in London, Birmingham and Edinburgh.

One of the most popular exotic tree-like plants for London front gardens, and relishing the warmth of the urban heat island, is Cabbage-palm *Cordyline australis*. Perhaps it reminds people of their summer holidays abroad, giving their gardens a touch of the Riviera. Originally from New Zealand, it eventually reaches tree-like proportions of 8m (26ft), but even young plants are capable of producing the large, branching flowerheads which are soon packed with seeds. These germinate where they fall on pavements and amenity areas, but the ugly brown seedheads are sometimes removed from garden specimens and dumped on waste ground, where plants become established. They've even been known to be thrown into the River Thames, where they get washed downriver leading to seedlings appearing on the riverbank (Mark Spencer pers. comm.).

London's intense heat island also benefits other exotic trees. One of the most prolific seeders, and a plant that could become quite problematic in the future, is Foxglove-tree *Paulownia tomentosa*. A native of China, this beautiful species has been grown in Great Britain since 1838 and is highly prized in gardens for its large, softly hairy leaves and spikes of exotic lavender flowers. It's an exceptionally

LEFT: Cabbage-palm fruiting prolifically in the warmth of central London. In its native New Zealand, the leaves have been used as a source of fibre for cloth, anchor ropes, fishing lines and baskets.

RIGHT: Foxglove-tree is an attractive and fast-growing species from China. In one ancient custom, seeds of the species would be planted on the birth of a girl. When she eventually got married, the tree would be felled and the wood carved to make beautiful objects for her dowry.

RIGHT: Seedlings of Foxglove-tree growing in a London street basement. Once established, these young plants are capable of growing up to 2m per year in good conditions.

fast grower, with young shoots capable of putting on nearly 2m (6ft) per year (a rate of growth that has attracted the attention of biofuel producers) and leaves that can reach 60cm (2ft) across (catching the eye of jungle-style gardeners). Although it's hardy to around -15°C, the flowers are produced before the leaves in April or May and are susceptible to late frosts. Only in milder areas and large cities do they regularly survive and produce seedpods, each of which releases up to 2,000 tiny, winged seeds into the air. In some parts of central London, it's now springing up all over the place and seedlings are surprisingly frequent along the base of walls, in pavement cracks and on path sides and waste ground. It even seems capable of invading dense urban woodland (Mark Spencer pers. comm.). This is certainly a species to watch out for in the future, and one that could easily become seriously invasive.

Another rather exotic species that's seeding well in parts of London is Mount Etna Broom *Genista aetnensis*. Originally from Sardinia and Sicily, including the slopes of Mt Etna at altitudes of 900–1,890m (3,000–6,000ft), it grows in open, stony and rather poor soil. It has been grown in British gardens since its introduction in 1823 but is only popular in southern areas and warmer cities. Plants are drought tolerant and fast growing, eventually reaching up to 9m (30ft), and look spectacular in full flower during July and August, when the thin, drooping branches are clothed with fragrant, yellow, pea-like blooms. Each pod contains two or three seeds, and in London at least it's seeding into areas of rough ground, path sides, parks and urban fallow land.

Two other trees in the pea family (Fabaceae) are also enthusiastic seeders. Laburnum *Laburnum anagyroides* needs little introduction, as its cascades of yellow flowers adorn countless suburban gardens, parks and roadsides. Its beauty attracted the attention of early

BELOW: A particularly impressive group of Mount Etna Broom growing in central London, with a large Buddleja *Buddleja davidii* and Tree-of-heaven *Ailanthus altissima* for company.

travellers, who brought it back from the mountains of central Europe by 1596, making it one of the first ornamental trees to be introduced to Britain. Hardy and tolerant of urban pollution, it seeds very freely onto roadsides, railways and urban fallow sites. Mapping the frequency of this species at the 2-km tetrad scale clearly shows London, Cambridge, Norwich, Birmingham, Manchester, Liverpool, Sheffield, Leeds, Newcastle upon Tyne, Edinburgh, Glasgow and Aberdeen. It's one of our most urban of alien trees.

Slightly more exotic is False-acacia from eastern North America. This looks rather like Laburnum but with shorter spikes of white flowers. A yellow-leaved variety 'Frisia' is particularly popular, despite the colour making it look like it's rather ill and suffering from chlorosis (it also genuinely suffers from a new die-back disease). The species arrived here a little later than Laburnum, in 1634, and is much less common but is frequent in and around London, Birmingham, Manchester and Liverpool. As well as seeding into pavements, roadsides, railway embankments and urban fallow land, it spreads aggressively by suckers. In many parts of Europe this is a highly invasive and problematic species, taking over urban waste ground, quarries, hedgerows and road verges and damaging valuable semi-natural habitats like grazing pastures and coppiced woodlands (Sitzia *et al.* 2016). Control is extremely difficult, especially because of its suckering habit (Vítková *et al.* 2017). Thankfully, the species doesn't behave quite so badly in our cooler oceanic climate yet, but it is nonetheless seeding and suckering prolifically in London.

Other exotic trees are also starting to seed themselves around in London, as well as other towns and cities. Indian Horse-chestnut *Aesculus indica*, a Himalayan species ranging from Afghanistan to Nepal, often seeds itself around in parks as an understorey tree. As well as being very attractive, it has the distinct advantage of not being affected by the Horse-chestnut Leaf Miner *Cameraria ohridella* that plagues common Conker trees. Despite its common name, Pride-of-India *Koelreuteria paniculata* is native to north-east China and Korea. It's a large tree with ash-like leaves and heads of yellow flowers. Seedlings are increasingly frequent in parks, pavements and on waste ground, and sometimes get established and grow to maturity.

Another dramatic urban tree is Indian Bean Tree *Catalpa bignonioides*, a large, spreading species native to the south-eastern United States (Alabama, Florida, Georgia, Louisiana and Mississippi). Introduced to Great Britain in 1762, it's popular in large

LEFT: Indian Bean Tree *Catalpa bignonioides* flowering in front of Big Ben. The genus name comes either from the native American Catawba tribe, or from the Muscogee word 'kathulpa' meaning 'head with wings', referring to the large, fringed flowers or the papery fringed seeds.

gardens and parks where it's grown for its heart-shaped leaves and spikes of white flowers. These are followed by narrow, cylindrical pods up to 40cm (16 inches) long that look like beans. They remain on the tree over winter and split open in spring, releasing thousands of winged seeds that disperse widely. There is a famous row of six magnificent Indian Bean Trees under the shadow of Big Ben, thought to have been planted in 1857 and now bearing wonderfully gnarled trunks. Seedlings were reported in Parliament Square as long ago as 1983 (Palmer 1983) and have now been spotted at several sites across London, and also in Cambridge. Again, this is a species that could increase in our warming climate.

Ailanthus altissima: a tree of many names

In 1743, Pierre Nicolas d'Incarville, a Jesuit priest, sent seeds of a promising new tree from Beijing to Paris. He thought it was a form of Chinese Varnish Tree *Toxicodendron vernicifluum*, a plant highly prized for its sap that dries to form a hard lacquer which has been used to protect wooden objects for at least 4,500 years. A few years later in 1751, seed was sent from Paris to three English gardeners: Peter Collinson, an avid plant collector known as the Peckham Botanist; Philip Miller, superintendent of the Physic Garden at Chelsea; and Philip Webb, a man described as having 'a curious exotic garden in Busbridge, London'. All three grew the tree under different names, creating huge confusion, but it was soon realised that the plant was an entirely novel species and, unfortunately, didn't yield any lacquer. Although recognised as an *Ailanthus* in 1788, taxonomic confusion reigned until 1916, when the plant's identity as *Ailanthus altissima* was finally settled. Our common name for it, **Tree-of-heaven**, is often said to come from the habit of the branches to grow rapidly skywards, but it actually comes from the Moluccan word for another species, *ailanto*, meaning 'a tree of heaven', after which the genus is also named (Hu 1979).

The new tree was held in high esteem by those early growers who admired its elegant foliage, rapid growth in polluted urban environments, and its luxuriant, exotic appearance. It became a favourite of gardeners by the end of the eighteenth century and through the nineteenth and twentieth centuries was widely planted across London. But then the 'heavenly' qualities of the species began to wane. When large trees are pruned to keep them manageable, they begin to sucker fanatically, pushing up paving slabs and breaking through concrete and tarmac. These suckers can sometimes appear as much as 27m (89ft) from the parent plant. As for the leaves, they might look beautiful but they emit a strong, foetid smell when crushed, while the male flowers also produce an evil-smelling stench, earning the tree another name, '**Stinking Sumac**'. The tree also launches chemical warfare on its neighbours, with leaves and bark leaching an allelopathic chemical, ailanthone, that can suppress the germination of other species – although this chemical has recently been shown to have strong anti-cancer properties (Ding 2020). As if all this wasn't enough, the tree can seed prolifically. Each flowerhead is capable of producing several hundred 'keys' with two wings that are twisted at each end. This causes them to helicopter like crazy when they fall, helping them travel far in the wind. Dispersal distances of more than 100m (330ft) have been measured, and turbulence from vehicles and trains also aids their spread (Kowarik and Säumel 2007).

Its enthusiastic suckering and seeding have turned Tree-of-heaven into a highly accomplished urban invader, regarded as a noxious weed in many parts of Europe, North America, Canada, Japan, South Africa and Australia (Nava 2014). Its fondness for taking over run-down urban areas has earned it the name '**Ghetto Palm**' in North America, while in Great Britain and Europe it has become known as the '**Tree-of-hell**'. Plants are particularly prone to growing in the most inappropriate places at the base of walls and in front of doors and windows, but curiously they often become admired by local residents who perhaps regard them as an exotic sign of nature reclaiming the urban landscape. The trees have an almost mystical ability to blend in wherever they sprout, brazenly growing so large so quickly that people think they must surely have been intentionally planted (Wood 2022).

This tree is clearly changing behaviour in our warming climate. In 2002, seed production was reported as rare (Preston *et al.* 2002), but by 2011 large crops of seed were being noted in warm summers in London and other parts of the south-east (Dehnen-Schmutz 2016). Today, seeding is an almost annual occurrence and spontaneous plants are encountered in urban areas with increasing frequency. Although the tree tolerates temperatures down to -33°C, seedlings are much more sensitive and can be killed in severe frosts of -10°C (Kowarik and Säumel 2007). Cosseted by the urban heat island, there has been a dramatic increase in records since 2000, especially in London, but self-sown seedlings have now been reported from Exeter, Bath, Weston-super-Mare, Cambridge, Wolverhampton, Nottingham and as far north as Sheffield.

In its native China, the tree is known as *Ch'un Shu* (pronounced a little like 'train' and 'sure') meaning '**spring-tree**'. This is not because its unfurling foliage is one of the first signs of spring, but rather because it's the last tree to come into leaf, the swelling buds a sign of release from severe winter cold and associated privation. This link is manifest in a rather alarming rural nursery rhyme, '*ch'un-shu mao tsuan, o-ti ch'ung-jên fan po yen*' – 'as the unfolding buds of ailanthus appear, the helpless white eyes of the starving people turn clear' (Hu 1979).

Whatever you call it, this is a tree that simply can't be ignored as it romps its way through the urban jungle.

Seedheads of Tree-of-heaven in central London.

Tree-of-heaven in a doorway, Skinner Steet, Islington, London.

Large specimens of Tree-of-heaven can reach more than 20m (60ft).

Urban Plants

The return of the epiphytes

During the 1950s and 1960s, when sulphur dioxide levels were at their highest, many epiphytic bryophytes that grow on trees just couldn't tolerate the relentless acid rain and soot of industry. Now that SO_2 levels are at their lowest levels for decades, many species are returning and, today, street trees provide wonderful habitats for epiphytic bryophytes. Located right beside the carriageway, though, they're now exposed to some of the highest levels of nitrogen pollution from vehicle exhausts, and only the most pollution-tolerant species can survive.

Because the trunks of street trees have been bare for so long, they haven't attracted much attention from bryologists. As Jeff Duckett and Silvia Pressel put it in their wonderful recent study of London street-tree bryophytes, there was a time when 'not even the most eccentric amongst us would have dreamt of spending any time at all looking at epiphytes along major urban roads in a large city accompanied by the almost constant roar of traffic, not to mention incredulous passers-by' (Duckett & Pressel 2019). How things have changed. Now, street trees are proving deeply rewarding hunting grounds for the prodigal mosses returning to our city centres.

In order to chart this change, Jeff and Silvia surveyed 504 mature trees lining 20 roads in London in 2018. Those with the best

RIGHT: One of the most common street-tree epiphytes in London is White-tipped Bristle-moss, forming small tufts studded with capsules. The long white hair on each leaf is very distinctive.

bryophyte floras were Plane, limes, maples and Ash, each supporting 29–31 species. Other trees were universally poor, with alders, birches, cherries, Ginkgo, oaks, and rowans and whitebeams all supporting very few or no bryophytes at all.

Across the survey, 36 different bryophyte species were recorded. The most common, found on more than 83% of trees, were White-tipped Bristle-moss *Orthotrichum diaphanum* and Capillary Thread-moss *Bryum capillare*, both of which are also common on other urban substrates like walls and concrete. Like many mosses, bring them under a ×10 hand lens and their astonishing beauty is revealed; it's difficult to pass Capillary Thread-moss without a closer look at its extraordinary capsules. After these two species, the most frequent were the equally beautiful Grey-cushioned Grimmia *Grimmia pulvinata*, which is also common on walls (see Chapter 8), and Wood Bristle-moss *Lewinskya affinis*, found on 60% and 54% of trees respectively.

Alongside these tufted (acrocarp) mosses, the most common mat-forming (pleurocarp) species was Cypress-leaved Plait-moss *Hypnum cupressiforme*, encountered on 44% of trees. This very widespread and frequent woodland moss often carpets entire trunks and branches with its flat, mid-green shoots. Each of these is clothed with tiny overlapping leaves, looking like a plait of hair. Other pleurocarpous mosses include Clustered Feather-moss *Rhynchostegium confertum*

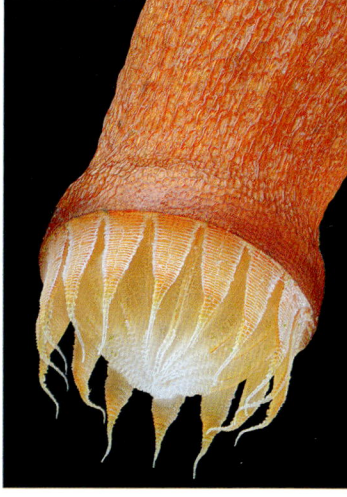

ABOVE: The spore capsule of Capillary Thread-moss is tipped with a ring of peristome teeth that fold in and out depending on humidity to control the release of spores. The diameter of the capsule is around 1.1mm.

LEFT: Cypress-leaved Plait-moss *Hypnum cupressiforme* is the most common mat-forming (pleurocarp) moss on street trees in London. The word *cupressiforme* means 'with the form of cypress' and the shoots do indeed resemble tiny versions of this conifer.

(24%), Creeping Feather-moss *Amblystegium serpens* (20%) and Velvet Feather-moss *Brachytheciastrum velutinum* (19%).

London's street trees have also been colonised by a fascinating group of screw-mosses *Syntrichia*. The most frequent is Small Hairy Screw-moss *S. laevipila* (38% of trees), followed by Marble Screw-moss *S. papillosa* (18%). A few decades ago, this latter species would have caused bryologists to squeal with excitement when discovered on mature hedgerow and roadside trees. Since the fall in SO_2 levels, it has made a dramatic recovery and is now much more common. It also seems to relish quite high levels of nitrogen, so urban trees have become a favourite haunt. One of the larger-leaved species, Water Screw-moss *S. latifolia* (9%), usually grows at the base of trees beside rivers where floods cover it with silt. Street trees therefore sound like an unlikely habitat, but it has found its own little niche around the bottom of trunks where it gets splashed by water from the road, full of grit and dust. It also colonises tarmac in this position. The final two species making up the group are Intermediate Screw-moss *S. montana* (9.3% – see Chapter 8) and Lesser Screw-moss *S. virescens* (5.2%). It's not just in London that these species are increasing. Marble Screw-moss is now abundant in Bristol (David Hawkins pers.

TOP: Clustered Feathermoss, a neat pleurocarpous moss of street trees. The abundant capsules appear in late autumn and winter.

CENTRE: Small Hairy Screw-moss is the most common of the genus on street trees in London, and readily identified by the blunt leaf tips that end in a very long, white hair.

BOTTOM: Once scarce enough to make some bryologists leap for joy, Marble Screw-moss is common on urban street trees now that SO_2 levels have fallen.

comm.), Cardiff and towns in Pembrokeshire (Bosanquet, 2010 and pers. comm.), while Small Hairy Screw-moss is also frequent. These species are common on street trees in Cambridge, too, but are outnumbered here by Intermediate Screw-moss and Lesser Screw-moss (Preston & Hill 2019).

As can be seen from this brief dip into street-tree bryophytes, these micro-niches offer much to discover. Many trees in London now support more than ten different species, the current record being a Plane tree with eighteen species. Even a tiny patch of bark can support eight or more different bryophytes, enough to entertain anyone with a hand lens and a few minutes to spare.

The dog-pee zone

The UK is home to around 13 million dogs (Anderson *et al.* 2023). As anyone with a male dog will know, marking their territory is a behaviour that borders on obsession. Any object will do, but trees are an absolute favourite target. And, since the main aim of urinating is to let other dogs know you're around, the same trees get sprayed repeatedly. In cities with large populations of dogs, trees on streets and in parks come in for particular attention, especially those outside blocks of flats, on street corners and entrances to parks. No one has yet measured the quantities involved, but some trees must take a lot of urine.

LEFT: A west highland terrier cocks his leg against a parkland tree, adding his contribution to the dog-pee zone (DPZ). Taller breeds would be able to reach about 40–50cm up the tree.

In response to all this activity, the dog-pee zone (DPZ) develops as a feature around the base of some urban trees. Because of the amount of ammonia and nitrogen produced by the urine, most bryophytes and lichens simply can't cope and the DPZ becomes dominated by a film of green algae (Duckett & Pressel 2019, Gilbert 1989). The most common species involved is *Rosenvingiella radicans*, a terrestrial, filamentous green alga that relishes nitrogen-rich sites (Michael Guiry pers. comm., Rindi *et al.* 2004). It's attached to the tree with small root-like rhizoids, and usually looks like a light to dark green covering of velvet on the trunk, though most people would probably describe it more prosaically as 'green slime'. On the soil around the base of the tree, other nitrophilous algae can grow, including *Klebsormidium flaccidum* and *Prasiola crispa* (Michael Guiry pers. comm.).

Several lichens that are extremely tolerant of nitrates and ammonium salts can survive in the DPZ, including *Myriolecis dispersa* and, in slightly less intense conditions, *Physcia tenella* and *Phaeophyscia orbicularis* (Gilbert 1989). A few nitrogen-tolerant mosses also survive. The most common and widespread of these include Capillary Thread-moss and Redshank, while the rarer Lesser Screw-moss is associated with the DPZ in London and Brighton (Duckett & Pressel 2019).

BELOW: The nitrate-loving alga *Rosenvingiella radicans* growing on a tree in Galway, Ireland, where lots of dogs pass nervously on their way to a veterinary practice nearby. Note the dense growth of bryophytes just above the DPZ.

It must be said that the DPZ is not always clearly developed on trees that get a lot of attention from dogs. Likewise, it can be present on trees where there are no dogs. Nitrogen levels are now more universally raised by vehicle emissions, so it may be that the effect is more generally spread out over the urban landscape than it used to be. Conversely, nitrogen levels from vehicle exhausts are at their highest within a few metres of the roadside. This nitrogen is deposited by rain and washed down trunks, becoming most concentrated at the base, encouraging the growth of algae. Many nitrogen-loving algae are also found on damp areas at the base of urban walls, including *Rosenvingiella radicans* and *Prasiola calophylla*. This latter species likes concrete where dogs leave their mark, and is particularly noticeable on walls around housing estates (Michael Guiry pers. comm.).

Tree pits

Trees planted in hard urban landscapes need somewhere to get their roots down into the soil, and the hole through the paving slabs, concrete or tarmac around the base of the trunk is known as a tree pit. This might be one of those cases where there's a whole world of engineering, hidden underground out of sight, that you never knew about. Tree pits aren't just important for trees, though: they provide extremely valuable areas of open soil in an otherwise unrelentingly impenetrable urban landscape, one of the few places where plants can actually get their roots in and grow.

One approach to planting trees in pavements is to dig as small a hole as possible, drop it in, pave or tarmac around the trunk, and hope for the best. This cheap and easy approach is, however, prone to failure. Many street trees planted this way die within the first few months as their roots are unable to move into the dry, compacted substrate around them. Those that do survive often go on to lift up the paving surface, creating trip hazards, injuries and costly insurance claims. Such trees inevitably end up being cut down and removed anyway.

A much better method is to construct something that will help the tree survive in its position for many years. Generally, young trees initially need around $3m^3$ of good topsoil in which to root, which isn't always available under a pavement (a mature tree will require more than ten times as much substrate as this, but it's a good start). Another big problem for street trees is soil compaction from pavement footfall and road traffic. Hard surfaces with heavy pedestrian or vehicle traffic exert huge forces on the soil below, destroying its structure, reducing aeration and creating an environment totally unsuitable for root growth. And, of course, getting enough water under an impervious surface is a critical challenge for water-hungry trees.

In order to combat these problems, various engineering options have been developed. These generally use mesh-sided modular plastic formers (rather like very large plastic crates) that are set in a large underground

BELOW: This poorly planted Plane (*Platanus*) tree is lifting the paving stones (known as paving heave) and creating a trip hazard. Unfortunately, the tree will probably be cut down and removed as a result.

Urban Plants

RIGHT: Installation of a modern tree pit. This large tree is being placed into a modular plastic former filled with topsoil. This supports the pavement above, which can come close to the trunk, preventing soil compaction. Additional engineering encourages irrigation of the roots.

BELOW: A tree pit in Llandudno Junction, Conwy, supporting Narrow-leaved Ragwort *Senecio inaequidens*, Herb-Robert *Geranium robertianum*, Hedge Mustard *Sisymbrium officinale* and Smooth Sow-thistle *Sonchus oleraceus*.

hole and filled with topsoil. A membrane is placed over the top and covered with the paving. This hard top surface is therefore supported by the plastic supports, keeping the topsoil open and aerated. The tree is planted into a cavity in the plastic formers, which often have additional barriers to help direct roots downwards and away from the paved surface. To improve irrigation, water is collected from the surface and directed towards the rootball, while stability is provided by underground guying attached to the plastic formers. Above ground, additional irrigation comes from permeable surfaces, while the tree is protected using metal grilles and vertical guards.

As well as ensuring the survival of street trees, tree pits offer small areas of open soil for other plants to establish. These tiny fragments of habitat, often little more than a metre square in size, might seem rather insignificant and unimportant. But in urban landscapes they can be critical in sustaining populations, reducing habitat fragmentation and providing refugia from which plants can recolonise the pavement. Often, they're the only remaining patches of green, especially in heavily paved city centres, and can be the most frequent green patches encountered by local residents (Vega & Küffer 2021).

It is likely that many of the hundreds of plant species that exist on pavements (see Chapter 7) grow in tree pits. Sadly, there are no studies of our own tree-pit flora, but Omar *et al.* (2018) have considered the plants growing around 1,474 trees on 26 streets in the Bercy district of Paris, France. They found 117 species in all, with each tree pit home to an average of 4.8 species. By far the most frequent was our ubiquitous urban friend, Annual Meadow-grass *Poa annua*, found in 80% of tree pits. Next, and rather a long way behind at 45%, were Canadian Fleabane *Erigeron canadensis* and Dandelion *Taraxacum* agg., with Wall Barley *Hordeum murinum* just behind at 40%. The top 12 was completed with eight species occurring in 8–26% of tree pits, namely Smooth Sow-thistle *Sonchus oleraceus*, Shepherd's-purse *Capsella bursa-pastoris*, London-rocket *Sisymbrium irio*, Common Chickweed *Stellaria media*, Scented Mayweed *Matricaria chamomilla*, Knotgrass *Polygonum aviculare*, Prickly Lettuce *Lactuca serriola* and Groundsel *Senecio vulgaris*. Most of the species (40%) were dispersed by wind, while others were mainly dispersed by gravity (28%) and by animals (22%). Tree pits with compacted soil had significantly fewer species (often only the trampling-tolerant Greater Plantain *Plantago major*), as did those covered with metal grilles.

Perhaps the most unexpected result was the influence the species of tree had on this flora. False-acacia supported the fewest species in each tree pit (an average of 2.8), probably because it's allelopathic, producing a cocktail of robinetin, myricetin and quercetin to suppress root and shoot growth of other species. Horse-chestnut supported just over three species, while cherries, hornbeams and limes all supported around four species. Tree pits around Plane trees were richer, with five species. The big surprise, though, is that the tree supporting most species was the alien invasive Tree-of-heaven (see box on pages 318–319), with an average of 6.4 species. Given that this species is also allelopathic, producing toxic ailanthone from its leaves to suppress germination of other plants, this result seems inexplicable. However, there's a very good reason behind it. The leaves of this tree are so large and make such a mess that the municipal services remove them from the pavement and around the base of trees as soon as they fall. The tree-pit soil is therefore left bare, providing optimum conditions for seedlings and plants to grow in autumn (Omar *et al.* 2018). This

ABOVE: A row of newly planted Chestnut-leaf Holly *Ilex koehneana* in Blackfriars, London. Although it looks an impossible situation in which to grow, the trees are rooting into large topsoil-filled cavities below ground. The tree pit creates a small spot where other plants can grow in an otherwise impermeable landscape.

is a good example of where a small and seemingly trivial activity can have a big impact on the urban flora.

In Zurich, Switzerland, Vega & Küffer (2021) studied the flora of 2,130 differently sized green 'patches' throughout the city. Three-quarters of the patches were less than 20m², and most of these were tree pits (or 'tree disks' as they call them). Remarkably, of the 166 species recorded in the whole survey, 154 (93%) were found in these small patches, showing just how important they are for urban plant diversity. Individual small patches were home to an average of nine species, but sometimes as many as 30. The biggest contribution these small patches make to urban diversity, though, is their heterogeneity. Smaller patches were found to be more dissimilar to each other than larger patches, so they add much more to overall plant diversity in the city than large patches. As the authors put it, they 'punch above their weight' in terms of contributing to overall plant diversity.

Importantly, the small patches were also much closer together (16m on average) compared to medium and large patches (55m and 106m respectively). This is critical for their contribution to fragmentation and how they function ecologically. If they are effectively connected to one another, species can move naturally between them and existing populations can be reinforced (Vega & Küffer 2021). Back in Paris, this is exactly what Omar *et al.* (2018) found, but not perhaps in the way we might expect. Contrary to expectations, the distribution of species wasn't correlated with seed weight or wind dispersal. Instead, they suggest that dispersal by people was much more important, as we carry seeds around on our clothes and in mud on our footwear and vehicles. Our role in dispersing seed (anthropochory) is likely to be supported by the longevity of the seed bank (see Chapter 7), with long-lived seed able to take advantage of small habitat patches as and when they become available. This seed-bank trait seems to be the main characteristic influencing the distribution of species among tree pits. Once again, by inadvertently moving plants around the urban landscape, we're playing much more of a role in their survival and the character of the urban flora than we might realise.

BELOW: A tree pit in Finsbury, London, supporting a dense population of Wall Barley *Hordeum murinum* and Black Medick *Medicago lupulina*. Note the two other tree pits in the background with the same species. Although small, these connected patches are essential in supporting urban diversity.

The future of the urban forest

Under the cover of darkness on 14th March 2023, the peace of Plymouth city centre was shattered by the sound of chainsaws. On Armada Way – a wide, tree-lined boulevard in the middle of town – trees were being cut down by council contractors. By late afternoon the following day, after 110 trees had been felled, work was stopped by an emergency High Court injunction from a local pressure group, saving the last 20 trees. The resulting local and national outcry cost the Conservative council leader his job and put the scheme on hold.

In Sheffield, an even larger felling programme began in 2012 after the recommendations of an environmental report into the state and condition of the city's street trees were misinterpreted by the council (which thought that all 'mature' trees needed to be removed). As a result, 17,500 mature trees, 50% of the city's total, were scheduled to be replaced over a period of 25 years. Due to the lack of public engagement, the scale of the plans weren't widely appreciated until 2014, when the removal of a veteran oak on Melbourne Road made the headlines. The Sheffield Tree Action Groups (STAG) was formed in 2015 to bring together local protesters in different parts of the city, and in 2016 opposition to the scheme became even more galvanised when eight mature trees on Rustlings Road were felled at 4.45am

BELOW: Armada Way, in the centre of Plymouth, remained a sight of devastation for months after work to fell trees was abandoned following local protests.

ABOVE: In Sheffield, this 150-year-old Huntingdon Elm on Chelsea Road was found to host a colony of White-letter Hairstreak *Satyrium w-album* butterflies. Designated to be felled in 2015, protestors finally fought off the chainsaws in 2018 and the tree is now protected.

one November morning. The council responded by becoming more entrenched and hardened in its position, and the police became involved with protests as tensions escalated throughout 2017. When the programme was finally halted in March 2018, 5,500 mature trees had been cut down. The (excellent) report from the subsequent inquiry describes how the situation arose, vividly recalls the depths of feeling on both sides, and shows how reconciliation can be achieved in even the most acrimonious of disputes (Lowcock 2023).

There have, of course, been many other examples of street trees being cut down in the face of local opposition, but few have hit the headlines or been met with quite so much national outrage as these two cases. More than anything, they demonstrate just how valuable urban trees are to local residents, and the importance of involving communities with decisions around their future. The inquiry in Sheffield noted that although most of the felled trees were replaced with young trees, this didn't necessarily resonate with residents, who placed most value on having large, mature trees in their neighbourhoods (Lowcock 2023). Plymouth and Sheffield have also proved to be direct catalysts for change. In November 2023, it became a statutory duty under the Environmental Act 2021 for all local authorities in England to consult with residents on the felling of trees on their streets (unless the trees are already dead, dying or preventing other emergency work; Legislation 2023). This is a huge change in the perception around street trees – they are there to benefit residents, not simply as adornments owned by the council – and places significant power in the hands of everyone living with them, at least in England.

As well as felling by chainsaw, street trees face other significant threats. The most pernicious are pests and diseases, some of which have been here for decades but others have recently arrived. Most mature elms, of course, have been wiped out by Dutch Elm Disease *Ophiostoma novo-ulmi*, the fungus that swept through much of Europe after arriving from Canada in the 1960s. Today, there are many millions of elms in Britain and Ireland, but most are small saplings or suckers. Once they reach a certain size, young trees can be detected by the Elm Bark Beetle *Hylurgopinus rufipes* that spreads the fungus. Different species and hybrids of elm vary in their susceptibility, and the few surviving trees (such as the famous Huntingdon Elm *Ulmus* × *hollandica* 'Vegeta' in Sheffield, pictured above) show full or at least partial resistance.

One of the most visible diseases is caused by Horse-chestnut Leaf Miner *Cameraria ohridella*. This moth originally comes from the Balkan region of south-eastern Europe, and its caterpillars bore into the leaves of Horse-chestnut and related species, causing severe browning of the leaves and early leaf fall. Although up to 75% of the leaf area can be attacked, trees rarely die because most of the damage is done in late summer and autumn; total annual carbon assimilation is reduced by 30–40%, stunting growth but not killing the tree (Forest Research 2020). Much more dangerous to Horse-chestnut is bleeding canker, caused by the bacterium *Pseudomonas syringae* pathovar *aesculi*, which arrived here by some unknown means from the Himalaya in the early 2000s. Before then, other bacteria were involved and infection rates were low, but the new strain is much more virulent and by 2007 it was found that 49% of trees in Great Britain were affected (Forest Research 2024a).

ABOVE: Horse-chestnut Leaf Miner is a tiny micro-moth, just 3–5mm long. Its larvae also feed on the leaves of Sycamore *Acer pseudoplatanus*.

The most serious recent arrival is Ash Dieback, caused by the fungus *Hymenoscyphus fraxineus* from eastern Asia. Although the disease was first noticed here in 2012, the pathogen may have arrived as early as 2006. The fungus initially infects young shoots and leaves, then spreading to whole branches and eventually girdling the trunk, killing the tree within 10–20 years (Forest Research 2024b). Millions of trees have already been lost, with the initial spread boosted by nurseries importing and distributing infected saplings for planting. Ash is a very important urban tree. In Cambridge, for example, there are thought to be 53,000 individuals, 22% of all the city's trees (Cambridge City Council 2024), while in Edinburgh there are around 42,720, 6% of the total (City of Edinburgh Council 2022). As well as the visual impact on the landscape and loss to biodiversity (the species hosts many bryophytes and lichens on its bark), infected trees pose a significant risk to the public as their branches and limbs become very brittle and liable to fall. For this reason, many towns and cities are mapping or have already mapped their Ash trees and are closely monitoring them so diseased individuals can be removed safely.

Urban street trees are often weakened by high levels of pollution, compacted soils and reduced water and nutrient availability, making them more susceptible to pests and diseases. This can be exacerbated by climate change, which not only affects the physiology of the tree but can also encourage the spread of newly arrived pathogens. In 2009, the first occurrences of Massaria disease *Splanchnonema platani* on living London Plane trees were identified in Bristol and London. The effects of this dieback disease, which is widespread in the Mediterranean, seem to be enhanced by hot summers. While it doesn't kill them outright, infected trees are prone to brittle limbs and branch fall, potentially placing exorbitant costs on municipal councils to make them safe (Forest Research 2024c). The same can't be said of Canker Stain of Plane (caused by the fungus *Ceratocystis platani*), which can kill Plane trees within 3–7 years. Although it hasn't reached the UK yet, it could transform some urban areas if it does. The fungus appeared in Europe during the Second World War, possibly on boxes of military supplies made of Plane wood from North America, and has spread rapidly in recent years with two new outbreaks in northern France (Forest Research 2024d).

Climate change also has a direct impact on urban trees. As well as warmer temperatures, they may be affected by the intensity and severity of heatwaves and droughts, and by phenological changes as the seasons shift around. Understanding how different species respond to these changes is important, allowing urban planners to account for future climate scenarios by planting more drought-resistant and heat-tolerant species. Many trees are already suffering. A recent study looked at 3,129 species of tree and shrub planted in 164 cities in 78 countries around the world. They found that well over half the species are living outside their 'comfort zone', with 56% and 65% respectively exceeding the heat and precipitation conditions they're adapted to in their native range. Even more alarmingly, all the trees in some cities, including Barcelona in north-eastern Spain, are already living in an 'unsafe' climate (Esperon-Rodriguez *et al.* 2022).

Urban temperatures are pushed to extremes even more by the urban heat island (see Chapter 5). Ironically, while trees suffer, they are also an integral part of the solution. The cooling effects of trees, through a combination of direct shading and increased evapotranspiration, are well known. In a study of 601 European cities, Marando *et al.* (2022) found that urban trees reduced average temperatures by 1.1°C (and sometimes up to 2.9°C), but in order to achieve 1°C cooling a tree canopy cover of 16% is needed. Encouragingly, in a survey of 5,749 urban wards in the UK, Forest Research found that the average urban tree cover is 17.3%, with a quarter of wards exceeding 20%. The highest regional levels of cover were in South Wales (19.2%) and

ABOVE: What will our urban forest look like in the future? With species potentially drawn from all around the world, it's difficult to say, but one thing is certain: urban trees are good for us, and we can't have too many of them.

south-east England (22.1%) (Forest Research 2024e). While this is good news, some suggest that canopy cover targets of 30% would be more realistic to protect against the worst effects of climate change.

As planting is stepped up in many towns and cities with future climate in mind, we need to ensure a high diversity of native and alien trees is selected, and that non-native species are appropriately screened for invasiveness and disease susceptibility. Current models suggest that species native to areas 2–5 degrees of latitude south of Great Britain could be considered suitable, as well as trees from equivalent climates elsewhere in the world. These include some interesting and attractive species such as Rauli *Nothofagus alpina* from Chile and Argentina, American Ash *Fraxinus americana* from central North America, Japanese Pagoda Tree *Styphnolobium japonicum* and Maidenhair-tree, both from China, and even Cider Gum *Eucalyptus gunnii* from Tasmania. We don't yet know what the future urban forest will look like, but one thing is certain – more trees can only ever be a good thing.

Part Four
Final thoughts

The future of urban plants

chapter twelve

It's a few months after my discovery of Willow-leaved Yellow-oxeye *Buphthalmum salicifolium* in Llandudno Junction and I'm on my way to the butchers in Conwy for some of their award-winning sausages. I park beside the magnificent castle and there, on a low stone wall beside the road, my eye is caught again by another out-of-place plant sprouting from the cracks between the stones. It's a large grass with distinctive reddish-bronzy leaves, glowing in the autumn sunshine. This time, I'm familiar with the plant. Pheasant's-tail *Anemanthele lessoniana* is a hugely popular grass widely grown in gardens and amenity planting. Originally from New Zealand, it's also known as New Zealand Wind-grass and some people probably know it better by its old scientific name, *Stipa arundinacea*. Very adaptable and easy to grow, it has a shocking ability to seed itself around, as anyone who's planted it in their garden will know. And this is where the alarm bells begin to ring.

Pheasant's-tail hasn't been in Britain and Ireland for long. The first records outside gardens, all dating from the early 2000s, come from widely scattered towns and cities including Taunton, Cambridge, Guildford and Leamington Spa in England, Banchory in Scotland, and Waterford and Dublin in Ireland. Today, it's been recorded from an astonishing 169 10-km squares, although it's probably overlooked in many areas. Most of these escapees grow along pavements, the base of walls, path sides, verges and urban fallow ground. However, it's never been recorded from Wales before, so I've just clocked up another first for the country!

This is clearly an alien in the early stages of invasion. Should we be alarmed? Will it become a dominant feature of the urban landscape? Will it act thuggishly, outcompeting other species, or fit in neatly

PREVIOUS PAGES:
A vibrant mix of Californian Poppy *Eschscholzia californica*, Common Poppy *Papaver rhoeas* and Austrian Chamomile *Cota austriaca* on a Brighton street.

OPPOSITE:
A shoot of Ivy (*Hedera helix*) growing across graffiti on an iron bridge in Bristol.

Urban Plants

RIGHT: Colourful Pheasant's-tail on a wall in Conwy along with the succulent foliage of Thick-leaved Stonecrop *Sedum dasyphyllum*.

alongside them, just another colourful new arrival at the urban plant party? Although we can look at their biology and ecology elsewhere in the world to see how they might behave, identifying these invasive species isn't easy. In a recent exercise to spot some of them, a sister species to Pheasant's-tail, American Needle-grass *Nassella neesiana* (formerly *Stipa neesiana*), was ranked in the top 20 likely invaders across all species groups, a risk that, as yet, has not been borne out (Roy *et al.* 2014, Stroh *et al.* 2023).

Compared to animals, invasive plants are slightly unusual, in that there's often a considerable lag between their initial arrival and subsequent spread. Many recent urban colonisers have behaved this way, with Water Bent *Polypogon viridis* taking 140 years to get going, Narrow-leaved Ragwort *Senecio inaequidens* taking 160 years and Canadian Fleabane *Erigeron canadensis* 270 years. Reasons for this lag include time needed to adapt to our climate, the arrival of more invasive forms, or climate change eventually producing more favourable conditions for spread. Compared to these species, Pheasant's-tail seems to have taken off at an alarming rate, within 20 years of its arrival. Now that new data on spread are available from *Plant Atlas 2020* (Stroh *et al.* 2023), maybe it's time for a reassessment of this and other species? And, more importantly, perhaps such assessments should include collaboration with the horticultural trade, so they don't stock our garden centres and nurseries with potential invaders?

As climate change gathers pace at an increasingly alarming rate, even more exotic species will start to survive and spread. For example, a surprising number of seedlings of Chusan Palm *Trachycarpus fortunei* (a species from central China, southern Japan, northern Myanmar and northern India) have been spotted since the late 1990s germinating close to parent plants in parks and gardens, mainly along the south coast of England and south-west Wales. Even more astonishing is the large colony of Lace Aloe *Aristaloe aristata*, a common succulent houseplant, found on a pavement in Castle Cary, Somerset, in 2016 and still growing, flowering and spreading nicely in 2024 (Helena Crouch pers. comm., McDonnell 2016). This plant seems to have escaped from the windowsill of a nearby house, but might occur as a naturalised plant more often as such succulents become increasingly popular in gardens.

We can, of course, expect more new surprises in the coming years, and more arrivals as we continue to move species around the world. Botanists are a curious and ever-vigilant bunch, and I'm sure we'll keep a careful eye on what's growing where, so we can monitor their spread and assess which species might become a problem or pose a threat in the future. To this end, the diligent recording of our flora by the Botanical Society of Britain and Ireland, the British Bryological Society and others (see 'Further study' on page 350) is critical, as it is only through their work that we can begin to understand how such species are behaving.

ABOVE: The succulent Lace Aloe, from South Africa and Lesotho, has been known growing on pavement in Castle Cary, Somerset, for seven years. The clump is increasing in size, with new rosettes even pushing up through the gravelly pavement.

Conservation of urban plants

All my life I've been a conservationist. This passion for preservation was ignited way back in the 1980s, when a small fragment of chalk grassland near my home was ploughed up and sown with fodder turnips for sheep. I was horrified. It was full of downland treasures like

ABOVE: Parkland Walk, a 4km-long linear nature reserve in London, follows the former railway line connecting Finsbury Park to Alexandra Palace. It includes regenerating woodland and scrub, veteran trees, fragments of acid grassland and wetland habitats.

Clustered Bellflower *Campanula glomerata*, Horseshoe Vetch *Hippocrepis comosa* and Autumn Lady's-tresses *Spiranthes spiralis*, and I reeled at the utter pointlessness and injustice of their loss. Since then, I've dedicated my working life to helping preserve and restore everything from heathlands to verges, cornfield flowers to hay meadows, and from rare ferns to orchids. Quintessentially rural, there are strong environmental, cultural and moral arguments to support the conservation of our highly threatened native flora. But what about our urban flora, dominated as it is by a handful of common natives and a plethora of unusual aliens?

Of course, the 'handful of common natives' is the very legacy of urbanisation, which has wrought a terrible toll on our native species. Across Greater London and Middlesex, for instance, 186 native and archaeophyte taxa are known to have become extinct, nearly 12% of the total. In addition, 156 species are on the Great Britain or England Red List, and several hundred other more common British plants (regarded as 'Least Concern' elsewhere) are facing the threat of extinction in the London area (Mark Spencer pers. comm.). In Glasgow, 9% of native and archaeophyte species had become extinct by 2000 (Dickson *et al.* 2000). Sadly, these tolls are, perhaps, rather inevitable. The spread of urbanisation is like a sledgehammer or a wrecking-ball, a destructive force that comes crashing into

The future of urban plants

ABOVE: Cardiff Bay Wetlands Reserve is an 8ha (20-acre) site created in 2002 to compensate for the loss of a saltmarsh SSSI permanently flooded by the construction of the Cardiff Barrage. It now boasts a diversity of habitats including reedbeds, freshwater ponds and lakes, grasslands and scrub woodland.

semi-natural habitats and leaves nothing untouched. Protecting the few remaining fragments of these precious habitats as they're engulfed is a daunting task, since they are inexorably altered by the changed landscapes encroaching upon them, and sites constantly come under huge pressure to be developed. But 'inevitable' and 'daunting' are never words to put off conservationists – in fact, they tend to galvanise them into action – and a host of individuals and organisations are fighting to protect what's left.

All sorts of mechanisms and designations exist to protect urban wildlife. They include Tree Preservation Orders (TPOs), Local Wildlife Sites (LWSs, which can also be called Sites of Importance for Nature Conservation, SINCs, Sites of Local Nature Conservation Importance, SLNCI, and Local Nature Conservation Sites, LNCSs), Sites of Special Scientific Interest (SSSIs) and both Local and National Nature Reserves (LNRs and NNRs). In the UK, around 11,653ha (28,795 acres) of SSSI are located within the urban boundary (ONS 2018), an extraordinary extent of green space that indicates the proximity of high-quality habitat to urban populations. Local Wildlife Sites (and their sister designations) are especially important for the protection of urban biodiversity. Although they don't have statutory protection, they are identified using local criteria and designated in partnerships between local authorities, local Wildlife Trusts and other conservation organisations, affording them a high level of protection within the planning system. In London, more than 1,600 SINCs have been identified, covering as much as 20% of the city and forming the core of London's ecological network (GIGL 2019), while in Glasgow there are more than 90 SINCs. Local Nature Reserves also provide a critical role and, in a survey of 27 urban local authority areas in England, the number of urban LNRs had trebled from 68 in 1993 to 215 by 2021 (Box 2021). Of course, designation doesn't necessarily mean protection – either in providing appropriate habitat or species management, or in guaranteeing that level of protection for ever – but the sheer number and scale of sites show just how valued these semi-natural habitats are in the urban landscape.

BELOW: Snapdragon *Antirrhinum majus* has been a highly successful coloniser of urban habitats. Still treated with contempt by some, alien species like this are simply plants we've distributed responding to an environment we've created, so perhaps deserve a bit more respect.

But, what of our alien urban flora? Is that worth protecting? In justifying the existence of such plants, we have more of a battle on our hands, and one that I find astonishing. Even today, many botanists pour scorn on alien species, shunning them as being unworthy of our attention, study or appreciation. You'll often hear comments like 'it's just a garden escape' or 'it doesn't really belong here', or 'it's invasive and needs to be controlled'. I have many problems with this attitude. Firstly, a long list of native plants are also invasive, but aren't treated with the same contempt. Secondly, some of these species have been here for hundreds or even thousands of years and are very much part of our wild flora, although I think we also need to relax the strict division between 'ancient' and 'new' introductions and give all these arrivals the respect they deserve. Thirdly, alien plants have their own fascinating biology and ecology, responding to our changing climate and environment just like the native flora. We can only predict what they might do in the future by studying changes in their distribution and understanding how they're spreading. And fourthly, but perhaps most importantly, I think the attitude of many people towards them is tainted by pure botanical xenophobia. In writing this book, I've developed a much deeper appreciation of, and respect for, our alien flora. Our attitudes towards these species are often

The future of urban plants

framed purely by their origin, by their 'foreignness'. This prejudice is deeply unfair, as they are, after all, simply plants that we've brought along with us, trying to grow in the places we've put them. They are part of our own story. They've overcome huge challenges to arrive, escape, survive and spread, and that alone makes them worthy of our admiration and study.

A few – and I mean a very few – of these arrivals have become genuinely problematic for some people in some situations. I'd put Buddleja *Buddleja davidii* in that category, along with Tree-of-heaven *Ailanthus altissima* and other highly invasive plants like Three-cornered Garlic *Allium triquetrum*, Green Alkanet *Pentaglottis sempervirens* and, of course, Japanese Knotweed *Reynoutria japonica*. The cost of controlling such species can be high, but isn't always an additional burden. Willows *Salix* spp. and birches *Betula* spp., for example, grow just as vigorously along railways as Buddleja, and all need good habitat management to keep them in check. After all, I'm afraid Buddleja is here to stay, folks, so rather than wishing we could send it back to China, we might as well learn to live with it (Chiles 2019).

But we shouldn't tar all these human-mediated arrivals with the same brush. The vast majority – probably more than 90% – are utterly benign, finding their place in the urban landscape and living happily alongside the native flora. Most, as we've seen, put in fleeting

BELOW: A dense stand of invasive Green Alkanet beside the river Cam in Cambridge. Originally from south-western Europe, it spreads mainly by seed, but also through its brittle roots that readily break into small fragments.

343

Urban Plants

RIGHT: We may use Garden Lobelia *Lobelia erinus* to brighten up our hanging baskets, but traditional shamanic healers in its native southern Africa use it to wash divination bones to improve the accuracy of their predictions. The plant has many names, including Impanjana in Zulu and Mahlo-a-konyana in SiSwati.

cameo appearances, like bright, ephemeral fireworks in the flora. Others stay with us a little longer, trusty companions on our journeys through the streets. All are worthy of the same respect and curiosity as our native flora.

The flowering of our streets

Although we now treat some ancient introductions, particularly our archaeophyte cornfield flowers like Corn Marigold *Glebionis segetum* and Common Poppy *Papaver rhoeas*, as honorary natives, we'll probably never consider our neophyte flora in the same way. Some, such as the London-rocket *Sisymbrium irio* that rose from the ashes of the Great Fire of London, may be elevated to protected status on cultural grounds. But I doubt most will ever hold Oxford Ragwort *Senecio squalidus* in the same regard, even though it's now in decline. That's not what I'm suggesting, though. Rather than selecting individual urban species for protection, I think we need to look instead at the communities of plants that develop in urban habitats. Across our pavements, walls, lawns, parks and streets, we should conserve the full spectrum of our urban flora, giving it the space and opportunity to flower, spread and flourish. These unique communities are incredibly important, not just for the ecosystem services they provide and their sheer biodiversity value in otherwise barren environments, but also as novel, highly adapted and extremely resilient forms of vegetation that can survive the worst of what we can throw at them. It is only by understanding and appreciating the ecology of these recombinant communities, made up of many different **extremophytes** adapted to thrive under conditions of extreme stress, that we can learn how they respond to such stresses, and therefore how we can live alongside them (Rotherham 2017). This will become particularly acute and urgent in the coming years as climate change takes a firmer grip and wreaks upon us whatever havoc it will bring. Unlike our meadow, woodland and heathland plants, we don't yet know how best to manage most urban plants – they tend to survive in spite of what we do, not because of what we do – and we need to change our attitude towards them from one of control and eradication to something much more fostering and accommodating.

ABOVE: Red Valerian *Centranthus ruber*, Purple Toadflax *Linaria purpurea*, Snapdragon *Antirrhinum majus* and Smooth Hawk's-beard *Crepis capillaris* brightening up Chapel Street in Conwy.

This is why the recent relaxation in herbicide use in many towns and cities brings so much hope. In Cambridge, for example, herbicide has been sprayed systematically along the city's streets since the turn of the millennium, but that stopped in 2023. This sudden release, combined with the very wet summer that year, saw a flowering of the streets like never before, with a huge 26% rise in species diversity (from 235 taxa in 1998–99 to 297 in 2023, Preston & Chater in prep.). It's a trend that's being repeated in many other places. Across the UK, over 100 local authorities have either stopped using herbicides in urban areas or are taking steps to do so (PAN 2024, see Chapter 7). This is a seismic shift in attitude towards our urban flora and demonstrates that councils and many residents really do want to step away from using harmful chemicals and allow wildlife the chance to return.

The greening of our streets isn't welcomed by everyone, however. Some residents are quick to complain, unhappy at the growth of weeds making neighbourhoods look unkempt or unloved. Reactions can be quite extreme, often generating a storm of criticism. Recent press commentary has run along the lines of: 'Weed-choked pavements anger residents as "rewilding" divides UK towns and cities' (Weston

2023), '"Like a war zone" – State of unkempt verges across borough is slammed' (Weeds 2024), 'Our streets are overgrown with weeds – something needs to be done' (Marsh 2024), and '"Never seen it looking so scruffy" – Llandudno speaks out for rest of North Wales as weeds take over' (Forgrave 2024), the latter article including the wonderfully flippant comment: 'You should see Gwydyr Road. There are zebras living in the undergrowth.'

This is, perhaps, understandable. When you've lived with 'neat-and-tidy' all your life, coming to accept 'not-so-neat-and-not-so-tidy' can be a challenge. Such adverse reactions are often linked to the sudden cessation of herbicide application and the feeling that all efforts to tame pavement plants in public areas have been abandoned, despite the fact that alternative methods of control (such as mechanical weeding) are often being explored (see Chapter 7). As always, effective communication is critical, especially to avoid accusations that halting the herbicide is simply a cost-cutting measure cynically dressed up as a conservation initiative.

The key to shifting attitudes is to start with local communities, garnering grassroots support to build a wider desire for change. Once empowered, residents can work with councils, demonstrating solutions

RIGHT: A rich community of natives, archaeophytes and neophytes along a pavement by Hobson's Conduit, Cambridge, including Wall Lettuce *Mycelis muralis*, Cat's-ear *Hypochaeris radicata*, Common Mallow *Malva sylvestris* and Red Valerian.

The future of urban plants

that balance the maintenance of public areas while at the same time nurturing the flora. This ambition is much easier to implement if everyone is involved with, and understands, the approach being taken. After all, there's a world of difference between what might be perceived as complete neglect and 'managed messiness', where people know that the luxuriant growth will be dealt with each year, once everything has had a chance to flower and set seed.

Perhaps we could learn some lessons from Paris? Like all towns and cities across France (as well as Denmark and Luxembourg), Paris has been free of herbicides since 2017 and, if the 2024 Olympic Games are anything to go by, the city doesn't appear to be disappearing beneath a canopy of weeds. Indeed, when former resident Emma Pavans de Ceccatty of Pesticide Action Network UK returned to the city in 2023, she was struck by how normal and well maintained the streets looked, as if nothing had changed. Paris, she notes, has embraced a balanced approach, whereby some areas are allowed to become wilder and overgrown, but others are more highly maintained through increased street cleaning. This includes regular sweeping to remove leaf litter and reduce the build-up of humus, and the removal of plants that damage infrastructure through hand weeding, hoeing

LEFT: Plants of Common Mallow *Malva sylvestris*, Bristly Oxtongue *Helminthotheca echioides* and Wall Barley *Hordeum murinum* spill onto a pavement.

347

or mechanical brush-cutting. The city now encourages its residents and municipal employees to 'work with natural cycles', and runs projects to help them learn about, look after and even map their street wildlife (Pavans de Ceccatty 2023). This shift in mindset didn't happen overnight – it has taken time, trial and error, and political will – but is an impressive achievement.

I find it fascinating that, in Britain, some people get so angry at what are, after all, just a few plants growing on their streets. It's ironic that we love to surround ourselves with flowers – from exuberant gardens, window boxes and houseplants, to rich floral patterns on our wallpaper, clothes, cushions and bedspreads – yet we can't tolerate them brightening up our pavements, walls and verges. Although we've lived alongside them for thousands of years, we've pushed them aside, rejecting them as members of the urban ecosystems we've created and of which we are part. Instead, we need to welcome them back into our daily lives, embracing them, valuing them and cherishing them for all they do for us. We seem to have a long way to go, but it's a road well worth travelling.

RIGHT: A breathtaking depiction of a Dandelion *Taraxacum* painted onto a high-rise tower in Göteborg, Sweden. Created by artist Mona Caron, the work is 'a tribute to the resilience of all those beings who no one made room for, were not part of the plan, and yet keep coming back, pushing through and rising up'.

ABOVE: A street junction in Clerkenwell, London, framed by a large self-sown Mount Etna Broom *Genista aetnensis*. We have built this entire environment and brought the tree here from Sardinia and Sicily, where it now luxuriates in the warm embrace of the urban heat island we've created.

A world of our own making

More than anything, writing this book has shown me just how closely our own lives are entwined with those of the urban plants around us. We are not passive observers, but active participants in their lives. As architects of their landscape, we destroy many of them but create huge opportunities for others; we allow them to escape from cultivation and inadvertently move and carry them around with us, we provide them with a myriad of places to grow, and we even cocoon them in urban warmth and fertilise them heavily with nitrogen pollution. More than we realise, every little thing that we do has an impact on them.

Every one of us has some sort of relationship with urban plants, whether it's admiring a tuft of moss on a wall, lounging on the grass in the park, enjoying a verge planted with cornfield flowers, or loathing the weeds on the street. If they matter to us, we'll notice them. And that's important, because not noticing them is the biggest danger of all.

Each of these plants is rooted in some way in our own turbulent history, our complex cultures, our ever-changing technology and our constantly evolving fashions. Urban floras never stand still; they are a world of flux within a world that's in flux. They are echoes of our past and prophets of our future. And for that alone, their stories are well worth listening to.

Further study

For anyone interested in learning about urban floras, studying them and getting to know the plants, four societies offer various opportunities for getting involved.

- The **Botanical Society of Britain and Ireland** (BSBI, bsbi.org) is interested in our native and introduced wild flowering plants, trees, ferns and related vascular plants. It organises local flora groups of people who study plants in their own particular county, as well as running national citizen science activities such as the popular New Year Plant Hunt. The society produces regular newsletters packed with information and discoveries, videos and blogs about our flora, and publishes a scientific journal, *British & Irish Botany*.

- The **Botanical Society of Scotland** (BSS, botsoc.scot) also deals with flowering plants, conifers and ferns and has been running its Urban Flora of Scotland project since 2015. Collecting records of plants, bryophytes, fungi and algae in any settlement with more than 1,000 residents, it leads field meetings, produces identification materials and is monitoring the change in urban species across Scotland.

- The **British Pteridological Society** (BPS, ebps.org.uk) is interested in ferns, clubmosses, quillworts and horsetails. It also organises field meetings, workshops and garden visits, and publishes several journals about ferns and the society, as well as a scientific journal, the *Fern Gazette*. It also organises exchanges of plants and spores, and arranges special-interest groups on the cultivation of ferns.

- The **British Bryological Society** (BPS, britishbryologicalsociety.org.uk) focuses on bryophytes, our non-vascular plants, i.e. mosses, liverworts and hornworts. A very active society, it arranges local meetings throughout the UK and Ireland to find and record bryophytes, as well as several extended fieldwork trips each year, and workshop weekends to help with identification and study. It produces an informal bulletin *Field Bryology*, as well the *Journal of Bryology* covering the latest research.

It's also worth checking your local **Wildlife Trust** (wildlifetrusts.org), as many organise walks, talks, courses and other activities on urban botany and other wildlife. Several are city-focused, including the London Wildlife Trust (wildlondon.org.uk), Birmingham and the Black Country (bbcwildlife.org.uk) and Sheffield and Rotherham Wildlife Trust (wildsheffield.com). Other organisations with resources in urban botany include the Field Studies Council (field-studies-council.org), the Royal Botanic Gardens, Kew (kew.org) and the Royal Botanic Garden Edinburgh (rbge.org.uk).

Glossary

Acrocarp (or 'acrocarpous'). A moss that grows with upright shoots, usually in dense tufts, mats or small cushions (cf. pleurocarp).

Alien. A species that has arrived in Britain or Ireland with the help of humans, either intentionally (e.g. many garden plants) or unintentionally (e.g. as grain impurities or through birdseed).

Allelopathic (and allelopathy). The production of certain biochemicals in the leaves and roots of one plant to suppress or inhibit the growth, survival, development and reproduction of neighbouring plants. It is a strategy employed by species such as Tree-of-heaven *Ailanthus altissima* to gain a competitive advantage over others.

Allochory. The dispersal of seed with some form of external assistance, such as an animal vector, the wind or water (cf. autochory).

Anemochory. The dispersal of seed through the wind, usually assisted by a special parachute or tuft of hairs attached to the seed. Well-known examples are Dandelion *Taraxacum* agg., Rosebay Willowherb *Chamaenerion angustifolium* and Spear Thistle *Cirsium vulgare*.

Annual. A plant that completes its life cycle within 12 months, germinating, growing, flowering, setting seed and then dying. Many annuals germinate in spring and die before winter, but **winter annuals** germinate in autumn or winter and die after flowering the following spring.

Annuality. A measure of the proportion of annuals that are found in a vegetation community. Annuality can be a proxy for the level of soil and habitat disturbance. Some urban plant communities have high levels of annuality.

Annulus. A band of thickened cells around the spore-bearing sporangia of ferns such as Polypody *Polypodium vulgare*. As the band dries out, the cells suddenly rupture and flick backwards, ripping the sporangium open and flinging the spores into the air.

Anthropedogenesis. The formation of urban soils through predominantly human processes (such as construction) that often include a high proportion of human-made materials like rubble and plastics.

Anthropochory. The dispersal of seed by humans. It usually refers to unintentional (rather than deliberate) dispersal, such as carrying seed in dirt on footwear or attached to our clothing. By contrast, **hemerochory** is the intentional dispersal of cultivated plants through horticulture and agriculture.

Archaeophyte. An ancient introduction; in other words, an alien plant that arrived before AD 1500, often appearing as a cornfield weed when agriculture spread here from Europe (e.g. Common Poppy *Papaver rhoeas*), or as a food crop (e.g. Horseradish *Armoracia rusticana*).

Autochory. The dispersal of seed without any external assistance, such as falling to the ground by gravity (cf. allochory).

Auxin. A plant hormone produced by the growing tips of shoots and roots. By controlling cell division and expansion, auxin influences many aspects of growth, such as the direction in which a stem grows.

Awn. A hair or bristle-like appendage attached to the seed of a grass. Awns are often barbed with tiny hooks that help them become attached to the fur of animals or to clothing. They aid dispersal of species such as Wall Barley *Hordeum murinum*.

Ballochory. The dispersal of seed through the explosive dehiscence (rupturing) of a fruit or seedpod, usually resulting from internal pressures or tensions generated as the fruit ripens or dries. A well-known example is

Glossary

the exploding seedpod of Himalayan Balsam *Impatiens glandulifera*.

Barochory. The dispersal of seed by gravity. One of the simplest forms of dispersal, it usually involves seeds falling to the ground directly from the seedpod.

Biennial. A plant that completes its life cycle within two years, germinating and growing in the first year, then flowering, setting seed and dying the next.

Bings. A term often used in Scotland for spoil tips or heaps derived from mining waste, especially coal. In time, coal bings can become well vegetated and home to many locally rare species such as orchids and ferns.

Bioreceptive. The ability of a surface, such as a brick wall or concrete pavement, to support life. Bioreceptivity tends to increase over time as surfaces weather.

Biotic homogenisation. The process through which urban floras in different cities come to resemble each other as the original native flora is reduced to a suite of similar generalist species, and these are augmented by introduction of a uniform suite of non-native alien species.

Calcicole. A plant that requires a lime-rich, calcareous soil in which to grow, usually chalk or limestone but also urban substrates such as mortar and concrete.

Calcifuge. A plant that requires an acidic soil or substrate on which to grow.

Capping (and **coping**). The topmost layer of a wall, designed to protect the structure from rain and to provide a decorative finish. Often made of contrasting brick, stonework or cement, a capping comes flush to the edge of the wall, while a coping comes out over the edge, helping to shed rainwater away from the wall.

Casual. An alien plant that doesn't persist in the wild but forms short-lived populations that arise from repeated introductions.

Chamaephyte. A shrub whose perennating buds are located on woody shoots close to the soil surface (e.g. some *Cotoneaster* species).

Chasmophyte. A plant that grows in the crevices, cracks and fissures between rocks. Many wall ferns, such as Wall-rue *Asplenium ruta-muraria* and Black Spleenwort *A. adiantum-nigrum*, grow in this way.

Cryptophyte. A perennial herb whose perennating buds are located just under the soil surface (e.g. Common Horsetail *Equisetum arvense*).

Dispersal kernel. The pattern of seed dispersal around a parent plant. Dispersal kernels may be restricted, with seed falling close to the parent, or involve long-distance dispersal to overcome fragmentation and colonise new sites. They may also include several phases where, for example, a seed is blown to one site and then moved to another by a bird.

Encapsulated countryside. A term used to describe small fragments of natural or semi-natural habitat, such as woodlands and grasslands, that have become surrounded by urban development.

Endozoochory. The dispersal of seed on the inside of an animal, usually by the ingestion of berries and seeds that pass through the digestive tract (cf. epizoochory). Birds often perch on the top of walls, for instance, and defecate seeds such as those of Hawthorn *Crataegus monogyna*, Elder *Sambucus nigra* and Yew *Taxus baccata* that can then become established on the wall.

Epiphyte. A plant that grows upon the surface of another plant. Mosses and ferns that grow on the trunks and branches of trees are classed as epiphytes (cf. lithophyte).

Epizoochory. The dispersal of seed on the outside of an animal, usually by attachment to the coat of an animal through hooked or barbed seeds (cf. endozoochory). Common examples include Cleavers *Galium aparine*, Burdock *Arctium* species and Wood Avens *Geum urbanum*.

Established (or 'naturalised'). An alien plant that escapes into the wild and forms persistent populations, reproducing by seed or vegetative spread.

Extremophyte. A plant adapted to thrive in an environment characterised by a high degree of abiotic stress, such as very high temperatures, extreme soil pH, severe drought or high levels of pollution.

Floricane. The short, lateral flowering shoots produced by brambles *Rubus fruticosus* agg. that carry blackberries in autumn. Floricanes grow from the arched portion of the long vegetative shoots produced the previous year (cf. primocane).

Footings. The foundation on which a wall sits. Footings are usually made from cement poured into a trench to provide a solid, level surface on which to build the wall.

Fragmentation. The gradual loss of large areas or patches of habitat until only small fragments remain in the landscape. Fragmentation leads to the isolation of populations, reducing the ability of species to interact with each other and increasing their risk of extinction.

Garbic. A component of urban soils derived from landfill, mainly including household and organic waste.

Habitat transformation. The gradual or sudden change of one habitat type into another. In the urban context, the transformation from natural and semi-natural habitats into the built environment is usually irrevocable.

Hemeroby. A measure of the degree of human influence on an environment, which increases as habitat degradation increases. It is generally taken to be complementary to the term 'naturalness'.

Hemicryptophyte. A perennial herb whose perennating buds are located at the same level as the soil surface (e.g. Dandelion).

Hydrochory. Dispersal of seed through moving water, for example by being carried on the surface of a river, washed along a roadside gutter or splashed around by heavy rain.

Lithophyte. A plant that grows on the surface of a rock or stone. **Epilithic lithophytes** attach themselves directly to the rock surface (e.g. mosses and lichens), while **endolithic lithophytes**, like many flowering plants, root into the cracks and crevices of the surface (cf. chasmophyte and epiphyte).

Myrmecochory. The dispersal of seeds through their deliberate movement by ants. Seeds of myrmecochorous plants have a special structure, a parcel of lipid- and protein-rich food known as an **elaiosome**. Ants collect the seeds and carry them back to their colonies where the elaiosome is fed to developing larvae. The intact seed may be discarded underground or near the edge of the nest at the surface.

Native. A species that has arrived naturally in Britain or Ireland without human help, either surviving through the last ice age or arriving since then.

Negative phototropism. The growth of a plant away from the light. Most plants usually grow towards the light (positive phototropism), but negative phototropism is sometimes deployed by plants growing on walls to direct developing seedpods (e.g. Ivy-leaved Toadflax *Cymbalaria muralis*) or stems (e.g. Ivy *Hedera* spp.) towards the shaded wall surface.

Neophyte. A new introduction, in other words an alien plant that has arrived since AD 1500. Most of our garden plants are neophytes, including all introductions from North and South America.

Pavement refugium. An area of pavement that is protected from constant trampling, footfall and disturbance, allowing plants to grow larger and more luxuriantly. Such refugia can be created by temporary railings and scaffold, as well as around lampposts and other street furniture. They often serve an important role by allowing plants to seed into more trampled areas of pavement.

Pedicel. The stem of a flower or seedpod.

Perennial. A plant that lives for several or many years. This includes trees and shrubs with permanent woody stems above ground, and herbaceous perennials with soft growth that dies back each winter, growing again in spring from underground roots or stems.

Pleurocarp (or 'pleurocarpous'). A moss that grows with laterally branching shoots, usually in wide spreading carpets or mats (cf. acrocarp).

Primocane. The long vegetative shoots produced by brambles that grow upright at first before arching over and bending down. They often reach the ground again, where their tips root to form new plants (cf. floricane).

Recombinant ecosystem. A novel association of plants and animals that has been created, either intentionally or unintentionally, by humans.

Rhizome. A horizontal stem that grows under the surface of the soil, often rooting from the nodes to produce new plants.

Ruderal. A species that tends to grow where the soil has been recently disturbed and is bare. Many annuals are ruderals, making the most of the opportunity that the bare soil gives them to germinate.

Ruderality. A measure of a species' ability to survive repeated soil and habitat disturbance. Some urban plant communities have high levels of ruderality.

Glossary

Sealed soils (and sealed surfaces). A term used to describe impervious surfaces of cement, tarmac, paving stones and other building materials that completely cover the ground and the soil below. Sealed soils suffer from reduced absorption of water and nutrients and impaired exchange of oxygen, carbon dioxide and other elements.

Semi-natural. A habitat that has undergone some modification by human-mediated management, such as grasslands grazed by livestock or coppiced woodland. As a result, species composition is likely to have changed from the original natural habitat.

Spikelet. A small cluster of seeds that make up the inflorescence of a grass. Arranged along a stem (the rachis), each spikelet is usually composed of several seeds and their associated bracts and awns.

Spoilic. A component of urban soils derived from industrial mining spoil, dredging and road construction.

Stolon. A horizontal stem that grows flat along the surface of the ground, often rooting from leaf nodes to produce new plants.

Succession. The process by which the habitat in an area evolves over time, with the gradual arrival of new species replacing or displacing previous communities. Each stage changes the current ecological conditions, allowing new species to become established until a climax stage (usually woodland) is reached.

Sward. The dense growth of grasses that, if cut short, creates a lawn, sports pitch, park or playing field. If left uncut, the sward can grow into a long-grass habitat such as meadow.

Taxon (plural taxa). A group that includes members of any taxonomic rank, such as species, subspecies, varieties, hybrids and microspecies.

Therophyte. An annual plant whose perennating buds are located inside seeds (e.g. Thale Cress *Arabidopsis thaliana*).

Tillering. The repeated growth of lateral shoots from the base of grass plants, usually stimulated by cutting or mowing. Tillering helps to create the dense sward found in lawns and parks.

Tree pit. An area of soil underneath a pavement into which a tree can root. A community of plants can develop where this soil comes to the surface around the tree trunk. Tree pits are often covered in metal grates to protect the trunk and soil. Tree pits are also known as tree halos and tree disks.

Urban adaptor. A species that is relatively tolerant of urban conditions. These tend to be early-succession, native and non-native species that are frequent in both urban and rural settings. They can withstand some habitat modification and disruption and remain frequent under moderate levels of urbanisation.

Urban avoider. A species that cannot tolerate any level of urbanisation. These tend to be native, late-succession habitat specialists. They are among the first species to disappear when their preferred environmental conditions are altered by disturbance and urbanisation.

Urban canyon. A lane or street flanked by very tall buildings on both sides, creating a deep, narrow gap between them.

Urban exploiter. A species that thrives best in urban habitats. These tend to be alien, early-succession species that are well adapted to disturbance and urban conditions. They are generally less frequently encountered in rural settings.

Urban fallow. Areas of urban land that are left abandoned for some years, often developing a rich and diverse flora before being cleared and built on again. Also known as urban waste ground, derelict land and brownfield, urban fallow is a less pejorative term, borrowing its terminology from agricultural fallow land.

Urbanity. A measure of the tendency for a species to occur in cities or areas of urban land.

Urbic. A component of urban soils derived from building rubble, construction waste and other human-made artefacts.

Xenicity. A measure of the proportion of non-native alien neophytes in a vegetation community. Some urban plant communities have high levels of xenicity.

References

Adams, K. J., and Preston, C. D. 1992. Evidence for the effects of atmospheric pollution on bryophytes from national and local recording. In *Biological Recording of Changes in British Wildlife*, edited by P. T. Harding, pp. 31–43. London: HMSO.

Ahrazem, O., Diretto, G., Argandoña, J., Rubio-Moraga, A., Julve, J. M., Orzáez, D., Granell, A., and Gómez-Gómez, L. 2017. Evolutionarily distinct carotenoid cleavage dioxygenases are responsible for crocetin production in *Buddleja davidii*. *Journal of Experimental Botany* 68: 4663–4677. https://doi.org/10.1093/jxb/erx277.

Alcock, J. P. 2011. *A Brief History of Roman Britain Conquest and Civilization*. London: Hachette.

Allen, M. 2023. Old Plant Communities in Urban Areas: British and Irish Botanical Conference video. 13th December. https://www.youtube.com/watch?v=VHajYU_5FUk. Accessed 13th March 2024.

Anderson, K. L., Casey, R. A., Cooper, B., Upjohn, M. M., and Christley, R. M. 2023. National Dog Survey: Describing UK Dog and Ownership Demographics. *Animals* 13: 1072. https://doi.org/10.3390/ani13061072.

Andersson, S., Nilsson, L. A., Groth, I., and Bergström, G. 2002. Floral scents in butterfly-pollinated plants: possible convergence in chemical composition. *Botanical Journal of the Linnean Society* 140: 129–153.

Angold, P. G., Sadler, J. P., Hill, M. O., Pullin, A., Rushton, S., Austin, K., Small, E., Wood, B., Wadsworth, R., Sanderson, R., and Thompson, K. 2006. Biodiversity in urban habitat patches. *Science of the Total Environment* 360: 196–204. https://doi.org/10.1016/j.scitotenv.2005.08.035.

Antonopoulos, N., Kanatas, P., Gazoulis, I., Tataridas, A., Ntovakos, D., Ntaoulis, V. N., Zavra, S.-M., and Travlos, I. 2023. Hot foam: Evaluation of a new, non-chemical weed control option in perennial crops. *Smart Agricultural Technology* 3: 100063. https://doi.org/10.1016/j.atech.2022.100063.

Aronson, M. F., La Sorte, F. A., Nilon, C. H., Katti, M., Goddard, M. A., Lepczyk, C. A., Warren, P. S., Williams, N. S., Cilliers, S., Clarkson, B., Dobbs, C., Dolan, R., Hedblom, M., Klotz, S., Kooijmans, J. L., Kühn, I., Macgregor-Fors, I., McDonnell, M., Mörtberg, U., Pysek, P., Siebert, S., Sushinsky, J., Werner, P., and Winter, M. 2014. A global analysis of the impacts of urbanization on bird and plant diversity reveals key anthropogenic drivers. *Proceedings of the Royal Society B: Biological Sciences* 281: 20133330. https://doi.org/10.1098/rspb.2013.3330.

Ashmore, M. R., Bell, J. N. B., and Mimmack, A. 1988. Crop growth along a gradient of ambient air pollution. *Environmental Pollution* 53: 99–121.

Atkinson, B. W. 1968. A preliminary examination of the possible effect of London's urban area on the distribution of thunder rainfall 1951–60. *Transactions of the Institute of British Geographers* 44: 97–118.

Austin, K. C. 2002. Botanical Processes in Urban Derelict Spaces. Unpublished PhD Thesis. Birmingham: University of Birmingham.

Baker, C. 2018. *House of Commons Library Research Briefing: City & Town Classification of Constituencies & Local Authorities*. London: UK Parliament. https://commonslibrary.parliament.uk/research-briefings/cbp-8322/.

Ballinger, B. 2020. 50 walls in Dundee. *Botany in Scotland*, 7th June 2020. https://botsocscot.wordpress.com/2020/06/07/50-walls-in-dundee/.

Banks, G. 1830. *The Plymouth and Devonshire Flora*. Devonport: W. Byers.

Barden, D. J., and Preston, C. D. 2009. Are *Polypodium interjectum* and *P. vulgare* increasing in Cambridgeshire (v.c. 29)? *Nature in Cambridgeshire* 51: 12–20.

Bark, S. 2020. *How We Made the Pavements Width Map.* Cambridge: Esri UK. https://resource.esriuk.com/blog/how-we-made-the-pavements-width-map/

Barthelat, F. 2019. CABI Digital Library. *Erigeron karvinskianus* (Karwinsky's fleabane). *CABI Compendium* https://doi.org/10.1079/cabicompendium.11420.

Bartlewicz, J., Vandepitte, K., and Jacquemyn, H. 2015. Population genetic diversity of the clonal self-incompatible herbaceous plant *Linaria vulgaris* along an urbanization gradient. *Biological Journal of the Linnean Society* 116: 603–613.

Baskin, J. M., and Baskin, C. C. 1970. Germination eco-physiology of *Draba verna. Bulletin of the Torrey Botanical Club* 97: 209–216.

Baskin, J. M., and Baskin, C. C. 1983. Germination ecology of *Veronica arvensis. Journal of Ecology* 71: 57–68.

Bassett, R., Young, P., Blair, G., Cai, X., and Chapman, L. 2020. Urbanisation's contribution to climate warming in Great Britain. *Environmental Research Letters* 15: 114014. https://doi.org/10.1088/1748-9326/abbb51

Bateman, R. M. 2022. Systematics and conservation of British and Irish orchids: a 'state of the union' assessment to accompany Atlas 2020. *Kew Bulletin* 77: 355–402. https://doi.org/10.1007/s12225-022-10016-5.

Baude, M., Kunin, W., Boatman, N., Conyers, S., Davies, N., Gillespie, M. A. K., Morton, R. D., Smart, S. M., and Memmott, J. 2016. Historical nectar assessment reveals the fall and rise of floral resources in Britain. *Nature* 530: 85–88. https://doi.org/10.1038/nature16532.

Bechtel, B., and Schmidt, K. J. 2011. Floristic mapping data as a proxy for the mean urban heat island. *Climate Research* 49: 45–58.

Beesley, S., and Wilde, J. 1997. *Urban Flora of Belfast.* Belfast: Institute of Irish Studies, The Queen's University of Belfast.

Bell, M. L., Davis, D. L., and Fletcher, T. 2004. A retrospective assessment of mortality from the London smog episode of 1952: the role of influenza and pollution. *Environmental Health Perspectives* 112: 6–8.

Berry, M. 2022. Adventive and aliens news 27. *BSBI News* 151: 34–41.

Berry, M. 2023a. Adventive and aliens news 28. *BSBI News* 152: 41–48.

Berry, M. 2023b. Adventive and aliens news 30. *BSBI News* 154: 31–41.

Birmingham Tree People. 2024. *Birmingham Tree People: Street Trees.* Birmingham: Birmingham Tree People. https://birminghamtreepeople.org.uk/trees-in-birmingham/street-trees/. Accessed 24th January 2024.

Blair, R. B., and Launer, A. E. 1997. Butterfly diversity and human land use: species assemblages along an urban gradient. *Biological Conservation* 80: 113–125.

Bodsworth, E., Shepherd, P., and Plant, C. 2005. *Exotic plant species on brownfield land: their value to invertebrates of nature conservation importance.* English Nature Research Reports Number 650. Peterborough, English Nature.

Bonthoux, S., Brun, M., Di Pietro, F., Greulich, S., and Bouché-Pillon, S. 2014. How can wastelands promote biodiversity in cities? A review. *Landscape and Urban Planning* 132: 79–88. https://doi.org/10.1016/j.landurbplan.2014.08.010.

Bonthoux, S., Voisin, L., Bouché-Pillon, S., and Chollet, S. 2019. More than weeds: Spontaneous vegetation in streets as a neglected element of urban biodiversity. *Landscape and Urban Planning* 185: 163–172. https://doi.org/10.1016/j.landurbplan.2019.02.009.

Bosanquet, S. D. S. 2010. *The Mosses and Liverworts of Pembrokeshire.* Pontypool: published by the author.

Boucher, A., and Partridge, J. 2006. *Urtica membranacea*, an annual nettle, in Warwick: a first British record? *BSBI News* 103: 29–30.

Box, J. 2021. Increasing numbers of Local Nature Reserves in urban areas in England over the past 30 Years. *In Practice: Bulletin of the Chartered Institute of Ecology and Environmental Management* 144: 12–16.

Bromwich, M. 2006. *The Culmstock Yew.* https://www.ancient-yew.org/userfiles/file/Culmstock_article.pdf. Accessed 28th February 2024.

BSS. 2024. *Botanical Society of Scotland. Urban Flora of Scotland – what grows in your street?* Botanical Society of Scotland https://www.botanical-society-scotland.org.uk/Urban_Flora_of_Scotland.

BTO. 2023. *Garden Bird Feeding Survey.* https://www.bto.org/our-science/projects/gbfs. Accessed 25th August 2024.

Buglife. 2023. *Brownfield Hub: Brownfields.* https://www.buglife.org.uk/resources/habitat-hub/brownfield-hub/. Accessed 10th November 2023.

Bullock, P., and Gregory, P. J. 1991. Soils: a neglected resource in urban areas. In *Soils in the Urban Environment*, edited by P. Bullock and P. J. Gregory, pp. 1–5. Oxford: Blackwell Scientific Publications.

Burton, R. M. 1983. *Flora of the London Area*. London: London Natural History Society.

Burton, R. M. 2012. Notes on *Pilosella flagellaris* (Willd.) P. D. Sell & C. West in the British Isles. *BSBI News* 148: 54–58.

Butcher, B., Carey, P., Edmonds, R., Norton, L., and Treweek, J. 2020. *UK Habitat Classifications – Habitat Definitions V1.1*. https://ukhab.org/.

Cadbury, D. A., Hawkes, J. G., & Readett, R. C. 1971. *A Computer-Mapped Flora: A Study of the County of Warwickshire*. London: Academic Press.

Cairney, J. W. G., and Meharg, A. A. 1999. Influences of anthropogenic pollution on mycorrhizal fungal communities. *Environmental Pollution* 106: 169–182.

Cambridge City Council. 2024. *Help us manage the city's trees: Ash trees*. Cambridge, Cambridge City Council. https://www.cambridge.gov.uk/ash-trees. Accessed 8th April 2024.

Cape, J. N., Tang, Y. S. van Dijk, N., Love, L., Sutton, M. A., and Palmer, S. C. F. 2004. Concentrations of ammonia and nitrogen dioxide at roadside verges, and their contribution to nitrogen deposition. *Environmental Pollution* 132: 469–478.

Chappelka, A. H., Kush, J. S., Runion, G. B., Meier, S., and Kelley, W. D. 1991. Effects of soil-applied lead on seedling growth and ecto-mycorrhizal colonization of loblolly pine. *Environmental Pollution* 72: 307–316.

Chater, A. O., Oswald, P. H., and Preston, C. D. 2000. Street floras in Cambridge and Aberystwyth. *Nature in Cambridgeshire* 42: 3–26.

Cheptou, P.-O., Carrue, O., Rouifed, S., and Cantarel, A. 2008. Rapid evolution of seed dispersal in an urban environment in the weed *Crepis sancta*. *Proceedings of the National Academy of Sciences of the United States of America* 105: 3796–3799.

Chiles, A. 2019. In the wastelands of Birmingham and Manchester, buddleia is a symbol of our national neglect. *Guardian Opinion*, 4th April https://www.theguardian.com/environment/commentisfree/2019/apr/04/in-the-wastelands-of-birmingham-and-manchester-buddleia-is-a-symbol-of-our-national-neglect.

City of Edinburgh Council. 2022. *The City of Edinburgh Council Ash Dieback Action Plan*. Edinburgh, City of Edinburgh Council. https://www.edinburgh.gov.uk/downloads/file/30585/ash-dieback-action-plan. Accessed 8th April 2024.

City of Westminster. 2017. *Westminster Walking Strategy 2017–2027*. London: City of Westminster.

Common, J. 2022. *An Urban Flora of Newcastle – Mapping Wild Plants in the City*. Common By Nature https://commonbynature.com/2022/10/20/an-urban-flora-of-newcastle-mapping-wild-plants-in-the-city/. Accessed 13th March 2024.

Common, J. 2023a. *Newcastle's Urban Flora – A Project Update*. Common By Nature https://commonbynature.com/2023/08/02/urban-flora-newcastle/. Accessed 13th March 2024.

Common, J. 2023b. Newcastle's Urban Flora: Botanical Society of Britain and Ireland video. *13 December*. https://www.youtube.com/watch?v=ddcgFttCtbl. Accessed 13th March 2024.

Cornelis, J., and Hermy, M. 2004. Biodiversity relationships in urban and suburban parks in Flanders. *Landscape and Urban Planning* 69: 385–401.

Cortizo, G. 2022. Santiago estudia el uso de hierba en el enlosado para controlar la temperatura e incidir sobre el clima urbano. Madrid: elDiario.es https://www.eldiario.es/galicia/santiago-estudia-hierba-enlosado-controlar-temperatura-e-incidir-clima-urbano_1_9194796.html.

Crouch, H. J. 2020. Ferns of Bath: past and present. *Bath Natural History Society Magazine* 53.

Daniel, P. P., Woodward, F. I., Bryant, J. A., and Etherington, J. R. 1985. Nocturnal accumulation of acid in leaves of Wall Pennywort (*Umbilicus rupestris*) following exposure to water stress. *Annals of Botany* 55: 217–223.

Darlington, A. 1981. *Ecology of Walls*. London: Heinemann.

De Prado, R., Lopez-Martinez, N., and Giminez-Espinosa, R. 1997. Herbicide-resistant weeds in Europe: agricultural, physiological and biochemical aspects, in R. De Prado, J. Jorrín, and L. Garcia-Torres, eds, *Weed and Crop Resistance to Herbicides*, pp. 17–27. Dordrecht: Kluwer Academic Publishers.

Defra. 2016. The *Rural Urban Classification*. London: Department for Environment, Food and Rural Affairs https://www.gov.uk/government/collections/rural-urban-classification.

Defra National Statistics. 2023a. *National Statistics: Air quality statistics in the UK, 1987 to 2022 – Summary*. https://www.gov.uk/government/statistics/air-quality-statistics/summary. Accessed 3rd April 2024.

Defra National Statistics. 2023b. *Emissions of air pollutants in the UK – Sulphur dioxide (SO2)*. London: Department for Environment Food and Rural Affairs https://www.gov.uk/government/statistics/emissions-of-air-pollutants/emissions-of-air-pollutants-in-the-uk-sulphur-dioxide-so2. Accessed 3rd April 2024.

Dehnen-Schmutz, K. 2016. *GB Non-native Organism Rapid Risk Assessment for Ailanthus altissima*. GB Non-native Species Secretariat. https://www.nonnativespecies.org/assets/Uploads/RSS_RA_Ailanthus_altissima.pdf.

Dickson, J. H., Macpherson, P., and Watson, K. 2000. *The Changing Flora of Glasgow Urban and Rural Plants through the Centuries*. Edinburgh: Edinburgh University Press.

Dines, T. D., Eaton, S., and Myers, C. 2012. *The wild things guide to the changing plant life of the British Isles*. London: Transworld Publishers/Channel 4 Books.

Ding, H., Yu, X., Hang, C., Gao, K., Lao, X., Jia, Y., and Yan, Z. 2020. Ailanthone: A novel potential drug for treating human cancer. *Oncology Letters* 20: 1489–1503. https://doi.org/10.3892/ol.2020.11710.

Dise, N. B., Ashmore, M. R., Belyazid, S., Bobbink, R., de Vrise, W., Erisman, J. W., Spranger, T., Stevens, C. J., and van den Berg, L. 2011. Nitrogen as a threat to European terrestrial biodiversity. In: *The European nitrogen assessment: sources, effects and policy perspectives*. pp. 463–494. Cambridge: Cambridge University Press.

Druce, G. C. 1927. *The Flora of Oxfordshire*. Oxford: Clarendon Press.

Duckett, J. G., and Pressel, S. 2009. London's changing bryophyte flora. *Field Bryology* 122: 35–51.

Duckett, J. G., and Pressel, S. 2019. The epiphyte flora of roadside trees in the London conurbation with a North American perspective on its possible future. *Field Bryology* 122: 35–51.

Ebeling, S., and Tallent-Halsell. 2009. *CABI Digital Library. Buddleja davidii (butterfly bush)*. CABI Compendium https://doi.org/10.1079/cabicompendium.1031.

Edgington, J. A. 2003. Ferns of the metropolis – a status report. *The London Naturalist* 82: 59–73.

Edgington, J. A. 2007. Dynamics of long-distance dispersal: the spread of *Asplenium adiantum-nigrum* and *Asplenium trichomanes* (Aspleniaceae: Pteridophyta) on London walls. *The Fern Gazette*: 18: 31–38.

Edgington, J. 2008. Urban ferns. *Pteridologist* 5: 5–7.

Effland, W. R., and Pouyat, R. V. 1997. The genesis, classification, and mapping of soils in urban areas. *Urban Ecosystems* 1: 217–228.

Ellenberg, H., Weber, E., Düll, R., Wirth, W., Werner, W., and Paulißen, D. 1992. *Zeigerwerte von Pflanzen in Mitteleuropa*. 2nd edition. Scripta Geobotanica 18. Göttingen: Verlag Erich Goltze.

Elmqvist, T., Alfsen, C., and Colding, J. 2008. Urban systems. *Encyclopedia of Ecology* (Second Edition) 4: 452–458.

English Heritage. 2022. *History of Silchester Roman City Walls and Amphitheatre*. Swindon, English Heritage https://www.english-heritage.org.uk/visit/places/silchester-roman-city-walls-and-amphitheatre/history/. Accessed 19th December 2022.

Esperon-Rodriguez, M., Tjoelker, M. G., Lenoir, J., Baumgartner, J. B., Beaumont, L. J., Nipperess, D. A., Power, S. A., Richard, B., Rymer, P. D., and Gallagher, R. V. 2022. Climate change increases global risk to urban forests. *Nature Climate Change* 12: 950–955. https://doi.org/10.1038/s41558-022-01465-8.

Fagot, M., De Cauwer, B., Beeldens, A., Boonen, E., Bulcke, R., and Reheul, D. 2011. Weed flora in paved areas in relation to environment, pavement characteristics and weed control. *Weed Research* 51: 650–660. https://doi.org/10.1111/j.1365-3180.2011.00878.x.

Falk, S. 2009. *Warwickshire's Wildflowers: The wildflowers, shrubs and trees of historic Warwickshire*. Redditch, Brewin Books.

Falk, S. 2020. *Introduction to brownfields*. Peterborough, Buglife https://cdn.buglife.org.uk/2020/01/Introduction-to-brownfields.pdf. Accessed 4th April 2024.

Farmer, A. M. 1991. The effects of dust on vegetation – a review. *Environmental Pollution* 79: 63–75.

Fitter, A. H., and Fitter, R. S. 2002. Rapid changes in flowering time in British plants. *Science* 31: 1689–1691. https://doi.org/10.1126/science.1071617.

Fitzky, A. C., Sandén, H., Karl, T., Fares, S., Calfapietra, C., Grote, R., Saunier, A., Rewald, B. 2019. The Interplay Between Ozone and Urban Vegetation—BVOC Emissions, Ozone Deposition, and Tree Ecophysiology. *Frontiers in Forests and Global Change* 2: 10.3389. https://doi.org/10.3389/ffgc.2019.00050.

Fokuhl, G., Heinze, J., and Poschlod, P. 2019. An ant–plant mesocosm experiment reveals dispersal patterns of myrmecochorous plants. *Forests* 10: 1149. https://doi.org/10.3390/f10121149.

Foo, C. L., Harrington, K. C., and MacKay, M. B. 2010. Comparison of weed control techniques to establish three ground cover species. *New Zealand Plant Protection* 63: 96–101. https://nzpps.org/_journal/index.php/nzpp/article/view/6542.

Forest Research. 2020. Pest and disease resources: Horse chestnut leaf miner (*Cameraria ohridella*). Farnham, Forest Research. https://www.forestresearch.gov.uk/tools-and-resources/fthr/pest-and-disease-resources/horse-chestnut-leaf-miner-cameraria-ohridella/. Accessed 8th April 2024.

Forest Research. 2024a. Pest and disease resources: Bleeding Canker of Horse Chestnut (*Pseudomonas syringae pv. aesculi*). Farnham, Forest Research. https://www.forestresearch.gov.uk/tools-and-resources/fthr/pest-and-disease-resources/bleeding-canker-of-horse-chestnut-pseudomonas-syringae-pv-aesculi/. Accessed 8th April 2024.

Forest Research. 2024b. Pest and disease resources: Ash dieback (*Hymenoscyphus fraxineus*). Farnham, Forest Research. https://www.forestresearch.gov.uk/tools-and-resources/fthr/pest-and-disease-resources/ash-dieback-hymenoscyphus-fraxineus/. Accessed 8th April 2024.

Forest Research 2024c. Pest and disease resources: Massaria disease (*Splanchnonema platani*). Farnham, Forest Research. https://www.forestresearch.gov.uk/tools-and-resources/fthr/pest-and-disease-resources/massaria-disease-splanchnonema-platani/. Accessed 8th April 2024.

Forest Research 2024d. Pest and disease resources: Canker stain of plane (*Ceratocystis platani*). Farnham, Forest Research. https://www.forestresearch.gov.uk/tools-and-resources/fthr/pest-and-disease-resources/canker-stain-of-plane-ceratocystis-platani/. Accessed 8th April 2024.

Forest Research 2024e. *I-Tree Eco: UK Urban Canopy Cover*. Farnham, Forest Research. https://www.forestresearch.gov.uk/research/i-tree-eco/uk-urban-canopy-cover/. Accessed 8th April 2024.

Forgrave, A. 2024. 'Never seen it looking so scruffy' - Llandudno speaks out for rest of North Wales as weeds take over. *Daily Post*, 20th July. https://www.dailypost.co.uk/news/north-wales-news/never-seen-looking-scruffy-llandudno-29576299. Accessed 1st October 2024.

Francis, R. 2011. Wall ecology: A frontier for urban biodiversity and ecological engineering. *Progress in Physical Geography* 35: 43–63.

Francis, R. A., and Hoggart, S. P. G. 2012. The flora of urban river wallscapes. *River Research and Applications* 28: 1200–1216. https://doi.org/10.1002/rra.1497.

Fraser, A. 1993. *King Charles II*. London: Arrow Books Ltd.

Friends of the Earth. 2023. *Mapping English tree cover: results, ranking and methodology*. London: Friends of the Earth. https://policy.friendsoftheearth.uk/insight/mapping-english-tree-cover-results-ranking-and-methodology.

Fry, K. 2023. *The Plants Of Nottingham – A City Flora – 25 years on Journal*. iNaturalist. https://www.inaturalist.org/projects/the-plants-of-nottingham-a-city-flora-25-years-on/journal.

Fuller, R. M. 1987. The changing extent and conservation interest of lowland grasslands in England and Wales – a review of grassland surveys 1930–84. *Biological Conservation* 40: 281–300.

Futter, K., and Raynes, P. 1989. *The Flora of Derby*. Derby: P. Raynes.

Garthwaite, D., Parrish G., and Ridley, L. 2020. *Pesticide Usage Survey Report 302: Amenity Pesticide Usage in the United Kingdom 2020*. York: Food and Environment Research Agency (FERA).

Gaston, K. 2010. Urban ecology. In Gaston, K. (ed.), *Urban Ecology* (Ecological Reviews, pp. 1–9). Cambridge: Cambridge University Press. https://doi.org/10.1017/CBO9780511778483.002.

Geerts, S., Rossenrode, T., Irlich, U. M., and Visser, V. 2017. Emerging ornamental plant invaders in urban areas – Centranthus ruber in Cape Town, South Africa as a case study. *Invasive Plant Science and Management* 10: 322–331. https://doi.org/10.1017/inp.2017.35.

Gerard, J. 1597. *The Herball or Generall Historie of Plantes*. London: John Norton.

Geschke, A., James, S., Bennett, A. F., and Nimmo, D. G. 2018. Compact cities or sprawling suburbs? Optimising the distribution of people in cities to maximise species diversity. *Journal of Applied Ecology* 5: 2320–2331.

Gilbert, O. L. 1968. Bryophytes as indicators of air pollution in the Tyne valley. *New Phytologist* 67: 15–30.

Gilbert, O. L. 1986. Field evidence for an acid rain effect on lichens. *Environmental Pollution* 40: 227–231.

Gilbert, O. L. 1989. *The Ecology of Urban Habitats*. London: Chapman & Hall.

Gilbert, O. L. 1990. Wild figs by the River Don, Sheffield. *Watsonia* 18: 84–85.

Gilbert, O. L. 1992a. *Rooted in Stone: The Natural Flora of Urban Walls*. Peterborough: English Nature.

Gilbert, O. L. 1992b. *The Flowering of Cities: the Natural Flora of Urban 'Commons'*. Peterborough: English Nature.

Gillespie, R. G., Baldwin, B. G., Waters, J. M., Fraser, C. I., Nikula, R., and Roderick, G. K. 2012. Long-distance dispersal: A framework for hypothesis testing. *Trends in Ecology and Evolution* 27: 47–56.

GIGL. 2019. *Greenspace Information for Greater London CIC: Show & Tell: SINCs and the City – how nature is protected in the urban landscape*. London: GIGL. https://www.gigl.org.uk/2019/03/29/show-tell-sincs-and-the-city/. Accessed 18th April 2024.

GIGL. 2022. *Greenspace Information for Greater London CIC: Key London Figures*. London: GIGL https://www.gigl.org.uk/our-data-holdings/keyfigures/. Accessed 23rd March 2023.

GLA. 2023. *Housing in London 2023. The evidence base for the London Housing Strategy*. London: Greater London Authority. https://www.london.gov.uk/sites/default/files/2023-10/Housing%20in%20London%202023.pdf. Accessed 24th March 2023.

Godefroid, S., Monbaliu, D., and Koedam, N. 2007. The role of soil and microclimatic variables in the distribution patterns of urban wasteland flora in Brussels, Belgium. *Landscape and Urban Planning* 80: 45–55. https://doi.org/10.1016/j.landurbplan.2006.06.001.

Gorton, A. J., and Shaw, A. K. 2022. Using theoretical models to explore dispersal variation and fragmentation in urban environments. *Population Ecology* 65: 17–24.

Gov.Scot. 2023. *Scottish Vacant and Derelict Land Survey 2022*. Edinburgh: Scottish Government. https://www.gov.scot/publications/scottish-vacant-derelict-land-survey-2022/pages/5/.

Grace, J. 2020. *Urban Flora of Scotland Newsletter February 2020*. https://www.botanical-society-scotland.org.uk/sites/default/files/UFP%20newsetter%20Feb2020%20Final.pdf.

Grace, J. 2022. Plant of the Week – 20th June 2022 – Rue-leaved Saxifrage – *Saxifraga tridactylites*. Botany in Scotland. https://botsocscot.wordpress.com/2022/06/19/plant-of-the-week-20th-june-2022-rue-leaved-saxifrage-saxifraga-tridactylites/.

Grace, J. 2023. Plant of the Week, 16th January 2023 – Fairy Foxglove, *Erinus alpinus* L. Botany in Scotland https://botsocscot.wordpress.com/2023/01/15/fairy-foxglove-erinus-alpinus-l/.

Grantz, D. A., Garner, J. H. B., and Johnson, D. W. 2003. Ecological effects of particulate matter. *Environment International* 29: 213–239.

Grime, J. P., Hodgson, J. G., and Hunt, R. 1992. *The Abridged Comparative Plant Ecology*. London: Chapman and Hall.

Guédot, C., Landolt, P. J., and Smithhisler, C. L. 2008. Odorants of the flowers of Butterfly Bush, *Buddleja davidii*, as possible attractants of pest species of moths. *The Florida Entomologist* 91: 576–582. https://www.jstor.org/stable/25434874.

Haigh, M. J. 1980. Ruderal communities in English cities. *Urban Ecology* 4: 329–338.

Hall, A. 2000. A brief history of plant foods in the city of York. In: White, E. (ed.), *Feeding a city: York. The provision of food from Roman times to the beginning of the twentieth century*. Totnes, Prospect Books, pp. 23–42.

Hall, P. C. 1980. *Sussex Plant Atlas: An Atlas of the Distribution of Wild Plants in Sussex*. Brighton: Booth Museum of Natural History.

Hansard. 1849. Sheffield Market. House of Commons Debate. *UK Parliament Hansard* 107: 492–514. https://api.parliament.uk/historic-hansard/commons/1849/jul/17/smithfield-market.

Hanson, C. G. 2000. Update on bird seed aliens (1985–1998). *Watsonia* 23: 213–220.

Hanson, C. G., and Mason, J. L. 1985. Bird seed aliens in Britain. *Watsonia* 15: 237–252.

Harris, S. 2024. *Oxford Plants 400: Cymbalaria muralis P.Gaertn., B.Mey. & Scherb. (Plantaginaceae)*. Oxford: University of Oxford. https://dps007.plants.ox.ac.uk/bol/plants400/Profiles/cd/Cymbalaria.

Harris, S. A. 2002. Introduction of Oxford ragwort, *Senecio squalidus* L. (Asteraceae), to the United Kingdom. *Watsonia* 24: 31–43.

Hayes, F., Williamson, J., and Mills, G. 2012. Ozone pollution affects flower numbers and timing in a simulated BAP priority calcareous grassland community. *Environmental Pollution* 163: 40–47.

Hayward, M. W, Scanlon, R. J., Callen, A., Howell, L. G., Klop-Toker, K. L., Di Blanco, Y., Balkenhol, N., Bugir, C. K., Campbell, L., Caravaggi, A., Chalmers, A. C., Clulow, J., Clulow, S., Cross, P., Gould, J. A., Griffin, A. S., Heurich, M., Howe, B. K., Jachowski, D. S., Jhala, Y. V., Krishnamurthy, R., Kowalczyk, R., Lenga, D. J., Linnell, J. D. C., Marnewick, K. A., Moehrenschlager, A., Montgomery, R. A., Osipova, L., Peneaux, C., Rodger, J. C., Sales, L. P., Seeto, R. G. Y., Shuttleworth, C. M., Somers, M. J., Tamessar, C. T., Upton, R. M. O., Weise, F. J. 2019. Reintroducing rewilding to restoration – Rejecting the search for novelty. *Biological Conservation* 233: 255–259. https://doi.org/10.1016/j.biocon.2019.03.011.

Heap, I., and Duke, S. 2018. Overview of glyphosate-resistant weeds worldwide. *Pest Management Science* 74: 1040–1049. https://doi.org/10.1002/ps.4760.

Heaviside C., Cai, X.-M., and Vardoulakis, S. 2015. The effects of horizontal advection on the urban heat island in Birmingham and the West Midlands, United Kingdom during a heatwave. *Quarterly Journal of the Royal Meteorological Society* 141: 1429–1441.

Highways England. 2021. *Design Manual for Roads and Bridges: CD 143 Designing for Walking, Cycling and Horse-riding. Version 2.0.1*. Standards For Highways. https://www.standardsforhighways.co.uk/tses/attachments/9b379a8b-b2e3-4ad3-8a93-ee4ea9c03f12?inline=true.

Hill, M. O. (ed.) 2022. *The Nature of Cambridge*. Newbury: Pisces Publications.

Hill, M. O, Roy, D. B., and Thompson, K. 2002. Hemeroby, urbanity and ruderality: bioindicators of disturbance and human impact. *Journal of Applied Ecology* 39: 708–720.

Historic England. 2018. *Oppida: Introductions to Heritage Assets*. Swindon: Historic England. https://historicengland.org.uk/images-books/publications/iha-oppida/heag213-oppida/.

Hoare, P. G., Vinx, R., Stevenson, C. R., and Ehlers, J. 2002. Re-used bedrock ballast in King's Lynn's 'Town Wall' and the Norfolk port's medieval trading links. *Medieval Archaeology* 46: 91–105. https://doi.org/10.1179/med.2002.46.1.91.

Hodge, S. J. 1991. *Urban Trees: A survey of street trees in England. Forestry Commission Bulletin 99*. London: Forestry Commission.

Hodkinson, D. J., and Thompson, K. 1997. Plant dispersal: the role of man. *Journal of Applied Ecology* 34: 1484–1496.

Hofbauer, W. K., and Gärtner, G. 2021. *Microbial life on Façades*. Heidelberg: Springer Spektrum Berlin.

Holderness, T., Barr, S., Dawson, R., and Hall, J. 2013. An evaluation of thermal Earth observation for characterizing urban heatwave event dynamics using the urban heat island intensity metric. *International Journal of Remote Sensing* 34: 864–884.

Holt, J. S. 1987. Factors affecting germination in greenhouse-produced seeds of *Oxalis corniculata*, a perennial weed. *American Journal of Botany* 74: 429–436.

Hope, D., Gries, C., Zhu, W. X., Fagan, W. F., Redman, C. L., Grimm, N. B., Nelson, A. L., Martin, C., and Kinzig, A. 2003. Socioeconomics drive urban plant diversity. *Proceedings of the National Academy of Science of the United States of America* 100: 8788–8792.

Hoste, I., and Verloove, F. 2010. Mediterranean container plants and their stowaways: A potential source of invasive plant species. Pp. 39–44 in: *Proceedings of a scientific meeting* on *Invasive Alien Species*. Brussels, Belgian Biodiversity Platform.

Hou, L., Wang, Y., Shen, F., Lei, M., Wang, X., Zhao, X., Gao, S., and Alhaj, A. 2020. Study on variation of surface runoff and soil moisture content in the subgrade of permeable pavement structure. *Advances in Civil Engineering* 2020: 8836643. https://doi.org/10.1155/2020/8836643.

Hoyer, M. A. 1908. *By the Roman Wall: Notes on a Summer Holiday*. London: David Nutt.

HTA. 2010. *Top plants & trees for amenity landscapes*. Reading: Horticultural Trades Association. http://www.hillandsons.co.uk/docs/HTA_top_plants_for_amenity_landscapes.pdf.

Hu, S. Y. 1979. Ailanthus. *Arnoldia* 39: 29–50.

Hulme, M., Jenkins, G. J., Lu, X., Turnpenny, J.R., Mitchell, T. D., Jones, R. G., Lowe, J., Murphy, J. M., Hassell, D., Boorman, P., McDonald, R., and Hill, S. 2002. *Climate change scenarios for the UK: The UKCIP02 Scientific Report*. Tyndall Centre for Climate Change Research, University of East Anglia.

Humphries, T., and Florentine, S. K. 2021. A comparative review of six invasive *Nassella* species in Australia with implications for their management. *Plants (Basel)* 10: 1036. https://doi.org/10.3390/plants10061036.

Hunt, H. V., Rudzinski, A., Jiang, H., Wang, R., Thomas, M. G., and Jones, M. K. 2018. Genetic evidence for a western Chinese origin of broomcorn millet (*Panicum miliaceum*). *The Holocene* 28: 1968–1978. https://doi.org/10.1177/0959683618798116.

Imperial War Museum. 2024. *The Blitz Around Britain*. Imperial War Museum. https://www.iwm.org.uk/history/the-blitz-around-britain

Independent. 2018. *Why cows still roam the commons of Cambridge*. London: Independent Digital News & Media Ltd. https://www.independent.co.uk/climate-change/news/cambridge-cattle-cows-commons-why-parks-livestock-countryside-urbanisation-a8460171.html#.

IPC Vegetation. 2017. *Ozone impacts on vegetation*. International Cooperative Programme on Effects of Air Pollution on Natural Vegetation and Crops. https://icpvegetation.ceh.ac.uk/our-science/ozone.

Ivimey-Cook, R. B. 1984. *Atlas of the Devon Flora*. Exeter: Devonshire Association for the Advancement of Science, Literature and Art.

Jackson, L. 2015. *Dirty Old London. The Victorian Fight Against Filth*. London: Yale University Press.

Jackson, L. 2012. London labour and the London poor 1851, 1861–2 Henry Mayhew: Street sellers of the green stuff. *Dictionary of Victorian London*. https://victorianlondon.org/publications/mayhew1-8.htm.

Jackson, P. W., and Skeffington, M. S. 1984. *Flora of Inner Dublin*. Dublin: Royal Dublin Society.

Jeanjean, A. P. R., Buccolieri, R., Eddy, J., Monks, P. S., and Roland, R. J. 2017. Air quality affected by trees in real street canyons: The case of Marylebone neighbourhood in central London. *Urban Forestry and Urban Greening* 22: 41–53. https://doi.org/10.1016/j.ufug.2017.01.009.

Jones, A. W. 1957. The flora of the City of London bombed sites. *The London Naturalist* 37: 189–210.

Johnston, M. 2017. *Street Trees in Britain: A History*. Oxford: Oxbow Books.

Kelley, E. J. 1999. The effects of soil moisture on pavement systems. Unpublished MSc thesis. Athens, Ohio University.

Kent, D. H. 1961. The flora of Middlesex walls. *London Naturalist* 40: 29–43.

Kent, M., Stevens, R. A., and Zhang, L. 2001. Urban plant ecology patterns and processes: a case study of the flora of the City of Plymouth, Devon, UK. *Journal of Biogeography* 26: 1281–1298.

Kershaw, T. 2017. The urban heat island (UHI). In *Climate Change Resilience in the Urban Environment*, T. Kershaw. London, IOP Publishing.

King, G. A., and Hall, A. 2008. Evaluation of biological remains from a Roman timber drain at 21 St Peters Street, Colchester (site code: 2007.124). *Reports from the Centre for Human Palaeoecology, University of York* 2008/15.

Kluge, M. 1977. Is *Sedum acre* L. a CAM plant? *Oecologia* 29: 77–83.

Kováts, N., Hubai, K., Diósi, D., Sainnokhoi, T., Hoffer, A., Tóth, A., and Teke, G. 2021. Sensitivity of typical European roadside plants to atmospheric particulate matter. *Ecological Indicators* 124: 107428. https://doi.org/10.1016/j.ecolind.2021.107428.

Kowarik, I., and Säumel. I. 2007. Biological flora of Central Europe: *Ailanthus altissima* (Mill.) Swingle. *Perspectives in Plant Ecology, Evolution and Systematics* 8: 207–237.

Lachmuth, S., Durka, W., and Schurr, F. M. 2010. The making of a rapid plant invader: genetic diversity and differentiation in the native and invaded range of *Senecio inaequidens*. *Molecular Ecology* 19: 3952–3967. https://doi.org/10.1111/j.1365-294X.2010.04797.x.

Lambdon, P. W., Pyšek, P., Basnou, C., Hejda, M., Arianoutsou, M., Essl, F., Jarošík, V., Pergl, J., Winter, M., Anastasiu, P., Andriopoulos, P., Bazos, I., Brundu, G., Celesti-Grapow, L., Chassot, P., Delipetrou, P., Josefsson, M., Kark, S., Klotz, S., Kokkoris, Y., Kühn, I., Marchante, H., Perglová, I., Pino, J., Vilà, M., Zikos, A., Roy, D., and Hulme, P. E. 2008. Alien flora of Europe: species diversity, temporal trends, geographical patterns and research needs. *Preslia* 80: 101–149.

Lambert, T. 2021. *Local Histories: A History of Towns*. https://localhistories.org/a-history-of-english-towns/. Local Histories.

Lambrinos, J. G. 2002. The variable invasive success of *Cortaderia* species in a complex landscape. *Ecology* 83: 518–529.

Lavin, J. C., and Wilmore, G. T. D. 1994. *The West Yorkshire Plant Atlas*. Bradford: City of Bradford Metropolitan Council.

Lee, D. O. 1992. Urban warming? An analysis of recent trends in London's urban heat island. *Weather* 47: 50–56.

Legislation 2023. *Environment Act 2021. Part 6: Tree felling and planting*. London, Legislation.gov.uk. https://www.legislation.gov.uk/ukpga/2021/30/section/115. Accessed 8th April 2024.

Leguil, S. 2020. A history of weeding. *More than weeds*. https://morethanweeds.co.uk/a-history-of-weeding/.

Leguil, S. 2021. Are we weeds? *More than weeds*. https://morethanweeds.co.uk/.

Lehmann, A., and Stahr, K. 2007. Nature and significance of anthropogenic urban soils. *Journal of Soils and Sediments* 7: 247–260.

Lehner, S., Schulz, S., and Dötterl, S. 2022. The mystery of the butterfly bush *Buddleja davidii*: How are the butterflies attracted? *Frontiers in Plant Science* 13: 994851. https://doi.org/10.3389/fpls.2022.994851.

Lengyel, S., Gove, A. D., Latimer, A. M., Majer, J. D., and Dunn, R. R. 2009. Ants sow the seeds of global diversification in flowering plants. *PLoS ONE* 4: e5480. https://doi.org/10.1371/journal.pone.0005480.

Leslie, A. C. 2019. *Flora of Cambridgeshire*. Peterborough: Royal Horticultural Society.

Levermore, G., Parkinson, J., Lee, K., Laycock, P., and Lindley, S. 2018. The increasing trend of the urban heat island intensity. *Urban Climate* 24: 360–368.

Liu, J., and Niyogi, D. 2019. Meta-analysis of urbanization impact on rainfall modification. *Scientific Reports*: 9: 7301. https://doi.org/10.1038/s41598-019-42494-2.

Llewellyn, T., Gaya, E., and Murrell, D. J. 2020. Are Urban Communities in Successional Stasis? A Case Study on Epiphytic Lichen Communities. *Diversity* 12: 330. https://doi.org/10.3390/d12090330.

LNHS. 2024. London Natural History Society: Botany – A constantly changing flora. *London Natural History Society* http://www.lnhs.org.uk/index.php/sections/botany.

Lodwick, L. A. 2017. Agricultural innovations at a Late Iron Age oppidum: Archaeobotanical evidence for flax, food and fodder from *Calleva Atrebatum*, UK. *Quaternary International* 460: 198–219.

London Assembly. 2022. *70 years since the great London smog*. London: London Assembly. https://www.london.gov.uk/programmes-strategies/environment-and-climate-change/environment-and-climate-change-publications/70-years-great-london-smog. Accessed 20th March 2024.

London Biodiversity Partnership. 2001. *Urban Wastelands Habitat Statement*. London: London Biodiversity Partnership https://www.lbp.org.uk/hswasteland.htm. Accessed 6th December 2024.

London Tree Map. 2024. *London Tree Map*. London: London Assembly. https://apps.london.gov.uk/street-trees/. Accessed 23rd November 2023.

Lowcock, M. 2023. *Sheffield Street Trees Inquiry*. Sheffield, Sheffield City Council. https://www.sheffield.gov.uk/sites/default/files/2023-03/sheffield_street_trees_inquiry_report.pdf. Accessed 8th April 2024.

Lowe, A. J., and Abbott, R. J. 2003. A new British species, *Senecio eboracensis* (Asteraceae), another hybrid derivative of *S. vulgaris* L. and *S. squalidus* L. *Watsonia* 24: 375–388.

Lowe, A. J., and Abbott, R. J. 2004a. Reproductive isolation of a new hybrid species, *Senecio eboracensis* Abbott & Lowe (Asteraceae).

Heredity 92: 386–395. https://doi.org/10.1038/sj.hdy.6800432.

Lowe, A. J., and Abbott, R. J. 2004b. Origins, establishment and evolution of new polyploid species: *Senecio cambrensis* and *S. eboracensis* in the British Isles. *Biological Journal of the Linnean Society* 82: 467–474. https://doi.org/10.1111/j.1095-8312.2004.00333.x.

Lubelli, B., Moerman, J., Esposito, R., and Mulder, K. 2021. Influence of brick and mortar properties on bioreceptivity of masonry – Results from experimental research. *Construction and Building Materials* 266: 121036. https://doi.org/10.1016/j.conbuildmat.2020.121036.

Luck, G. W., and Smallbone, L. T. 2010. Species diversity and urbanisation: Patterns, drivers and implications. In *Urban Ecology* edited by K. Gaston, pp. 88–119. Cambridge: Cambridge University Press.

Luck, G. W., Smallbone, L. T., and O'Brien, R. 2009. Socio-economics and vegetation change in urban ecosystems: patterns in space and time. *Ecosystems* 12: 604–620.

Lundholm, J. 2011. Vegetation of urban hard surfaces. pp 93–102 In: Nie-melä, J., Breuste, J., Elmqvist, T., Guntenspergen, G., James, P., and McIntyre, N. (eds) *Urban Ecology: Patterns, Processes and Applications*. Oxford: Oxford University Press.

Mabey, R. 1996. *Flora Britannica*. London: Sinclair-Stevenson.

Mao, Q., and Huff, D. R. 2012. The evolutionary origin of *Poa annua* L. *Crop Science* 52: 1910–1922. https://doi.org/10.2135/cropsci2012.01.0016.

Marando, F., Heris, M. P, Zulian, G., Udías, A., Mentaschi, L., Chrysoulakis, N., Parastatidis, D., and Maes, J. 2022. Urban heat island mitigation by green infrastructure in European Functional Urban Areas. *Sustainable Cities and Society* 77: 103564. https://doi.org/10.1016/j.scs.2021.103564.

Margottini, C., and Spizzichino, D. 2014. How Geology Shapes Human Settlements. In *Reconnecting the City: The Historic Urban Landscape Approach and the Future of Urban Heritage*, edited by F. Bandarin and R. van Oers, pp. 47–84. Hoboken: Wiley Blackwell.

Marren, P. 1982. *A Natural History of Aberdeen*. Finzean, Robin Callander.

Marsh, A. 2024. Harrow Council slammed by former councillor for street weeds. *Harrow Times*, 12th September. https://www.harrowtimes.co.uk/news/24578203.harrow-council-slammed-former-councillor-street-weeds/. Accessed 1st October 2024.

Marshall, C. A. M., Wilkinson, M. T., Hadfield, P. M., Rogers, S. M., Shanklin, J. D., Eversham, B. C., Healey, R., Kranse, O. P., Preston, C. D., Coghill, S. J., McGonigle, K. L., Moggridge, G. D., Pilbeam, P. G., Marza, A. C., Szigecsan, D., Mitchell, J., Hicks, M. A., Wallis, S. M., Xu, Z., Toccaceli, F., McLennan, C. M., and Eves-van den Akker, S. 2023. Urban wildflower meadow planting for biodiversity, climate and society: An evaluation at King's College, Cambridge. *Ecological Solutions and Evidence* 4: e12243. https://doi.org/10.1002/2688-8319.12243.

Marston, C., Rowland, C. S., O'Neil, A. W., Morton, R. D. 2022a. Land Cover Map 2021 (10m classified pixels, GB). NERC EDS Environmental Information Data Centre. https://doi.org/10.5285/a22baa7c-5809-4a02-87e0-3cf87d4e223a.

Marston, C.; Rowland, C. S.; O'Neil, A. W.; Morton, R. D. (2022b). Land Cover Map 2021 (10m classified pixels, N. Ireland). NERC EDS Environmental Information Data Centre. https://doi.org/10.5285/e44ae9bd-fa32-4aab-9524-fbb11d34a20a.

Mason, B. 2016. *Bomb-Damage Maps Reveal London's World War II Devastation*. https://www.nationalgeographic.com/science/article/bomb-damage-maps-reveal-londons-world-war-ii-devastation.

McDonnell, L. 2017. *Somerset Rare Plants Group, 2016 Newsletter*. Somerset Rare Plants Group. https://www.somersetrareplantsgroup.org.uk/wp-content/uploads/2017/06/2016-Newsletter-17-FINAL-amended-June-2017-.pdf. Accessed 18th April 2024.

McIntyre, N. E., Knowles-Yanez, K., and Hope, D. 2000. Urban ecology as an interdisciplinary field: differences in the use of 'urban' between the social and natural sciences. *Urban Ecosystems* 4: 5–24.

McKee, J., and Richards, A. J. 1998. Effect of flower structure and flower colour on intrafloral warming and pollen germination and pollen-tube growth in winter flowering *Crocus* L. (Iridaceae). *Botanical Journal of the Linnean Society* 128: 369–384.

McKinney, M. L. 2008. Effects of urbanization on species richness: A review of plants and animals. *Urban Ecosystems* 11: 161–1769.

McKinney, M. L., and Lockwood, J. L. 1999. Biotic homogenization: a few winners replacing many losers in the next mass extinction. *Trends in Ecology and Evolution* 14: 450–453.

Meier, I. C., and Leuschner, C. 2008. Leaf size and leaf area index in *Fagus sylvatica* forests: competing effects of precipitation, temperature, and nitrogen availability. *Ecosystems* 11: 655–669.

Melzer, B., Steinbrecher, T., Seidel, R., Kraft, O., Schwaiger, R., Speck, T. 2010. The attachment strategy of English ivy: a complex mechanism acting on several hierarchical levels. *Journal of the Royal Society Interface* 7: 1383–1389. https://doi.org/10.1098/rsif.2010.0140.

Mentaschi, L., Duveiller, G., Zulian, G., Corbane, C., Pesaresi, M., Maes, J., Stocchino, A., and Feyen, L. 2022. Global long-term mapping of surface temperature shows intensified intra-city urban heat island extremes. *Global Environmental Change* 72: 102441.

Merrett, C. 1666. *Pinax rerum naturalium Britannicarum*. London.

Mesnage, R., Székács, A., and Zaller, J. G. 2021. Herbicides: Brief history, agricultural use, and potential alternatives for weed control. Pages 1–20 in *Emerging Issues in Analytical Chemistry: Herbicides, Chemistry, Efficacy, Toxicology, and Environmental Impacts*, edited by R. Mesnage and J. G. Zaller. Oxford: Elsevier.

Met Office. 2023. The Great Smog of 1952. London: Met Office https://www.metoffice.gov.uk/weather/learn-about/weather/case-studies/great-smog. Accessed 2nd February 2023.

Middleton, R. 2000. *The Plants of Hull: A Millennium Atlas*. Hull: Hull Natural History Society. http://www.hullnats.org.uk/millennium/index.htm.

Mills, G. 2008. Luke Howard and the climate of London. *Weather* 63: 153–157.

Mimet, A., Pellissier, V., Quénol, H., Aguejdad, R., Dubreuil, V., and Rozé, F. 2009. Urbanisation induces early flowering: evidence from *Platanus acerifolia* and *Prunus cerasus*. *International Journal of Biometeorology* 53: 287–298.

Mittal, H., Sharma, A., and Gairola, A. 2018. A review on the study of urban wind at the pedestrian level around buildings. *Journal of Building Engineering* 18: 154–163.

Mucina, L. 1990. Urban vegetation research in European Comecon countries and Yugoslavia: a review. In: *Urban Ecology: Plants and Plant Communities in Urban Environments*, edited by H. Sukopp, S. Hejny, and I. Kowarik, pp. 23–43. The Hague: SPB Academic Publishing.

Mundell, T. 2000. *Conyza bilbaoana* is on its way to you. *BSBI News* 87: 62–65.

Muratet, A., Machon, N., Jiguet, F., Moret, J., and Porcher, E. 2007. The role of urban structures in the distribution of wasteland flora in the Greater Paris area, France. *Ecosystems* 10: 661–671. https://doi.org/10.1007/s10021-007-9047-6.

Muratet, A., Lorrillière, R., Clergeau, P., and Fontaine, C. 2013. Evaluation of landscape connectivity at community level using satellite-derived NDVI. *Landscape Ecology* 28: 95–105. https://doi.org/10.1007/s10980-012-9817-1.

Nash, D. L. 1976. *Erigeron* Linnaeus. In: Nash, D. L. and Williams, L. O. (eds). Flora of Guatemala. *Fieldiana: Botany* 24(11.4): 156–159.

Nava, S. C. 2014. CABI Digital Library. *Ailanthus altissima* (tree-of-heaven). CABI Compendium. https://doi.org/10.1079/cabicompendium.3889.

Nevado, B., Harris, S. A., Beaumont, M. A., and Hiscock, S. J. 2020. Rapid homoploid hybrid speciation in British gardens: The origin of Oxford ragwort (*Senecio squalidus*). *Molecular Ecology* 29: 4221–4233. https://doi.org/10.1111/mec.15630.

Nowak, D. J., and Greenfield, E. J. 2020. The increase of impervious cover and decrease of tree cover within urban areas globally (2012–2017). *Urban Forestry and Urban Greening* 49: 126638. https://doi.org/10.1016/j.ufug.2020.126638.

OECD. 2022. Organisation for Economic Co-operation and Development: Glossary of Statistical Terms. http://stats.oecd.org/glossary/index.htm. Accessed 16th November 2022.

Oke, T. R. 1982. The energetic basis of the urban heat island. *Quarterly Journal of the Royal Meteorological Society* 108: 1–24.

Old Lawnmower Club. 2024. *The Old Lawnmower Club: Mower History* https://oldlawnmowerclub.co.uk/mowers/aboutmowers/history. Accessed 4th January 2024.

Omar, M., Al Sayed, N., Barré, K., Halwani, J., and Machon, N. 2018. Drivers of the distribution of spontaneous plant communities and species within urban tree bases. *Urban Forestry & Urban Greening* 35: 174–191. https://doi.org/10.1016/j.ufug.2018.08.018.

ONS. 2018. *Office for National Statistics. UK natural capital: ecosystem accounts for urban areas.* London: Office for National Statistics. https://www.ons.gov.uk/economy/environmentalaccounts/bulletins/urbannaturalcapitalaccountsuk/2023.

ONS. 2020. *Office for National Statistics. One in eight British households has no garden.* London: Office for National Statistics. https://www.ons.gov.uk/economy/environmentalaccounts/articles/oneineightbritishhouseholdshasnogarden/2020-05-14.

ONS. 2023. *Office for National Statistics. Urban natural capital accounts, UK: 2023.* London: Office for National Statistics. https://www.ons.gov.uk/economy/environmentalaccounts/bulletins/urbannaturalcapitalaccountsuk/2023.

Palliser, D. M. 2000. *The Cambridge urban history of Britain. Volume 1 600–1540.* Cambridge: Cambridge University Press.

Palmer, R. 1983. Red Indian Bean Tree in Westminster. *BSBI News* 35: 16. https://archive.bsbi.org.uk/BSBINews35.pdf.

PAN. 2021. Alternatives to herbicides. A Guide for the Amenity Sector. Brighton: Pesticide Action Network. https://www.pan-uk.org/site/wp-content/uploads/Alternatives-to-herbicides-a-guide-for-the-amenity-sector.pdf.

PAN. 2022. Where are we with a national ban on urban pesticides in the UK? Brighton: Pesticide Action Network. https://www.pan-uk.org/where-are-we-with-a-national-ban-on-urban-pesticides-in-the-uk/. Accessed 8th November 2022.

PAN. 2023. Greener Cities. A guide to the plants on our pavements. Brighton: Pesticide Action Network. https://issuu.com/pan-uk/docs/greener_cities_-_a_guide_to_our_pavement_plants.

PAN. 2024. Calling for councillor support to ban urban pesticides. Brighton: Pesticide Action Network. https://www.pan-uk.org/calling-for-councillor-support-to-ban-urban-pesticides/. Accessed 18th April 2024.

Parker, E. 2022. Weeding women: shaping England's gardens. *English Heritage* 2022. https://english-heritage.org.uk/learn/histories/women-in-history/weeding-women/.

Pavans de Ceccatty, E. 2023. Pesticide-Free Paris: It didn't take a revolution. Brighton: Pesticide Action Network. https://www.pan-uk.org/pesticide-free-paris/. Accessed 1st October 2024.

Payne, R. J, Dise, N. B., Field, C. D., Dore, A. J., Caporn, S. J. M., and Stevens, C. J. 2017. Nitrogen deposition and plant biodiversity: past, present, and future. *Frontiers in Ecology and the Environment* 15: 431–436.

Payne, R. M. 1978. The flora of walls in south-eastern Essex. *Watsonia* 12: 41–46.

Payne, R. M. 2005. The flora of walls and buildings in the Isle of Ely. *Nature in Cambridgeshire* 47: 43–58.

Pemberton, R. W., and Irving, D. W. 1990. Elaiosomes on weed seeds and the potential for myrmecochory in naturalized plants. *Weed Science* 38: 615–619. https://doi:10.1017/S0043174500051584.

Pescott, O. 2016. A systematic florula of a disturbed urban habitat: Pavements of Sheffield, England. *Biodiversity Data Journal* 4: e10658. https://doi.org/10.3897/BDJ.4.e10658.

Pilkington, S. 2011. Beginners Corner. Confusing urban mosses part 2: mortar-dwellers. *Field Bryology* 105: 50–55. https://www.britishbryologicalsociety.org.uk/wp-content/uploads/2020/12/FB105_Confusing-urban-mosses-part-2.pdf.

Plantlife 2017. *We need to talk about nitrogen.* Salisbury, Plantlife. https://www.plantlife.org.uk/wp-content/uploads/2023/10/We-need-to-talk-Nitrogen-Plantlife.pdf. Accessed 7th May 2024.

Plants In Action 2018. 3.1.1. The power of turgor pressure. *Plants In Action.* Australian Society of Plant Scientists, New Zealand Society of Plant Biologists, and New Zealand Institute of Agricultural and Horticultural Science 2010–2018. https://www.rseco.org/content/311-power-turgor-pressure.html. Accessed 17th October 2023.

Preston, C. D. 1988. The spread of *Epilobium ciliatum* Raf. in the British Isles. *Watsonia* 17: 279–288.

Preston, C. D. 2000. Engulfed by suburbia or destroyed by the plough: the ecology of extinction in Middlesex and Cambridgeshire. *Watsonia* 23: 59–81.

Preston, C. D. 2020. The phenology of an urban street flora: a transect study. *British and Irish Botany* 2: 1–26. https://doi.org/10.33928/bib.2020.02.001.

Preston, C. D. 2022. How 'natural' are our alien species? Botanical Society of Britain and Ireland video. 2 December. https://www.youtube.com/watch?v=pWgVZMq2KUc. Accessed 13th March 2024.

Preston, C. D., and Chater, A. O. 2024. Street floras in Cambridge and Aberystwyth revisited. *Nature in Cambridgeshire*. in prep.

Preston, C. D., and Hill, M. O. 2019. *Cambridgeshire's Mosses and Liverworts – a Dynamic Flora*. Newbury: Pisces Publications.

Preston, C. D., Pearman, D. A., and Dines, T. D. 2002. *New Atlas of the British and Irish Flora*. Oxford: Oxford University Press.

Preston, C. D., Pearman, D. A., and Hall, A. R. 2004. Archaeophytes in Britain. *Botanical Journal of the Linnean Society* 145: 257–294. https://doi.org/10.1111/j.1095-8339.2004.00284.x.

Primavesi, A. L., and Evans, P. A. 1988. *Flora of Leicestershire*. Leicestershire Museums Publication no. 89. Leicester: Leicestershire Museums.

Qasem, J. R., Alfalahi, A. O., Alsubeie, M. S., Almehemdi, A. F., and Synowiec, A. 2023. Genetic Variations among Fleabane (*Conyza bonariensis* (L.) Cronquist) populations in Jordan and their susceptibility levels to contact herbicides. *Agriculture* 13: 435. https://doi.org/10.3390/agriculture13020435

Qin, Y., Zhang, X., Tan, K., and Wang, J. 2022. A review on the influencing factors of pavement surface temperature. *Environmental Science and Pollution Research* 29: 67659–67674. https://doi.org/10.1007/s11356-022-22295-3.

Rai, P. K. 2016. Impacts of particulate matter pollution on plants: Implications for environmental biomonitoring. *Ecotoxicology and Environmental Safety* 129: 120–136.

Raunkiær, C. 1934. *The Life Forms of Plants and Statistical Plant Geography*. Oxford: Oxford University Press.

Ray, J. 1670. *Catalogus plantarum Anglae, et insularum adjacentium*. John Martyn: London.

Rebel Botanists. 2024. Street Graffiti or Urban Education? *Rebel Botanists* https://rebelbotanists.org/.

Rega-Brodsky, C. C., Aronson, M. F. J., Piana, M. R., Carpenter, E., Hahs, A. K., Herrera-Montes, A., Knapp, S., Kotze, D. J., Lepczyk, C. A., Moretti, M., Salisbury, A. B., Williams, N. S. G., Jung, K. Katti, M., MacGregor-Fors, I., MacIvor, J. S., La Sorte, F. A., Sheel, V., Threfall, C. G., and Nilon, C. H. 2022. Urban biodiversity: State of the science and future directions. *Urban Ecosystems* 25: 1083–1096. https://doi.org/10.1007/s11252-022-01207-w.

Reisch, C. 2007. Genetic structure of *Saxifraga tridactylites* (Saxifragaceae) from natural and man-made habitats. *Conservation Genetics* 8: 893–902. https://doi.org/10.1007/s10592-006-9244-4.

Reynolds, S. 1997. *Conyza bilbaoana* also in Ireland. *BSBI News* 74: 44–46.

Richardson, D. M., Pyšek, P., Rejmanek, M., Barbour, M., and Panetta, F. W. C. 2000. Naturalization and invasion of alien plants: concepts and definitions. *Diversity and Distributions* 6: 93–107.

Ridding, L. E., Redhead, J. W., and Pywell, R. F. 2015. Fate of semi-natural grassland in England between 1960 and 2013: A test of national conservation policy. *Global Ecology and Conservation*: 516–525. https://doi.org/10.1016/j.gecco.2015.10.004.

Rindi, F., and Guiry, M. D. 2002. Diversity, life history, and ecology of *Trentepohlia* and *Printzina* (Trentepohliales, Chlorophyta) in urban habitats in western Ireland. *Journal of Phycology* 38: 39–54.

Rindi, F., and Guiry, M. D. 2004. Composition and spatial variability of terrestrial algal assemblages occurring at the bases of urban walls in Europe. *Phycologia* 43: 225–235.

Rindi, F., McIvor, L., and Guiry, M. D. 2004. The Prasiolales (Chlorophyta) of Atlantic Europe: an assessment based on morphological, molecular, and ecological data, including the characterization of *Rosenvingiella radicans* (Kutzing) comb. nov. *Journal of Phycology* 40: 977–997. https://doi.org/10.1111/j.1529-8817.2004.04012.

Rishbeth, J. 1948. The Flora of Cambridge Walls. *Journal of Ecology* 36: 136–148.

Rizwan, A. M., Dennis, Y. C. L., and Liu, C. 2008. A review on the generation, determination and mitigation of the Urban Heat Island. *Journal of Environmental Sciences* 20: 120–128.

Roberts, H. A., and Lockett, P. A. 1978. Seed dormancy and periodicity of seedling emergence in *Veronica hederifolia* L. *Weed Research* 18: 41–48.

Roberts, H. R., Warren, J. M., and Provan, J. 2018. Evidence for facultative protocarnivory in *Capsella bursa-pastoris* seeds. *Scientific Reports* 8: 10120. https://doi.org/10.1038/s41598-018-28564-x.

Robinson, B. S., Bennie, J., Inger, R., Early, R., and Gaston, K. J. 2018. Sweet flowers are slow and weeds make haste: anthropogenic dispersal of plants via garden and construction soil. *Journal of Urban Ecology* 4: juy004. https://doi.org/10.1093/jue/juy004.

Robinson, J. M., Mavoa, S., Robinson, K., and Brindley, P. 2022. Urban centre green metrics in Great Britain: A geospatial and socioecological study. *PLoS ONE* 17(11): e0276962. https://doi.org/10.1371/journal.pone.0276962.

Rodwell, J. S. 2006. *NVC Users' Handbook*. JNCC, Peterborough.

Roetzer, T., Wittenzeller, M., Haeckel, H., and Nekovar, J. 2000. Phenology in central Europe – differences and trends of spring phenophases in urban and rural areas. *International Journal of Biometeorology* 44: 60–66.

Rogers, K., Sacre, K., Goodenough, J., and Doick, K. 2015. *Valuing London's Urban Forest. Results of the London i-Tree Eco Project*. London: Treeconomics London.

Rotherham, I. D. 2017. *Recombinant Ecology – A Hybrid Future?* Cham, Switzerland: Springer. DOI: 10.1007/978-3-319-49797-6.

Roy, H. E., Peyton, J., Aldridge, D. C., Bantock, T., Blackburn, T. M., Britton, R., Clark, P., Cook, E., Dehnen-Schmutz, K., Dines, T., Dobson, M., Edwards, F., Harrower, C., Harvey, M. C., Minchin, D., Noble, D. G., Parrott, D., Pocock, M. J. O., Preston, C. D., Roy, S., Salisbury, A., Schönrogge, K., Sewell, J., Shaw, R. H., Stebbing, P., Stewart, A. J. A., and Walker, K. J. 2014. Horizon scanning for invasive alien species with the potential to threaten biodiversity in Great Britain. *Global Change Biology* 20: 3859–3871. https://doi.org/10.1111/gcb.12603.

Rumsey, F. 1998. *Adiantum raddianum* Presl in London. *BSBI News* 78: 60.

Rumsey, F., and Crouch, H. J. 2008. Brake out! *Pteris* go wild in the British Isles. *Pteridologist* 5: 31–35.

Salisbury, A., Gallagher, F. J., Parag, H. A., Meneses-Florián, L., and Holzapfel, C. 2021. Plant diversity increases in an urban wildland after four decades of unaided vegetation development in a post-industrial site. *Urban Ecosystems* 24: 95–111. https://doi.org/10.1007/s11252-020-01018-x.

Salisbury, E. 1961. *Weeds and Aliens*. London: Collins.

Sansom, M., Saborido, A. A., and Dubois, M. 2013. Control of *Conyza* spp. With glyphosate – a review of the situation in Europe. *Plant Protection Science* 49: 44–53.

Santamouris, M., Georgakis, C., and Niachou, A. 2008. On the estimation of wind speed in urban canyons for ventilation purposes – Part 2: Using of data driven techniques to calculate the more probable wind speed in urban canyons for low ambient wind speeds. *Building and Environment* 43: 1411–1418.

Santos, G., and Sayers, S. 2020. *Epipactis dunensis* (Orchidaceae): a confirmed new addition for the Irish flora. ResearchGate https://www.researchgate.net/publication/340065625_Epipactis_dunensis_Orchidaceae_a_confirmed_new_addition_for_the_Irish_flora Accessed 18th March 2024.

Satterthwaite, D. 2020. *An urbanising world*. London, International Institute for Environment and Development. https://www.iied.org/urbanising-world.

Save Bloomsbury. 2020. A forgotten part of London's heritage. *Save Bloomsbury*, 27th March 2020. https://savebloomsbury.co.uk/2020/03/27/a-forgotten-part-of-londons-heritage/.

Schadek, U., Strauss, B., Biedermann, R., and Kleyer, M. 2009. Plant species richness, vegetation structure and soil resources of urban brownfield sites linked to successional age. *Urban Ecosystems* 12: 115–126. https://doi.org/10.1007/s11252-008-0072-9.

Schmidt, K. J. 2014. *Plants in urban environments in relation to global change drivers at different scales*. PhD thesis. Hamburg: University of Hamburg. https://d-nb.info/1054422796/34.

Schwarz, L. 2001. London 1700–1840. In *The Cambridge Urban History of Britain*, edited by D. M. Palliser, P. Clark, and M. Daunton. Cambridge: Cambridge University Press.

Shah, M. A. 2010. Effect of arbuscular mycotrophy on growth and invasiveness of some alien plants of Kashmir Himalaya with particular reference to phosphorus nutrition. PhD thesis. Kashmir: University of Kashmir.

Shah, M. A., Callaway, R. M., Shah, T., Houseman, G. R., Pal, R. W., Xiao, S., Luo, W., Rosche, C., Reshi, Z. A., Khasa, D. P., and Chen, S. 2014. *Conyza canadensis* suppresses plant diversity in its nonnative ranges but not at home: a transcontinental comparison. *New Phytologist* 202: 1286–1296. https://doi.org/10.1111/nph.12733.

Shaukat S. S., Munir N., and Siddiqui, I. A. 2003. Allelopathic response of *Conyza canadensis* (L.) Cronquist: a cosmopolitan weed. *Asian Journal of Plant Science* 14: 1034–1039.

Shaw, M. 1988. *A Flora of the Sheffield Area (Two Hundred Years of Plant Records)*. Sheffield: Sorby Natural History Society.

Shepherd, P. A. 1992. Botanical Studies of the Synanthropic Urban Vegetation in Central England. Unpublished PhD thesis. Nottingham: University of Nottingham.

Shepherd, P. A. 1998. *The Plants of Nottingham: A City Flora*. Sheffield: Wildtrack Publishing.

Shimwell, D. W. 2009. Studies in the floristic diversity of Durham walls, 1958–2008. *Watsonia* 27: 323–338.

Sitzia, T., Cierjacks, A., de Rigo, D., and Caudullo, G. 2016. *Robinia pseudoacacia* in Europe: distribution, habitat, usage and threats. In: San-Miguel-Ayanz, J., de Rigo, D., Caudullo, G., Houston Durrant, T., Mauri, A. (eds.). *European Atlas of Forest Tree Species*. Publ. Off. EU, Luxembourg, pp. e014e79+.

Smith, C., Dawson, D., Archer, J., Davies, M., Frith, M., Hughes, E., and Massini, P. 2011. *From green to grey; observed changes in garden vegetation structure in London, 1998–2008*. London Wildlife Trust, Greenspace Information for Greater London, and Greater London Authority.

Smith, C. L., Webb, A., Levermore, G. J., Lindley, S. J., and Beswick, K. 2011. Fine-scale spatial temperature patterns across a UK conurbation. *Climatic Change* 109: 269–286.

Smith, R., Hodgson, B., and Ison, J. 2016. *A New Flora of Devon*. Exeter: The Devonshire Association.

Solbreck, C., and Andersson, D. 1987. Vertical distribution of fireweed, *Epilobium angustifolium*, seeds in the air. *Canadian Journal of Botany* 65: 2177–2178.

Stamp, N. E. 1984. Self-burial behaviour of *Erodium cicutarium* seeds. *Journal of Ecology* 72: 611–620.

Stanley, P. 1996. *Conyza bilbaoana* J. Rémy – New to South Hampshire (VC11) and to Britain. *BSBI News* 73: 47–49.

Starry, O., Lea-Cox, J. D., Kim, J., and van Iersel, M. W. 2014. Photosynthesis and water use by two *Sedum* species in green roof substrate. *Environmental and Experimental Botany* 107: 105–112.

Stevens, R. A. 1990. *A Provisional Flora and Habitat Atlas of Plymouth*. Nature Conservancy Council, Plymouth.

Stroh, P. A., Walker, K. J., Humphrey, T. A., Pescott, O. L., and Burkmar, R. J. 2023. *Plant Atlas 2020: Mapping Changes in the Distribution of the British and Irish Flora*. New Jersey: Princeton University Press.

Stroh, P. A., Leach, S. J., August, T. A., Walker, K. J., Pearman, D. A., Rumsey, F. J., Harrower, C. A., Fay, M. F., Martin, J. P., Pankhurst, T., Preston, C. D., and Taylor, I. 2014. *A Vascular Plant Red List for England*. Bristol: Botanical Society of Britain and Ireland.

Sukopp, H. 2003. Flora and vegetation reflecting the urban history of Berlin. *Die Erde; Zeitschrift der Gesellschaft für Erdkunde zu Berlin* 134: 295–316.

Sukopp, H. 2002. On the early history of urban ecology in Europe. *Preslia* 74: 373–393.

Tackenberg, O., Poschlod, P., and Kahmen, S. 2003. Dandelion seed dispersal: The horizontal wind speed does not matter for long-distance dispersal – it's updraft! *Plant Biology* 5: 451–580.

Tallent-Halsell, N. G., and Watt, M. S. 2009. The Invasive *Buddleja davidii* (Butterfly Bush). *Botanical Review* 75: 292–325. https://doi.org/10.1007/s12229-009-9033-0.

Thiele, J., and Otte, A. 2007. Impact of *Heracleum mantegazzianum* on invaded vegetation and human activities. In P. Pyšek, M. J. W. Cock, W. Nentwig, and H. P. Ravn (eds). 2007. *Ecology and Management of Giant Hogweed (Heracleum mantegazzianum)*. Wallingford: CAB International.

Thompson, K., Hodgeson, J. G., Smith, R. M., Warren, P. H., and Gaston, K. J. 2004. Urban domestic gardens (III): Composition and diversity of lawn floras. *Journal of Vegetation Science* 15: 373–378.

Thompson, K., and McCarthy, M. 2008. Traits of British alien and native urban plants. *Journal of Ecology* 96: 853–859. https://doi.org/10.1111/j.1365-2745.2008.01383.x.

Torra, J., Montull, J. M., Calha, I. M., Osuna, M. D., Portugal, J., and de Prado, R. 2022. Current status of herbicide resistance in the Iberian peninsula: future trends and challenges. *Agronomy* 2022: 929. https://doi.org/10.3390/agronomy12040929.

Treasure, E., Gröcke, D., Caseldine, A., and Church, M. 2019. Neolithic farming and wild plant exploitation in western Britain: archaeobotanical and crop stable isotope evidence from Wales (*c.* 4000–2200 cal BC). *Proceedings of the Prehistoric Society* 85: 193–222.

Trimen, H., and Dyer, W.T.S. 1869. *Flora of Middlesex*. London: Hardwicke.

Troy, A. R., Grove, J. M., O'Neil-Dunne, J. P. M., Picken, S. T. A., and Cadenasso, M. L. 2007. Predicting opportunities for greening and patterns of vegetation on private urban lands. *Environmental Management* 40: 394–412.

Turner, W. 1548. *The Names of Herbs* (1965 Facsimile). London: The Ray Society.

Unsolved Murders. 2023. Mabel Greenwood. http://www.unsolved-murders.co.uk/murder-content.php?key=108&termRef=Mabel%20Greenwood.

van der Kooi, C. J., and Stavenga, D. G. 2019. Vividly coloured poppy flowers due to dense pigmentation and strong scattering in thin petals. *Journal of Comparative Physiology. A, Neuroethology, Sensory, Neural, and Behavioral Physiology* 205: 363–372. https://doi: 10.1007/s00359-018-01313-1.

Vega, K. A., and Küffer, C. 2021. Promoting wildflower biodiversity in dense and green cities: The important role of small vegetation patches. *Urban Forestry & Urban Greening* 62: 127165. https://doi.org/10.1016/j.ufug.2021.127165.

Vítková, M., Müllerová, J., Sádlo, J., Pergl, J., and Pyšek, P. 2017. Black locust (*Robinia pseudoacacia*) beloved and despised: a story of an invasive tree in Central Europe. *Forest Ecology and Management* 384: 287–302. https://doi:10.1016/j.foreco.2016.10.057.

von der Lippe M., and Kowarik I. 2007. Long-distance dispersal of plants by vehicles as a driver of plant invasions. *Conservation Biology* 21: 986–996. https://doi:10.1111/j.1523-1739.2007.00722.x.

Walker, K. J. 2007. The last thirty five years: recent changes in the flora of the British Isles. *Watsonia* 26: 291–302.

Walker, K. J., Stroh, P. A., Humphrey, T. A., Roy, D. B., Burkmar, R. J., and Pescott, O. L. 2023. *Britain's Changing Flora: A Summary of the Results of Plant Atlas 2020*. Durham: Botanical Society of Britain and Ireland.

Warwick, S. I., and Briggs, D. 1978a. The genecology of lawn weeds I. Population differentiation in *Poa annua* L. in a mosaic environment of bowling green lawns and flower beds. *New Phytologist* 81: 711–723.

Warwick, S. I., and Briggs, D. 1978b. The genecology of lawn weeds II. Evidence for disruptive selection in *Poa annua* L. in a mosaic environment of bowling green lawns and flower beds. *New Phytologist* 81: 725–737.

Warwick, S. I., and Briggs, D. 1979. The genecology of lawn weeds III. Cultivation experiments with *Achillea millefolium* L., *Bellis perennis* L., *Plantago lanceolata* L., *Plantago major* L., and *Prunella vulgaris* L. collected from lawns and contrasting grassland habitat. *New Phytologist* 83: 509–536.

Warwick, S. I., and Briggs, D. 1980a. The genecology of lawn weeds IV. Adaptive significance of variation in *Bellis perennis* L. as revealed in a transplant experiment. *New Phytologist* 85: 275–288.

Warwick, S. I., and Briggs, D. 1980b. The genecology of lawn weeds V. The adaptive significance of different growth habit in lawn and roadside populations of *Plantago major* L. *New Phytologist* 85: 289–300.

Warwick, S. I., and Briggs, D. 1980c. The genecology of lawn weeds VI. The adaptive significance of variation in *Achillea millefolium* L. as investigated by transplant experiments. *New Phytologist* 85: 451–460.

Weeds, J. 2024. People in Great Yarmouth frustrated with overgrown verges. *Great Yarmouth Mercury*, 10th June. https://www.greatyarmouthmercury.co.uk/news/24377817.people-great-yarmouth-frustrated-overgrown-verges/. Accessed 1st October 2024.

Westermann, J. R., von der Lippe, M., and Kowarik, I. 2011. Seed traits, landscape and environmental parameters as predictors of species occurrence in fragmented urban railway habitats. *Basic and Applied Ecology* 12: 29–37. https://doi.org/10.1016/j.baae.2010.11.006

Weston, P. 2023. Weed-choked pavements anger residents as 'rewilding' divides UK towns and cities. *The Guardian*, 26th August. https://

www.theguardian.com/environment/2023/aug/26/civic-wars-break-out-over-rewilding-town-centres-age-of-extinction. Accessed 1st October 2024.

Whild, S. J., Godfrey, M. F., and Lockton, A. J. 2011. *A Flora of Shrewsbury*. Shrewsbury: Shropshire Botanical Society and the University of Birmingham.

Whitney, H. M, Bennett, K. M. V., Dorling, M., Sandbach, L., Prince, D., Chittka, L., and Glover, B. J. 2011. Why do so many petals have conical epidermal cells? *Annals of Botany* 108: 609–616. https://doi.org/10.1093/aob/mcr065.

WHO. 2000. Air quality guidelines for Europe. Second edition. Copenhagen: WHO Regional Publications, European series No 91. https://www.euro.who.int/__data/assets/pdf_file/0016/123091/AQG2ndEd_10effso2.pdf.

Wichmann, M. C., Alexander, M. J., Soons, M. B., Galsworthy, S., Dunne, L., Gould, R., Fairfax, C., Niggemann, M., Hails, R. S., and Bullock, J. M. 2008. Human-mediated dispersal of seeds over long distances. *Proceedings of the Royal Society B: Biological Sciences* 276: 523–532. https://doi.org/10.1098/rspb.2008.1131.

Williams, N. S., Schwartz, M. W., Vesk, P. A., McCarthy, M. A., Hahs, A. K., Clemants, S. E., Corlett, R. T., Duncan, R. P., Norton, B. A., Thompson, K., and McDonnell, M. J. 2009. A conceptual framework for predicting the effects of urban environments on floras. *Journal of Ecology* 97: 4–9. https://doi.org/10.1111/j.1365-2745.2008.01460.x.

Witcher, R. 2013. On Rome's ecological contribution to British flora and fauna: landscape, legacy and identity. *Landscape History* 34: 5–26. https://doi.org/10.1080/01433768.2013.855393.

Wittig, R. 2004. The origin and development of the urban flora of Central Europe. *Urban Ecosystems* 7: 323–339.

Wood, P. 2022. *London is a Forest*. London: Quadrille Publishing Ltd.

Woodell, S. R. J., and Rossiter, J. 1959. The Flora of Durham Walls. *Proceedings of the Botanical Society of the British Isles* 3: 257–273.

Woods Ballard, B., Wilson, S., Udale-Clarke, H., Illman, S., Scott, T., Ashley, R., and Kellagher, R. 2015. *The SuDS Manual*. London: Ciria.

World Bank. 2022. *The World Bank. Urban Population – United Kingdom*. https://data.worldbank.org/indicator/SP.URB.TOTL?locations=GB and https://data.worldbank.org/indicator/SP.URB.TOTL.IN.ZS?locations=GB. Washington: World Bank Group.

Woźniak, G., Sierka, E., and Wheeler, A. 2018. Urban and industrial habitats: how important they are for ecosystem services. In *Ecosystem Services and Global Ecology*, edited by Hufnagel, L. London: IntechOpen. 10.5772/intechopen.75723.

Wurzell, B. 1988. *Conyza sumatrensis* (Retz.) E. Walker established in England. *Watsonia* 17: 145–148.

Wurzell, B. 1994. A history of *Conyza* in London. *BSBI News* 65: 34–38.

Wyka, T. P. 2023. Negative phototropism of the shoots helps temperate liana *Hedera helix* L. to locate host trees under habitat conditions. *Tree Physiology* 43: 1874–1885. https://doi.org/10.1093/treephys/tpad077.

Yang, X., Li, Y., Luo, Z., and Chan, P. W. 2017. The urban cool island phenomenon in a high-rise high-density city and its mechanisms. *International Journal of Climatology* 37: 890–904.

Zhang M. J., Liu M. Z., Prest, H., and Fischer, S. 2008. Nanoparticles secreted from ivy rootlets for surface climbing. *Nano Letters* 8: 1277–1280. http://dx.doi.org/10.1021/nl0725704.

Zipper, S. C., Schatz, J., Singh, A., Kucharik, K. J., Townsend, P. A., and Loheide, S. P. 2016. Urban heat island impacts on plant phenology: intra-urban variability and response to land cover. *Environmental Research Letters* 11: 054023. http://dx.doi.org/10.1088/1748-9326/11/5/054023.

Illustration credits

All photographs and figures are copyright © the author or are understood to be out of copyright, except for those listed below.

Bloomsbury Publishing would like to thank those listed below for providing illustrations and for permission to reproduce copyright material within this book. While every effort has been made to trace and acknowledge copyright holders, we would like to apologise for any errors or omissions, and invite readers to inform us so that corrections can be made in any future editions.

Key: l = left; r = right; t = top; c = centre; b = bottom; tl = top left; tr = top right; ct = centre top; cb = centre bottom; bl = bottom left; br = bottom right; i = inset.
Alamy = Alamy Stock Photo; Getty = Getty Images; NPL = Nature Picture Library; SS = Shutterstock.

2–3 Matthew Taylor / Alamy; 11 Marie Aymerez / Biosphoto / Alamy; 12–13 Mark Pedley / Colouria Media / Alamy; 14 Michael Hutchinson / NPL; 17 Arco / A. Scholz / Imagebroker / Alamy; 18 (all) Mark Patterson; 19 l Botanical Society of Britain and Ireland; r Zoonar / J. Ehrlich / Zoonar GmbH / Alamy; 22 Greg Balfour Evans / Alamy; 23 Andrew Cole / Alamy; 24 Howard Walker / Alamy; 25 Based upon LCM2021 © UKCEH 2022. Contains Ordnance Survey data © Crown Copyright 2007 Licence number 100017572, Land & Property Services © Crown Copyright and database right 2007 VARCA 100513. Reproduced with kind permission of the UK Centre for Ecology and Hydrology; 26 Nigel Burkitt / Getty; 27 Robert Stainforth / Alamy; 28 A.P.S (UK) / Alamy; 29 Greenspace Information for Greater London (GiGL, CIC); 30 i4images rm / Alamy; 34 Heritage Images / Getty; 36 l rustamxakim / SS; r shapencolour / Alamy; 37 t Paul R. Sterry / Nature Photographers Ltd / Alamy; b Heritage Image Partership Ltd / Alamy; 38 Hulton Deutsch / Getty; 39 t Harry Todd / Getty; i blickwinkel / Bala / Alamy; 40 Michael Hutchinson / NPL; 43 Jude Wood; 44, 45 (all) James Common; 46, 47 Elizabeth Richmond, Founder of Rebel Botanists; 48–49 FLPA / Alamy; 50 FLPA / Alamy; 52 Altaf Shah / SS; 53 Rebecca Wheeler; 55 amomentintime / Alamy; 56 b Jim Horsfall; 58 t Sue Martin / SS; b Chris Preston; 60 t Henry Miller; b Helena Crouch; 61 t Fred Rumsey; c John Edgington; b Fred Rumsey; 62 Daniel Hepenstrick; 63 Holger Kirk / SS; 64 Clare Gainey / Alamy; 65 b Peter Turner Photography / SS; 68 P.Cartwright / SS; 69 Uellue / SS; 70 Chiara Salvadori / Getty; 72 Gerald Mills; 73 Reproduced with kind permission of Inter-Research. Redrawn by Julian Baker; 74 fotoVoyager / Getty; 75 Greater London Authority and River Thames data © Crown Copyright / database right 2011. An Ordnance Survey / EDINA supplied service. Image courtesy of Tomas Holderness; 76 imageBROKER / Daniel Kuehne / Alamy; 77 Reproduced with kind permission of Inter-Research; 78 l Helen McCarthy; 79 t traction / SS; b Manfred Ruckszio / Alamy; 80 gerard ferry / Alamy; 81 William Barton / SS; 84 Rebecca Cole / Alamy; 86 blickwinkel / H. Bellmann / F. Hecker / Alamy; 87 Michał Długosz / CC BY-SA 4.0; 88 Anatoliy Berislavskiy / SS; 89 PA Images / Alamy; 90, 91 t Claire Halpin; b Sharon Pilkington; 92 Rudmer Zwerver / Alamy; 93 Andrew Michael / Alamy; 95 Justin Kase z12z / Alamy; 97 Hazel Plater / SS; 99 Isabel Hardman; 100 t Jonathan Need / Alamy; 102 Dave Ellison / Alamy; 104 Ryzhkov Serhii / SS; 105 Bob Gibbons / Alamy; 107 t simona pavan / SS; b V. Tarasenko / SS; 112 Richard Bradford / SS; 114 Orest Lyzhechka / SS; 117 blickwinkel / F. Hecker / Alamy; 120–121 PCJones / Alamy; 122 BRIAN MITCHELL / Getty; 128 R. Knapp / SS; 130 t

Ismael Garcia Bentancor / SS; b Ryco Montefont / SS; 133 (all) Miguel Serrano, Department of Botany, University of Santiago de Compostela; 136 b, 137 l, 138 Chris Preston; 142 DT Holyoak; 144 Sandiwild / SS; 145 t Hans Stuessi / Alamy; b Dmitriev Mikhail / SS; 146 l Tomas Heller; r Solvin Zankl / mauritius images GmbH / Alamy; 147 Hans Stuessi / Alamy; 148 l Val Duncan / Kenebec Images / Alamy; r Irina Boldina / SS; 152 l Bob Gibbons / Alamy; r imageBROKER / Marko Koenig / Alamy; 153 r Chris Preston; 154 tl Michael Hutchinson / NPL; 155 t Bubushonok / SS; b blickwinkel / F. Hecker / Alamy; 156 Bob Gibbons / Alamy; 159 r JBShots / Alamy; 162 The History Collection / Alamy; 163 The History of Advertising Trust Archive / Heritage-Images / Heritage Image Partnership Ltd / Alamy; 164 Andrew Shaw, rarebritishplants.com; 165 t Alex Prendergast; b Andrew Shaw, rarebritishplants.com; 167 Nahhana / SS; 169 (all) Chris Preston; 172 Eddie J. Rodriguez / SS; 173 Rio Hermantara / SS; 174 t Hervé Lenain / Alamy; b iPlantsman / SS; 176 Mark Waugh / Alamy; 179 tr Ron Ellis / SS; 183 olko1975 / SS; 184 l Stescha / SS; 185 t Peter Turner Photography / SS; 186 t Henrik Larsson / SS; 188 t Claire Halpin; b Robert Yaxley; 189 t Sam Bosanquet; ct Mike Ball; cb DT Holyoak; b Claire Halpin; 190 Henri Koskinen / SS; 191 b Forest & Kim Starr / CC BY 3.0; 193 Omelchuk Yevhenii / SS; 194 Mick Rock / Cephas Picture Library Ltd / Alamy; 195 Chris Jeffree; 196 r Frank Fox, mikro-foto.de / CC BY-SA 3.0; 197 t Ole Schoener / SS; bl Chris Preston; 200 Martin Fowler / SS; 206 Beekeepx / SS; 209 t Zoonar / Harald Biebel / Alamy; b blickwinkel / fotototo / Alamy; 212 l Beverley Glover; 213 Peter Turner Photography / SS; 215 t Ivanita / Alamy; 219 t Stephen F Granville / SS; 223 Taxomony / SS; 224 Construction Photography / Avalon / Getty; 227 derek oldfield / SS; 228 t David Cheskin / PA Images / Alamy; b derek oldfield / SS; 229 Peter Lopeman / Alamy; 233 KerrysWorld / SS; 237 Steven Falk; 238 Sophie Boxall; 239 t Greg Smith (Friends of Burgess Park); 240 Harry Todd / Stringer / Getty; 241 t FLPA / Alamy; b Frank Fischbach / SS; 242 l Przemyslaw Muszynski / SS; r Bob Gibbons / Alamy; 243 b Cyrustr / SS; 244 Mike Kemp / Getty; 245 MGn42 / SS; 246 l Alex Manders / SS; r Emilio100 / SS; 247 t ShorelineGalesPhotography / SS; c Manfred Ruckszio / SS; b Yegor Larin / SS; 249 Lubos Chlubny / SS; 255 t Wut_Moppie / SS; b Ashleigh Whiffin; 256 l Franco Barbadoro; r Hulton Archive / Getty; 257 l Greg Walter; 258 l Orest lyzhechka / SS; r kristof lauwers / SS; 259 aga7ta / SS; 260 t George Pollock / Alamy; b Alan Keith Beastall / Alamy; 261 Ashleigh Whiffin; 263 Martin Allen; 264 Rebecca Wheeler; 265 Dr James Lowman; 267 Olaf Doering / Alamy; 269 Jeff J Mitchell / Getty; 275 Altaf Shah / SS; 276 Stephen Sykes / Alamy; 277 Julia At One / SS; 281 (all) Richard Bradford; 283 t David Chapman / Alamy; b Gary K Smith / Alamy; 284 t Sean Cole; 285 l Isabel Hardman; r Kevin Walker; 287 mike jarman / Alamy; 290 jax10289 / SS; 292 Andrew Fox / Alamy; 294 l Peter Byrne / PA Images / Alamy; r Geoff Drake, drakephotography.co.uk; 295 Joe Giddens / PA Images / Alamy; 297 t Peter Dench / Getty; b John Gough / Alamy; 301 The Natural History Museum / Alamy; 302 The Natural History Museum / Alamy; 304 Imagery ©2025 Airbus, Maxar Technologies, Map data ©2025; 305 Paul White - North West England / Alamy; 306 John Prior Images / Alamy; 307 t Paul Wood / Alamy; b Colin Underhill / Alamy; 309 t ChWeiss / SS; 310 (all) Deborah Vernon / Alamy; 311 l Tim Gainey / Alamy; 314 STUDIO75 / Alamy; 317 BrettPetrillo / iStock; 320 Sharon Pilkington; 321 t Des Callaghan / CC BY-SA 4.0; b Claire Halpin; 322 t Claire Halpin; c Jonathan Sleath; b Sharon Pilkington; 323 A. Kiro / SS; 324 M.D. Guiry, AlgaeBase; 325 Justin Kase z03z / Alamy; 326 t Frosts Landscapes; 327 Paul Wood / Alamy; 329 Roy Perring / Alamy; 330 Matthew Taylor / Alamy; 331 blickwinkel / G. Kunz / Alamy; 333 Monica Wells / Alamy; 334–335 Simon Dack News / Alamy; 336 Steve Taylor ARPS / Alamy; 339 Helena Crouch; 340 Michael Heath / Alamy; 341 graham bell / Alamy; 346 Jill Whitelock; 347 Lulah Ellender; 348 Mona Caron.

Acknowledgements

I am deeply indebted to many people for helping me write this book. Chris Preston, who I'm fortunate to count as a good friend, has guided me throughout, providing me with his considerable wit and wisdom as well as several deeply enjoyable field days in the very fine city of Cambridge. He also read and commented on early copies of the manuscript (rightly capping the number of times I used the word 'exciting'), provided me with his street survey data and, being one of the best bryologists in Britain, was my main 'moss man' throughout. Entertaining conversations with Mark Spencer on the botany of London also proved invaluable and informative, and I will never forget our exciting whirlwind tour of the English capital in blisteringly hot weather, where I encountered many rare urban plants for the first time. Another dear friend, Arthur Chater, kindly provided the data of his street surveys from his hometown of Aberystwyth, and guided me in the early outline of the book.

Others BSBI county recorders have very generously provided me with valuable data or information about their local urban flora, including James Common (Newcastle upon Tyne) and Jonathan Shanklin (Cambridge), and especially Mark Woods (Nottinghamshire) for a rare copy of *The Plants of Nottingham* by Peter Shepherd. I'm also grateful to both Fred Rumsey and Helena Crouch for sharing their experience and knowledge of urban ferns, and Mick Crawley for his help with urban street trees.

This book would not have existed had Katy Roper (Senior Commissioning Editor at Bloomsbury Wildlife) not approached me to write it. Thank you, it's changed my life. Huge thanks also to my wonderful editor at Bloomsbury, Kate Dickinson, and my copyeditor, David Hawkins, who both considerably improved the text by kicking it around the neighbourhood until it made sense. I'm also deeply indebted to my designer, Susan McIntyre, who turned my dull manuscript into something beautiful.

I'd like to extend a personal thank you to everyone that has generously provided their own photographs, especially those that spent hours searching thousands of files to find the pictures I was after. Urban botany isn't always photogenic (and believe me there's a dearth of photos of urban street 'weeds'), but many talented souls have helped make the pages of the book shine.

Finally, special thanks are due to Carry Akroyd for the stunning artwork that graces the cover of this book. Far removed from the beautiful plants, birds and animals of meadows, woodlands and heathlands she normally depicts for this series, I know the urban theme presented her with a considerable challenge. But by recycling fragments of her old artworks, she has created a wonderful collage based on a scene in Kelvingrove, Glasgow, and it's just perfect.

Index

Page numbers in **bold** refer to illustrations.
Page numbers in *italics* refer to tables.

Aberdeen 100, 316
Aberystwyth 42, 149–150, *151*, 157, 222–223
air pollution 70, 72, 84–94, 106
   oxides of nitrogen 85–86, **86**, 142–143, 192–193, 324
   ozone 87–88, **87**
   particulate matter (PM) 86, 93–94, **93**, 98
   pavement plants and 142–143
   sulphur dioxide 88–93, **88**, **89**, **90**, **91**, **92**, 193, 195
   volatile organic compounds (VOCs) 86–87
   wall plants and 192–193, 195
Alder 64, 221, 300, 306
   Grey 312, **312**
   Italian 44, 312
algae 186, 193, 196–197, **196**, 324, **324**
Alkanet, Green 57, 262, 343, **343**
allochory 144
Allseed 248
   Four-leaved 136, **136**
Aloe, Lace 339, **339**
amenity planting 64–67, **65**, **66**, 106
   wildflower meadows 291–296, **292**, **294**, **295**, **297**
anemochory *see* wind dispersal
annuality 112
ant dispersal 146–147, **147**, 192, **192**, 212, 214
anthropedogenesis 96
anthropochory 62–63, 145, **145**, 238–239, **238**, **239**, 328
Aphid, Lime 308–309
Apple 76, 242–243, 268, 306
   Crab 31, 268
Apple-of-Peru 64, **64**
Arabis, Garden 68
archaeophytes 31–33
   defined 31
   extinctions 340

   numbers and proportions of 118, *118*
Ash 20, 141, 167, 199, 217, 221, 268, 269, 299, 300, 306, 308
Ash Dieback 331
Aspen 87, 269
Aster, Mexican 243, 292
Aubretia 57, **58**
autochory 144
Avens, Wood 52, 144, 145, **145**, 153, 220, 221
Avocado 57, 78–79, **78**
awns 144–145, 146, **146**

Bacopa 108, **108**
ballochory 144, 145–146, **146**, 190–191, **190**, 268
Banana
   Darjeeling 78
   Japanese 78, **78**
Barberry, Thunberg's 64, **65**, 267
Barley, Wall 33, 144–145, **145**, 153, **154**, 163, 201, 242, 252, 255, 327, **328**, 347
barochory 190, 212, 214
bats 296
Bean, Broad 55, 150
Beard-grass, Annual 62, 137, **137**
Beard-moss
   Cylindric 90, 128
   Lesser Bird's-claw 186, **186**, 253
Bedstraw, Lady's 27, 242, 275
Bee
   Ashy Mining 287
   Common Carder 287
   Honey 309
   Ivy 181
   Large Yellow-face 236, **237**
   Tawny Mining 287
Beech 76, 87, 217, 306
bees 181, 212, 214, 236, **237**, 251, 283, 287, 291, 309

Beetle
   Elm Bark 330
   Tumbling Flower 236
Belfast 42, *118*, 303
Bellflower
   Adria **6**, 205, *208*, **209**
   Clustered 295
   Trailing 57, 175, *208*, **209**
Bent
   Black 277
   Common 264, 276
   Creeping 236, 245, 248, 264, 276
   Water 137, **137**, 157, 166, 338
Berlin 62–63, 238, 248
Berwick-upon-Tweed *203*, 204
Bindweed, Hedge 236, 249
biological volatile organic compounds (BVOCs) 86–87
bioreceptivity 95, 178, 180
biotic homogenisation 113–114
Birch **8**, 88, **199**, 217, 227, **244**, 267, 269, 300, 306, **308**, 343
   Chinese Red 310, **310**
   Downy 266, 308
   Erman's 310, **310**
   Himalayan 310
   Silver 167, 266, 308, **310**
bird dispersal 191–192, 218–219, 267
bird food 63–64, **63**, **64**
Bird's-foot-trefoil, Common 88, 264, 274, 282, 288, 289, **289**
Birmingham
   Big City Plan 39, **244**
   street trees 306–307, 313, 316
   urban botany 42
   urban fallow 244, **244**, 245
   urban flora 106, 108, 112, 113, *118*
   urban heat island (UHI) 75
   see also West Midlands urban fallow surveys

Index

Bitter-cress
  Hairy 53, 146, *151*, 153, 154, 156, 222
  New Zealand 62
Bittersweet 236, 262
Black-bindweed 31
Blackberry, Giant 268
bleeding canker 331
Blitz see bomb sites
Blois, France 129–130, **130**, 156
Bluebells, Spanish and Hybrid 57, 118, **119**, 300
bomb sites 38, **39**, 240–244, **240, 241, 242, 243**
Bonfire-moss 90, **91**, 253
botanic gardens 68–69, **69**
Botanical Society of Britain and Ireland (BSBI) 106–108, 124, 350
Botanical Society of Scotland (BSS) 42, 114, 350
Bougainvillea 78
Bracken 35, 242
Brake
  Jungle 60
  Spider 60
  Tender 60, **60**
Bramble 191–192, 207, 217, **226**, 267–268, 300
  Parsley-leaved 268
Bremen, Germany 248
Brighton *118*, 324
Bristle-moss
  Anomalous 91, 188, **188**
  Smooth 91
  White-tipped 85, 91, **320**, 321
  Wood 321
Bristol 38, 99, 322–323, 332
British Bryological Society (BBS) 351
British Pteridological Society (BPS) 350
Brome
  Barren 153, 156, 166, 255, **261**
  Californian 69
  Compact 163
Broom 268
  Mount Etna 315, **315**, **349**
Brown, Meadow 287
brownfield sites 225, 231–232, 235
Brussels 236–237, 238, 252
bryophytes
  air pollution and 85, 90–91, **90, 91**, 193
  on pavements 128, **142**, 143, **155**, 166
  on street trees 320–323, **320, 321, 322**, 324, **324**

in urban fallow 253, 265–266, **266**
on walls 101, **180**, 186, **186**, 188–189, **188, 189**, 190, 193, **197**, 198
Bryum, Bicoloured 166, 253
BSBI News 'Adventives and Aliens' 106–108, 124
Buckwheat 63, **63**
Buddleja 19, **19**, 20, 57, 63, 98, 112, **112, 132**, 141, 156, 167, 191, 199, 217, 221, **226**, 227, **227**, 236, **244**, 248, 249, 250–251, **250, 251**, 252, 254, 266, 267, **315**, 343
Bumblebee
  Buff-tailed 287, 309
  Early 291
  Garden 291
bumblebees 212, 287, 291, 309
Burnet-saxifrage, Greater 205
Burnet, Six-spot 287
Busy Lizzie 63, 150
Buttercup
  Creeping 35, **270**, 271, 274, 278, 282, 288, 289
  Meadow 86, 113, 290
butterflies 251, 287

Cabbage-palm 313, **313**
Cabbage, Wild 145
Caernarfon *203*, 204
Calleva (Silchester) 34–35, **34**
Cambridge
  air pollution 193
  King's College wildflower meadow 295–296, **295, 297**
  pavement plants 149, 150, *151*, 157, 159
  phenology study 152–153, **152, 153**
  street-tree bryophytes 323
  street trees 303, 316, 331
  urban botany 41, 42
  urban fallow 229–230, **230**
  urban flora 117, *118*
  urban grasslands 278, **279**
  wall plants 202, *203*, 216, 220, 222
  weed control 169, **169**, 345
Cambridge Natural History Society 41
Canker Stain of Plane 332
Cape-jewels **125**
capping 177

Cardiff 323, **341**
Carrot, Wild 253
Catchfly
  Nottingham 99, **100**
  Sticky 99, **99**
Cat's-ear **122**, 156, 157, 262, 289, **346**
Celandine, Greater 35, 118, 147, **147**, 153, 206, **206**
chamaephytes 139
Chamomile, Austrian 160, 295, **334–335**
chasmophytes 175
Chepstow *203*, 204
Cherry 64, 242–243, 306
  Bird 267
  Dwarf 76
  Kanzan 310
  Wild 76, 305
Chester *203*
Chestnut, Sweet 300
Chichester *203*, 204
Chickweed, Common 31, 35, 117, 141, 142, *151*, 152, 154, 193, 255, 327
Chicory **240**, 242
China Doll 78
Chinese-lantern 243
Chives 172
Cleavers 142, 144, 145, 193, 221
climate change 74, 183, 263, 339, 345
  flooding and 82, 129
  orchids and 282, 283, 284
  street trees and 319, 332–333
Clover
  Hare's-foot 247, **247**
  Red 89, 242, 282, **293**
  White 86, 139, 244, 248, 264, 271, 274, **274**, 282, 288, 289, **289**, 290
Cock's-foot 88, 221, 248, 261, 264, 275
Cockspur 85, **86**, 142, 163
Colt's-foot 240, **243**, 244
conservation 339–344
Conwy 200, *203*, 204
coping 177
Corncockle 32, 35, 295
Cornsalad
  Common 135, **135**
  Keeled-fruited 157
Corydalis, Yellow 57, 153, 180, 192, **192**, 199, *208*, 243
Cotoneaster 44, **45**, 57, **65**, 139, 192, 219, 267

377

Wall 217, **219**, 222
Couch, Common 252, 264, 275
Coventry 38, 42
Cowslip 87, 282, 295
Crane's-bill
    Cut-leaved 146, **146**
    Dove's-foot 153
    Shining 185
Crassulacean Acid Metabolism (CAM) photosynthesis 184
Cress
    Thale 135, 139, 166, 185, 198
    Tower 216
Crocus 75
Crouch Oak, Sussex 300, **301**
cryptophytes 139
Cudweed, Jersey 62, 136–137, **136**
Culmstock Yew, Devon 218, **219**
Curry-plant 44, **45**
Cypress, Lawson's 217, 312–313

Daisy 86, 139, 153, 157, **270**, 271, 274, 282, 288, 289–290
    Oxeye 27, 35, 242, 262, 282, 290, **297**
Dandelion **40**, 83–84, **84**, 86, 112, **128**, 139, 147–148, *151*, 152, 155, 156, 205, *205*, 222, 244, 248, 249, 264, 271, 274, 282, 288, 289, 327
Dead-nettle, Red 33, 118, 147, 152, **152**
Delaware, Ohio 134
Denbigh *203*
Derby 42, *118*
derelict land see urban fallow
diseases, street trees 330–332
dispersal
    on animals 144–145, **145**
    by ants 146–147, **147**, 192, **192**, 212, 214
    by birds 191–192, 218–219, 267
    explosive 144, 145–146, **146**, 190–191, **190**, 268
    fragmentation and 107
    by gravity 190, 212, 214
    in horse fodder and dung 241–242, **241**, **242**
    by humans 62–63, 145, **145**, 238–239, **238**, **239**, 328
    pavement plants 143–149, **144**, **145**, **146**, **147**, **148**
    in soils 98
    street trees 308, 311, 318
    tree-pit flora 327–328

urban fallow plants 235, 238–239, **238**, **239**, 241–242, **241**, **242**, 266, 267, 268
on vehicles 62–63, 145, 238–239, **238**, 328
wall plants 190–192, **190**, **191**, **192**, 212, 214, 218–219, 221
in water 148, 221
by wind 83–84, **84**, 147–148, **148**, 190–191, **190**, **191**, 214, 235, 238, **239**, 241, 266, 308, 311, 318
dispersal kernel 107, 143–144
Dock
    Broad-leaved 85, 221, 249, 252, 264
    Fiddle 272, **273**
dog-pee zone 323–324, **323**, **324**
Dog-violet, Common 52, **53**, 147
Dog's-tail, Crested 264, 277
drainage, pavements 127, 128–129, **128**, **129**, 134
Dublin 42, 117, *118*
Dundee 185–186
Durham 203–204, *203*, 216, 221–222
Dutch Elm Disease 330

Edinburgh 24
    botanic garden 68, 69
    geology 99, **99**
    street trees 303, **309**, 313, 316, 331
    urban grasslands 274, **274**
elaiosomes 146–147, **147**, 192, 214
Elder 157, 192, *205*, 217, 219, 222, 267
Elm 300, 301, 306, 330, **330**
encapsulated countryside 51–52, **52**
endolithic lithophytes 175
endozoochory 191–192, 218–219
epilithic lithophytes 175
epizoochory 144–145, **145**
Eryngo, Field 99
Evening-primrose 243, **243**, **255**
    Common 254
    Large-flowered 112
Everlasting-pea, Broad-leaved 246–247, **247**, 248
Every Flower Counts survey 281–282, 289
Exeter 42, *118*
explosive dispersal 144, 145–146, **146**, 190–191, **190**, 268
extremophytes 345

fallow land see urban fallow
False-acacia **8**, 63, 246, **246**, 249, 268, 306, 316, 327
Fat-hen 35, 153, 237
Feather-moss
    Clustered **266**, 321, **322**
    Common 90, 186, 266, **266**
    Creeping 186, **186**, 190, 265, 322
    Silky Wall 90, 101, 189, **189**, **197**
    Tufted 128
    Velvet 322
Fennel 238, **238**
Fern
    Adder's-tongue 282
    Button 61
    Maidenhair 187
    Male 205, *205*
    Rasp 61, **61**
    Ribbon 60, **60**
    Sickle 61, **61**
Fern-grass 135, 185
    Sea 157
ferns 52
    air pollution and **92**, 93, 193
    dispersal 190–191, **190**
    houseplants 59–61, **60**, **61**
    urban fallow 228
    walls **92**, 93, 101, **101**, 175, 176, **186**, 187, 192, 193, 198, 200, **200**, **201**, 205, *205*, 207, 208–209, *208*, 210–211, **210**, **211**, 223
Fescue
    Chewing's 276
    Hard 276
    Meadow 237
    Rat's-tail 255
    Red 207, 264, 276
    Tall 277
Feverfew 222, 262
Field-speedwell
    Common 152, 255
    Green 152
Fig 58, **59**, 62
Figwort
    Common 262
    Water 205
Fleabane
    Argentine 158–159, **159**, 163
    Bilbao 67–68, 82, **124**, 156, 158, **159**, 207, 254
    Canadian 20, 53, 62, 82, 83, 112, 113, 153, 156, 158, **158**, 159, 163, 207, 240, 248, 252, 254, 327, 338

Index

Guernsey 156, 157, 158, 159, 163, 221, 254
Mexican 57, 118, **132**, 153, 175, 191, **191**, 192, *208*, 209, 212–213, **213**
flooding 82, 95, 98, 129
footings 177
Forsythia 76, **76**
Fox-and-Cubs 286, **286**
Foxglove 254
  Fairy 173, **173**, 192, *208*
Foxglove-tree 313–315, **314**
Foxtail, Meadow 242, 276
fragmentation 105–106, 107, **107**
Fuchsia 217, 268
Fumitory, Common 138, 147, 255
fungal diseases 330, 331, 332

garbic materials 96–97
garden escapes 19, 54–55, 57–59, **58**, **59**, 106–108, 123–124, 173, 243
Garlic, Three-cornered 57, 147, 343
geology 98–101, **99**, **100**, **101**
Ginkgo 306, 310, **311**
Glasgow 42, *118*, 316, 340, 342
Goat's-rue 113–114, 243, 246, **246**
Goldenrod, Canadian 57, 63, 112, 113, **114**, 248, 249, 262
Gorse 35, 268
gradient of diversity 114–116, **115**
Grantham Oak, Lincolnshire 300
grassland habitats **270**, 271–296, **273**, **274**, **275**
  grasses 275–277, **276**, **277**
  grazing 277–278, **279**
  long-grass habitats 287, **289**, 290–291
  mowing and cutting 277–279, **279**
  nectar and pollen production 289–290
  #NoMowMay 280–286, **281**, **283**
  orchids 282–285, **283**, **284**, **285**
  short-grass habitats 287–289, **289**
  wildflower meadows 291–296, **292**, **293**, **294**, **295**, **297**
green algae 193, 196–197, **196**, 324, **324**
green spaces see urban green spaces
Grimmia
  Grey-cushioned 11, 188, **188**, 321
  Sessile 91

Thickpoint 189, **189**, 193
Groundsel 31, 53, 113, 142, *151*, 152, 154, 156, 164, 205, *205*, 221, 222, 244, 253, 274, 327
  Welsh 164–165, **165**
Gum, Sweet 306, 307, **307**

habitat fragmentation 105–106, 107, **107**
habitat transformation 104–105
Hadrian's Wall 171–173, **172**
Haematococcus pluvialis **196**, 197
Hairstreak, White-letter 330
Hamburg 76, **76**, 77, **77**, 82
Harebell 85, 87, 205, 248, 272
Hart's-tongue **48–49**, 93, 176, 187, 210, 211, 223
Hawk's-beard
  Beaked 156, 248
  Marsh 245
  Smooth 264, **345**
Hawksbeard, Holy 107, **107**
Hawthorn 31, 192, 217, 267, 306, **307**
Hazel 31, 267
heat
  pavements 133–134, **133**, **134**
  see also urban heat island (UHI)
Heath-grass 35, 272
heavy metals 86, 93, 94, 98
Helleborine
  Broad-leaved 285, **285**
  Dune 44, 285, **285**
hemeroby 112
hemicryptophytes 139
Hemlock 85, 262
Hemp-agrimony 187, 220, 262
Henbane 32
Herb-Robert **40**, 124, 146, 152–153, 157, 192, **326**
herbicides 18, 21, 125, 129–130, 161–169, **163**, **166**
  herbicide resistance 151, 156, 159, 163, 166, **167**
  phenology and 153
  reduced use of 46, 129–130, 168–169, **169**, 345–348
  succession and 166–167, 200
  urban grasslands 279, 294
Hogweed 187, 261
  Giant **261**, 264–265, **264**
Holly 267
  Chestnut-leaf **327**
Holly-fern
  Fortune's 60
  House 60

Hollyhock 243
Honeysuckle, Wilson's 64
Hop 243
Horehound
  Black 35
  White 33, **36**
Hornbeam 305
Horse-chestnut 305, 306, 327, 331
  Indian 316
Horseradish 33, 262
horses 241–242, **241**, **242**
Hound's-tongue 33, **36**
House-leek 192, **193**
houseplants 59–61, **60**, **61**
Hoverfly, Marmalade 287
Hull 42, *118*, **233**
Hull Natural History Society 42
human dispersal 62–63, 145, **145**, 238–239, **238**, **239**, 328
Huntingdon Elm, Sheffield 330, **330**
hydrochory 148, 221

Indian Bean Tree 316–317, **317**
invertebrates
  Buddleja and 251
  limes and 308–309
  tree pests 316, 330–331, **331**
  urban fallow 236, **237**
  urban grasslands 283, 287, 291
  walls 181, 212, 214
  wildflower meadows 293, 296
Iona Abbey **175**, 176
Iris, Bearded 262, **263**
Iron Age 31–32, 34–35, **34**, 155
Ivy **174**, 181, **181**, 182, **182**, *205*, 217, 221, 236, **336**

Kew Gardens **60**, 68–69, **69**, 164, 250, 295
King's College, Cambridge 295–296, **295**, **297**
Knapweed, Common 27, 35, 113, 262, 290
Knotgrass 35, 139, *151*, 153, 236, 274, 327
Knotweed 84
  Japanese 249, 343

Laburnum 268, 315–316
Lady's-mantle, Garden 57, 262
Lady's-tresses, Autumn 282, **283**
lawns see grassland habitats
Leaf Miner, Horse-chestnut 316, 331, **331**
Leeds 42, *118*, 316

Leek, Round-headed 99
Leicester *118*
Leptinella 286
Lettuce
    Great 240
    Prickly 33, 112, 163, 248, 327
    Wall 153, 175, **346**
Leuven, Belgium 107
Lichen
    Inflated Beard 92
    Sea-storm 92
    Shield **88**, 89
lichens
    air pollution and **88**, 89, 92
    on street trees 324
    on walls 197–198, **197**
Lime 301, 305, 306, 308–309, **309**
    Large-leaved 308
    Small-leaved 308, 309
lithophytes 175
Liverpool **294**, 295, **305**, 316
Liverwort, Common 186
liverworts see bryophytes
Lobelia
    Garden **43**, 57, 153, 157, 206, **344**
    Lawn 286
Local Nature Reserves (LNRs) 25, 341, 342
Locust, Honey 307
London
    air pollution 88, **89**, 92
    bomb sites 38, **39**, 240–244, **240**, **241**, **242**, **243**
    canal boats 110–111, **110**
    conservation **340**, 342
    Great Fire 36
    plant extinctions 340
    rainfall 80–81
    rural–urban gradient 29, **29**
    street-tree bryophytes 320–323, **320**, **321**, **322**, 324
    street trees **300**, **302**, 303, **304**, 305–306, **307**, 313–315, 316, 332
    urban botany 41, 42
    urban fallow 229, **231**
    urban flora 117, *118*
    urban heat island (UHI) 71–72, **72**, 74, **75**, 78–79, **78**, **79**
    wall plants *203*, 220–221, **220**
    weed control 160–161, 168–169
London Natural History Society 41
London-rocket 344
    False 148
Loosestrife, Dotted 54, 262

Loquat 79, **79**
Lucerne 54, 242, 247, **247**
Lupin, Russell 112, 245, 262

Madison, Wisconsin 77
Maidenhair, Delta 61, **61**
Maidenhair-tree 306, 310, **311**
Mallow, Common **120–121**, 153, **153**, **230**, 237, **261**, 262, **346**, **347**
Manchester 74–75, 303, 316
Maple 64, 306
    Norway 305
Marigold
    Corn 295, 344
    French 245
    Pot 54, 243, 292
Marsh-orchid
    Northern 44, **45**
    Southern 282
Massaria disease 332
Mat-grass 272
Mayweed
    Scented 327
    Scentless 139, 255, 274
Meadow-grass
    Annual 53, 116–117, **117**, **124**, 139, 143, 145, 151, *151*, 152, 154, **154**, 156, 163, 166, 185, 204, *205*, 206, 221, 222, 236, 242, 253, 274, 276, 288, 327
    Early 62, 136, **136**, 140, 151, 157
    Flattened *208*
    Rough 145, 276
    Smooth 276
Meadowsweet 27, 35, 220
Medick
    Black 248, 264, 288, **328**
    Toothed 99
Melilot
    Ribbed 20, 112, 258–259, **258**
    White 112, 113, 258–259, **258**
Mercury, Annual 33, 236
Michaelmas-daisies 112, 248, 262
Mignonette, Wild 236
Millet, Common 55, 63
Mind-your-own-business 82, 166, **167**, 208
Mint, Water 35, 221
moisture
    pavements 134–138
    walls 183–187, **183**, **184**, **185**, **186**, 190
Montpellier, France 107

Moonwort 228
mortar 100–101, **101**, 177, 178, 179–180, **179**
mosses see bryophytes
Moth, Mullein 236
moths 236, 251, 287, 291, 293, 316, 331, **331**
Mouse-ear
    Common 274
    Sticky 156, 157, 185
Mouse-ear-hawkweed 255
    Spreading 69
Mugwort 20, **224**, 236, 242, 244, 245, 248, 249, **254**, 259, 262
Mullein 236
    Great **170**
    Purple 106–108
Mustard
    Black 145
    Hedge 148, 255, **326**
    Hoary **254**
mycorrhizal fungi 94, 159
myrmecochory 146–147, **147**, 192, **192**, 212, 214

Nasturtium 54, **55**
National Nature Reserves (NNRs) 25, 341
National Vegetation Classification (NVC) 24, 252
natural history societies 41–42
Navelwort 36, 184, **185**, *208*, 223
nectar production 289–290
Needle-grass
    American 338
    Argentine 66, 150, 263
negative phototropism 182, 214, **215**
nematodes 149
Neolithic 31, 55, 155
neophytes
    defined 31
    numbers and proportions of 54, 117–118, *118*
    random introductions 113–114
    xenicity 112
Nettle
    Common 85, 112, 142, 145, 220, 221, 237, 248, 249, 260, 261, 262, 278, 300
    Mediterranean 62, **62**, 134, **134**
    Small 35, 152, 255
Newcastle upon Tyne 41, 44–45, **44**, **45**, 82, 90, *118*, 316
Nightshade, Black 157
Nipplewort 153, 221

Index

nitrogen pollution 85–86, **86**, 142–143, 192–193, 324
#NoMowMay 280–286, **281**, **283**
Norwich 203, 316
Nottingham 42, 99, **100**, *118*
Nottinghamshire Wildlife Trust City Local Group 42

Oak 87, 269, 300
    Pedunculate 87, **301**
Oat-grass
    False **141**, 261, **261**, 262, 264, 275
    Yellow 242, 264, 277
Onion, Wild 245, **245**
Orchid
    Bee **44**, 283, **283**
    Early-purple 282
    Fly 284
    Lady 284
    Lizard 284–285, **284**
    Man 284
    Pyramidal **26**, 27, 282
Oregon-grape 57, 64, **65**, 217
origins of urban plants 51–69
    alien species 19, 52–69
        accidental hitchhikers 62–63, **62**
        amenity planting 64–67, **65**, **66**, 106
        bird food 63–64, **63**, **64**
        botanic gardens 68–69, **69**
        gardens 19, 54–55, 57–59, **58**, **59**, 106–108, 123–124, 173, 243
        houseplants 59–61, **60**, **61**
        ports 67–68, **68**
    native species 51–52, **53**, 56, **56**
        encapsulated countryside 51–52, **52**
Oxtongue
    Bristly **347**
    Hawkweed 249
ozone 87–88, **87**

Palm, Chusan 62, 339
Pampas-grass 66–67, **66**
Pansy, Mountain 275
Paris 234, 235, 238, 248–249, 327–328, 347–348
Parsnip, Wild 86
particulate matter (PM) 86, 93–94, **93**, 98
Passionflower, Blue 79, **79**, 160
pavements **122**, 123–169, **124**, **125**
    changes in street flora 157–160

dispersal 143–149, **144**, **145**, **146**, **147**, **148**
drainage 127, 128–129, **128**, **129**, 134
heat 133–134, **133**, **134**
materials and construction 127–131, **127**, **130**, **131**
micro-niches 131–132, **132**
moisture 134–138
nitrogen pollution 142–143
pavement refugia 140–142, **141**, 326–328, **326**, **327**, **328**
phenology 152–153, **152**, **153**
succession 166–168
top 12 pavement plants 149–156, *151*, **154**, **155**, **156**
trampling 138–140, **140**
weed control 125, 129–130, 160–169, **161**, **162**, **163**, **166**, **169**, 345–348
width 125–126
Pear, Callery 306
Pearlwort
    Procumbent 139, 143, *151*, 155, **155**, 156, 166, 198, 207, 221, 242
    Sea 157
Pellitory-of-the-wall 152, **166**, 184, 192, 199, **201**, *208*, 221, 223
Pesticide Action Network 46, 168
Petunia 57, 160
Pheasant's-tail 337–338, **338**
phenology 152–153, **152**, **153**
Phoenix, Arizona 109
phototropism
    negative 182, 214, **215**
    positive 214
physical urban environment
    geology 98–101, **99**, **100**, **101**
    rainfall 80–82, **80**, **81**
    soils 96–98, **97**, 106
    surfaces 94–95, **95**, 106
    wind turbulence 82–84, **84**, 106
    see also air pollution; urban heat island (UHI)
Pimpernel, Scarlet 135, 242
Pincushion
    Common 91, **91**
    Frizzled 91
Pineappleweed 68–69, **127**, 138, 140, **140**, 145
Pink
    Clove 216
    Maiden 99
Plait-moss, Cypress-leaved 90, 321, **321**

Plane 327
    London 76, **298**, 301, **302**, 303, 305, 306, **306**, 310–311, 323, 332
Plant Atlas 2020 **19**, 103–104, 201, 338
Plantain
    Greater 139, 145, *151*, 153, 155, **155**, 156, 157, 236–237, 252, 264, 288, 327
    Ribwort 112, 117, 163, 248, 249, 264, 288
Plantlife 280–282, 286, 289
Plymouth 42, 99, 115–116, *118*, 303, 329, **329**
pollen production 289–290
pollinator seed mixes 291–293, 294–295
pollinators
    Buddleja and 251
    limes and 309
    urban fallow 236, **237**
    urban grasslands 283, 287, 291
    walls 181, 212, 214
    wildflower meadows 293
pollution *see* air pollution
Polypody **186**, 190–191, 193, 209, 211
    Common 187, **190**, **210**, 211, 216
    Intermediate 210, 211, 223
    Southern 200, **200**, 211
Poplar, Black 87, 300, **300**
Poppy
    Atlas 57, 124
    Californian 57, 291, **334–335**
    Common 32, 35, 118, 138, 206, 237, 242, 255, 292, 295, **334–335**, 344
    Opium 32, 35, **137**, 138, 142
    Welsh 56, **56**, **132**
ports 67–68, **68**
positive phototropism 214
Pratia, Matted 286, **287**
Pride-of-India 316
protocarnivory 149
Purple-loosestrife 27, 187, 220

Quaking-grass 277, 295

Ragged-Robin 27, 35
Ragweed 44, **45**, 64
Ragwort
    Common **120–121**, 207, 221, **239**, 264, **265**, 290
    Narrow-leaved 44, **45**, 55, 236, 249, **326**, 338

Oxford 14, 20, 38, 53, 83, 112, 142, 157, 164, *205*, 206, 222, 240, 244, 248, 254, 256–257, **257**, 344
York 164, **164**, *165*
rainfall 80–82, **80, 81**
#RebelBotanists 46, **46, 47**
recombinant ecosystems 53
Redshank 90, 253, 324
refugia, pavement 140–142, **141**, 326–328, **326, 327, 328**
Rennes, France 76
rewilding 227
Ribbon-fern, Variegated 60
Rock-cress, Bristol 99
Rocket
  London 36, **37**, 327
  Tall 148
Roman Britain 32–33, 34–35, 171–173, **172**
Romulea, Crocus-leaved 108
Rosenvingiella radicans 324, **324**
Rotherham 291–292
Rowan 64, 217, 267, 306
Royal Botanic Garden Edinburgh 68, 69
ruderality 112
rural–urban gradient 27–29, **28, 29**
Rustyback 101, 192, *208*, 210, 211, **211**
Rye-grass, Perennial 154, 163, 245, 248, 274, **274**, 275, 276
Ryegrass, Perennial 139

Salisbury Cathedral 272, **273**
Sandwort, Thyme-leaved 156, 185, 288
Sanicle 111, 300
Santiago de Compostela, Spain 133–134, **133**
Saxifrage, Rue-leaved 93, 135, 185, 186, **186**, 194–195, **194, 195**, 198, 253
Scabious, Small 44, 88
Scalewort, Dilated 91
Screw-moss
  Great Hairy 189, **189**
  Intermediate 91, 189, **189**, 193, 322, 323
  Lesser 322, 323, 324
  Marble 85, 322–323, **322**
  Small Hairy 322, **322**, 323
  Wall 90, 101, **180**, **186**, 188, **188, 197**, 198
  Water 322
Scurvygrass, Danish 84, 135, 157

Sea-buckthorn **244**, 267, **267**
Sea-spurrey, Lesser 157
sealed soils/surfaces 82, 95, **95**, 106, 115, **115**, 127, 128, 134–135
Selfheal 147, 274, 282, 288, 289, **289**
semi-natural habitats 24, 26–27, 29, 115
  brownfield sites 225, 231–232, 235
  encapsulated countryside 51–52, **52**
  habitat transformation 104–105
  protecting 341–342
  urban grasslands 26, 271–272, 288
  urban green corridors 239
  urban woodlands 26, 299–300, 303
settlements, classification of 22–23, **22, 23**, *23*, **24**
Sheffield
  pavement plants 150, *151*
  street trees 303, 306, 316, 329–330, **330**
  urban botany 42
  urban fallow 244–245
  urban flora 106, 112, 113–114, *118*
  urban grasslands 272, 276, 282
Shepherd's-needle 242
Shepherd's-purse 31, 117, 138, 139, 148–149, **148**, *151*, 152, 154, 155, 237, 255, 274, 327
Shrewsbury 42, *118*
Silver-moss 128, **142**, 143, 166, 253
Sites of Importance for Nature Conservation (SINCs) 341, 342
Sites of Special Scientific Interest (SSSIs) 25, 341
Skullcap **220**
Snapdragon 192, 200, 205, *208*, 209, 212, **212**, 222, **342, 345**
  Cape 124
  Trailing *174*, **174**
Snowdrop 76
social media 39, **43**, 124–125, 292
socio-economic factors 109–111, **110**, 304, **305**
soils 96–98, **97**, 106
  pavements 128
  urban fallow 232, 234, 235, 236–237
  urban grasslands 273, 274–275

Soldier, Gallant 68, **69**
Sorrel, Common 290, **297**
Southampton *203*
Sow-thistle
  Prickly **148**
  Smooth *151*, 156, 163, 193, 205, *205*, 206, 255, **326**, 327
Speedwell
  Germander 288, 289
  Ivy-leaved 147, 192, 201, 216
  Slender 286
  Thyme-leaved 288
  Wall 185, 207, **207**, 222, 288
Spleenwort
  Black 176, 193, 207, *208*, 210, 211, **211**, 223
  Forked 99
  Green 210, **210**
  Maidenhair 52, 93, 101, **101**, **174**, 192, 193, 198, **201**, 207, *208*, 210, 211, 223
  Sea **175**, 176, 210
spoilic materials 96–97
Spotted-orchid, Common 27, 245, 282
Spurge
  Mediterranean 65, **65**
  Petty 118, **132**, 138, 147, *151*, 152, 154, **154**, 155, 255
  Sun 138, 147, 152, **152**, 242
St John's-wort, Marsh **105**
Stonecrop 183–184
  Biting 183, **183**, 192
  Caucasian 183, **184**
  English 183
  Reflexed 183, **184**, *208*
  Rock 183, 192
  Thick-leaved 183, 200, **338**
  White 183, 192, *208*, 223
Stork's-bill, Common 146, **146**
street trees **298**, 299–333, **300, 301**
  biological volatile organic compounds 87
  bryophytes 320–323, **320, 321, 322**, 324, **324**
  climate change and 319, 332–333
  diversity 305–307, **306, 307**
  dog-pee zone 323–324, **323, 324**
  felling 303, 329–330, **329, 330**
  numbers of 303–304, **304**
  pests and diseases 316, 330–332, **331**
  planting 301–302, **302**
  seeding trees 308–319, **308**,

          309, 310, 311, 312, 313,
          314, 315, 317, 319
    socio-economic factors 304, **305**
    tree pits 140, 325–328, **325,
          326, 327, 328**
    winds and 83
  stress tolerance 112
  succession
    pavements 166–168
    urban fallow 227, 234, 235–236,
          252–269
      Buddleja Scrub-woodland
          Stage 266–269, **267,
          269**
      Coarse Grass Stage 264–266,
          264, 265, 266
      Oxford Ragwort Pioneer
          Stage 253–258, **254,
          255**
      Rosebay Willowherb Tall-
          herb Stag 258–263,
          **258, 259, 260, 261,
          263**
    walls 196–201, **196, 197, 199**
  sulphur dioxide 88–93, **88, 89, 90,
          91, 92,** 193, 195
  Sumach, Stag's-horn 245, **249**
  Sundew, Round-leaved 104, **104**
  Sustainable drainage systems (SuDS)
        129, **129**
  Sycamore 20, 141, 167, **205,** 217,
        222, **230,** 268, 269, 300, 306,
        308

  Teasel, Wild 254, **254**
  Tenby *203*
  therophytes 139
  Thistle
    Creeping 20, 85, 112, 147, 240,
          244, 248, 249, 252, 261,
          262, 278
    Plymouth 99
    Spear 141, 142, 147, **239,** 240,
          262
  Thread-moss
    Capillary 90, 166, 321, **321,** 324
    Golden 90
    Pale Glaucous 253
    Wall 189, **189**
  Throatwort 124
  thunderstorms 80–82, **80**
  Thyme-moss, Swan's-neck 90, **90**
  tillering 276, 288
  Timothy 277
  Toadflax
    Common 107, **107**

    Corsican 215
    Italian 215
    Ivy-leaved **12–13, 132,** 153, **174,**
          175, 180, 192, 198, **201,**
          205, 208, 209, 214–215,
          214, 215, 221, 222, **223,**
          243
    Malling 124
    Purple 53, **124,** 153, **153,** 208,
          243, 248, **254,** 345
  Tobacco, Tree 78
  Tomato 55, 57–58, **58,** 243
  Tongue-orchid
    Heart-flowered 284, **284**
    Lesser 17–18, **18,** 284
  Toothwort 228
  Tormentil 35, 85, 111, 275
  trampling 138–140, **140**
  Treasureflower 106
  Tree-of-heaven 79, 141, 167, 240,
          249, **315,** 318–319, **319,** 327,
          343
    tree pits 140, 325–328, **325, 326,
          327, 328**
    trees and shrubs
      on urban fallow land 266–269,
          267, 269, 300
      on walls 199–200, **199,** 217–
          219, **219**
      see also street trees
  Trefoil
    Hop 275, 288
    Lesser 288, 289
  Tulip-tree **87,** 307

  urban
    defining 21–25, **22, 23,** *23,* **24, 25**
    rural–urban gradient 27–29,
          28, 29
  urban adaptors 111–113, **111**
  urban avoiders 111, **111**
  urban botany 41–46, **43, 44, 45,
          46, 47**
  Urban Boundary Layer 73, **73**
  Urban Canopy Layer 73, **73**
  urban canyons 72–74, **74,** 82–83, 84
  urban exploiters **111,** 113
  urban fallow **224,** 225–269, **226,
          228, 229, 233**
    defining 231–233
    dispersal 235, 238–239, **238,
          239,** 241–242, **241, 242,**
          266, 267, 268
    factors influencing plant diversity
          234–239, **239**
    plants species 240–252, **241,**

          242, 243, 244, 245, 249
    redevelopment of **227,** 229–
          231, **230, 231**
    soils 232, 234, 235, 236–237
    succession and communities 227,
          234, 235–236, 252–269
      Buddleja Scrub-woodland
          Stage 266–269, **267,
          269**
      Coarse Grass Stage 264–266,
          264, 265, 266
      Oxford Ragwort Pioneer
          Stage 253–258, **254,
          255**
      Rosebay Willowherb Tall-
          herb Stag 258–263,
          **258, 259, 260, 261,
          263**
  urban flora 15–21, 103–119
    conservation 339–344
    diversity 116–118, *118*
      gradient of 114–116, **115**
    future of urban plants 337–349
    history of urban plants 31–39,
          36, 37, 38, 39
    processes shaping
      anthropogenic modifications
          106
      biotic homogenisation
          113–114
      fragmentation 105–106, 107,
          107
      habitat transformation
          104–105
      human preference 106–108
      plant responses to urban
          stresses 111–113, **111,
          112**
      random introductions
          113–114
      socio-economic factors
          109–111, **110**
    see also grassland habitats;
          origins of urban plants;
          pavements; street trees;
          urban fallow; walls
  Urban Flora of Newcastle project
        41, 44–45
  Urban Flora of Scotland project 114
  urban green corridors 239
  urban green spaces 26, 27, **27,** 29,
        29, 77, 115, 230
    see also grassland habitats; semi-
          natural habitats
  urban habitats
    defining 23–25, **25**

383

mosaic of 26–27, **26, 27**
see *also* grassland habitats;
   pavements; urban fallow;
   walls
urban heat island (UHI) **70**, 71–80, 106
   in British cities 71–72, **72**, 74–75, **75**
   causes of 72–74
   dynamic structure of 73, **73**
   impacts on plants 75–80, **76, 77, 78, 79**
Urban Surface Layer 73, **73**
urbanity 112
urbic materials 96–97, **97**

Valerian, Red 83, 113, 153, **166, 174**, 175, 184, **185**, 191, **191**, 199, 200, *208*, 222, 223, **226**, 243, **345, 346**
vehicles
   air pollution 85–86, 93, 142, 192–193, 324
   bryophytes on **142**
   dispersal by 62–63, 145, 238–239, **238**, 328
Vernal-grass, Sweet 242, 277
Vervain, Argentinian 153, 263
Viper's-bugloss 254, **255**
volatile organic compounds (VOCs) 86–87

Wall-rocket
   Annual 175
   Perennial 243
Wall-rue 52, 93, 192, 207, *208*, 211, **211**, 223
Wallflower 192, 193, 200, *208*
walls **170**, 171–223, **173, 174**
   accidental species 206, 216
   algae 186, 193, 196–197, **196**, 324
   bioreceptivity 178, 180
   bomb sites 243
   bryophytes 101, **180**, 186, **186**, 188–189, **188, 189**, 190, 193, **197**, 198
   changes in walls flora 221–223, **223**
   cleaning and repair 200–201, **200, 201**

companion species 206–207, **207**
construction 177, **177**
dispersal 190–192, **190, 191, 192**, 212, 214, 218–219, 221
ferns **92**, 93, 101, **101**, *175*, 176, **186**, 187, 192, 193, 198, 200, **200, 201**, 205, *205*, 207, 208–209, *208*, 210–211, **210, 211**, 223
Hadrian's Wall 171–173, **172**
interior walls **175**, 176
light and aspect 187–190
materials 100–101, **101**, 177, **177**, 178–180, *179*
numbers of species 201–204, *203*
nutrients and air pollution 192–193, 195
retaining walls 176, **176**, 187
specialist species 207–215, *208*, **209, 210, 211, 212, 213, 214, 215**
succession 196–201, **196, 197, 199**
surfaces 180–182, **180, 181, 182**
top 12 wall plants 204–206, *205*
water supply 183–187, **183, 184, 185, 186**, 190
waterside walls 220–221, **220**
woody plants 199–200, **199**, 217–219, **219**
waste ground see urban fallow
water dispersal 148, 221
water supply
   pavements 134–138
   walls 183–187, **183, 184, 185, 186**, 190
waterside walls 220–221, **220**
Weld 236, **237**, 254, **255**, 261
West Midlands urban fallow surveys 234, 238, 245–248, 252, 259–260, 266, 268
Whitebeam 306
   Bristol 99
   Swedish 267, **311**, 312
Whitlowgrass
   Common 131, 135, 152, 156, 185, **186**

Wall 175
wildflower meadows 291–296, **292, 293, 294, 295, 297**
Wildlife Trusts 351
Willow 267, 269, 300, 343
   Eared 266
   Goat 254, 266, 308
   Rusty 167, 217, 266, 308
Willowherb
   American 83, *151*, 155–156, **156**, 205, *205*, 222
   Broad-leaved 157, *205*
   Great **141**, 153, 187, **227, 230**, 262
   Hoary 157, 237
   Rosebay 20, 38, **39**, 83, 157, *205*, 206, 222, **227**, 240, **240**, 244, 248, 254, 259–262, **260**, 264, **265**
wind dispersal 83–84, **84**, 147–148, **148**, 190–191, **190, 191**, 214, 235, 238, **239**, 241, 266, 308, 311, 318
wind turbulence 82–84, **84**, 106
Wood-rush, Field 274
woodlands, urban 299–300
   area of 26, 303
   on urban fallow land 266–269, **267, 269**, 300
Wormwood 33, 112, 113, 236, 238, 259, **259**
Woundwort, Hedge 143, 262

Xanthoria parietina 197–198, **197**
xenicity 112

Yarrow 35, 288
Yellow-oxeye, Willow-leaved 16–17, **16, 17**, 21
Yellow-rattle 35, 290, 291
Yellow-sorrel
   Least 286
   Procumbent **124**, 143–144, **144**, 145, 156, 157
Yew 192, 218, **219**, 267, 300
York 33, 164, **165**, *203*, 204, 205–206
Yorkshire-fog 222, 245, 248, 255, 260, 261, 264, 275, 276, **276**

Zurich 328